Transcending the State-Global Divide

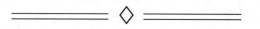

Critical Perspectives
on World Politics

◇

R. B. J. Walker, Series Editor

Transcending the State-Global Divide

A Neostructuralist Agenda in International Relations

◇

edited by

Ronen P. Palan
Barry Gills

Lynne Rienner Publishers ◆ Boulder & London

Published in the United States of America in 1994 by
Lynne Rienner Publishers, Inc.
1800 30th Street, Boulder, Colorado 80301

and in the United Kingdom by
Lynne Rienner Publishers, Inc.
3 Henrietta Street, Covent Garden, London WC2E 8LU

Library of Congress Cataloging-in-Publication Data
Transcending the state-global divide : a neostructuralist agenda in
    international relations / edited by Ronen P. Palan & Barry Gills.
    (Critical perspectives on world politics)
    Includes bibliographical references and index.
    ISBN 1-55587-395-2 (alk. paper)
    1. International relations—Philosophy. 2. Structuralism.
I. Palan, Ronen P., 1957– . II. Gills, Barry, 1956– .
III. Series.
JX1391.T73   1993
327'.01—dc20   93-8935
                                                                   CIP

British Cataloguing in Publication Data
A Cataloguing in Publication record for this book
is available from the British Library.

Printed and bound in the United States of America

       The paper used in this publication meets the requirements
 ∞ of the American National Standard for Permanence of
       Paper for Printed Library Materials Z39.48-1984.

Contents

Foreword
Susan Strange

In and out of universities people are looking for new ways to think about global problems. The horizons of thinking, caring people today are no longer limited to their own national backyards. The suffering of strangers and the degradation of the planet are brought before their eyes every evening on TV. Every morning, the newspapers report on and discuss social and economic problems that, clearly, are not limited to any one state but are shared by many. Yet, solutions and remedies are fewer than the problems and conflicts of opinion.

That is probably why discussion of these problems today is joined by representatives from all the social sciences. Sociologists and geographers, economists and lawyers all are adding to the mounting babel of voices. While their interpretations may be contradictory and confusing, the escalating dialogue confirms the impression among students of world politics that they are accurate in being dissatisfied with the conventional paradigms of international relations. All of these familiar paradigms now seem part of a bygone age. Just how, in the post–Cold War era, are we to think or make decisions about these global problems and issues?

This book points in a number of new and forward-looking directions. Indeed, an alternative subtitle could have been "Signposts to the Study of International Relations." To be sure, not all the signposts point in the same direction; the end result would have been suspiciously contrived if they had done so. Some authors hint that, despite the demise of the so-called socialist states, we should turn more to the left, whatever that means nowadays. Others, pointing to the economic success and early harbingers of political change in South Korea or Taiwan, would have us lean more to the right. But the differences among their final policy preferences and proposals are less important for readers than the shared determination about where to start. Common to all is a belief in the indefensibility of any arbitrary separation of domestic political economy and global political economy. There is also a shared determination to stop artificially separating the study of economics, politics, and society, as well as the local from the planetary. Karl Popper once said that the divisions of the social sciences were all monuments to the administrative convenience of university bureaucrats now long retired or buried; these divisions and disagreements came to be—literally—set in concrete as scholars increasingly occupied discrete buildings, wrote for separate specialist journals, and advised their students not to stray into neighboring fields.

Today's students and readers who rightly reject such narrow, self-serving advice will find that eclecticism requires more awareness and knowledge, not less, about, for example, the details of national constitutions or institutions. Students of international relations must know more about the internal politics of at least the major (and some minor) states, just as students of comparative government cannot get by without some awareness of the global structures of security, finance, and production. Figuring out—as voters, politicians, businesspeople, or commentators— the options for a government or party requires both micro- and macroperspectives, as well as the indispensable sense of what is feasible and what is not. Politics is still the art of the possible, within relatively unchanging power structures. These structures, moreover, now require awareness of the state of markets—for the factors of production, for products, and for services. That, in turn, requires some sensitivity to the implications of rapidly changing technology—an aspect of political economy that social scientists, who for the most part have limited expertise in elementary science, persistently overlook.

Building an eclectic social science appropriate to the twenty-first century is what this "signpost" book is about. Never mind if, like me, the reader may not be sure what it means to be "neostructural"; as with "postmodern," it is only a word that means different things to different people. The important question is not "neo-what?" but "ante-what?" What comes next? What is all this ante to?

The adventurous reader, undeterred by a dash of academic jargon, will surely find in what follows some useful pointers for thinking about the future.

Acknowledgments

The ideas for this book were first discussed at a seminar organized by Susan Strange at the European University Institute, Florence, May 1990. The participants in the seminar felt that what we have dubbed here as neostructuralism has in fact been around for some while, but its implications for International Relations have only become manifest in the past few years. This seminar was followed by a discussion, chaired by Susan Strange, held at the British International Studies Association annual meeting at Newcastle in 1990, and yet another meeting, convened by Sandra Halperin, held during the International Studies Convention in Vancouver in 1991. These and subsequent conversations laid the foundations for this book.

Since then the "neostructuralist agenda" has become an important line of thought contributing to the development of the new journal, the *Review of International Political Economy* (RIPE), organized by the two editors of this book along with Ash Amin and Peter Taylor. Several contributors to this volume are on the editorial board of RIPE.

In organizing this book we relied heavily for advice and support on Brook Blair, to whom we would like to extend our special thanks. We have also gained from the insights of Robert Denemark, who made a number of valuable comments on the manuscript. The Department of Politics, University of Newcastle Upon Tyne, assisted with the funding of the manuscript preparation, for which we are very grateful. Additional thanks are due to the editor of the *International Social Science Journal,* Ali Kazancigil, for granting us permission to print a revised version of A.G. Frank's article, originally published in the *ISSJ* (February 1992), and to Steve Barr, Kate Watts, and the team at Lynne Rienner Publishers.

Lastly, we would like to thank all of the contributors to this volume for bearing with us throughout the numerous changes it has gone through before reaching publication.

Ronen P. Palan
Barry Gills

Introduction:
The Neostructuralist Agenda in International Relations
Barry Gills & Ronen P. Palan

For most of this century the discipline of International Relations was normally presumed to treat the relations _between_ states, the latter viewed as cohesive social actors driven by their desire for power and prestige. The raison d'être of the discipline was originally to provide a social science explanation and solution for the pressing problems of war and peace plaguing the modern world order. As political acts of sovereign states, war and peace focused attention on the interaction state A had with state B, and with state C and so on, in terms of narrowly defined "political relations." International Relations theory was about understanding the patterning of these relations, conceived of at the level of high politics; usually diplomacy, alliances, and war behavior. In this burning concern with human destiny, given greater urgency with the advent of nuclear weapons, there seemed to be little place for scholastic squabbling over the finer aspects of state theory, let alone what appeared to be esoteric methodological debates. The internal workings of states, as policymaking units and actors in international relations, were often scrutinized, no doubt, but with a definite reluctance to go beyond certain limits. The intricate nature of the domestic political process was therefore recognized from time to time, but recognition never extended to the essential theoretical framework. In practice International Relations appeared increasingly complex and multifaceted, but in "theory" it was still about the interactions of volitional unities seeking power and prestige.

With mounting evidence to the contrary, it was not simply the fantasy of an utterly cohesive state sharing human sensibilities—"sensitive and vulnerable" (according to Keohane and Nye); endowed with "survival instincts" (Waltz); "friendly," "distrustful" (Wolfers)—which began to be questioned (but seldom challenged). It was also the myth of the utility of the "billiard ball" model which had been exploded—and comprehensively so. In recent debates it has been more widely recognized that in order to adequately address these central questions, so defined, economic and

1

socioeconomic relations are fundamental elements of any explanatory framework. For some, however, the critical question remains: What *is* the appropriate subject matter of the discipline of International Relations? Neorealism moved a step closer to addressing a wider set of economic and societal relations that are seen as partly determinant of the outcomes in high politics among state actors. But the neorealists addressed these wider issues, it seems, in order to neutralize them: already announcing that the "survival instinct (of states) rules the world," one has no recourse but to accept all other potential political concerns—profit, for instance—as secondary. But the neorealists never convincingly proved that "survival instincts" (*whose* instincts exactly is never clear) indeed rule the world.

To some, neorealists and regime theorists represent the state of the art of mainstream International Relations. However, the agenda of International Relations has been further broadened in recent years and its fundamental questions are posed entirely anew by an entirely different tradition. However, like the flickering transmission of stars from another galaxy, we hear only fragments of thoughts of this tradition: names such as Fernand Braudel, Karl Polanyi, Antonio Gramsci, and even Michael Mann and Nicos Poulantzas are mentioned. But there is no apparent logic or history to this tradition—nor is it entirely clear what its implications are for the discipline of International Relations.[1] One sometimes hears of dependency theory and world-systems analysis: but much has happened since Frank published his seminal book on *Development and Underdevelopment in Latin America* (1967) and Wallerstein his *Modern World System* (1974).

In our view, some of the most exciting recent contributions to the study of globalization and the states system have originated in this theoretical space. It is the expressed design of this book to bridge this gap by attempting to unite these scattered flickerings into something approaching a coherent agenda. In organizing this collection, our purpose has been twofold: first, we wanted to bring together some of the more innovative thinkers on these issues. The reader will find that these are not necessarily names that will immediately be associated with International Relations— rather they are drawn from a variety of disciplines, each concerned with certain aspects of the international system. Second, and perhaps more importantly, by presenting them together in a single work, we hope to demonstrate that amongst apparently disparate studies a new consensus may be emerging around certain key concepts and methodological questions.

* * *

What, then, is the nature of this common agenda? In our view, the contributors seek to bridge several important gaps in the International Relations literature. First and foremost, the emerging new agenda entails a shift in focus from the interaction between supposedly discrete unities to the dynamics of social development within the international system as a whole. Formerly, the dominant theories of state transformation took each state to be an ontologically distinct and organic entity. The preponderance of theoretical work during the postwar period was unilinear and evolutionary, privileging endogenous factors of change over exogenous or "external" "international" stimuli of transformation. These dominant theories of state and societal transformation identified each state with a single society which, however, evolved according to the pattern preestablished by the most advanced states. What was in fact a theory derived from this specific world-historical time frame presented itself as universal and timeless. Both modernization theory and even much of what passed as orthodox "development" were examples of this tendency.

The structural approach represented by both dependency theory and world-system theory sought to counter these prevailing orthodoxies. They shifted the analytical focus away from the single nation or state-society and toward what were posited to be governing processes of state and societal transformation occurring globally. These world processes were largely determinant of processes at lower levels in the structural hierarchy of the world. Though this counterattack was welcomed by many, it still suffered from a tendency to focus too intently on the governing processes on the world scale without always sufficiently problematizing the domestic level of response and transformation. This gave rise to a positional preoccupation, which though often useful and explanatory in many ways, sometimes contributed to holding back further extension of the sociological agenda of inquiry into the state/society transformations occurring at other levels.

Partly as a result of the well-known criticism of structuralism, structuralist research is now moving into a new era that may be called neostructuralism.[2] Neostructuralism, however, is not a compromise between past structuralist and neorealist positions. It is an attempt to redefine the very focus of inquiry within a new conceptualization of International Relations. Neostructuralism asks how global processes interact with other processes of state/societal transformation occurring at many other levels of the world system. It posits that the subject matter of International Relations is not only foreign policy or power patterns, as in realism and neorealism, nor only economically derived positional relations, as in much structuralist analysis. All of the above are constituent elements in larger state/societal transformative processes of the world as a whole. All states and societal forces in the modern world participate in these global governing processes and in the many levels of response to them. Therefore, the first-order questions of neostructuralist approaches to International Relations are on the order of how state/society transformation at level A is affected by and in turn affects the transformations at level B, and C, and so on. *It is the transformative processes themselves that are placed at the center of analysis.*

The neostructuralist approach suggests an entirely new conception of the real subject matter of International Relations. Rather than the mere relations among states—narrowly defined as governments—the subject matter is an overall transformative process wherein all states and societal forces are constantly being transformed through participation in the world system as a whole in terms of their fundamental characteristics and structure. Neostructuralism seeks to analyze and explain the social and structural forces, including the conjunctural, arrayed in these transformative processes.

In this sense International Relations in neostructuralist terms can be regarded as a *vast transmission mechanism* and stimulus for state and societal transformations: stimulated by and responded to at the global level as well as at many other definable levels, all of which are intricately interwoven. The "strong" as well as the "weak," and the "advanced" as well as the "backward" all mutually participate in this transmission of transformative pressures. The specific patterns of these transformative processes are therefore the proper empirical subject matter of International Relations. This is the main idea we wish to advance in this volume. This approach transcends any strict dichotomies between levels of the world system and does not restrict the category "state" to discrete territorial "nation-states," nor does it restrict the category "society" or social forces to the single-state framework. Indeed, it does not adhere to any of the former sacrosanct discrete systems boundaries. Thereby it counteracts both the unilinearity of evolutionary theories bounded by the state and its endogenous factors on the one hand, and offers a new antidote to the dangers of oversystematizing the world processes identified by structural theories, without abandoning some of the useful aspects of either.

By refocusing on the transformative processes, the neostructuralists seek—and this is the second plank of neostructuralism—to *problematize* the concept of the state. Indeed, the entire approach is rooted in, and enters into dialogue with, state theory. This contrasts sharply with both traditional International Relations and the structuralist approach, which have often tended to take the state for granted. But in placing the stress on the state and state theory, the neostructuralists distance themselves also from the more recent neo-Weberian approaches. This edited collection may remind some readers of an earlier collection edited by Evans, Rueschmeyer, and Skoçpol titled *Bringing the State Back In* (1985). The contributors to this present volume share many of the ideas and concerns voiced by the contributors of that earlier volume. Furthermore, our aim is somewhat similar to theirs in that we wish to strengthen the link between sociological theories of the state and International Relations. Nonetheless, the group of contributors assembled here differs from that of Evans et al. in three vital respects. First, whereas Evans et al. hold to a "Weberian" or "statist" theory of the state, the neostructuralists are, by and large, nearer to what Bob Jessop described as the "relational theory of the state" (1985).

The main difficulty we find with the neo-Weberians' perspective is that it shares the traditional realists' perception of the state as a cohesive actor, albeit this time the state is no longer equated with society at large, but with the bureaucratic machinery that is legally defined as the state (Auster and Silver 1979; Gilpin 1987; Hall and Ikenberry 1989; Halliday 1987; Krasner 1978; Mann 1984; Skoçpol 1979). In doing so, the neo-Weberians are making a number of critical but unwarranted assumptions: they idealize the state-bureaucracy, its aims and functions, and yet possess at the same time an exaggerated perception of its powers. They appear to accept what Wallerstein called "the ideology of statism" at face value, namely, the self-glorification of the bureaucracy as a functionally neutral social body solely concerned with the pursuit of the common good and the "national interest." Krasner, for instance, argues that it can be demonstrated empirically that: "The objective sought by the state cannot be reduced to some summation of private desires. These objectives can be called appropriately the national interest" (1978, 5). Mann repeats the famous Weberian theme of the enabling, socially (and implicitly class-) neutral state:

> The four most persistent types of state activities are:
>   1. The maintenance of internal order. . . .
>   2. Military defence/aggression, directed against foreign foes. . . .
>   3. The maintenance of communications infrastructures. . . .
>   4. Economic redistribution: the authoritative distribution of scarce material resources . . . different ecological niches, age-groups, sexes, regions, classes, etc. (1984, 120, 121).

This view idealizes, reifies, and mystifies the state: it is far too one-sided. Braudel's position, which may be regarded as broadly representative of the views taken by the contributors to this volume, provides what we regard to be a more accurate picture of the role of the state: "The state was there to preserve inequality, the cornerstone of the social order. Culture and its spokesmen were generally on hand to preach resignation to one's lot" (1979, II, 515). Mann and Skoçpol do concede, as an afterthought, that the state plays a significant class role. Skoçpol, for instance, accepts that "states usually do function to preserve existing economic and class structures" (1979, 30). But their theoretical framework is not attentive enough to the subtleties of political power and process: of the nature of political power, its attainment and maintenance. The very assumption of the unity of function and purpose of the bureaucracy stands in the way of the more difficult task of understanding the intricate character of political power.

At the same time, the neo-Weberians credit the bureaucracy with a large measure of autonomy. Naturally, the greater the degree of autonomy and cohesiveness attained by the bureaucracy, the lesser the importance attached to the domestic political processes. Like traditional realists, neo-Weberians therefore often ignore or downplay the importance of the domestic political process. As a consequence, the relations between domestic processes and global processes are not explored properly.

In contrast to the neo-Weberians, the neostructuralists stress the secondary role of the government and regime in relation to socioeconomic structures. The state itself is no longer seen as a set of institutions or a cohesive actor but as a type of social relations, an articulation of class interests within a given territorial context. Several of the neostructuralists prefer to talk of the "social formation" rather than the state. We may say that the neostructuralists focus on state theory, not on the state. Consequently, as the focus is brought back to the state, the state as a *category* is likewise deprivileged and placed within a wider sociological context transcending discrete state boundaries. In the best tradition of sociological investigation of state and power, states are disaggregated into classes, social forces, institutions, individuals, genders, races, peoples, regions, localities, and so forth. It is then reassembled not as a unified consciousness, but as a complex play of forces that shapes and is in turn reshaped by socioeconomic forces, domestic and international culture, and ideologies.

It is important to bear in mind, therefore, that when the contributors to this volume speak of "the state," they do not have a political subject, let alone an object, in mind. To neostructuralists, the "state" cannot be a volitional subject: it has no needs, it does not pursue "power and prestige," it does not possess a unique agenda. It is not an "it." Indeed, the very question "What is the state?" although undoubtedly a legitimate one, may set us on the wrong course. For the question implicitly suggests that we are dealing with a unit, a phenomenon, whereas in reality, the only way of understanding the state as a working concern is to view it as "the heart of political power" (Poulantzas 1978, 81). It is, as Lipietz in this volume approvingly quotes Marx and Engels: "the apparatus by which society equips itself in order that the different groups of which it is constituted do not exhaust themselves in a struggle without end."

State policies therefore cannot be explained in terms of a volitional being: the state does not pursue a "national interest," it possesses no distinct "reason of state." State policies must be explained therefore by other means. Central to the neostructuralist agenda is the concern with the interrelation between policies and the wider socioeconomic and ideological domestic and international setting.

Finally, the neostructuralists share a common perception of the notion of totality or the "international system." We have been accustomed in International Relations to view the entire globe as a single unidimensional framework of activities. The organizing concepts of such a globalized system range from the "international society" (Bull 1977), the "system of states" (Morgenthau 1967; Wight 1977), the "world-system" (Wallerstein 1974), and so on. Each of these organizing concepts suggests that the entire international system operates to the tune of one logic and uniform rhythm. The neostructuralists share a common concern to correct this one-dimensional theory of the international system. The essence of neostructuralism lies in the conviction that there are inherent limitations in the capacity of global or international patterns to create totalizing systems. The reason being that any one-dimensional global system negates, by its very nature, the myriad of transformative processes, be they at the local, national, or global level, which are at the heart of this analysis.

Since the neostructuralists reject the notion of one unifying transnational totality, they are naturally faced with the question of how the "separate" levels and instances relate to each other in any given situation. The neostructuralists respond to this problem by elevating the concept of the historical conjuncture. The "whole," or what the structuralists call the world-system, is thought by the neostructuralists to consist of a multiplicity of factors. Each of these factors needs to be understood at one and the same time in isolation, i.e., as a separate system—thus, Strange, for instance, talks of four systems: security, finance, production, and knowledge—but at the same time, in relation to the wider picture. The conjuncture is the historical moment where these various factors meet and combine to produce specific outcomes. The conjuncture therefore suggests that any given historical event must ultimately be explained in its given historical context. There must be, in other words, a certain distance between theory and history.

Ultimately neostructuralism may be read as a call for more modesty on the part of theorists: theory can help explain so much but no more. What we therefore hope the reader will find in this collection is less a new unified theory of International Relations and more a new spirit of dialogue among scholars from a variety of disciplines concerned with a similar set of issues. This spirit is animated by an underlying basic methodological and philosophical affinity as to their view of the underlying forces shaping the international system. It is this affinity that creates the basis for a common agenda. While the unsuspecting reader might be prone to see neostructuralism as just another approach to a discipline that already appears to be in general disarray, we feel, on the contrary, that these essays signal a more profound movement toward a set of issues different from those that have traditionally occupied the discipline of International Relations. In other words, neostructuralism is here to stay. For not only have the methodological and philosophical concerns of the neostructuralists been incorporated to varying degrees by existing approaches, but now, with the end of the Cold War, these concerns at last have an opportunity to blossom into a consistent body of thought in its own right. But even more so, neostructuralism is bound to flourish because, paradoxically, although it may appear at first sight to make a sharp break from traditional International Relations theories, it draws its strength in fact from a renewal of the classical tradition of political economy. It was this very break with the classical tradition of political economy that severely impoverished the discipline of International Relations throughout the Cold War period. And as shown throughout history, it is often by way of a creative return to the classics that we come to gain a more profound understanding of the present.

* * *

In formulating this book we strove to represent the two sides of the neostructuralist project: the comprehensive and interdisciplinary nature of the theoretical perspective, and the commitment to a critical historical research attentive to the intricacies of the political economy. The task became difficult as we found out, to our dismay as editors but to our delight as critical thinkers, that neostructuralist literature is not amenable to such a division: some of the "theoretical" pieces contain superb historical analyses, and some of the "case studies" may prove equally informative at theory as much as history. A better approach was then to let the chapters guide us slowly from the abstract to the concrete: from the early chapters which represent generalized observations about the nature of the key concepts of "capitalism," "system," and "state" to the articulation of the neostructuralist understanding of these categories in a given situation.

More than anything this collection of articles represents a dawning awareness of a new territory in International Relations. It is more a signpost than a mapping. In his opening chapter, Warren Mason shows us that the neostructuralist agenda is more of an opening of a space between world-system analysis and what may be described as the postmodernist project. The postmodernists reject the "grand narrative" of state, capital, and teleology. They do so because capitalism is no longer a regulated system. Capitalism, instead of being a grand narrative, is now seen as a play of forces, a "set of sets" without an overarching system of regulation to unify it. Mason maintains that the discovery of this space is contingent on placing the "state" as the locus of the transformative processes in the world economy. We think Mason is correct: the chapters of this collection may be understood to take place within a space between them, i.e., within a more flexible system of capitalist development.

The second chapter by Alain Lipietz sets the tone for this shift in perspective. Instead of relying on state and capital, Lipietz raises the idea of the local—grassroots movements. But he does not replace the global with the local. The neostructuralist perspective draws heavily on the French school of regulation, which, in turn, may be regarded as a political economy interpretation of the "relational state." More than anyone else, Lipietz has been extending the regulationists' interpretation simultaneously toward the international and the local. In his chapter, he unifies these two interests by taking us beyond the current purview of state theory. Lipietz suggests that the very spaciality of "the state," and the manifestation of social and cultural practices, play an important political role nationally and globally. The local is a materialization of capital, a regional organization of the Fordist mode of regulation, which, however, in turn becomes an intervening force in its own right in the capitalist system. Therefore, for Lipietz, capitalism can never be a unified concept. Rather than a system of the iron laws of the dialectics of capitalist development, one finds a more flexible system with different types of actors.

Palan discusses one of the fundamental problems that Lipietz's chapter raises: the rejection of a facile dichotomy of internal and external causation. Instead of the assumed determination of the internal by the external or vice-versa, the neostructuralists seek to articulate the relationships between them. This raises fundamental questions about the nature of social closure and indeed the significance of the social formation. Like Lipietz, Palan talks about capitalism, but again, no longer as a unified system. In the Marxist tradition the task of the state lies in the rationalization and organization of capitalist interests. The state is therefore crucial to capitalist development. In that sense we have to acknowledge the plurality of capital. Capitalism is rooted in a system of states, no doubt, but the system of states itself is merely a framework within which socioeconomic forces compete. How does a hierarchical and competitive "system of states" rationalize capitalist interests? How can there be, in other words, a world market? The traditional answer always came on the side of the dominant power: imperialism or "hegemonic stability": the "embedded liberal orthodoxy" placed, maintained, and transformed by U.S. power. Palan argues that instead of a top-down organization of capital, intersocietal linkages generate a certain homogenizing effect upon the political organization of the transnational system. Intersocietal structural relationships complement, therefore, our understanding of the nature of transnational orders.

The theme of internal and external causation is explored further by Sandra Halperin in her study of the rise of nationalism in the nineteenth century. Halperin sees the rise of nationalism or the nation-state not as the mere cause or result of the capitalist system, but as a vector through which capitalist interests expand and maintain order through newly developed principles of International Relations. Nationalism is a uniquely nineteenth-century phenomenon, but also one that cannot be understood outside of a specific moment in the acceleration of the capitalist process. Nationalism created the ideology of a unity between state and society, at a time when the acceleration of history born of capitalism was about to break them down. The ideology of unity was then taken at face value in International Relations and the state assumed quasi-ontological properties. But Halperin shows us that at the very moment of nationalist unity, classes were actually involved in defining their own system of hierarchies within the nineteenth-century European system. The cohesive, "infrastructural" nation-states of the nineteenth and twentieth centuries are political responses to the problem of capitalist dislocation.

Christopher Chase-Dunn's contribution is a broad historical discussion of the role of technology in determining transformation in "modes of accumulation." His approach, as developed in *Global Formation* (Chase-Dunn, 1989), extends the neostructuralist agenda precisely because he attempts to transcend limiting debates over "internal" versus "external" causation. Chase-Dunn deploys a sophisticated analytical framework based on the interactive dynamics of local/national social formations and the world-system, or global political economic processes. His far-reaching analysis of the role of technology in this chapter ranges from competition among core states for control of peripheries in the ancient world, to the "ways in which states and the larger system of states have been transformed by capitalism," and finally to a stimulating predictive analysis of the trends in core competition and the prospects for a renewal of socialism, particularly in industrialized semiperipheral countries in the future. Interestingly, much of Chase-Dunn's discussion is critically addressed to the "flexible accumulation" approach.

The neostructuralist agenda contains a number of important debates. Lipietz, Palan, and Cerny stress the emergence of a new capitalist phase which began in the 1970s. Chase-Dunn represents an opposing view that finds "no major structural or processual changes in the world-system in the last few decades" that cannot be interpreted as the "largely predictable continuation of cycles and trends long in operation." His incisive comments on the continuing rigidity of the core/periphery hierarchy, the reintegration of the socialist economies into the capitalist world-system, and the attacks on labor in the core and its attendant ideological expressions, are elegantly subsumed in his dialectical model of the "spiral of capitalism and socialism."

Peter Taylor contributes a penetrating and systematic explanation of the "creative tension" that can be generated between world-system analysis (seen as a theory of globalization) and theories of the state. In his review of how the state "captured" politics and succeeded in harnessing nationalism he explicitly rejects the "state-national society" equation of the prevailing state-centric analyses, while recognizing that the state is the "basis of formal power" within the world-system. However, states are not treated by Taylor as "given," but rather "they are created as part of the operation of the world-economy and are a consequence rather than a cause of the system."

Taylor re-poses the important question of whether we should assume there is only one world economic entity in which there are still many states presiding over fragments of this one economy, or whether there is a simple juxtaposition of quite discrete nation-state social formations. His attempt to bridge this global/state divide generates a clear formulation of a world-system's concept of state maneuverability within structural and world-scale constraints, as well as a stimulating predictive hypothesis on the future of the contradiction between accumulation and legitimation.

Moseley seeks to reproblematize the mutual relations between world economy, classes, state system, and states. She does so through a critical review of debates concerning the rise of capitalism in Europe and the subsequent development process in the Third World. She organizes the discussion through three major positions: world-system, Marxist-structuralist, and state-centered views. In her treatment of the contemporary context, she contrasts "nationalist" and "globalist" camps. She contrasts the structuralist tendency to underestimate the effects of larger state structures and/ or networks of exchange to the state-centric proclivity to adopt a position of "true" autonomy of the states.

Moseley's review of development theories begins from the critical observation that most of the debate centers on achieving something called development, and the focus is therefore on the relative efficacy of states and markets in this regard. Whether "national development" is desirable in the sense of being indefinitely feasible or as an emancipatory goal is being re-posed and debated between "nationalist" and "globalist" positions. Her conclusions are addressed mainly to the world-system approach, whereby she suggests the unpacking of the world-system concept, restoring the analytic autonomy of capitalism and the states.

With Andre Gunder Frank's chapter we reach the area of analysis of concrete conditions. Perhaps more than any other contributor to this volume, Frank re-privileges the worldwide economic context and world economic causality in his wide-ranging analysis of recent events in Europe. He attacks the notion that economic policy is a true cause of events. Frank's provocative thesis is that policy is largely independent of political ideology and usually results in effects opposite to its intended result. His analysis of the causes of the crisis of Eastern Europe concentrates on how the world economic crisis, rather than national ideology, policy, or "social system," spelled the doom of the "socialist" economies. Likewise, the ongoing policies of accelerated economic integration and marketization of the East are again more effect than cause, according to Frank.

His analytical contribution to this volume is precisely in his re-privileging of the world economic context, and the global economic crisis in particular, in a manner that locates the causes of the political realignments and restructuring of Europe, East and West, in the same economic crisis. He finds it remarkable that the current violent nationalist and ethnic upheavals of Europe are not being explained by reference to underlying economic causes. Frank predicts that reliance on free-market ideology will fail to address the real problems in the economy and will sharpen economic social and political polarization, while the lessons of how the last world economic crisis produced fascist movements in Central, Southern, and Eastern Europe seem not to be well remembered.

Kees van der Pijl's study of the trends of West German unification is again a political economic interpretation of recent events. In contrast to Frank, however, van der Pijl emphasizes the materiality of culture and ideology and therefore extends historical materialist analysis beyond the "rule of the market." In van der Pijl's chapter, the appearance of a unified world of the "system of states" is broken down into two types of statecraft—the Lockean heartland and the Hobbesian state—which manifest themselves in politics and economics. Here a crucial step is taken beyond mere ideological ideas of the nature of states and markets, showing their embedding in material reality through a set of techniques and practices that in turn provide a system of government and societal regulation. The German social formation is treated as discrete, and yet as part of a larger transnational order. The beauty of this approach is that these supposedly merely philosophical concepts are now helping us to understand the development of the German social formation in the late twentieth century.

Lawrence Wilde then takes a look at one of the disappointments of recent years. Socialists in Europe and the world have grown accustomed to look upon Sweden as the model for the gradual transition from social democracy to socialism. Lawrence Wilde documents how during the 1980s Sweden was no longer able to shield itself from the international pressures of capitalism. The threat of erosion of the competitive position of Swedish industry destroyed the corporate consensus on which Swedish social democracy had been based. The great mistake of the Swedish socialists, for which they paid dearly, was to underestimate the vulnerability of the Swedish economy to international pressures. The theoretical mistake of the Swedish socialists was grounded, in other words, in the rigid traditional dichotomy of "in" and "out." Wilde's chapter demonstrates the concrete implications of the neostructuralist's problematic of internal and external causation.

Gills' contribution is an attempt to compare the explanatory value of a neostructuralist interpretation of a specific East Asian case, South Korea, with the more dominant conventional state-centric approaches. The chapter seeks to explain the critical historical transition to the now-well-known model of state-led, export-oriented industrialization of South Korea, as well as of Taiwan. His approach is explicitly conjunctural and analyzes the unique emergence of the Korean trajectory within its specific domestic, regional, and global situation in the late 1950s and early 1960s. The conjunctural explanation of the shift to export-oriented industrialization focuses on the convergence of class and state interests among elites in Japan, the United States, Korea, and Taiwan that offered the latter two countries a special structural opportunity to industrialize and promoted specific state forms. The framework of analysis assumes an ongoing interpenetration and mutual transformatory restructuring between the global and the domestic structures. Gills's conclusions undermine the claim—made from a state-centric perspective—that there is any true national model of development in East Asia that could be adopted or emulated elsewhere. The origin of the so-called "East Asian model" was a product of a conjuncture and its highly specific convergent class interests, hegemonic influences and goals, and structural opportunities within the international division of labor.

Finally, Cerny's chapter is a neostructuralist foray into the new debates on the role and function of international finance. Cerny sidesteps the old and fruitless debate on whether there is a zero-sum game between state and capital, i.e., whether the predominance of one necessarily implies a giving way by the other. On the contrary, Cerny suggests that steps toward global reorganization in the financial structure are in turn effecting changes in the technologies of state. Whereas once one assumed a territorial sovereign state, one now finds a state that must adapt to development and the deployment of capital—thus the competition state.

In Cerny's interpretation the relative functional unity between the circuits of capital—production, trade, and finance, created by the liberal trading system of the *pax americana*—was broken not because of any inherent "capitalist contradictions," but ultimately because of the success of the liberal trade regime. One cannot help being reminded of Marx and Engels's prediction: "The bourgeoisie has through its exploitation of the world market given a cosmopolitan character to production and consumption in every country. To the great chagrin of reactionists, it has drawn from under the feet of industry the national ground on which it stood" (Marx and Engels 1973, 71, 72). Already in 1848 Marx and Engels had foreseen that day when the globalization of the world market would reach the stage in which the entire gamut of social and political institutions of capitalism would be placed in contradiction. Perhaps the neostructuralist message is that we have reached this stage.

NOTES

1. On Gramscian theory, which had been an important input in the neostructuralist perspective, either in the form of Poulantzas and his followers' reading of Gramsci, or through the work of Cox and Gill, see the latest collection edited by Gill (1993).

2. Or as one of us termed it elsewhere, "second structuralism" (Palan [1992a]).

1

What Is New
in Neostructuralism?

Warren Mason

Political scientists—and particularly those in the United States—are only beginning to realize the extent to which the Cold War shaped the attention and theoretical orientation of the discipline. The dominant positivist paradigm of the postwar period has given ground only hesitantly, if at all, to the challenges of the social activists of the 1960s and 1970s, and to the so-called radical theorists rooted primarily in Latin American scholarship (Frank 1967; Dos Santos 1970; Cardoso and Faletto 1979) and secondarily in a long-established European tradition of critical scholarship (Myrdal 1969; Galtung 1967). Frequently inspired by the Marxist tradition, these challenges to postwar orthodoxy had to struggle against the resistance of established social science frameworks and methods on the one hand, and on the other, against an ideological conservatism suspicious of models without pluralist and neoliberal implications (Ricci 1984, 23–25).

The high stakes of the Cold War confrontation probably made it inevitable that the value preferences of liberalism would find safer anchorage among the theories and methods of positivistic rationalism than among those of dialectical historicism. In an atmosphere in which the geopolitical adversary took comfort from one set of assumptions and interpretations, it was reasonable for the West to avoid them in order to build an intellectual consensus to support the economic and military struggle. The fact that positivism was also linked with the triumphs of the natural sciences only added to the certainty of the choice.

It may be symbolic that analyses of development/underdevelopment focusing on the Third World represented the main point of contact between the orthodox, rational-positivist paradigm and the radical, conflict-based historicist paradigm. Intellectually as well as militarily, it seems, this was the active battleground of the Cold War.

The essays in this volume are written in a post–Cold War context. This fact is liberating in itself. Many of the old issues raised in these pages may be evaluated freshly, without the inhibitions of Cold War confrontation.

15

Some of the neostructuralists presented here extend the debate by pushing the discussion into new areas or by reaching for a more systematic and integrated conception of global politics. The neostructuralist work represented in this volume goes beyond the concerns of international politics to invite a rethinking of the core ideas of the discipline.

STRUCTURALISM AND NEOSTRUCTURALISM

However familiar to those scholars operating in the Marxist tradition, the structuralist perspective is somewhat elusive for many who operate within the mainstream positivist perspective. As so often in discussions of this kind, it is quite possible—even probable—that the understanding with which we are working will not match precisely the concepts specified or implied in these essays. All the same, identifying some of the common core of ideas on which these essays build will be useful to see the direction in which these efforts may be pointing.

At base, the structuralist approach—at least in the social sciences —appears to draw upon the Marxist tradition that holds for the primacy of social relations deriving fundamentally from the structure of the economy. A well-known summary of comparative theory offers the following definition:

> The fundamental thesis of the structuralist perspective is that the functions of the state are broadly determined by the structures of the society rather than by the people who occupy positions of state power (Gold, Lo, and Wright, quoted in Chilcote 1981, 195).

The requisites of the liberal market economy (capitalism) are seen, in this perspective, to shape the normative and behavioral characteristics of the state. It is the structure of society, rather than the actions of individuals, interest organizations, and classes that is the focus of attention. While individual actors are not the focus of this approach, the psychology of material interest is controlling in the long term no matter what other elements may deflect attention in the short term. Since these interests are more acutely important to those who benefit or lose most in the economic process, the beneficiaries create social structures to reinforce and preserve their interests while at the same time assuring the repression or at least quiescence of those likely to be motivated by their material loss.

Among these structures is the state. While fundamentally dependent on the pattern of social relations that is the theoretical source of its existence, the state also acquires a certain degree of autonomy with respect to those same social structures. Indeed, a prominent representative of this approach holds that the state organizes and gives cohesion to the interests of the capitalist class and that it regulates the "global equilibrium" of the social system (Poulantzas 1973a, 44–56). This would appear to give the state at least tactical autonomy, but structuralists tend to be suspicious of the viability of any state that is diverted too far for too long from the material interests of the beneficiary class. Hence, politics, while it may be specialized and professionalized and while it may be committed to the stability and expansion of the state, is ultimately an artifact of social forces that mold it, not in concrete detail but in underlying direction.

The question of the autonomy of the state is a central issue for the structuralists insofar as they are committed to the primacy of influences emanating from society. The degree to which the state acts autonomously from social influences is the degree to which structuralists must sacrifice a deterministic understanding of politics. So the question of autonomy is urgent. At most, only a relative or partial autonomy can be attributed to the state.

While poorly defined in most writing, structuralism relies on the concept of the state. Rich with connotation from its long history in political theory, the idea of the state has been criticized for its tendency to encourage reification and anthropomorphization. Consequently, the Political Science discipline has tended to prefer concepts like "government" or "political system" that permit clearer specification of the activities encompassed by the older term. The insistence upon the concept of the state, however, is important to the structuralists' emphasis upon the total network of relations that define the society. The term does not invite disaggregation, and this is precisely because structuralists wish to focus attention upon the configuration of relationships essential to social coherence. It is characteristic of the approach that domination is seen in the arrangement of structures rather than in particular activities (Poulantzas 1973a).

Neostructuralism, as implied in this collection of essays, extends the logic of structuralism to encompass a global concept of politics. In doing so, a considerable complexity is introduced into the analysis. As the requisites of technology and economic efficiency extend the economy to global dimensions, neostructuralism must contend with social influences that are both internal and external. As economic interests expand and the domestic economy becomes a derivative of the global economy, the nation-state is placed in a difficult and contradictory position. It must, in neoliberal societies (and there are ever-fewer exceptions to the category), promote the efficiency of global resource exploitation and at the same time meet an expanding array of domestic responsibilities. In short, fundamental economic (and sociocultural) relations are increasingly structured at the global (or at least regional) level, while pressures on the state to assure the security and prosperity of domestic society are also increasing.

The neostructural project carries forward the tendency toward monistic explanation found in the world-system and dependency traditions (cf., summary critique in Almond 1990). For several of these writers, there is virtually no departure from the dogmatism and sweeping generalizations associated with those traditions. The structure of the global economy becomes a closed system that explains all. The dominance of the center drives weaker regions always into greater and greater poverty and dependence as the center, in turn, bloats on an economic system that cannot survive without exploitation. Hence, the world moves constantly toward a breaking point, a revolutionary catharsis, from which a new (socialist) world economic order will emerge. Too often, the certainty that accompanies closed-system thinking leads to assertions (e.g., the distribution of income is becoming increasingly polarized, or ethnic conflict arises from economic crisis) that, in the absence of evidence or a strategy to investigate them, must be called global dogmatism.

The unfortunate aspect about this tendency toward dogmatism is that theoretical insights that could be provoked by postulating the structure of the global economy tend to be lost. An explanatory structure should not be imposed in ways that force the rich complexity of history to conform to its outline. The power of such general formulations lies in their capacity to suggest fresh relationships and to create a general framework that will allow creative inquiry to add detail and complexity to understanding. Above all, structure should not be allowed to devalue other elements that may be vital aspects of a social situation and that may be nearer to the psychological reality of actors than structural generalizations.

Other neostructural writers seem more inclined to use this perspective to tease out new theoretical insights and to begin an open-ended dialogue, both logical and empirical, with history (e.g., Chase-Dunn 1989). It is a positive conceptual contribution, for example, to grapple with the problem of the nation-state in a world of increasingly transnational social relations. To call attention to the heightened importance of transnational firms and regional or global regimes invites new thinking about sovereignty and forms of political organization. An attempt to emancipate the relationship between society and politics from the purely national context—to move toward more general theory—is a positive and exciting product of neostructuralist thinking. When the structure becomes a prelude to a genuinely open inquiry that can lead to a revised structural concept, neostructuralism can escape scholasticism and contribute to a new phase of theoretical development in the discipline.

TOWARD A POSTMODERN POLITICS

If the modern period since World War I has been characterized by the ascendancy of rationalistic positivism, the emergence of the omnicompetent nation-state, and economic, military, and ideological polarization, the present era calls for a basic redefinition. Paradigmatic pluralism in the social sciences, challenges to the nation-state that have grown even faster than its capabilities, and the dramatic easing of Cold War confrontation have fundamentally changed the context of inquiry about political phenomena. It is tempting to call this new condition the postmodern era, although the term is hazardously multifaceted. One postmodern theorist insists that no comprehensive social transformation has taken place and that no coherent and shared postmodern theory exists. He argues, however, that the essence of the postmodern perspective is to call attention "to new trends and social conditions that require a loosening up and development of our old theories and that might be productive for new theoretical syntheses" (Giroux 1991, 61). In this spirit, neostructuralism would appear to point toward the possibility of a postmodern politics.

The postmodern project—if that is not too grand a term for something so tentative—must begin, as far as political inquiry is concerned, with an attempt to engage in dialogue the major social science paradigms of our time, rationalistic positivism and dialectical historicism. As David Apter has suggested, it is both intellectually parochial and counterproductive for an intelligent approach to the world's pressing problems not to search for relationships, and possibly syntheses, between the major analytical traditions (Apter 1987). The neostructuralist approach invites development of a number of such points of contact. Among the most promising are a common focus on the concept of the state with its related questions of autonomy and sovereignty, the beginnings of epistemological convergence between the major analytical approaches, and the gradual emergence of a language of accommodation.

Orthodox or mainstream political science operating in the positivist tradition has focused its analytical attention on the arena of social forces, of which politics was characteristically seen as a dependent variable. Gabriel Almond's vigorous retort that positivist political science always included an important attention to the autonomous action of the state (conceptualized as bureaucracy, government, polity, and the like) is accurate but oblique to the point (Almond 1988; Almond 1990). The main thrust of a political science concerned with inputs from the social environment, outputs from government, and feedback effects upon the environment was to see how social influences *structured* the operation of the political system. "Withinputs" and similar concepts have been, in any fair assessment of the tradition, a distinctly secondary emphasis of analysis. In fact, a perception that political science has paid too little attention to the structuring impact of governmental institutions upon society appears to have motivated a large group of mainstream political scientists to risk declaring a renewed interest in so hydra-headed a concept as the state (e.g., Rosenau 1989). The reappearance of the state as an analytical category among writers in the positivist tradition suggests a productive point of cross-paradigmatic contact (Caporaso 1989).

The importance of the state autonomy question for neostructuralist writers has already been noted. Emphasis and terminology varies among them, but the center of gravity in this matter appears to be that the state, while fundamentally structured and sustained by the civil society in which it is immersed, nonetheless acquires some measure of autonomy. The Marxist tradition sanctions the idea of the state as the mobilizer, articulator, enforcer, and so on, of class interest, and neostructuralists influenced by that tradition have found in the state at least a relative autonomy or an autonomy of maneuver. Indeed, for them the state institutionalizes and maintains the network of social relations that is the operative expression of the dominant power relationship in each historical epoch. Their hesitation about a full-blown autonomy, however, seems very near the dominant view of mainstream analysts: both are impressed with the "ultimate" power of social forces that provide an environment for political structures even if their understanding of those forces is divergent. Even the realist theorists in international relations who tend to take the autonomous state for granted do so only by focusing on the instrumental values that states project into the international arena. They are not much concerned with the question of which substantive interests are being served.

"Sovereignty," says Steven Krasner, "is a term that makes the eyes of most American political scientists glaze over. It has lost its meaning and analytical relevance" (Krasner 1989, 88). Yet, he argues that the disjunction between the responsibilities and capabilities of states has made it necessary to reexamine two aspects of sovereignty: final authority within a territory and control of transborder movements (ibid., 88–89). An important trend that may be characterized as postmodern is the lack of congruity between the territorial organization of political authority and the subterritorial and transterritorial mobilization of social forces. The idea of sovereignty anchored in the nation-state has consequently come under pressure. As orthodox political science grapples with the relative autonomy of the state vis-à-vis both internal and external social groupings, neostructuralists investigate the primary structural influence of global forces (economic and cultural) upon politics.

The disintegration of the USSR and the consolidation of the European Community are only two titanic instances in which the question of sovereignty has burst its national bounds. The North American Free Trade Area, the Palestinian "entity," Kuwait and Iraq, Hong Kong, Northern Ireland, and Quebec all appeal in somewhat different ways for creative thinking about sovereignty. Compared with their mainstream counterparts, the neostructuralists have taken a more relativistic and disaggregated view of sovereignty. The latter tend to see the nation-state as having aggregated political power into more-or-less stable units suited to the requisites of a particular technology and level of economic development. As technology fosters the globalization of the economy (and to a significant degree, of culture), decisive authority disaggregates partially toward both subnational and transnational groups and institutions. It is this partial disaggregation suggesting the possibility of a layered or parallel concept of sovereignty that appears to have strong links with mainstream functionalist thought.

Method is another area of potential postmodern convergence. Positivist method has been the defining characteristic of mainstream political science. The search for analytical precision in empirical research brought concepts like the state and sovereignty into disrepute in the first place. A kind of methodological determinism—if you can measure it, it's real; if not, it's not—even created tension between the high abstractions of general theory and the imperative values of positivist method. For those operating in the historicist tradition, on the other hand, the essential realities were configurative—networks, patterns, and macrocosmic relationships—and, consequently, disaggregative methods threatened to dissolve the key variables of the political universe. These analysts required a greater tolerance for ambiguity (general tendencies rather than specific instances), configurative intuition based on immersion in historical detail, and inductive logic. Analytic positivism was often seen as a way to obscure, and therefore deny, the most important generalizations about politics.

Insofar as the neostructural project represents the new thinking of the historicist tendency, the dissent from positivist methods appears to be falling away. Raymond Duvall and others have already made a start in this direction (Duvall et al. 1981; Sylvan et al. 1983). The key development of neostructuralism is an effort to work out the composition rules—systematic links—that integrate subnational, national, and transnational politics. Among the writers in the present volume, there appears to be an emerging openness to empirical methods tied to an integrated set of concepts. At the same time, movement toward questions of state autonomy and sovereignty among the positivists suggests the basis, at least, for brushing epistemological shoulders if not for a more intimate relationship. Indeed, several writers have noted the prospect of a convergence between "culturalist" and "structuralist" perspectives and have called for a "disciplined eclecticism" (So 1990, 261–268). Charles Ragin has suggested some empirical strategies by which this effort of synthesis might be pursued (Ragin 1987; see also Sylvan and Glassner 1985).

Finally, we come to the need for a language of accommodation. The rhetorical style of some of the existing literature suggests strongly that the last vestige of the Cold War may be the confrontational tone of intellectual discourse. Philosophical positions have always been protected by semantic battlements, and it seems likely that the erstwhile geopolitical struggle further increased the stakes of engagement. Even before the Cold War dissipated, however, scholars reacting to trends we have called postmodern began to change the rhetorical rules. Apter's Modernization I and Modernization II is a clear example but there are others as well (Apter 1987;

Chilcote 1981; Sylvan et al. 1983). Precisely because there are so many points of intellectual contact between the neostructuralist perspective and that of mainstream political science, the dialogue seems likely to produce a language that will de-emphasize confrontation and look toward an intellectual cross-pollenization of enormous potential benefit both to the discipline and to the human community it serves. It is toward this postmodern effort to find creative theoretical syntheses that the neostructuralist project is properly directed.

2

The National and the Regional: Their Autonomy Vis-à-vis the Capitalist World Crisis

Alain Lipietz

Some fifteen years after the onset of what numerous authors have identified as the "general crisis of the Fordist development model," an orthodox response seems to have taken shape in the media, among certain mainstream economists, and even among left-wing intellectuals in the industrialized countries. We can summarize the proposed orthodox solution to the crisis in two broad points:

1. The crisis could potentially be resolved through worldwide technical cooperation and interlinked markets with an appropriate social support system.
2. The operationalization of such a solution would require a suppleness and flexibility that could only be ensured at the local level.

The difficulty with this orthodox strategy is that it presupposes that there is one, and only one, possible form of post-Fordist social organization, determined, as it were, by the technological revolution that itself was informed by the crisis of Fordism. This technological revolution implies a worldwide and flexible social organization. The orthodox proposal also entails an important political consequence, for it implies that the national state, as an institution and as a geographical construct, must fade away to the benefit of alternative worldwide and local authorities.

From its very beginning this orthodox solution ran into lively criticism from certain groups on the left who identified weaknesses in the argument. They highlighted two general criticisms:

1. Its technological and economic determinism, which arose no doubt from an uncritical acceptance of the Marxian orthodoxy of the Second and Third International: a view of human destiny somehow dictated by the blind and impersonal forces of "progress"—a progress that is nevertheless dictated by specific social forces.

23

2. The loss of relevance of the national as an appropriate level for social change, which undercut labor and other progressive forces that,
in spite of the unhappy claims of "proletarian internationalism,"
have never found anything better than the nation-state as an unavoidable instrument for change.

Valuable as these criticisms from the left may be, they should not
mask the fact that similar criticisms have often been associated with nationalistic and conservative forms of attachment to social gains; such criticisms have frequently and perhaps unwittingly led to a rejection of authentically progressive aspirations to rid societies of a state perceived as
alienating, in favor of communities more closely bound to the individual
and better rooted within the conscience of a collective destiny—aspirations that in the past have often been suppressed by the nation-state. Ironically, therefore, this left-wing Fordist reaction to the decline of national
Fordism reinforces precisely the position that it purported to combat in the
first place, thus instituting an absurd polarization (e.g., between "the national" and "the local," between the closing and opening of the national
economy, between the state and the individual). The end result is that a
fraction of the left thus became identified with the Fordist era, an era not
only transcended by the dominant capitalist evolution, but also rejected by
the very same popular forces not so long ago mobilized against the cen-
tralist tutelary state that regulates the Fordist model.

The purpose of the present text is to develop a general theoretical argument, based upon the French "Regulation" approach,[1] which might sur-
mount this absurd polarization between the over- and underestimation of
locally rooted social compromises. First, I reflect on the concept of
"space" or "spatiality"[2] and use it to suggest a number of basic notions
that clarify the specificity of "the regional" in relation to "the national."
Next, I revisit the Fordist model in its international and interregional dimensions, and with respect to its crisis issues. In this fashion I evaluate the
autonomy of the national and the regional in view of actual tendencies,
looking for different ways out of the crisis. In conclusion, I evoke the relevance of these two levels of political decisionmaking to the search for a
progressive solution to the crisis in Fordism.

SOCIAL RELATIONS AND SPACE: SOME DEFINITIONS[3]

From the Modes of Production to Space-in-Itself

Each social formation is a complex structure of social relations intertwined at the economic, politico-juridical, and ideological instances. It
presents itself as an articulation of modes of production: typical mixtures

of social relations such as capitalism, petty commodity production, and domestic production. This articulation, however, represents something more than a mere combination of these relations.

On the one hand, the form of existence of each of the forms of production depends largely upon the role attributed to it by the reproduction of the dominant mode in the social formation (i.e., capitalism). On the other hand, the conditions of existence of the dominant mode of production itself presupposes the presence of other modes of production, serving, for example, as reserves of labor power and outlets.

If, a priori, each mode of production has its own developmental dynamics and logic, which is generally in contradiction to that of the other modes, the dominance of the capitalist mode of production imposes on the whole structure its unity (i.e., its mode of functioning), which thereby manifests itself as a coherent whole. Thus, every practice and social relation figures within a concrete totality that is always already given and that determines that relation as its condition of existence. This totality, to the extent that it has materiality, carries a spatial dimension, for example, the separation of the producer from his/her means of production and the division of labor. As soon as this separation is realized—becomes physically established—it allows for the reproduction of the relation and, consequently, of the separation itself. Though all relations contribute to the constitution of social reality, every singular practice takes social reality—and hence spatiality—for granted. This is what may be called the "ecological paradox": for although the socioeconomic space is a product of practices, it appears, however, as somehow externally given for each individual practice or interaction (Lipietz 1989).

In other words, to the extent that it is not a historical transformation of the conditions of existence (i.e., of a revolutionary or long-term nature), the material existence of social reproduction also plays the part of a "social mold" determining the "habitus" (Bourdieu 1978), anticipations, behavior, and opportunities of the social formation as a whole. The social space, therefore, is one of the dimensions (the spatial dimension) of this social mold that one could call "the habits of history" (Lipietz 1987). In this light, social space should not be comprehended as the reflection (or support of the reflections) of social relations that would exist "elsewhere"; nor should it be perceived as a milieu, a field of deployment of regular practices constituting these relations. But in social reproduction the material space appears either as a result or as a determinant of these relations and practices. One can state that the social space is a "moment" of social reproduction. In this respect—and in this Hegelian terminology— the social "space-in-itself" is a "reflection" of social relations. This space-in-itself is the objective foundation of the empirical space in which social practices seem to take place, are embedded, and deployed.[4]

From Hegemony to Space-for-Itself

It is to the merit of Antonio Gramsci to have made, within the Marxian approach, significant progress in reflecting on the passage from "society as a field of relations" to "society as an agreement or struggle for the conservation or the establishment of a field of relations."[5] He did so precisely on the issue of the regional and national question, suggesting the notions of "social bloc" and "hegemonic bloc." A social bloc is a convergence of social groups or fractions belonging to certain groups.[6] A hegemonic bloc is the social bloc capable of representing or dictating (i.e., imposing) its project as that of society as a whole.[7] A space-for-itself is the spatial dimension of a social bloc, of its hegemony, or of the open struggle between such blocs.

Spaces-for-themselves might include such cases as the following: a nation, recognized or seeking to be recognized (e.g., Palestine or Sahara); or a more restrained space, still affirming its specificity (a region defined by a regional movement); or a wider space materializing in a community seeking a certain mode of life ("the Umma," the "Free World"). Notice first that a space-for-itself can as easily express positions of either a conservative, modernist, reactionary, or progressive nature. And second, a space-for-itself may be defined in any instance (e.g., economic, ideological, religious, political, and linguistic options). Hence conflicts of legitimacy and the possibility of shifts: One can experience oneself as a Yugoslavian (against Stalin) and then as a Croatian (as a Catholic); one can experience oneself as an Arab nationalist, but also as Lebanese, and, then again, as a Sunni; and so forth. Notice finally that, as a result, the borders of a space-for-itself do not necessarily coincide with the space-in-itself proper to a particular social relation, nor with the language community or the citizenship.[8] In contrast, few social movements exist without a spatial dimension, whether nationalist or regionalist. Conversely, a region that acquires a consciousness-of-itself cannot avoid having an ideological dimension: elegy for a re(li)gion, writes Francisco de Oliveira (1977) speaking of the northeast of Brazil.

Economic Regions, Regional Armatures, Nation-States

An homogeneous area consisting of articulation of modes and forms of production will be defined henceforth as an "economic region."[9]

"Homogeneous" here should not imply that we disregard subregional differences, the most evident of which are urban-rural divisions, or that we neglect economic and social divisions in the urban spaces or urban hierarchies within the region. Considering the totality of these relations (urban and rural; workers and bourgeois neighborhoods), it may be said that the form of articulation of these relations "individualizes" the region. In an economic region, a definite subregime of accumulation evidently exists that maintains relations with its exterior. The choice of scale (i.e., of the social relations under consideration) can be somewhat artificial; the "Industrial North," for instance, is a global economic region, whereas the Great West of France and the northeast of Brazil form economic regions within national spaces.

Yet such illustrations of space-in-itself do not necessarily provide a sufficient basis for the articulation of a space-for-itself. For example, while the North-Western part of the world and the Brazilian *nordeste* provide illustrative cases, for the time being at least, the Great West of France does not. Evidently, there is some question as to the existence of the hegemonic social bloc and the institutional forms that grant a space for its personality. And it is precisely at this point that the question of the state can no longer be avoided: the state as "the apparatus by which society equips itself in order that the different groups of which it is constituted do not exhaust themselves in a struggle without end," as Marx and Engels defined it in *The German Ideology*. The topology of state relations—i.e., the topology of relations of sovereignty (or national borderlines)—relentlessly divides the scale of spaces among the national, the local, and the global.

We will call "regional armature" a space-for-itself where the dominant classes of the hegemonic bloc mobilize ideological and political apparatuses enabling the appropriate regulation at this level of some aspect or another of the socioeconomic conflict. Several regional armatures can divide an economic region, and certain parts of an economic region can appear as deprived of a significant regional armature. (Think of the specificity of Wales in relation to Sussex, for example.) Yet, the regional armature must be sharply distinguished from the nation-state, the territory of which is characterized by the universality of law (social law in particular), the uniqueness of its currency, and the monopoly of legitimate violence (sovereignty).

Let us limit ourselves to the economic aspects. It is only at the national scale that a policy of social compromise can become durably stable. For it is only within the totality of a state that social reproduction—and, in particular, the regime of accumulation—can make use of all the forms of compensatory mechanisms and of monetary, nonexchange transfers (e.g., taxes and social revenues). It is the privilege of the state to issue the general equivalent: the national currency that each holder of an income can exchange for an output realized at every location in the national territory, in an expedient fashion for both the individual and society. But this is also its limit. The exterior or balance of trade constraint requires that a distributed income exchanged for a foreign output should almost simultaneously have its counterpart in an equivalent exportation. A region (subnational), in contrast, does not face an exterior constraint.[10] This fundamental difference between the national and the local inevitably leads to political consequences; struggles and compromises can only be settled at the national level or, more precisely still, can only be settled at the level of regional armatures at the mercy of conditions warranted at the national level. A regional armature can extract the conditions for local compromises from the rest of the nation (in France, for example, le Midi Viticole, the industrial regions in decline). But it is certainly a national compromise (the maintenance of a "culture of the vine," of industries unprofitable from a capitalist point of view), at the charge of the nation, to make this compromise respected within the context of its exterior constraints.

But what about supranational spaces-for-themselves? Are there supranational forms of regulation, embedded in an international consensus among classes? Of course such forms exist, but until recently they have been rather weak forms of implicit hegemony, such as the dollar standard and "virtuous configurations" of complementarity between the national regimes of accumulation (Lipietz 1987). I will return to this issue later, when dealing with the European question.

Interregionality

First of all, a fundamental point needs to be clarified: the statute of interregionality in the definition of regions. In other words, one must ask: Is a region defined by itself, by the type of articulation of social relations that characterize it (see the definition above), or in relation to the others by the relation that opposes it to the other regions? Or yet more problematically: Is this "homogeneity" ascribed to the economic regions solely the product of the history of socioeconomic relations in these regions, or is it the impact of the position that regions take in an interregional division of labor? In brief: Is the interregionality derived from the regions, or vice versa? This is a decisive theoretical question for the problem at hand, irrespective of the degree of autonomy of the space-for-itself that grounds the economic region under investigation. If one adopts a global or an international theoretical perspective, then the potential for recognition of local, regional, or national socioeconomic transformations is very small. If, however, one adopts a regional standpoint, then everything evidently changes.

Despite the decisive nature of this issue, the answer will be voluntarily ambiguous.[11] First of all, it is evident that there exists a spatial division of labor internal to the economic region and that this very division in turn defines the subspaces (e.g., urban-rural). On the other hand, it is evident that there exists at the supraregional level a de facto spatial division of labor between the economic regions as soon as they become articulated among themselves: different-type regions neither produce nor exchange the same things. The only question lies in knowing whether the difference between regions (i.e., between the types of internal articulation that characterize them) is the product of different internal (genealogical) causalities, or whether it is the outcome of interregional relations. To this specific question, I answer: Both at the same time, according to a varying importance, and depending upon the topology proper to the division of labor corresponding to the most developed forms of contemporary capitalism, but leaving to internal causation an irreducible importance that always conserves its primacy in the case of a space identified with a given nation-state. To put things differently, the interregional division of space develops in correspondence with the current tendencies of the capitalist division of labor and on the basis of a checkerboard of regions having their internal "Okinawa"-social features inherited from the past (this is the "coarseness" or rather the "viscosity" of space, as evoked by Milton Santos, 1978). Thus, the development of the interregional division of space also takes into account the possibilities and willingness of the hegemonic social bloc in the concrete regions to adapt or resist. More simply still: The interspatial relations of the center-periphery type are the results, not the causes, of the socioeconomic characters of the peripheral spaces. The ultimate causes should be traced back to the internal dynamics of peripheral spaces, in the understanding that the forms of colonization should be considered as a part of these internal dynamics, and that the relations between the internal hegemonic bloc and the exterior weigh heavily on its proper dynamics.[12]

THE CRISIS OF FORDISM

Let us briefly review the notion of Fordism—the regime of intensive accumulation with mass consumption under monopolist regulation—that dominated in the North-West of the world from 1945 to 1970.

As a regime of accumulation, Fordism is based upon an organization of labor that combines Taylorism (separation of conception and execution, parceling and standardization of tasks) and mechanization (by incorporating the social know-how systematized in the machine system). The consequence of this process is a rapid growth of the apparent productivity of labor and of fixed-capital per capita. The outlets for this increased productivity are established through this same growth of per capita capital, on the one hand, and an increase in the real wage level corresponding to gains in productivity, on the other. Regulation of this regime of accumulation is in the first instance based on regulation of the wage-labor relation: coercive institutional forms (generalized collective agreements, growing minimum-wage levels, the welfare state) controlling parallel growth of demand stemming from the wage-laborers and capitalist production. To these one must add the consolidation of a pure credit currency with legal tender, issued in function of the involvements of private capital.

The Spacial Arrangement of Triumphant Fordism

There is an immediately striking and intimate relationship between Fordism and national space. Never before has the space of capital been so closely identified with the national framework, characterized by the validity of the legal-tender credit-currency and the redistribution of revenues in the welfare state. It was in the mid-1960s that the relation between exports and the domestic markets for manufactured goods reached its historical depth in most capitalist countries. Still, the exchange flows took place most essentially inside supranational continental blocs (e.g., the EC, U.S.A.–Canada). After that date, these exchanges tended to intensify and, as such, badly affect the efficiency of national regulation.

During the "Golden Age" of Fordism, the interregional division of labor forming the regional spaces tended to modify itself. In the preceding stages of capitalism these relations corresponded essentially to the spatial dimension of exchange relations between modes of production (external articulation) or between sectors of economic activity. It was the classical spatial division of labor between primary goods and manufactured products that also held sway in the international domain.

But Fordism allowed for a spatial disjunction, a new topology of its own productive process, according to the tripartition of:

1. Tasks of conception
2. Skilled tasks of production
3. De-skilled tasks of assembly

This disjunction did not necessarily adopt an interregional dimension, but could only do so once the firms found, within the old division of labor, the pools of labor power differentiated according to skills, costs, traditions of struggle, and—in the corresponding regional armatures—the social forces available to support such an industrialization strategy. Of course, during the two decades after World War II, this "new interregional division of labor" modified the regional armatures themselves.

The Crisis of Fordism

Nevertheless, after the mid-1960s, Fordism began to run out of breath. The Fordist operational modes engendered declining productivity gains while the technical composition of capital increased. This resulted in a fall of profitability that simultaneously diminished the capacity to accumulate; at the same time, accumulation led to less and less employment. As a consequence, the financing of the welfare state went into crisis. This, in turn, also decelerated the rhythm of accumulation.

The first reaction of firms was to counter the fall in profitability and the increase in the cost of the welfare state by seeking to implant "type III" activities in the economic regions external to the national Fordist social-formations in southern and eastern Europe and in the Latin American or East Asiatic Third World. This strategy, which extended the Fordist interregional division, succeeded all the better as it matched the division of local hegemonic blocs. Therefore, this strategy is called "primitive Taylorization" (cf. Lipietz 1985). But this strategy, in effect, served also to accelerate the internationalization of production and markets, and in this way it paralyzed the national monopolistic regulation to an increasingly greater degree. The external constraints entered into contradiction with the principles of the monopolist regulation of the wage-labor relation: In order to be competitive, the domestic wage-labor costs needed to be compressed. But what was consequently a cost to the domestic market could not automatically be regained through growing exportations.

In a first configuration of the crisis (1974–1979), the internal stimulation of the central markets continued to prevail by means of the credit system and gave certain newly industrialized countries access to a form of "peripheral Fordism" (Lipietz 1987). But more fundamental, within the industrialized countries themselves the wage-labor relation had to face two important inflections, the first one being regressive, the second one potentially progressive.

First of all, conditions for the reproduction of labor power were challenged. During economic growth, the coupling of productivity and wage level to one another had played the principal part and the welfare state a supportive part. As the welfare state continued to develop, securing for the wage-laborers and their families a kind of permanent income, enterprises tried to get rid of the heavy contractual bonds that were linking them directly to their wage-laborers. The "hard core" of labor (the permanent workers) began to break down, while a world of statuteless, low-paid, short-term, and part-time workers began to develop. These workers live primarily on the welfare state and only occasionally on a salary. This peculiar form of wage-labor relation, being an attractive solution to each individual enterprise, became a burden upon population and enterprise as a whole, for, in fact, social security and payroll taxes increased substantially. Moreover, this evolution even further disarticulated the consensus on Fordism. The last remainders of "statute" or "craftsmanship" disappeared among the young, condemned as they were, upon entry into the job market, to "bit (odd or small) jobs" and welfare.

The second tendency, evidently more interesting, was the search for new deposits of productivity. These sources were looked for within the work process itself, in the promising potential of the electronic "technological revolution" and the challenge to Taylorist principles: redefining tasks, and individual or collective involvement (through the "quality circles") of producers in search of efficiency.

But these germs of the future, just like Taylorism before them, could only develop in a favorable macroeconomic and social framework. This was clearly rejected by the monetarist shock. At the end of the 1970s, the social hegemonic bloc in the North-West of the world openly resigned itself of policies aimed at stimulating domestic demand. The restriction on credit and the challenge to social legislation drove this economic region into a succession of sharp business cycles resulting by 1979 in industrial stagnation. This contraction of credit and outlets by the "Center" has had disastrous effects on the whole of the old periphery, but it hit certain countries of peripheral Fordism particularly hard.

It is as if, having correctly identified the origin of the crisis in the fall of profitability, the world hegemonic bloc confined the search for its solution to a technological revolution liberated from the obstacles of national monopolistic regulation, and social legislation in particular. Yet, one should think more carefully about the real contribution of the technological revolution. Between technology and the model of development are a series of linkages established throughout social relations: from technology to technical operationalization and direct production relations (i.e., who decides how the collective work process will be organized?); and the overall socioeconomic relations from production to the economy (i.e., will there be enough consumers or, conversely, investors? what will they produce? which form of full employment?). In other words, a new regime of accumulation and a new mode of regulation, especially with respect to the wage-labor relation (or other relations of production) remain to be invented. In addition, the development should also be compatible within some new international configuration. I will briefly examine these three series of problems.

The Great Liberation of the 1980s?[13]

What does informatics offer? It offers not so much a gain in productivity per second of utilized machine-time, but rather the possibility of making full-time use of the machines on the workfloor and also of making that workfloor more flexible (Coriat 1984). A Fordist plant, based on the double-specialization of machines and people, makes uneconomic use of their time, for example, waiting-times between two operations, intermediary buffer stocks that pile up, and the impossibility of balancing work positions. The automatic control of a workfloor allows for a leap forward in the flexibility of the production process and hence for the economic use of constant capital. This is the large source of profitability that informatics offers. Information systems are quite expensive in initial investments, yet these investments can be used at full capacity.

There is more to consider. Electronics, especially, allow for increased flexibility in the system of machines. It was indeed a long while ago that the principle of automation entered the workshop: people created machines that, by themselves, would repeat their movements, such as in production lines in automobile processing or in print shops. But in order to produce the same uniform product, these enormous machineries could only perform a well-defined series of movements. In contrast, the robot can adapt itself and shift from one task to another by means of rapid reprogramming. As such, the robotized workshop can adapt itself to a fluctuating demand, jumping from one small series of tasks to another.

First bifurcation. Two evolutionary axes open up for the post-Fordist reorganization of the labor process. Automating the administration of the production process opens the temptation to separate still further the theoretical concept of the process from the executing acts of the collective worker. The operating workers would then become mere flesh and blood in the automated process of production. A majority of U.S. as well as some European plants, especially in Spain, France, and the U.K., follow this path. In contrast, however, automation can give rise to a partial reskilling of the collective worker, the practical knowledge of the operators having not only a real-time involvement in the process itself, but also in the permanent tuning of the equipment. This route seems to be being pursued by the majority of Japanese and European plants, especially in Germany and Scandinavia (Aoki 1985). This bifurcation is the scene of an immense social struggle over a new social compromise dealing with worker involvement and distribution of increased gains in productivity.

Second bifurcation. One should also know how these gains in productivity are to be utilized. The first variant in the post-Fordist alternative will mobilize even more capital than the aging Fordism itself. Productivity gains will be reserved as profit, and final demand will not grow. The flexibility, in itself, of computerized processes allows for the profitability of large-scale investments—by a succession of limited series of products—meant for segmented and capricious consumption by well-to-do clients. But these gains in productivity, in the absence of an extension of mass consumption, will also entail the growth of unemployment and the risk of a three-tiered division of society: a dominant class benefiting from the new gadgets of the electronic revolution; a stable but limited core of permanent employees; and a growing mass of increasingly more precarious wage-laborers marginalized by significantly weakened social protection, and finding only provisional access to service jobs during cyclical upswings. This seems to be the route being followed at present in the United States.

The other trajectory is the negotiated redistribution of gains in productivity, with mass access to the new consumption commodities that themselves require consumption time (e.g., cultural, optical, and acoustic hardware, home computers). These low-cost commodities (in comparison to automobiles) call for a division of gains in productivity in the sense of a substantial decrease of working time. Of course, a development model based on mass extension of nonpecuniary activities (e.g., leisure, creative activities, or intellectual enrichment) risks becoming translated into greater uncompetitiveness (in terms of the hourly wage-labor cost) compared to a model based on the intensification of labor without redistribution of gains in productivity. Yet, this way is being followed by Germany, Scandinavia, and, lately, even Japan. Consequently, there is a new bifurcation: Does the configuration of the world economy, the choices of the most powerful states, and the forms of interregional and international regulation leave certain spaces-for-themselves (regional armatures or nation-states) sufficient degrees of autonomy to explore new social relations? This question leads to the core of the subject, and the experience of previous years already gives some indication as to future possibilities.

THE AUTONOMY OF SPACES IN CRISIS

A Little More Theory

In order to face a crisis of the regime of accumulation and/or the mode of regulation at the local, national, or world level, it is important to understand that the social formation breaks down into not two but at least three basic postures that, in turn, can give birth to social blocs:

1. Defenders of the prevailing order up until the crisis itself (i.e., the conservative bloc);
2. Advocates of change in the capitalist hegemonic system (i.e., the modernist bloc);
3. Protagonists of a profound revolutionizing of existing social relations (i.e., the radical bloc); and also, in most cases, a fourth posture:
4. Those favoring a return to the mythical "golden age" preceding the regime in crisis (i.e., the reactionary bloc).

This very general typology is concretely materialized by ideological currents and social movements that combine these four postures in an often inextricable manner. Moreover, social classes are themselves divided between these different postures, hesitating as they are between the different routes and between the different blocs being formed and aspiring to hegemony.

It would be easy to illustrate this phenomenon of typological breakdown in its political reality.[14] But what about its spatial dimension in terms of spaces-for-themselves? At the regional as at the national level it can happen that the brutality of the transformations turns the whole of participating parties in the old bloc (of the exploiters as well as the exploited) against the project of monopolistic capital and of the centralized state (as in the case of declining regimes). The projected modernist space seems to enter openly into conflict with the old concrete regional space; the modifications of the juridical space, implied by the new project, appear despoiled, while the new classes fostering the changes appear as invaders. In these circumstances, the struggle between classes assumes a very distinct form: It opposes, at least initially, the defenders of the "old space" to the "new space" (or to the new mode of development), which is perceived as imposed by the "foreign state" and rejected as a whole. This is a phantasmagoric figure, where the whole population of a real, concrete space fights a virtual and abstract space.

In correspondence with the facilities they apparently offer, these struggles raise very difficult problems of hegemony in the social movement. At first they appear as indeed legitimate and unanimous—legitimate because humans must fight to save a land they have modeled with their own hands and also for the right to live and work in this country; unanimous because the enemy is elsewhere, at a distance, foreign and abstract. And additionally, as the enemy is monopoly capital and the state that regulates it (in the case of regional struggle) or, more precisely still, multinational capital, one could think that these struggles automatically embody the possibility of forming a radical, anticapitalist social bloc. But it is not so simple. For the old space is itself the very space that articulates social relations, which are themselves relations of exploitation. The regional social armature (or the national state) is de facto under the hegemony of the social conservative bloc. The legitimacy of the struggle may therefore only be the legitimation of the old way of exploitation, and the unanimity of the struggle may mask the direction of the struggle by the old exploiters belonging to the regime in crisis, or even to the preceding regime of accumulation. These are typical cases of nationalist or regionalist reactions, where radical and conservative or even radical and reactionary aspirations become mixed up with one another.[15]

There also exists an inverted image of this mix of reactions. A project of local, regional, or national compromise is difficult to accomplish within the existing interregional and/or international relations. It unites the radical refusal of the old order and the modernist aspirations of the new elites. The opposition between projected and real space then adopts the form of a progressive nationalism or regionalism that perceives exterior dependence as an obstacle to progress. This latter form generally covers situations in which the new seeks to be born, while the former mix of radical and conservative reactions refers back to situations in which the old dies out. In this way, the developmentalist nationalism of Europe and Latin America in the 1950s combined the search for social conquests guaranteed by the state and the more or less successful establishment of the Fordist regime of accumulation. Today's regionalist struggles against industrial restructuring or for protectionist maintenance of social gains in a national support system combine the workers' refusal to be treated as chess pieces and the conservative reaction of state functionaries, the employers' associations, and labor unions belonging to the Fordist compromise. The liberal-modernist current presently affecting the North-West of the world combines the libertarian refusal of the heavy forms of state administration in the Fordist compromise and the projects of multinationalization of a capital disembodied from social legislation.

This observation helps in understanding the absurd polarization that is tearing apart the left in Western industrialized countries, divided as it is between attachment to social-democrat compromises that have become conservative, on the one hand, and a subordinate affiliation to a new modernist bloc, on the other. The conservative avenue is by definition without outlet, even if it remains a feasible practice in the medium term.[16] It is economically condemned by the crisis of Fordism and its forms of national regulation, and, since the mid-1960s, politically rejected by the potentially progressive forces, even before the opening of the economic crisis. But is the modernist solution, as presented by the liberal orthodoxy, really a solution? This will now be briefly examined in order to stress the spatial aspects of the problem.

The Shortcomings of Modernist Liberalism and the Question of the Spaces of Regulation

The thrust of the liberal-modernist current lies in the first instance in the more or less theorized weakness of the Fordist modes of regulation, and especially of the national welfare state. Although too expensive for the productive system, the state organizes for its beneficiaries an economy of distribution in the absence of production. Moreover, the bureaucratic regulations, satisfactory to pilot the capital-widening growth of mass production and free of major innovations, are incapable of detecting and putting into operation the strategic lines of a new productive model still to be discovered. This exploration needs total flexibility and is stimulated by the largest possible competition, at the same time without really knowing if flexibility is required only in the exploratory stage or if it actually constitutes a durable feature of the future model.

The weakness of this current of thought is its total silence with respect to regulation, or rather that global competition would play the part of regulation. For neoliberalism, the future regime of accumulation would be already inscribed in the germs of the "third industrial revolution," and the individual agents (the firms) would adapt, on their own, through a process of struggling for their own existence and natural selection. The spatial consequence would be a reshuffling of the hierarchy of spaces (worldwide/national/local) that Fordism would have concentrated, now more than ever, at the national level. Schematically, the economic would be played out more directly at the world level, and the administration of the social (i.e., of the reproduction of labor power, whether in capitalist employment or otherwise) would be played out at the local level. Less schematically, the local would also have a role as the breeding ground for new productive forces. In a poorly defined continuum, the region would simultaneously be the site of the self-organization of survival through the mechanisms of civil society (e.g., the family, the informal economy) and of the emergence of innovative enterprises (corresponding to the myth of the replicability of Silicon Valley). The role of the state would not disappear; it would assist national firms in facing the world scene. From an organizer of society, it would become a cooperative or a syndicate in the service of local coalitions of private capital in the midst of worldwide competition. But this new role granted to the national state definitely discards the old distinction between nationalist and internationalist fractions of dominant classes. In the countries that became "central Fordisms" during the 1950s and 1960s —thanks to their developmental nationalism—the cooperative state reconciles matters between those advocates of a retreat of the welfare state and those defending state support of industry.[17] In newly industrialized countries led to peripheral Fordism by dictatorships, the democratic pressures stemming from the workers as well as from the interior bourgeois sometimes dissolve into the ascension to power of very moderate social democrats pursuing modernization without necessarily jumping ahead to the welfare state. In fact, these social democrats refuse to sacrifice the internal conditions for external competitiveness.[18]

Obviously, this model shows weaknesses on both sides. At the world level, at least without reservations too numerous to ignore, the argument is full of sophisms: In order to move away from the crisis, each national economy would merely have to become more competitive. This is the illusion of a world market that would function as a thermostat, capable of absorbing all the outputs, as if the competitiveness of some would not subtract from that of the others. The 1982 and 1991 economic slumps and the latent debt crisis of the worldwide economy have, however, demonstrated the instability resulting from an uncontrolled coupling of national economies. At the local level, new responsibilities assigned to civil society bypass by far what is possible within a regional armature devoid of a political apparatus; these include the disaggregation of the family and the local communities as well as the incapacity of the informal economy to provide the professional training corresponding to the proclaimed needs of the technological revolution. If the capacities of local regulation are not reinforced (i.e., if a local political society is not constituted), all of these allow one to foresee a disappearance of the social rather than its regeneration at the local level. As a result, the mode of regulation implicit to this model (within the bifurcation tree originating from the technological revolution outlined earlier) privileges the most regressive sides: aggravation of the separation, internationally as well as interregionally, between designers and executing manual workers; and aggravation of the social dichotomy between the beneficiaries of gains in productivity and the rejected economic agents now oscillating between the regular domestic economy and the bit (small) jobs. In this way, the spatial displacement of the instances of regulation can turn out to determine the evolution of the work process and the regime of accumulation.

Still, it is undeniable that—at the regional as well as at the national level—social blocs and political projects exist that proclaim themselves as "free trade" while still promoting progressive compromises between workers and management and, with respect to the command of technical change, pretend to search for a means for the local administration of the social, the forms of which would be mutually beneficial to society and the individual (e.g., think of the behavior of the Communist Party at Emilia-Romagna). But the success obtained by these modernist blocs often translates into the opposite of what liberal ideology would like to demonstrate. Spaces-in-themselves that are particularly well organized, equipped with intense internal forms of regulation without market character and practicing a protectionism more efficient than it is tacit ("cultural," as one says of Japan), often reveal themselves as the best adapted to world competition. In any case, these spaces (regions or nations) remain reliant on the global economic conjuncture upon which they themselves have no impact, whence the appeal to the national as the only space of explicit regulation possible at present, or the appeal to a supranational, worldwide, or continental (European) regulation.

In this fashion, the shortcomings of modernist liberalism and its economic defeat in the 1980s tend to revive two spatial instances that have had their time of glory but at the moment are doubtless facing a new youth: the federal state and the multinational bloc. These instances oblige us to refine the spatial scale suggested in the first part of this chapter.

By federative state we do not mean so much a juridical form of the state (although it is necessary) but a form of articulation of the national hegemonic system. Since the state cannot seek to assure everywhere the same form of macroeconomic regulation (and because this is not even desirable), the issue is to equip the regional armatures with more powerful instruments of economic and social regulation and to reserve for the nation-state the administration of the external relation (support to industries, administration of foreign exchange). In comparison to Fordism, which is above all and by definition "national," this new division of capacities between the national and the regional means a contraction of the national legislation and collective agreements and a larger variability for the regional armatures in their choice of the social protection level, as, for example, in Ronald Reagan's United States. With respect to peripheral Fordism, this development means that certain regions are abandoned to underdevelopment while others situate themselves for a globally oriented form of modernization (e.g., Brazil and China could follow this route). At the other side of the national level, a multinational bloc confers certain attributes of overall macroeconomic administration on supranational authorities, translating transnational compromises between forces that can themselves be transnational, multiregional alliances. The creation of the European Economic Community has typically represented the constitution of such a bloc. It translated not only the hegemony of the Fordist national blocs of all its participants, but also foresaw forms of collective regulation of the articulation of the modes of production (e.g., the Common Agriculture Policy) and compromise measures for transnational forms of particular regional armatures (e.g., the Mediterranean Programs).

In any case, the crisis of Fordism makes the radical insufficiency of the European Economic Community overt. Being a free-trade zone without common social policy (e.g., there is only the implicit common engagement in the treaty of 1957 to assure interregional equilibrium through an accelerated growth in the standard of living), its institutions condemn the different nations in the community to administer against each other their external constraint by a competitive stagnation resulting in an extended general stagnation. No internal policy—and the social-communist French experience of 1981–1984 is the best example thereof—can escape this iron law.[19] Orchestrated stimulation policy and the coordinated reduction in work time seem to be dictated by common sense, but they imply societal choices, among which are the formation of true hegemonic systems equipped with attributes of sovereignty: something approaching the constitution of a European nation that would eventually adopt the form of a federal state. But the experience of Italian or German unification shows that a nation is not formed coldly and objectively, without civil and foreign wars, even in the favorable case of the language community. In contrast, the experiences of Austria-Hungary or the U.S. Civil War show the great instability of a federal, yet regionally differentiated, state when it is not bound together by a common hegemonic system. Therefore, the purely technological European undertakings, such as the Eureka Project, incur the same risk as the "Parallel Action" in Musil's novel.[20] And the "cold revolution" of European unification through the Maastricht Agreement could eventually lead to similar tensions and outcomes, as in the cases of past unifications such as Yugoslavia or Czechoslovakia.

CONCLUSION

The articulation of the spaciality proper to the Fordist regime, centered on regulation of the nation-state with its virtuous international configuration and its internal differentiations in regional armatures, is at present as outmoded as the corresponding regime of accumulation. The spatiality corresponding to the modernist-liberal ideological current, based upon the coupling of the worldwide or the local with a national state carrying reduced responsibilities, appears at the same time macroeconomically unstable as well as socially regressive. The amendments that the formation of federative states and multinational blocs could offer appear themselves as fragile and unstable. But are all these reasons sufficient to reject such improvements in a progressive strategy?

The problem, as we have seen, is the lack of specialized sovereign authorities to guarantee the compromises institutionalized in the core of a hegemonic system. Whether one likes it or not, struggles and fundamental social compromises are still settled at the national level. But it is not necessarily desirable that the nation-state should keep the quasi-monopoly of the stabilization process and control of historical and social innovations.

For precision's sake, it is important to form an idea of an up-to-date and progressive solution to the crisis. In the absence of credible revolutionary perspectives, it would consist of a form of compromise equivalent to the social-democratic compromise facing the crisis of the 1930s (but necessarily different), more or less opening the road to radicalization. The latter would entail the increased capacity of the administration by the producers and the citizens of their way of life and work, while still pushing back alienation as much as possible through market exchange and forms of state exploitation and oppression, be it capitalist or in a family setting. Such compromises would orient the technological revolution toward increased skills and mastery as well as more conscious cooperation by participants in the productive process, increased control of the social consequences of technical change, and, in particular, of the distribution of gains in productivity in the form of a substantial reduction of work time. In the same sense, while maintaining or improving the level of social protection, such a compromise would seek to increase productivity (in terms of use-value) of the welfare state's funds. The latter would serve to finance alternative (e.g., community-wide, cooperative) forms of collective goods and services, to the detriment of moonlighting and the exploitation of women.

It is clear that such a model, which implies a "reterritorialization" of the relation between skills and jobs and between production and social use, will need nonmarket, democratic forms of regulation, as close as possible to the grassroots and thus regional levels. These forms will imply (while the converse does not) the gradual federalization of the nation-state. The central state should keep its responsibility to lay the minimum thresholds for regional social legislation and guarantee a general realignment of social welfare in order to limit the perverse effects of competition among regions. At the international level, the formation of multinational blocs matching their nonrecessive, macroeconomic policies, bringing together scientific and technical means, and allowing for social innovation, can only play a beneficial role in the continuation of national progressive experiences.

But a reasonable skepticism excludes the possibility that the different nations of a bloc adopt straightaway the same social compromises. Moreover, this is probably not desirable. In a progressive alliance between Europe and certain nations in the Third World, the first may allow the reduction of working time while the others opt to maximize production. One should rather aim at institutional forms within the bloc that would allow or even encourage the social advances, even if they are insulated from each of its members (a kind of Pareto optimality principle), without, however, excluding the coordination of progressive politics.[21] But the political willingness can only be imposed through social movements that are themselves transnational and through social experiences that are themselves regionalized.

NOTES

1. The theory of regimes of accumulation and of modes of regulation (Aglietta 1979; Boyer and Mistral 1978; Lipietz 1979) was first developed in France by making provisional abstraction of the articulation of the modes of production, regional specificities, and international relations, although these preoccupations had been by and large present in the spirit of the authors before the development of this theory and were even at the basis of its development. In any case, the relation between articulation of the modes of production and regimes of accumulation, the regionalization and the internationalization of these concepts, have hardly been pushed later on (but see Lipietz 1987).

2. The term *space* should be understood here in the more general and concrete French meaning, and not only in the abstract (Kantian) English acceptation. For French economists and geographers, space is what is specifically spatial in the notion of territoriality.

3. This theoretical part, as in the next one on Fordism, repeats, summarizes, and develops considerations presented earlier within the context of my work on space and the crisis of the regime of accumulation (see Lipietz 1977, 1987). I repeat intentionally each time when possible my initial formulations relative to both conceptual fields, in order to explore their compatibility.

4. The concepts of "space-in-itself" and "space-for-itself" are developed along lines similar to those found, for example, in the master/slave dialectics of Hegel's *Phenomenology of Mind* and in Marx's early writing. A space-in-itself would be purely objective (empirical) and prereflective conditions, as determined by the mode of production, whereas space-for-itself would imply a subjectively self-conscious region both in terms of territory and goal-oriented praxis (Editors' comment).

5. Society is not just the automatic reproduction of a structure of relations. These relations are relations of practices that, in addition to their routine character, can have an innovative ambit and, to the extent that the relations are contradictory (i.e., opposing individuals and the groups to one another at the same time as unifying them), can even carry a revolutionary or at least transformative vocation. The political is exactly the instance whereby this dialectical reproduction/transformation is condensed; and the ideological is the instance in which this tension is represented.

6. Or, more precisely, defined in themselves by the socioeconomic relations centered upon the project of maintaining or modifying the form of the existing relations.

7. Notice that a social class in itself can be divided among several competing blocs, and that inside a bloc the materiality of the convergence of interests inherent to one group with the interests of the bloc in general may be either more or less disputable. Therefore, it is necessary to distinguish between ruling groups and allied or related groups (Poulantzas 1973a).

8. See on this point the criticism by E. Terray (1973) against the empirist definitions of the nation (for example, Stalin's definition).

9. I intentionally use the vague term "form," first to leave room for the forms of production that the reader would refuse to acknowledge as a real mode of production, but also to take into account that every mode has adopted and adopts a number of forms, which can rival on the same territory.

10. This is a very important point. The "purchasing power" of a region against the overall product of an economic whole is certainly limited by the sum of the budgetary constraints (and the credit capacity) of its members, but this sum can be totally different from the "exportable" production of the region, if the interregional transfers are sufficient.

11. This is the criticism that D. Massey (1978) has addressed to me since the beginning: "The definition of the regions by Lipietz (1977) oscillates between that constructed through historical analysis and that relevant to the actual spatial division of labor."

12. This is the thesis that I defend (1987) in the case of international relations. The example of the relations U.S.A.–Mexico (two spaces created by colonization; then both become politically independent in the same period) is particularly illustrative. The analysis "starting from internal causes" sketched by Octavio Paz (1985) seems much clearer to me than the powerless invocation to "dependence."

13. I repeat here the conclusion in Lipietz (1984b). More recent developments are found in Leborgne and Lipietz (1987) and Lipietz (1989).

14. One can, for example, think of the breakup of the old Roosevelt alliance in the U.S. Democratic party in 1984 between Jackson, Hart, and Mondale, representing roughly the three basic attitudes. This breakup was not yet resolved by the election of 1992.

15. The rise of Muslim integrism can often be interpreted as a "radical-reactionary" reaction to the development of primitive Taylorization or peripheral Fordism. It has all the more success because the secular "radical-modernist" alliances of the preceding period (e.g., Nasserism) pretended that modernization and "progressism" are foreign aggressions.

16. One can interpret the decline of Great Britain and Argentina during the years 1950–1970 as the result of incapability to "modernize" their hegemonic system, facing the growing success of Fordism. Notice that now the conservative route can be embodied by labor or social-democratic parties (in the North) or by "developmentalist" parties (in the South).

17. I have analyzed, under the name "Saint Simonisme" (1984a) the strength of this current in France, well represented by A. Minc (1982) and his formula: "less state-protector (for the wage-labors), more state-shield (for industry facing worldwide competition)."

18. Rereading Poulantzas in the light of the theory of peripheral Fordism, I have called the leading class of this regime of accumulation "interior bourgeoisie." I have analyzed (1987) its hegemony over the democratic transition in Southern Europe in the seventies and in Brazil and Korea at present.

19. See Lipietz (1984b, 1989). One finds more and more analyses of this "perverse effect" in terms of game theory (cf. "prisoner's dilemma"); see, for example, Oudiz (1985). Note that these same perverse impacts can be found in interregional competition for foreign investments.

20. In *The Man Without Quality,* intellectuals from Austria-Hungary seek to riposte by a "parallel action" to the growing prestige of ally-rival Prussia. Their wild imaginings end in an order by the Austrian army to the merchants of Prussian guns.

21. More details on these dreams are in Lipietz 1989.

3

State and Society in International Relations

Ronen P. Palan[1]

Sometime in the early 1970s, the world economy entered what I would regard as a new capitalist phase, commonly referred to as *globalization*. The trend toward globalization of the world market is neither comprehensive nor complete. Porter (1986), for instance, believes that only a select number of manufacturing sectors have become fully globalized. He makes a distinction between multidomestic and global industries.[2] Even the financial markets, a sector commonly thought to have globalized entirely, in reality present a more complex picture: 98 percent of Japanese savings remain in Japan, and the figure stands at 96 percent and 83 percent for the U.S. and U.K. respectively (Lake and Graham 1990). Nonetheless, there is little doubt that the world economy already envelops the globe. This has direct impact on the state and the system of states. As Dendrinos observes:

> These interactions render national boundaries and the political notion of sovereignty obsolete to a great extent. Inter-spatial flows of commodities, labour, capital and information, among other stocks, cross national borders under various degrees of easiness. *De facto* limits rather than *de jure* boundaries become largely effective (1992, 56).

Many have concluded on the basis of similar observations that the vestiges of the old "national" order founded on a fragmented political authority (the "system of states") are an anachronistic residue of the past soon to be discarded.

I would not dispute Dendrinos's comments. Nonetheless, like other contributors to this volume (Cerny; Lipietz), I would advise against jumping to conclusions. As Cerny observes, the state is not about to "wither away" under the impact of a globalizing economy. On the contrary, the state is changing and transforming itself in such way that "the concept of the national interest itself is expanding to embrace the international dimension in new ways" (see Chapter 10).

Unfortunately, the debate about the role of the state in an increasingly global economy has all too often been conducted without due attention paid to either state theory or to the history of state formation. The operating assumption had been an image of the state drawn from the writings of the nineteenth-century idealists (Palan and Blair 1993). These represent the state as a discrete social entity, an ontological body (politic) whose territorial boundaries mark a clear separation in social interactions. Since states are believed to exert (or to have exerted at some unspecified point in the past) full control over "their" economy and society, a transnational market appears to have eroded and indeed shaken the very foundation of the state.

This fashionable, common-sense representation of the state neglects, however, the reality, which is that states are not, nor have they ever been, mere "units": egos confronting other egos in some synthetic "international arena." It is naturally convenient to think of "The State" as a cohesive body operating not unlike human beings. The difficulty is that whenever the state is represented as a definable social entity, as if it were one type of unit or another, the very processes that make up the state—the processes that sustain it as a viable social format—are downplayed almost to the point of disappearance. It then becomes a matter of constantly reminding ourselves that the units of our imagination are mere constructs. It is for this reason that several state theorists have found it far more appropriate to treat the state as a series of processes linked together by political interests (Jessop 1990; Poulantzas 1973a; see also Lipietz in this volume). This image may appear diffused and difficult to grasp (Easton 1981); however, it brings us closer to the actual dynamics of the state and the political processes of which it is composed.

What I would like to show in this chapter is that, from the perspective of the "relational" state theory, the study of relations between the state and the world economy assumed radically different significance. Put crudely, the state may be viewed as a form of articulation of class power. In a context of a globalized world economy, the *territoriality* of the state is significant not as the source of quasi-ontological needs and desires but because the state is the primary political organizational mechanism of social order and transformation. As Lipietz argues in this volume: "Whether one likes it or not, the struggles and the fundamental social compromises are still settled at the national level." In other words, irrespective of the fact that the economy is globalizing, political processes are still very much territorially circumscribed. Undoubtedly, the growing imbalance between a transnationalizing world economy and the politically fragmented system of nation-states poses difficulties in the regulation of capital (and hence to the prospects and fate of capitalism). But nonetheless, it would be foolhardy to pronounce at this stage the coming end of the state and of the state system.

The study of the relation between the state and the global economy must not be founded, therefore, on the premise of an inherent contradiction between them (Gilpin 1987). Markets (let alone "the economy," which is an abstraction) do not possess the capacity for self-regulation, but rather require extensive political and ideological support. This has been the message of writers from Adam Smith to Marx and Keynes.

The very fact that the world economy has been globalizing for an extended period of time (the past five hundred years, according to Wallerstein), within the context of the state system, suggests that there are perhaps less-visible mechanisms by which such political and ideological support are "transnationalized" as well.[3] The mechanisms of synchronization of political and ideological support may not be perfect, smooth, or of necessity functional, but they merit attention and explication.

Recently, the discipline of International Relations has been increasingly concerned with the nature of such mechanisms. The theories of hegemonic stability, imperialism and neocolonialism, world-system analysis, regime theory, structural power, the Gramscians, and transnational class alliances suggest, each in its own way, mechanisms by which a transnational informal order may come into being. To these works I would like to add a discussion of the intersocietal dimension of a transnational order.

STATE FORMATION AND THE EUROPEAN MARKET

Historically, the growth of the European and then global market can be correlated with the expanding role of the state. The relationships between the two structures, however, was never linear or deterministic. Four points in particular are worth bearing in mind.

1. The European state system emerged as the principal form of social organization in a specific historical context. State forms have of course existed for millennia (Claessen and Skalnik 1978). Nonetheless, in Europe the post-Carolingian state system was "swallowed," to use Sorokin's phrase, "by the feudal social bodies, and an enormous number of relationships just dropped out of the state system" (Sorokin 1941, III: 57). The state reemerged from the throes of feudalism as the political format that proved successful in providing political order. As Cole explains:

> The first and clearest necessity which the critical events of the sixteenth century pointed to was that of shifting to a particular system of maintaining order. . . . During the Middle Ages . . . [s]poradic violence was chronic in the entire system. When finally, the schism within the religious community occurred, it became evident that the old order was doomed. The only alternative was to accept the dismembered parts as self-sufficient units with which to rehabilitate strong government (Cole 1948, 17).

The concept of sovereignty, articulated by Jean Bodin in the late sixteenth century ([1576] 1986), gave the legal foundation of a fragmented political order, based on precedents in biblical and classical texts, to the new political and social order.

I would propose, therefore, that the rise of state format in Europe was in essence a *political* response to a political problem, the problem posed by violence and civil disorder.[4]

2. The modern state system, however, cannot be divorced or dissociated from the momentous event of the rise of capitalism. For unlike previous state formats, the rise of the modern state system from around the sixteenth century took place *in the wider context of the rise of contractual relationships.*[5] There is a great measure of truth in the claim that the modern state is rooted in, or can be "derived" from, the separation between workers and the means of production (Holloway and Piccioto 1978; Pashukanis 1983; Poulantzas 1973a). Indeed, Simon Clarke suggests that our first point may be linked to the second:

> The rise of capitalism precipitated a crisis in the political and ideological forms of the pre-capitalist state, which was resolved by the reconstitution of the state on the basis of the radical separation of the state from civil society and of the social power of money from the political power of the state (1988, 17).

This statement, although representative of a common Marxist interpretation, oversimplifies. If embryonic forms of the modern state can be traced back to the kingdom of the two Sicilies (and even before) and the beginning of the separation of state from "civil society" in the late fifteenth century, then capitalism is commonly believed to have become established as a dominant mode of production toward the end of the eighteenth century. Clarke is obviously pushing the cart before the horse. But if we replace the concept of capitalism with that of the market or more properly "the markets," then, as Braudel and a number of other writers have suggested, the emergence of a pan-European market and the colonial markets may have hastened the breakdown of feudal order (founded on the principle of the two universal rulers, the pope and the Holy Roman Emperor) and accelerated the emergence of a new political order.

3. Our modern sense (or myth) of society as a closed circuit of social activity emerged only following the industrial revolution (Hall 1986). In the opinion of Mary Kaldor (1991), the state has not been an effective tool of economic policy since the 1920s. From then on, only alliances of states and transnational cartels exercised a measure of control. The same period, however, also saw an unprecedented expansion of the state's functions and activity in society and economy. Indeed, broadly speaking, the increase in

the role and function of the state appears to be functionally related to the degree of transnationalization achieved by the world economy. A globalized economy generates more demands on the state, not the other way around.

4. Therefore, it is impermissible to assume that the state and the state system simply serve the needs of capital. At minimum there is tension, as van der Pijl observes, between ". . . the unifying force of world capital and the centrifugal effect of its 'national' fraction . . ." (1989, 11). Since self-organization implies a certain autonomy, for the self-organizing entity must be treated as a closed circuit, state policies cannot be entirely subsumed under the concept of capitalist relationships. State and international politics are complicating factors that deserve separate theoretical attention.

It is, therefore, not sufficient to recognize either the separability of state and market, or, conversely, their interconnectedness. A theory of international relations needs to demonstrate how and on what levels they overlap.[6]

THE UNDERLYING UNITY OF POLITICS AND ECONOMICS

To pursue a more holistic interpretation of the relations between politics and economics, and to begin to understand the interrelation between state and market, we must start from the basis that "politics" and "economics" are conceptual abstractions. Whether one is aware of this or not, these concepts are intelligible when a prior theoretical space is assumed in which they were not separated. There is, in other words, an underlying unity to economics and politics. In the annals of the social sciences this underlying space is called "society."

When a perception of society as an interdependent set of relationships—a system or complex set of *functionally* interdependent processes—began to emerge in the seventeenth century, first implicitly and then explicitly (Benseler 1980), then politics, economics, and culture (and then ideology) began to be viewed as separated and yet interdependent sets of practices.[7] In the writings of Hegel, for instance, successful or powerful societies were assumed to have resolved (for a given historical period or "moment") the problem of functional interdependence among these practices. These societies achieved perfect harmony between the needs and desires of their individual members, the level of their economy, and the character of the state. Subsequently, the field of administration explicitly sought to produce such interdependence and harmony among the economy, society, and politics. The same "structural-functional" ideas also permeate Marxist political discourse. As Poulantzas maintains, a strong and democratic state is a state in which the structures (politics, economics, and ideology) are properly articulated; fascism and military dictatorships are evidence of a noncorrespondence between these practices (Poulantzas 1974, 1975).

The very concepts of politics and economics therefore evoke, although implicitly, a *potential* functional relationship between them. The problem, however, is that the two concepts work within an implicitly bounded space, i.e., society. Hence, there are particular problems that the spatial incongruity between political and economic practices injects into the analysis. Attentive reading of political process theories, however, shows that such an interpretation is misleading. The theories of the political process can serve the study of international relations equally as well as they do the study of domestic politics.

By using the language and concepts of politics and economics, we already assume a certain functional interdependence between them. But what is the nature of this interdependence? We have been accustomed to think of economics in terms of a pure, nonterritorial, closed system of interaction; hence the discipline of Economics tends to neglect the social, political, and—more broadly, although perhaps less so in the past decade —the spatial dimensions of economic activity. Economic models relate, for example, changes in productivity, interest rates, wages, and so on, linking them in turn to other factors in the production process. A model treats the economy as an interdependent system.

The world market, the spatial framework that is the locus of economic activity, is not an organization but what Braudel calls a "social set" (Braudel 1979) and Mann a "social network" (Mann 1986). Unlike the state, which is a social organization, the world market may be thought of as a social network, i.e., a milieu of opportunities and constraints of actors' activities operating essentially outside the scope of individual will. As Marx describes it, the market maintains "[t]he mutual and universal dependence of individuals who remain indifferent to one another" (Marx 1980, 66). The market, therefore, is a framework that relates individuals, however indifferent they may be to each other.

In studying this market, the discipline of Economics owes its success in part to the fact that the economic system, or the market, is treated as an informational system wherein economic factors are viewed as "messages." The modern market is actually a metaphor. We think of traditional marketplaces at the center of the village where people meet each other face-to-face and exchange goods. The modern market is not such a "place"; there is very little face-to-face contact in this market. The modern market has been in reality *dis-placed*, although it has maintained the element of exchange of information. As Piore and Saville observe:

> every economy must have mechanisms to coordinate the actions of the separate decision-making units of which it is composed. Those mechanisms must balance supply and demand in individual markets. . . . In capitalist countries the most familiar form of microeconomic regulation is the price system (1984, 50).

The economic system may be viewed, then, as a communication device transmitting messages about the structure of opportunities and constraints open to individuals and companies.

Political studies have not achieved such sophistication. But contrary to popular belief, they are not far behind. Like economic ones, political studies have adopted similar informational-flow models. Dunleavy and O'Leary captured the point well when they observed that "analyzing politics in terms of 'the state' directs our attention to a single central problem, the interrelation between governing institutions of a country and other aspects of that society" (1987, 320).

The "pure" studies of politics and economics have established, in other words, two sets of informational flows or two systems of messages. They can be combined because, at base, the raw material (information) of the political system is not different from the information that lies at the base of the economic system. Indeed, most political scientists would readily accept that, at base, political power and economic power are one and the same. Similarly, the basic categories of economics, such as wages, interest rates, productivity, and profit, are political-economic categories. Politics and economics converge, therefore, at the base.

Awareness of the underlying common denominator in the two types of informational systems has been at the root of some of the more exciting research in the social sciences. Dependency theory, for instance, demonstrated that the concepts of comparative advantage and the international division of labor assume different significance when seen in a political and social context. A comparative advantage in a particular sector such as banana exporting translates politically into a ruling class that is unlikely to be of much assistance for the broader industrialization needs of a country. Similarly, the French school of regulation demonstrated that what Poulantzas called the "articulation of structures in the state" has concrete implications for regulating the economy and hence for economic growth.

SOCIETY AS AN INFORMATIONAL SYSTEM

Although it is customary to speak of the economic system as a system of informational flow, the notion of the state as an informational system requires clarification. This again can be best understood in an historical perspective. Feudal disintegration provoked the collapse of the universal medieval cosmology and precipitated a new political philosophy centering on the political communities. Pluralism thus became an attractive ideology to many of these communities (Gierke 1939: Nisbet 1974). Nonetheless, proponents of the pluralist thesis experienced difficulties explaining precisely why a permanent state of conflict is the best method of organizing a community. Consequently, racial and religious homogeneity of the social base was thought by some to be instrumental in maintaining order, hence the great expulsions of the Moors, Jews, and the Huguenots and other non-conformist Christian denominations. Similarly, Renaissance political science celebrated smallness and civic culture: the bigger the state, went the argument, the more potential existed for civil unrest and factionalism.

The pluralists lacked a firm foundation for their prognosis. Unexpected assistance came in the twentieth century from the new science of cybernetics. Cybernetics demonstrated that one of the keys to the homeostasis of complex systems is, among other things, an efficient flow of information between the components (Foerster 1968; Wiener 1948).

Under the twin impact of pluralism and cybernetics, twentieth-century Sociology began to conceive of society as an informational system. Democracy was then perceived as the best social order because it assures efficient transmission of information between society and state. Political Science followed the lead by developing schemes in which politics is discussed as an informational flow. Open expression of ideas and political interests were encouraged because they expedite the efficient flow of information. David Easton (1953) identified this fundamental shift in concern and coined the term, *political process*. Politics, he argued, is not simply about power and prestige, as Hans Morgenthau (1967) maintained, nor is it about subjects' desires, as Lasswell (1977) would have us believe. On the contrary, politics is essentially a system of relationships among groups whereby resources and values are allocated.

Easton, however, confused the subject of politics with its consequences. He defines politics (the subject) as he imagines its consequences (value allocation) to be; thus it appears that his underlying notion of the political system is of an extended transmission system communicating demands and support from civil society and translating these via the governing apparatus into operative goals. In contrast to the prevalent opinions in the nineteenth century—which, as argued above, informed international relations theories' perception of the state—the main feature of the political process is the absence of teleology. In modern thought, states and societies are not considered volitional subjects. On the contrary, only through the political process do societies formulate objectives, which are always in a sense short term.

FROM THE POLITICAL SYSTEM TO RELATIONAL THEORY

Easton's scheme is only of limited utility for political analyses. The reason is simply that the structural-functionalist concept of the political process is context-free, whereas politics is context-laden (Ake 1982). Easton's contribution lies, therefore, primarily in the study of administration and government. Nicos Poulantzas (1973a) was strongly influenced by these ideas and incorporated them into a Marxist framework. Vulgarization of the Marxist concept of determination aside, let us provisionally accept that the fundamental notion of Marxist political science is that economic and political power are intimately connected. Nonetheless, if politics were solely a reflection of economic interests, as some Marxists appear to argue, this would imply that politics is a purposeless and inconsequential activity, which both Marx and Lenin vigorously denied.

Poulantzas understood this point very well. He maintained that the concepts of economy and politics must be viewed as heuristic tools. They are defined by, and hence perceived as, functionally interdependent: politics is a mode of organizing economic interests, and economics shapes the political scene. People do not forget their politics and culture when they go to work; conversely, their position in the production process defines their class position, i.e., their politics and ideology. This is in contrast to the dominant, action-based thesis stating that politics, economics, religion, culture, and so on are of different action orientations and hence ontologically separable (Weber 1978). Considering, however, that politics may be regarded therefore as a structure possessing its own unique language and rhythm and hence, to some extent, is driven by internal dynamics, it must be recognized, he argued, that politics is *relatively autonomous.*

According to Poulantzas, social classes exert power through the organizational matrix of the "political scene" (the latter term is Poulantzas's version of the structural-functionalist political system). Poulantzas maintains that a full scheme of the political process must include additional information. Political maneuvers ultimately reflect class interests, and class interests are born, in turn, of the socioeconomic structure of a society. Demands and support operate, therefore, not only within the compound of the abstracted political system, but are the political manifestations of economic interests. Put differently, economic structures do not simply generate demands and support; the socioeconomic structure also *structures* the political system: it contains powerful interests that shape the political agenda. This implies, in turn, that changes at the level of the political scene make an impact both upon social classes and the economic structure as well, and vice versa.

Poulantzas's "relational" theory of the state was basically a superimposition of the Marxist perspective upon a functional-structuralist theory. The synthesis of the two generated a dynamic scheme of the political process, linking the economy with politics and ideology. This synthesis is, in my view, still at the heart of the modern theory of the state.

INTERACTIONS AMONG SOCIAL FORMATIONS

Poulantzas's theory provides a framework for research into the manner in which "inputs"—be they political, economic, or ideological—spread laterally throughout the social formation. It tells us what occurs once an external input penetrates the territorial boundaries of the state, but it does not inform us *how* it does so. It is clear, however, that "foreign" factors play a significant role in the development of any society. Indeed, there is a less-visible secondary line of contacts between societies operating and underpinning the formal world of supposedly independent states. Frank, for instance, holds that

> metropolitan centre-peripheral satellite relationships like the process of surplus expropriation/appropriation, run through the entire world capital-ist system in chain-like fashion from its uppermost metropolitan world centre, through each of the various national, regional, local and enterprise centres (1967, 10).

Many believe that this "invisible world" is, in fact, by far the more signif-icant. Cardoso and Faletto, for instance, maintain that these invisible con-nections are at the root of the modern world:

> There is no [sic] metaphysical relations of development between one na-tion and another, between one state and another. The relations are made possible through a network of interests and coercion that bind some so-cial groups to others, some classes to others (1979, 173).

But how does this informal world of intersocietal contacts interact with the domestic political processes? I would argue that "external" inputs, of what-ever form, forge one of the two following links between societies (some-times concomitantly): They either create a direct link, whereby a group re-siding in one society is tied to a group residing in another—we may call these vertical links—or alternatively, they generate horizontal links, those that occur when a group or organization residing in one society finds itself in relations of competition with groups or organizations in another. (This is based on the assumption that as competitors tend to modify their behav-ior or their structure in order to achieve a better position, their destiny be-comes, to some extent, linked.) It may be said that this invisible world of intersocietal interactions is crossed by an infinite number of such links, which, when combined, create an informal socioeconomic network of enormous spatial dimensions.

VERTICAL OR HIERARCHICAL LINKS

Dependency theory demonstrates that transnational links serve to maintain a social structure unfavorable to the long-term requirement of de-velopment of dependent formations. Translated into the language of state theory, the international division of labor "disarticulates"—to use a Pou-lantzian expression—peripheral social formations and reinforces their underdevelopment.

As seen above, in Frank's view, market relationships generate a series of binary contacts between societies cascading from the center to the periphery. He calls them center-peripheral satellite relationships (C-P). Since both the center and the periphery are not given conditions but mutually defining, mutually structuring relationships, they are in effect what philosophers call processes of becoming: active processes in which the center is constantly recentralizing by subordinating the periphery.

Dependency often falls into a tautological trap: observing that there cannot be a center without a periphery, and vice versa. Thus, causes and effects are not differentiated: the conditions of dependency are equated with the concrete links that create a dependency situation. This led many to conclude, incorrectly, that dependency theorists maintain that all C-P links inevitably result in underdevelopment. Since it is not difficult to show that C-P types of relationships are as typical of relationships between advanced countries (Canada, for instance) as between advanced and peripheral formations, a popular rebuff of the dependency theory maintained that it is empirically invalidated by the Canadian experience (Brym 1989). To avoid confusion, I suggest, therefore, that the expression "dependency" be reserved to describe a condition of a country, whereas I will use the more cumbersome concept of the "vertical link" to describe the concrete tie that may indeed lead to a situation of dependency.

The vertical link may be defined therefore *as situations whereby individuals, companies, and organizations residing in one formation are attached by some common purposes or interests to a group residing in another.* For instance, when Volkswagen expanded its operation in Brazil, the Brazilian work force, managers, and marketing force found their fate directly linked to the headquarters in Germany.

Such links do not necessarily cause underdevelopment (or to be more empirical, lower the average standard of living among the population); vertical links characterize not only C-P relationships. They are indeed far more prevalent among C-C relationships (center to center), or what is conventionally called the internationalization of production. They may be found also among P-C (periphery-center) types of linkages: Third World companies' direct or indirect investment in advanced countries. Countless studies have shown that such links produce important political and socioeconomic effects. Clearly, the internationalization of production, the exponential growth of direct and indirect foreign investment, and the growth of international trade have all generated powerful interests in the free-trade regime whose political expression helped reshape the political map of the world. The relative success of some Third World multinational enterprises is generating similar interests in these countries as well.

In this definition the vertical link is a pervasive type of social relationship, so pervasive, in fact, that some may feel it is rather redundant as a heuristic tool. Indeed, dependency may be regarded as a subspecies of a pervasive type of informal link between societies. I would argue, however, that a broad definition is useful because it brings to light the universality of such links, and more so, the similarity of patterns they produce in their interrelation with the domestic political process. The vertical link and its effects are by no means exclusive to capitalist societies or capitalist relations. Indeed, viewed from the perspective of state theory and the political process, trade and investment generate social relationships similar to those found in many other forms. "Patron-client" relationships, for instance, produce similar patterns in preindustrial civilizations. Amnsbury describes patron-client relationships as similar to C-P vertical relationships:

> All pre-industrial civilizations are peasant-based societies. The peasants' patrons might be landlords, gentry, merchants, moneylenders, politicians, banks, or warlords collecting taxes a generation in advance. All peasant-based societies are patron-client structures with pyramidal organized networks. . . . These networks are based on dyads, which are groups of two. Each person, in pursuit of personal autonomy, must enmesh himself in the web (1979, 83).

Vertical links are not exclusively of economic nature as well. Indirect rule, a strategy adopted by the Portuguese, Dutch, and British colonialists, recreates the pattern as well:

> At almost all times it has been a fundamental axiom of Dutch policy to utilize wherever possible the existing native chiefs or headmen, operating through some modified version of the existing institutions, as the intermediaries between the supreme Dutch authority and the mass of the population (Emerson 1964, 411).

Indeed, kings and princes employed the same principle in constructing states and empires as much as in maintaining their colonies. Elias describes the process in the following manner:

> The emperor and king . . . sent trusted friends and servants into the country to uphold the law in his stead, to ensure the payment of tributes and the performance of services, and to punish resistance. He did not pay for their services in money. . . . The earls or dukes, or whatever the representatives of the central authority were called, also fed themselves and their retinue from the land with which the central authority had invested them (1983, 16).

These "trusted friends" served as the nucleus of a hierarchical bureaucratic structure. A pattern spread throughout Europe: it underpinned the English political system, with its justices of the peace and sheriffs acting as independent and self-financing arms of the state down to the late nineteenth century (G. R. Smith 1984). In France a different arrangement, although based on a similar principle, was established toward the end of the

Hundred Years' War, A vertical bureaucratic structure (later reformed by Richelieu) centered around the *intendants* (the intendants of justice, police, and finances), who were functionaries dispatched with omnibus powers into the provinces (Anderson 1974a, 96). The *intendantur der Armee,* again based on the same principle, developed as the nucleus of a new, central government in Prussia (Bruford 1970).

HORIZONTAL LINKS

When two agents, be they individuals, companies, or states, are competing, they tend to modify their behavior or restructure themselves in order to gain advantage. Competition fosters changes within the two social formations. Thus, competition becomes an "input" into the domestic political process.

Competition, referred to here as the "horizontal link," functions as a channel by which societies structure each other, often unintentionally. The fiercer the competition the greater likelihood of fundamental change.

The horizontal links, or links of competition, may be discussed under two separate headings:

1. Commercial competition both (i) between companies residing in different formations and (ii) between states;
2. Military competition between states.

1. *Commercial competition.* There is a vast literature concerned with the interrelation between government policies and commercial competition that goes under the term of "restructuring." When German autoworkers demand a reduction in working time, they are watched carefully by workers, managers, and government officials all over the world, for German work practices have global implications. Because of its success (or supposed success), the Japanese Ministry of International Trade and Industry (MITI) became a model organization imitated worldwide. The pro and cons of industrial policy are discussed even in the Thatcherite heartland. The lineage of the Single European Act can be traced to the actions of two businesses and two businessmen in particular, Philips of Netherlands and Volvo of Sweden, with Wisse Dekker and Pehr Gyllenhammar (Franko 1990). These two are representative of industries that felt the burden of American and Japanese competition and were driven, as a result, to advocate a new political arrangement in order to recover commercial ground (Dumont 1990). These are well-known cases of the socioeconomic implications of commercial competition.

2. *Military competition.* Historically, military competition between states has been one of the most effective channels of communication of

techniques and technologies. Furthermore, states wishing to survive as a viable political force must counteract the administrative developments of their more successful neighbors. States that failed to do so, such as seventeenth-century Poland's failure to follow her neighbors' slide into absolutism, found themselves torn apart.

It is not totally accidental that periods of heightened political tension have also been periods of rapid administrative and constitutional changes. The two main models of the European state, France and England, emerged from a common war, the Hundred Years' War. Similarly, the unprecedented degree of rapidity of administrative changes throughout Europe in the final decade of the sixteenth century was unquestionably related to the unfortunate decision of Charles VIII's of France to march on Italy in 1494. The centralizing tendencies of the English state evolved in response to Henry VIII's dispute with the pope and the Hapsburg empire. The Act of Supremacy (1534) gave the king those doctrinal powers over the Church that the French kings were seeking. The Thirty Years' War, in turn, transmitted modern techniques of statecraft and warfare to the European peripheries, including Brandenburg-Prussia, which subsequently became a major European power. The wars of Louis XIV acted as a catalyst to the English financial revolution that was at the heart of the industrial revolution.

In all these cases, military competition generated change among the competitors: they became "linked" to one another.

THE POLITICAL PROCESS,
VERTICAL AND HORIZONTAL LINKS

I have posed two questions in this paper. The first: How does the state, as a place of articulation of social and political interests, interrelate with an increasingly globalized economy? To my mind, nationalistic and patriotic rhetoric apart, the state is significant in the world economy because it defines the geographical boundaries of the political process. Since the political process shapes the relationships between the socioeconomic structure of society and its political apparatuses, the same political process, by its very nature, relates the world economy to the state.

I have argued that transnational or global interactions together with the domestic political processes forge two types of social links, vertical and horizontal. I will presently demonstrate that an implicit concept of either the vertical or horizontal linkages permeates the literature. Two brief examples may be helpful at this point.

My first example is drawn from Marx's *Grundrisse*. In his comments on trade between England and the Netherlands in the sixteenth and seventeenth centuries, Marx states:

In England the import of Netherlands commodities in the sixteenth century and at the beginning of the seventeenth century gave to the surplus of wool which England had to provide in exchange, an essential, decisive role. In order then to produce more wool, cultivated land was transformed into sheep-walks, the system of small tenant-farmers was broken up, etc. , clearing of estates took place, etc., thus agriculture lost the character of labour for use value. . . . At certain points, agriculture itself became purely determined by circulation, transformed into production for exchange value. Not only was the mode of production altered thereby, but also all the old relations of population and of production, the economic relations which correspond to it, were dissolved (Marx, Grundrisse, 257).

In fact, this paragraph draws on an implicit notion of an interface between the vertical link and the social formation:

1. The Dutch exported surplus commodities to England (a vertical link);
2. England exported surplus wool as a means of obtaining foreign currency (further vertical linkages);
3. To produce more wool, cultivated land was transformed into sheep walks, the system of small tenant farmers was broken up, clearing of estates took place (the vertical linkages interrelate with domestic political processes);
4. At certain points, agriculture itself became purely determined by circulation, transformed into production for exchange value.
5. Not only was the mode of production altered thereby, but also all the old relations of population and of production—the economic relations that correspond to it—were dissolved.

The implications of Marx's analysis are that the evolution of England from an agrarian society to capitalism was inspired by the importation of Dutch commodities. Elsewhere (Palan 1992b) I have argued that the same theoretical framework underpins Marx's theory of the rise of capitalism.

In a different case, the focus is the horizontal link. Rubinson's (1978) brilliant analysis of German unification contains implicitly the notion of an interface between the horizontal linkages and the domestic political process:

Bismarck was able to unify Germany by bringing the opposing interests of Junkers and industrialists together in a compromise that was initially minimally acceptable to both. The Junkers grudgingly accepted it because it insured their political dominance within a united Germany; while the industrialists accepted Prussian rule because it gave them economic prosperity by establishing many elements of their economic goals. The peasants and urban working class, having previously learned that neither Junkers nor liberal were their allies, went along under the inducement of social security and the vote . . . this arrangement still very precarious, but with changes in the world economy favoured the coalition. The opening of American grain with trains, etc. . . . . To maintain their economic position, the Junkers were forced into a policy of economic protection and political supports for grain. This worked in two ways. One, a policy of tariff protection to protect the home market; and two, a policy of grain subsidies to allow Prussian grain to compete. . . . This shift to agriculture protection allied the economic interests of the Junkers with the industrialists, who had always been for protection. . . . This marriage of iron and rye became economically cemented with the Great Tariff of 1879, in which both interests combined around protection (50–53).

In this analysis, Rubinson demonstrates that the fragile German union was strengthened because of unforeseen worldwide conjunctural factors:

1. German unification was a grudging compromise between the Junkers and the industrialists. (A domestic political process is at a critical point. Rubinson makes no reference to the nationalistic movement sweeping through Europe, and Germany in particular, undoubtedly a reaction to the French Revolution—in my terms, a "horizontal effect");
2. The Junkers accepted the union because unification ensured their political dominance; industrialists accepted it because many of their economic goals were attained; peasants and urban workers are induced to accept because of the promise of social security;
3. The opening of American markets posed threats to the Junkers (a horizontal link);
4. They respond by erecting tariffs and subsidizing grains (a horizontal link interrelates with the domestic political process);
5. Protectionism was useful to industrialists as well (the domestic political process is affected by the horizontal linkages);
6. The marriage of iron and rye was cemented with the Great Tariff of 1879.

This brings me to my second question: Are there less-visible mechanisms by which political practices spatially correspond with economic practices? It is clear that a great number of economic, political, or cultural categories, such as the international division of labor, comparative advantage, competition, the domino effect, puppet regimes, and Westernization, are in fact coded terms to describe processes by which societies restructure each other. A division of labor, for example, suggests a degree of *structural* interdependence among those societies that participate in such division. I am not alone in suggesting that an accumulation and amalgamation of such structural interdependencies forms the basis of this informal "global society."

The daunting task of making sense of the myriad of transnational structural relationships could be made clearer by placing them in the context of what I have described as vertical and horizontal linkages. Putting the state in this context places it in an entirely new light: the state, i.e., the political process, not only reacts to external stimuli—military threat, economic competition, economic hierarchy—but, in reacting, internalizes these stimuli. The "outside" becomes the "inside," and the "inside" becomes inseparable from the "outside." The problem of causation, which assigns predominance to either the domestic or the international, is misdirected. The evolution of a system comes about by internal responses to outside circumstances that are in turn re-affective in relation to the general environment as a whole. The environment, or the system, is therefore both the aggregate of the parts and a sum total that must be differentiated from these parts. Nonetheless, the sum in no way negates these parts.

The state operates, then, as a type of transmission mechanism: the various political, economic, and cultural messages are processed, codified, and "internationalized." The end result is a far more synchronized set of social formations that seem to move and develop with greater uniformity than the anarchic configuration would suggest. It therefore becomes appropriate to discuss notions such as the Fordist mode of regulation in the global sense, while at the same time, each state represents a particular variation on the global pattern.

The vertical and horizontal framework offers an empirical framework for tracing the actual linkages between societies, and thus for charting the developmental course of the international system as a whole. It is here that one actually comes to grips with the constitutive dynamics of what we call the international system.

NOTES

1. I would like to thank Brook Blair, Robert Denemark, and Barry Gills for their useful comments on this chapter.

2. Also see Hood and Vahlne (1988) for debate.

3. If anything, the commitment to sovereign equality, and with it the commitment to the states system, has been extended under the UN charter.

4. The various solutions adopted by these new states for the problem of order was complex and multifaceted. Much had been learned from the "prepolitical" landpeaces and truces of gods experimented with in eleventh- and twelfth-century Germany. These were essentially voluntary agreements to limit killings and theft to a few days in a week. See Fisher 1898 for discussion.

5. "The contractual relationships compose a considerable part of the network of social relationships of many and various social groups beginning with the 'employers and the employees,' 'buyers and sellers,' 'owners and tenants' and ending with many a religious, political, state, occupational, educational, artistic, scientific and even familial groups and associations" (Sorokin 1941, III: 34).

6. It is, of course, the task of theory to show the underlying commensurability of things and events that otherwise appear unrelated. There is little in common, for instance, between Bach's music, coffee seeds, and motorbikes, and yet the discipline of economics correlates them as use-values, i.e., within an abstract economic space whose contours are defined by value (Aglietta 1974). Similar arguments can be made for international relations. Commensurability in the international sphere needs to be accomplished, however, without compromising the nonhomogeneous character of the international field, i.e., without postulating a one-dimensional "international system" or a "world-system."

7. Although the functional separateness of politics is traced to much earlier, perhaps the thirteenth century.

4

State Autonomy Versus Nationalism: Historical Reconsiderations of the Evolution of State Power

Sandra Halperin

Most recent perspectives on the state converge on some variation of the state autonomy thesis. According to this thesis, the state is to be understood as a set of administrative and coercive structures or institutions that is wholly, "relatively," or "potentially" autonomous from social forces. The state is considered autonomous, in this view, because it rules and controls society by virtue of capabilities that differentiate it from social groups.

In explaining the process through which the state gains autonomy, most theories of state autonomy offer a variation of the same theme: compelled by the imperatives—of modernization (e.g., Huntington 1968); industrialization (e.g., Gellner 1983); class conflict in capitalist society (e.g., Poulantzas 1973a, 1973b, 1975, 1976; Evans et al. 1985; Wright 1976; Therborn 1978); the division of labor in the world capitalist system (Wallerstein 1974); or the international environment and advances in military technology (Skoçpol 1979; Hintze 1975; Kaiser 1990; Downing 1992)—differentiated political centers emerge whose distance from society and control of resources give them autonomy relative to social forces. Successive forms of state—absolutist, national—are understood as representing progressive phases in this evolution. In this view, then, nationalism and its embodiment in the nation-states is seen as representing an evolutionary advance in the growth of rationalized, differentiated, and autonomous state structures.

This chapter takes issue with the state autonomy thesis. Specifically, it argues that to view successive forms of state as representing progressive phases in the growth of state autonomy misconceives the nature of nationalism and its relationship to the evolution of state power.

Nationalism arose historically as a reaction *against* the growth of state autonomy. Policies of the absolutist state designed to bring about greater state autonomy—to make state institutions autonomous from the feudal landowning and clerical elite—triggered the nationalist revolutions and movements of the nineteenth and twentieth centuries in Europe. The aim

63

of these revolutions and movements was to establish a specific form of socioeconomic and political reorganization designed to eradicate state autonomy.

In the following sections, and after pointing out the irremediable weaknesses with standard interpretations of nationalism, this paper will endeavor to show that nationalism and the establishment of nation-states represented a new mechanism of control, conceived by traditional elites as a means of safeguarding their power and privileges through the eradication of state autonomy.

NATIONALISM: A REAPPRAISAL

Nationalism and National Sovereignty

Standard liberal interpretations of nationalism associate the rise of nationalism with the quest for ethnic or popular sovereignty, with democracy, the establishment of liberal institutions, and the extension of liberty. But the rise of nationalism in Europe had little do with ethnic or popular sovereignty and was illiberal and undemocratic from the start.

There is scant evidence to support the notion that nationalism in European history represented the aspirations of distinct ethnic or cultural groups to form their own state. The establishment of nation-states was not the result of the quest for national self-determination in the sense of freedom from foreign rule. In fact, in numerous cases successful nationalist movements were capped by placing a crown on the head of a foreign aristocrat. The Walloons and Flemish peoples of Belgium rose up against what they perceived as undesirable rule by the alien Dutch, but the leaders of the Belgian nationalist movement offered the Belgian crown first to a royal heir of France and then to a German prince. The Great Powers assigned a Bavarian prince as monarch of the new state of Greece, but when Otto was overthrown in 1862, the Greeks replaced him with a Danish prince. Romania gained independence in 1877, but continued to be ruled until 1914 by Prince Charles of Hohenzollern-Sigmaringen, who had ruled as prince since 1866. Bulgarian nationalism arose in opposition to Russian control of the Bulgarian administration, but after gaining independence, Bulgarian leaders offered the Bulgarian throne to the German Prince Alexander of Battenberg; the throne was later offered to Prince Ferdinand of Saxe-Coburg-Gotha, who reigned until 1918. In 1905, the Norwegians separated from the Swedes and then voted to have a Danish prince as king of their new state.

Nor were national states created on the basis of preexisting national cultures. "National" cultures were created by dominant groups as a means of establishing claims to territory and monopolizing control over resource domains. In the epoch of the nation-state, the possession of a distinctive culture legitimated aspirations of groups to secure control over territory by forming a separate state. In the pursuit of this end, nationalist movements undertook the task of creating cultures by which to set apart a certain territory and population as a political entity. These movements sometimes used preexisting cultures, often obliterated them, sometimes invented them.

National movements in Europe began with philological revivals, the political function of which was to prove the possession of a language fit for literature and, consequently, the right to national sovereignty. The purely cultural national movement was almost everywhere accompanied by a political ambition.

The political ambition that attended nationalist movements was rarely limited to the achievement of national sovereignty. The nationalist movements that arose in Europe during the nineteenth and early twentieth centuries called not for "nation-states"—states congruent with a national community or culture—but for the resurrection or creation of empires. Nationalist writers (e.g., Fichte, Treitschke, Mazzini, Garibaldi, D'Annunzio, Kossuth, Obradovich, Danilevsky) called for the resurrection of the historical empires of Byzantium and Rome, of Charlemagne, Caesar, Dushan, and Simeon.[1] Even where there was no imperial past to recall, nationalists did not demand political independence of national communities within national frontiers. They called for the widest possible extension of national boundaries, regardless of ethnic considerations and in fundamental opposition to the national idea. Napoleon's Continental system, the Great Germany crusade, the Russian Pan-Slav movement, the Fascist crusade to recreate a Roman empire, the movements for a Greater Serbia, a Greater Bulgaria, a Great Slav state, a Greater Greece, and a Greater Romania, are only a few examples. There were also movements for a Greater Macedonia and, within the pan-Slav movement, a Greater Croatia movement; a pan-Celtic movement to unite Gael, Welsh, and Bretons was formed in the late nineteenth century.

In fact, nationalism in its essence, its origins, and its methods was similar to colonialism and imperialism, and its impact on large populations within Europe was similar to the impact of colonialism on Third World populations.

National territories were created through a process that bore all the characteristic features—political, economic, cultural, and military—of colonialism and imperialism. Nation building in Europe had the same objective and the same end as imperialism: control over the resources of a territory, including its population, their activities, and the goods they produced.

The creation of Great Britain began with London. From the sixteenth century, England was created and directed by London, and unification proceeded with the provincial economies becoming satellites of the capital (Braudel 1979, 365). England then expanded into the Celtic periphery:

Ireland, Scotland, and Wales—remote and mostly pastoral countries with Celtic populations usually hostile to English culture. Ireland was totally subjugated to the English market (Plumb 1950; Cullen 1968; Hechter 1975) and sank into the position of a "peripheral" country.

France developed through a similar process of territorial expansion from a political-military "core." The French nation grew through the violent subjugation and incorporation of numerous territories by the Ile de France, the region around Paris. From this center the French state expanded until it reached its modern frontiers.

Germany, from its first stages of development, did not conform at all with the accepted understanding of a nation-state in regard to nationalities. The borders of the German Empire established in 1871 actually split the German nation, dividing it between Austria and the new "national" state of Germany, and putting together the Germans and the racially distinct peoples in territories annexed from Poland, Denmark, and France.

German unity was the work of Bismarck, who was not a German nationalist but a promoter of Prussian interests. The acquisition of Schleswig-Holstein from Denmark, Alsace-Lorraine from France, and parts of Poland through military conquest was followed by germanization, or forced cultural assimilation.

The unification of Italy proceeded under the direction of the militaristic and paternalistic Piedmont. Piedmont was not considered by the greater number of its inhabitants to be an Italian province.[2] The process of "national unification" was, in fact, more accurately a process of "Piedmontization." This process involved the conquest and annexation of other regions. Its outcome was a country divided into two economies: a highly developed north, with many features similar to the industrialized countries like Britain and France, and a much poorer agrarian south, which was treated as an area for quasi-colonial exploitation by the north.

Russia expanded outward from a Russian political core, creating what was essentially a colonial empire. The Russians treated the backward nations of their empire as the colonial powers treated the natives of Africa and Australia (Macartney 1934, 85).

Given this history of the formation of national states in Europe, it is not surprising that today's territorial states are not congruent with national communities. One analyst has calculated that the total number of people living today in a state congruent with their ethnic community is less than 4 percent (Connor 1973).

Nationalism and Democracy

Some theorists of nationalism maintain that states were constituted by the will or consent of the populations of various territories, irrespective of ethnic considerations, to form or belong to a state. According to this view, nationalism in Europe emerged in association with the quest for popular sovereignty and democracy.

But nationalism in Europe was undemocratic, illiberal, violent, and aggression-bent from the start. States were created not by popular will but by force.[3] Movements to form states excluded large segments—usually, the vast majority—of the population. Nationalist leaders generally depended for their support on wealthy, elite elements and made little effort to appeal to the masses. And when state independence was won, rights were not extended to other classes or national groups.

In Italy the revolutions of 1848 were conducted substantially over the heads of an inactive rural population; throughout the Risorgimento, the loyalties of the masses remained local or regional but not national (Oriani 1908; Gramsci 1971, 100–103; Smith 1971, 36, 219–220, 273, Chap. 12). Germany was unified by Prince Otto von Bismarck and the Prussian army. The national movement in Poland was led by the serf-owning nobility in the face of peasant suspicion, distrust, or indifference (Reddaway 1941: II, 378, 383; Goriely 1948). The Hungarian nationalist movement, led by the Magyar aristocracy, found a weak response among the Slav peasantry (Fejtö 1948, 312–349). The Romanian revolution in 1848 sought the extension of political rights for the upper classes and, thus, alienated the peasantry (Tihany 1976, 163; Djordjevic and Fischer-Galati 1981, 111–112). Russian nationalism was the work of the government and of a small class of bureaucrats and intelligentsia. On the question of nationalism, the Russian masses were either almost indifferent, or, in the case of a few revolutionary thinkers, in active revolt against the policy of their government (Macartney 1934, 134). Of all the Serbian nationalist organizations advocating insurrection, unification, and the formation of a large state, none worked out any meaningful social and economic programs that would appeal to the masses (Djordjevic and Fischer-Galati 1981, 127).

* * *

The older nation-states of Western Europe were formed by conquering groups who colonized territories and subjugated, massacred, expelled, or forcibly assimilated the native populations. Later national movements were led by groups who, as the self-declared representatives of some ethnic or cultural "nation," and with funds and military or other assistance provided by existing states, organized crusades aimed at acquiring a territory for which it had created and advanced cultural or other claims.

After statehood was achieved, the ruling nation in the new multinational state often finished the work of expelling, exterminating, or forcibly assimilating ethnic minorities and other portions of the population with separate territorial claims or with the potential power to challenge the rule of the dominant group.

Nation-states did not represent an extension of liberty or an advance in human welfare. In many respects they were less liberal, less tolerant, and more oppressive than the absolutist states and empires they replaced.[4] After national independence was won, the leaders of the nationalist movements did not extend rights to other classes or nationalities; in nearly all states, the franchise remained highly restricted until well into the twentieth century.

Nationalism, Capitalism, and the Capitalist Bourgeoisie

Marxist theories hold that nationalism and its embodiment in the nation-state represented the coming to power of a new capitalist class. Nationalism, according to this view, was motivated by the desire of the bourgeoisie to secure for itself an internal or domestic market for its own commodity production, and to establish the political and legal framework necessary to ensure its class rule and the development of capitalism.[5]

The role attributed to the bourgeoisie, however, in the rise of nationalism and of nation-states (and its strength, unanimity, and omnipotence, generally) has been vastly overdrawn. In much of Europe, the bourgeois were often foreign classes within European societies. Elsewhere, they were weak and regionally confined, and consequently dependent on the monarchy, the Church, or the landholding aristocracy.

The bourgeoisie did not play the central role in the English revolutions of the seventeenth century, usually considered to be the first full manifestation of modern nationalism (Hexter 1961; Stone 1981; Hill 1981; Clark 1985, 1986). Many scholars reject the view that the French Revolution was a bourgeois revolution, inspired by bourgeois ideas, initiated, led by, and, in the end, redounding to the benefit of the bourgeoisie (e.g., Cobban 1971; Dawson 1972; Lucas 1973; Furet 1978; Schama 1989). Nor is the bourgeoisie generally ascribed a central role in the movement for German national unification. The German unification movement was dominated by the Prussian Junkers, a class of landowning aristocrats who controlled the imperial government. This same class continued to control the machinery of government in Germany after national unification (Veblen 1942; Dahrendorf 1967; Stern 1977). The movement for Italian national unification, as Engels and others noted, was marked by the absence of a politically and economically powerful bourgeoisie (Engels 1894, 1895; Gramsci 1949). Rosa Luxemburg wrote that in Poland, "the national idea was a class idea of the nobility, never of the bourgeoisie" (Luxemburg 1976, 176). In much of Central and Eastern Europe, the capitalist bourgeoisie consisted of foreign colonists—German, Jewish, Greek, Polish, or Italian—who could hardly claim to represent the nation (Macartney 1934; Kedourie 1960).

Far from being bound up with bourgeois aspirations, the dominant feature of nationalism is its determination to exclude from any significant share of power or wealth the foreign and minority groups that, in Europe and elsewhere during the nineteenth and twentieth centuries, formed a significant portion of the bourgeoisie.

The establishment of nation-states in Europe was the outcome of a violent, illiberal, and aggressive enterprise conducted, not by a new, rising, liberal-capitalist middle class but by traditional elites.

National territories were created through a process that bore all the characteristic features—political, economic, cultural, and military—of colonialism and imperialism. Nation-states are really multinational territories acquired through imperial expansion. Nation building and empire building are both phenomena in the struggle for the control of territory. Nation building and imperialism have the same objective and the same end: control over the resources of a territory, including its population, their activities, and the goods they produce.

Neither in Europe nor elsewhere was nationalism associated with the rise of a new capitalist bourgeoisie. In the course of absolutism, the feudal nobility had gained in strength, absorbing elements of the rising capitalist class into its ranks. No separate capitalist bourgeoisie emerged. In fact, the capitalist bourgeoisie within most European countries was either a foreign element or politically and economically weak, as well as dependent on the nobility.

Nationalist rebellions and movements to form nation-states were not bound up with the rise of a new capitalist bourgeoisie, as Marxist theoreticians assert. In fact, nationalism was the project of the traditional nobility.

The next section will endeavor to clarify the nature and aims of the nationalist project and to show, as well, the consequences of this project: The establishment of nation-states did not inaugurate the rule of a new capitalist class; rather, it consolidated the power of the traditional nobility.

NATIONALISM: A REINTERPRETATION

Historically, the first European nationalisms were conceived in opposition to centralized bureaucratic reform. Nationalist revolutions and movements were initiated by elites in reaction to attempts by absolutist monarchs to solve state fiscal crises through the imposition of redistributive and liberal reforms. It was a rearguard movement by privileged classes to reduce the leveling effects of bureaucratic absolutism, to safeguard traditional privileges, to restore the union of state and aristocracy, and to limit the growing autonomy of the state.

In the seventeenth and eighteenth centuries, absolutist rulers, faced with fiscal crises, sought to centralize and increase their authority and to reduce the powers and privileges of the nobles, urban patricians, the Church hierarchy, guild masters, and other semifeudal corporate institutions. To increase revenues and production, they sought to end some of the fiscal privileges of nobles and corporate institutions. Attempts to end internal customs dues and break up entailed estates, and to eliminate complex feudal regulations and customs that hampered economic progress, threatened aristocratic institutions. In order to effect these measures and to gain autonomy over powerful local groups, rulers attempted to gain control of the bureaucracy and the army, as well as to raise revenues through the use of mercenaries and foreign and minority bureaucrats, industrialists, and commercial classes.

In self-defense, the aristocracies of Europe advanced the oldest and most enduring of conservative ideas: the state must not be allowed to expand its powers at the expense of local groups and corporate interests (Weiss 1977, 9). The whole ideology of nationalism, with its theme of cultural regeneration and renewal, is centered on this idea.

Historically, the "nation" referred to the nobility or the ruling class (Zernatto 1944; Seton-Watson 1977). For centuries, the concept of the nation was bound up with the nobility and the clerical elite. In the eighteenth century, "nation" referred to those classes possessing wealth and education who considered themselves alone capable of government, prestige, and power (Barzun 1932; Zernatto 1944; Hertz 1947; Kedourie 1960; Snyder 1964).

A nation thus came to be understood as that body of persons who could claim to represent, or to elect representatives for, a particular territory at councils, diets, or estates. In the 1760s, the French *parlements* (bodies of magistrates drawn from the privileged classes) announced that they constituted a single united magistracy representing the whole country. Thereafter, the term "nationalists" was applied to the parlements (Palmer 1944, 105). Thus the idea of "nationalism" came to be understood as rule by aristocrats (Zernatto 1944, 361). The leaders of the French Revolution struggled against absolutism in the name of the "nation" (Lefebvre 1947, 30, 36, 51). Their quest was to achieve "national sovereignty"—that is, the establishment of the "nation" (the aristocracy) as the ultimate source of authority.

Throughout the eighteenth century the nobility had encroached steadily upon official posts. With footholds established in the local and central administration, they gained fiscal and tax exemptions that helped push France to the verge of bankruptcy. By the late 1780s, falling real wages, rising inflation, increasing feudal burdens, and bad harvests made it impossible to squeeze more from the common people. Faced with financial crisis, the monarchy proposed a reform program that included the abolition of feudal rights and guild restrictions and the introduction of a general property tax.

These proposals to stimulate economic activity and increase the taxable wealth represented more than a threat to the nobles' tax privileges. At stake was the growth of state autonomy; for, as LeFebvre notes, "if a budgetary balance could be restored, and maintained through the growth of national wealth, there would be no more need of erratic fiscal expedients and the king would escape from the control of the *parlements*" (LeFebvre 1947, 24–25). Thus, the aristocracy refused to pay without an extension of their privileges, and precipitated the revolution in 1789 by forcing the king to recall that relic of feudalism, the Estates-General. It demanded that the king recognize that the aristocracy alone had the necessary rank to advise him and to command in his name, and that he grant them a monopoly of employments compatible with that rank (LeFebvre 1947, 15).

Hungarian and Czech nationalism emerged under similar conditions and sought to achieve similar ends. As with French nationalism, these nationalist movements were initiated by the noble class in reaction to monarchical reforms.

At the end of the eighteenth century, Joseph II (1765–1790) and Leopold II (1790–1792) attempted to reform the empire. Joseph II, in 1781 and 1785, decreed the abolition of serfdom and the guilds, and toleration for the denominations. The nobility, however, was able to block serious land and tax reform, as well as state investment to aid the mass of peasants. Measures intended to improve the peasants' lot were rescinded completely after Joseph's death.

In December 1846, the central government issued a decree providing for the replacement of statute labor and feudal rights by certain taxes, in order to lighten the burden carried by the peasants.

During the 1848 revolution, Magyar nationalists extracted from Ferdinand V (1835–1848) a constitution; this constitution, however, was repudiated by Ferdinand's successor, Francis Joseph (1848–1916). The monarchy then sought to crush the Magyar nationalists by backing a rebellion of the minorities under Magyar domination.

Following their defeat in the Revolution of 1848–1849, the Hungarian nobility lost their exemption from taxation; income and other taxes were made applicable to the whole of the empire and interior customs barriers were abolished.

During the Austro-Prussian War of 1866, and in order to forestall a revolutionary rising of Magyar peasants and workers and of national minorities, the Magyar nobility accepted the *Ausgleich* or "Compromise of 1867." This compromise represented a compact of the Austrian emperor with the Hungarian feudal classes in order to secure Magyar hegemony over the Slav majority.[6] Hungarian nationalism obtained for the Magyar nobility a position of equality, in some respects of privilege, in the new state of Austria-Hungary.

* * *

Nationalist revolutions and movements in the Balkans during the nineteenth and twentieth centuries followed the same pattern as the Magyar.

Balkan nationalist movements, and their Great Power sponsors, sought to portray the Balkan movements as rebellions of oppressed Christians against Turkish Muslim overlords. By far the largest part of the population of the Balkans was non-Turk and Christian. But before the nineteenth century, Turkish rule over alien peoples of Christian religion had not caused much difficulty. It was only in the nineteenth century, when the Ottoman state passed a series of measures to liberalize the status of the peasant and to allow for economic freedom of the merchants, that elites, in an effort to defend their feudal privileges, began to search for support among the masses through religious and ethnic-national identification.

Most of the "nationalist" rebellions in the Balkans were either uprisings of peasants against their own (ethnic) Mohammedenized nobility—local notables who had become Muslims after the fifteenth century in order to retain their land and other privileges—or revolts by the nobility against Ottoman reforms designed to benefit the peasants. In Bosnia and Herzegovina, for example, the local feudal nobility, converts to Islam though Serbian by race, ruled the country in an oppressive fashion with the aid of the Janissaries (a privileged corps of troops). In the 1840s, the Porte struggled to remove the Bosnian nobles from local military positions, to eliminate requirements for forced labor, and to codify the owner-tenant relationship. The Islamized and Turkicized landowning classes in the provinces greatly resented these reforms, which promised to undermine their privileged feudal position. At the same time, dissatisfaction was widespread among the Christian population because of the Porte's slowness in implementing reforms to improve their social and economic status. It was the nobles' revolts against the sultan's reform measures, however, that eventually metamorphosed into the nationalist revolutions and movements in the Balkans in the nineteenth and twentieth centuries.

In the eighteenth and nineteenth centuries the local notables (*ayans*) came to rule entire provinces in the Balkans, challenging the central government. As the economic value of land began to increase as a result of the growth of trade with the West, the ayans attempted to take over the lands of the Balkan Christian peasants by force or to impose a series of new taxes on them, in open violation of the traditional Ottoman regulations (Stavrianos 1958; Stoinovich 1963). This form of neofeudalism (known as the *chiflik* system), which was not sanctioned by law, violated the existing order and undermined trust in the central government. The feudalistic provincial military wing of the Ottoman bureaucracy began to act, not as enforcers of the sultan's laws but as a social group bent on achieving economic power to the detriment of the peasants (Karpat 1973).

The efforts of Selim III (1789–1807) and Mahmud II (1808–1839) to abolish the Janissaries, to establish a modern army, and to reorganize government institutions were aimed at curbing the power of the ayans. Mahmud II destroyed the big ayans and confiscated their lands. In 1839, he issued a reforming edict (the Hatti-Sherif of Gülhane), which was to be the first of the reforming decrees that became collectively known as the *Tanzimat*, or "Reorganization." This edict was the earliest constitutional document in any Islamic country and was, in effect, a charter of legal, social, and political rights. The Tanzimat guaranteed freedom and security of life, honor, and property; a regular method of assessing and collecting taxes and the abolition of tax farming; an equally regular method of levying and recruiting the armed forces and of fixing their duration of service; and finally, fair public trial under the law, and no punishment without legal sentence.

The Tanzimat Edict promised equality between Christians and Muslims in a gradual effort to establish Ottomanism as a legal tie common to all subjects. The rights contained in the edict were to be applied equally to all Ottoman subjects, regardless of race or creed, and thus were intended to eliminate all legal distinction between Muslim and non-Muslim (Lewis 1961, Chap. 3; Davison 1973, Chap. 1; Shaw 1977: II, Chap. 2). The *Islahat Fermani* (Reform Charter) of 1856 was a follow-up of the edict. Among the reforms in this charter was a provision for giving fixed salaries to the clergy, thereby abolishing the dues that prelates collected from their flocks (Davison 1973, 114ff.). Its principal aim, however, was to achieve the equality between Muslims and Christians that had been promised in 1839.

The goal of the Tanzimat and the policies that followed afterward were to rationalize and liberalize the central state administrative apparatus; to reassert the authority of the central government both internally and internationally; to create a functional government that would assume a series of new responsibilities; to regulate activities and to harmonize and resolve the conflicts in the social body; to provide security of life and to property to all groups, but notably to the masses, and eventually to rely upon them against the local notables; and to create new sources of revenue through a more rational exploitation of natural resources, including the adoption of a more liberal economic policy (Inalcik 1973).

If carried to their logical conclusion, these reforms would have destroyed the independent power of notables throughout the empire. Following the proclamation of the Tanzimat Edict, hardly a decade passed without some violent uprising of the nobility against attempts by central government officials to apply and implement the reforms.

* * *

The growing autonomy of the state and its institutions and personnel was, historically, the central concern of nationalism. In most cases, the catalyst to national revolt was bureaucratic reforms undertaken by absolutist states, which challenged the prerogatives of the traditional nobility: the threat of liberal reform in France triggered the French Revolution, the liberal policies of Hapsburg monarchs gave rise to Magyar and Czech nationalism; reform-minded royalty of the Austro-Hungarian Empire fueled German nationalism in the empire; Ottoman reforms precipitated Balkan nationalisms and the Young Turk movement.

Movements to form national states were aimed at a specific form of socioeconomic and political reorganization designed to eradicate state autonomy. It achieved this end by systematically depriving the state of various bases of potential state autonomy. The next section will show how nationalism was used by traditional elites as a means of gaining control of state resources and institutions.

NATIONALISM: DISTRIBUTION OF POWER

Under absolutism, various resources and institutional bases of power were developed and eventually brought under the control of the state in its efforts to gain autonomy from dominant groups within society. Nationalism, however, sought to gain control of these resources and institutions in order to divest the state of sources of potentially autonomous power. Its success ensured that civil servants would be drawn from local privileged groups. It also eliminated extrasocietal sources of military power. It deprived foreigners and minorities of their economic power and position and reduced their role in finance, commerce, and trade. Finally, it consolidated its own power by wresting from the Church control of education, and using it as the ideological and cultural means to ensure its own continuity.

The Bureaucracy

State bureaucracies were originally developed by rulers in order to destroy the competing power of the aristocracy. Throughout history, in order to exercise power over their subjects and to gain autonomy from their internal adversaries, rulers have sought to develop an apparatus that operates independently of their subjects. Rulers could not, to any significant degree, establish—and govern by means of—a group of non-noble "bureaucratic" officials lacking the property rights that would define them as members of the ruling class. Officials who could somehow prevail over the feudal lords used their position to constitute themselves as members of the lordly class; thus, the monarch, by raising them to power, would ultimately reconstitute the feudal ruling class. What was required were servants who were completely independent of society.

"From the viewpoint of the central state, the major danger, as Plato recognized so long ago, is the acquisition, or retention, by its military or clerical office-holders, of links with particular kin groups, whose interests are then liable to sway the officers from the stern path of duty" (Gellner 1983, 15). In order for the sphere of public authority to become distinct from the sphere of private social relations, the state must have servants who have severed their ties to other social groups. Thus, in various times and places, rulers have maintained control of their central administration over local officials by the use of eunuchs or celibate priests, state-owned slaves, and members of otherwise disenfranchised or excluded groups. Whenever possible, rulers recruited their officials from foreigners, whose kin links were distant and who were completely dependent upon him.

Under absolutism, the local nobility encroached steadily upon official posts. Its incorporation into the administrative apparatus of the state ultimately brought about the "feudalization" of the state bureaucracy and forestalled its development as an autonomous institution.

* * *

Max Weber asserted that with the end of patrimonialism—the administrative system that developed under absolutism in which the state bureaucracy was private property—the state becomes a distinct institution within society. It differentiates itself from civil society and becomes institutionalized. Men and jobs are impartially matched; thus, authority relations are impersonal and serve the collectivity as a whole. But the rise of national states did not bring about the end of the absolutist administrative system.

And, in fact, Weber's historical analyses show that the administrative apparatus of the nation-state was closely linked to the aristocracy during the nineteenth and early twentieth centuries. In England, he writes, the state "remained an administration of notables" (Weber 1946, Chap. 8). Until relatively recently, the administration was drawn from men who first attended one of the public schools and later Oxford or Cambridge. During the nineteenth century, the German bureaucracy was unable to achieve independence from the Prussian Junker aristocracy who, during the eighteenth century, had controlled the entire country through the state apparatus (Weber 1946, 373; Rosenberg 1958, 43, 44, 199). Late-nineteenth-century Sweden rivaled Germany in the perpetuation of late-medieval political forms (Lipset 1983). In Russia the governmental apparatus was dominated exclusively by the nobility (Beetham 1974, 199). In France during the Second Empire, the bureaucracy fell completely into the hands of the ruling classes, which used it as a tool for furthering their own interests. The bureaucracy, rather than functioning as a necessary ingredient of the state's autonomy, was reduced to a "parasitic excrescence. " At the inception of the Fourth Republic, the state bureaucracy still recruited from the privileged social strata (Badie and Birnbaum 1982, 113–114).

* * *

It has been argued that eventually, in the course of the development of the nation-state, state elites became a separate stratum with a clearly separate identity and with interests and goals both distinct from and even in conflict with those of the ruling class. According to this view, state elites (1) comprise a separate and cohesive stratum, a new "class," with (2) identifiable interests, ideas, and policies, (3) opposed to those of the dominant groups within society, and with (4) the capacity to pursue their own interests and projects independently of and, if necessary, over the opposition of other social interests.

While state officials may tend to constitute self-conscious groups, this does not mean that they identify themselves as distinct from or in conflict with the ruling class. As Leroy-Beaulieu stressed, "the state is not society's brain; it has no qualification, no aptitude, no mission to lead society or to blaze its trails" (Leroy-Beaulieu 1911, 520, quoted in Badie and Birnbaum 1982, 110). A bureaucracy has a high organizational capacity but cannot set its own goals. Rationalized systems of social organization do not create values, as Max Weber recognized; they only function as a means to the furtherance of existing values (Weber 1978, 1402).

While the state can create new bureaucratic classes, it is not necessarily able to give them political strength (Leca 1990). Thus, even if state functionaries do eventually form a distinct stratum and can and do discover interests different from or in conflict with those of the dominant class, they would not find themselves capable on a long-term basis of imposing policies that threatened the interests of that class.

Some theorists have posited that state officials can bring about a "revolution from above" to transform society and create the socioeconomic conditions for modern economic development, against the interests of the old dominant classes (e.g., Trimberger 1978). But a revolution from above, by a faction of the state apparatus (e.g., the military), cannot bring about a transformation of economic and political structures. A revolution from above, as Barrington Moore notes, implies modernizing carried out under the leadership of the aristocracy without changing the social structure (Moore 1966, 442).

The transformation of social-property relations is usually beyond the ambition and means of any group of politicians and state officials. Even if they develop the ambition, politicians and bureaucrats cannot change the fundamental rules and overturn the distribution of power within society without the backing of a formidable social movement (Mann 1984). Short of a total overthrow of the old regime, reforms must be carried out in the context of existing institutional structures.

The Military

The state's autonomy is based not only on its control of the state bureaucracy, but also on its control of coercive instruments and its monopoly of the legitimate use of force within the territory over which it claims sovereignty. Monarchs have sought, throughout history, to raise troops in order to establish their power over political subjects. Thus, monarchs sought to gain autonomy from social groups, not only through developing a state administrative apparatus that operated independently of their subjects, but by raising and maintaining armies recruited from disenfranchised elements or foreigners.

Military forces were developed by rulers to disarm potential competitors for domination. These were not primarily other states—such states were usually ruled by family members or close relations—but local groups.

Because the primary threat to the ruling power came from within, rulers preferred to recruit mercenaries who were completely alien to the subjects and thus could neither seek nor find close ties with them. In the Middle Ages, powerful lords employed patrimonial slaves as personal troops. The caliphate relied for centuries on armies of purchased slaves. The Abbasids became independent of the national levy by buying and militarily training Turkish slaves who, as tribal aliens, were wholly tied to the ruler's domination.[7] In the fourteenth century, the Ottoman rulers freed themselves of levies by conscripting boys (*devshirme*) from conquered peoples' tribal or religious aliens (Bulgarians, Bedouins, Albanians, Greeks). These became the Janissaries.

Whenever rulers did not recruit their army from aliens but from subjects, they exempted from conscription the wealthy and powerful and based their military power on the propertyless or nonprivileged masses (Weber 1978, 1015–1020). In Europe, the aristocracy lost one of its key sources of power when nonaristocratic social groups became responsible for carrying out military functions.

A professional army dominated by mercenaries and controlled by civilian intendants appointed by the king, and generally chosen outside the great aristocratic families, gave the state a redoubtable power and consequently a considerable degree of autonomy (Kiernan 1957). At the end of the eighteenth century throughout Europe, a peacetime army with a large contingent of foreigners was the norm (Thompson 1990); a pure citizen army was an anomaly. Nationalism eliminated these mercenary armies; it ensured that the coercive apparatus would not have purposes and goals different from those of the dominant classes. In some newly established nation-states (e.g., Italy) the personal armies of the noble landowners became the foundation for the new national army.

The Economy

The power position of rulers depends on their autonomous control of resources. Kings could not avoid making concessions to the local nobility so long as they were not in a position to establish their own armies and bureaucracies and to pay both from their own treasuries (Weber 1978, 1057).

They needed revenue to maintain their bodyguard, patrimonial armies, mercenaries, and especially officials (Weber 1978, 1092). One way of gaining revenue was to extend market privileges and establish cities in order to obtain high ground rents and subjects capable of paying high taxes.[8] Ambitious to break the power of feudal lords and the estates and to unify their dominions under a centralized, bureaucratic rule, absolute monarchs in the seventeenth and eighteenth centuries pursued a policy of attracting foreign ethnic or religious groups both to raise the national average and to undermine the position of resident groups.

Monarchs also gained autonomy through direct regulation of economic resources and activities. In France, the state adopted an interventionist policy with regard to industry that worked primarily to make the productive apparatus dependent on the state or subject to its control (Nef 1967, 58ff.). First under Richelieu and then under Colbert, the state set up manufacturing enterprises, offered subsidies and privileges as a way of orienting production, and regulated both foreign and internal trade. Later, states obtained outside sources of revenue by allowing a high degree of foreign ownership of industry and a variety of credit, ownership, technological, and marketing dependency relationships with international capital.

Nationalism targeted foreign and minority elements. It transferred economic power to a dominant "national" group through restrictions on land ownership and confiscation of properties owned by groups now defined as foreigners or minorities within the national territory. Other restrictions followed to limit the mobility of labor and capital within the national territory. The state apparatus was used to regulate, control, and restrict the mobility of productive factors internationally and domestically, in order to protect local groups.

State autonomy from social forces implies that the state defines and articulates collective rather than particular interests. The policies of nation-states in Europe throughout the nineteenth century, however, created the conditions that permitted the survival of various forms of corporatism and monopoly. Corporate structures were used to prevent the popular sector from gaining access to the state and, at the same time, open up to dominant groups channels of access to the state. By gaining privileged access to the state, dominant classes were able to extract recurring unequal advantage from the state and all the resources at its command.

The abolition of guilds or corporations was central to the establishment of state autonomy. Guild and corporate structures, however, were never fully abolished; they were suppressed in 1776 by Louis XVI's finance minister, Turgot, but were restored after his fall (Lefebvre 1947, 45. The National Assembly suppressed the guilds and all other corporations of artisans and workmen. In the *Decree upon the Organization of Trades and Professions* of June 14, 1791 (Anderson 1904, 43–45), the assembly forbade all combinations, strikes, and agreements between workmen to refuse to work or between employers to refuse to give work except on specified conditions. Under the regime of Napoleon, however, quasi-corporations approximating the character of guilds were allowed to be established and to dominate a number of important fields of industry. On the other hand, the nineteenth century was far advanced before this restrictive policy was relaxed with respect to labor, and trade unions were legalized.

In the nineteenth century, corporatist structures were used to control and impede industrialization in the Hapsburg territories. Throughout the century, guild structures remained relatively intact in Denmark. In Germany, corporate structures were used to engineer industrial society. Italy turned to corporatism in the 1920s. In both countries, as well as in Portugal and Spain, corporatism culminated in variants of fascism. Fascist corporatism was aimed at ensuring that economic modernization would be contained within traditional hierarchical social forms (Linz 1963, 105–6; Crouch 1986, 193).

Corporate forms persisted because of their usefulness to dominant industrial and capitalist interests. The industrial and commercial upper classes favored economic freedom, as Weber noted, "only up to the point that some of them succeed[ed], through the purchase of privileges from the political authority or simply through the power of capital, in obtaining for themselves a monopoly for the sale of their products or the acquisition of their means of production, and in thus closing the market on their own part" (Weber 1978, 638). "What finance capital wants," Rudolf Hilferding wrote in a similar vein, "is not liberty but domination. It has no sympathy for the independence of the individual capitalist. . . . It abhors the anarchy of competition and demands organization in order to be able to engage in the struggle for competition at an ever-higher level. To achieve this, it requires the state" (Hilferding 1981, 451).

Corporate forms were permitted to survive throughout the nineteenth century as the result of state policy.[9] By the beginning decades of the twentieth century, lines of industry "in which the sharpest competition" had prevailed were "forced by state action into uniformity and single control" (Robbins 1939, 45–80). The sale of agricultural products, which in the absence of positive regulation by states would be highly competitive, was largely if not predominantly monopolistic. "The world of manufacturing industry," was "a world in which competition, in any effective sense, ha[d] virtually ceased to exist" (Robbins 1939, 59). Legislation and government action created monopolies in large areas of extractive industry where conditions had been highly competitive.[10]

An increasing trend toward industrial concentration and away from individual competition took place in all countries following World War I (Maier 1975). Some of the most important branches of industry were combined into cartels in Austria, France, Belgium, and Russia; most German enterprises were run by cartels (Romein 1978, 180–191). Cartelization, a salient feature of Eastern European economies before the war, became more extensive during the interwar period (Berend 1974; Teichova 1974).

As monopolies developed, they came more and more to control the governments of the various states; eventually "national" policy became essentially the product of their influence. By the early years of the twentieth century, capitalist interests had established a highly centralized organizational system. Large corporations increasingly made use of the state (Lenin 1932). Trusts obtained state help in capturing new markets abroad and dealing with their labor force. The interaction of industry and state during World War I harnessed the state to big business (Hardach 1977, 105–107). The state and capital became completely intertwined, with no clear dividing line between the trust or cartel, on the one hand, and the semipublic economic sector.

Education

In the years leading up to the French Revolution, the aristocratic literature had complained, above all, that the king had despoiled them of their sovereign power over the peasants (Lefebvre 1976, 19). In an effort to preserve their traditional privileges, the nobility enlisted the support of the people in their struggle against the absolute monarchy. They did this by extending to them the status of "nation," which had previously been an exclusive category.

Nationalism identified the main sources of national life with the traditional forms of life of the rural population.[11] It extolled the socially conservative peasant mass as the genuine mainstay of the national culture. In order to become the popular leaders of the rural masses, old German or Italian aristocratic families concealed their knowledge of Latin, French, or German and began to speak Tzechish or Slovenian when they were in the countryside (Naumann 1916, 88). The nationalist nobility revived peasant costumes, dance, and celebrations.

Control of the population had always been a source of power for rulers and ruling groups. Charismatic leaders gain autonomy because they are able to gain control of the population and thus deprive traditional power holders of its major resource; however, the problem becomes one of institutionalizing or, in Weber's terms, "routinizing" charismatic power. Until the emergence of nation-states, the Church had been the most successful instrument for institutionalizing control of the masses, but the eighteenth-century philosophers made the Church the object of continual attack. In 1762, the state in France closed down the Jesuit schools and proceeded to secularize education and place it under state control.

Control of education had provided the Church with a vital social resource for ensuring its own continuity. It became, for the nobility, the ideological, cultural, and organizational means of defining and articulating the national collectivity.

State education was used to legitimate the nation and perpetuate the ideology of the nation-state. The central position of national education in the work of the state is a theme that runs through nationalist writing. In the first of his "Addresses to the Nation," Fichte summed up his program: "It is a total change of the existing system of education that I propose as the sole means of preserving the existence of the German Nation. "He argues that it is the business of the state to further *Kultur* among the people. In this way the culture of each state will acquire national characteristics.[12] The French historian, Jules Michelet (1798–1874) considered it his vocation to teach French children "France, as faith, and as religion" (Michelet 1846, 242). Nationalism substituted "the nation for the role of God and his saints, the flag for the cross or the crescent, anthems for hymns, and national heroes for ancient prophets" (Smith 1976, 8).

Nationalist policies were designed to systematically bring institutional, economic, and ideological sources of autonomous state power under the control of traditional elites. Nationalism ensured that civil servants would be drawn from local privileged groups. It also eliminated extrasocietal sources of military power. It deprived foreigners and minorities of their economic power and position and reduced their role in finance, commerce, and trade. It gained control of industrial development and channeled it into noncompetitive, ascriptive, monopolistic forms. Finally, it wrested from the Church control of education and used it as the ideological and cultural means of consolidating its control of the population. It extended its hegemony throughout society by converting the cultural and ideological apparatus of the Church into the institutions of the nation-state.

CONCLUSIONS

According to the state autonomy thesis, successive state forms—absolutist and national—represent progressive phases in the development of differentiated and autonomous state structures.

But this chapter has shown that the rise of nationalism and the emergence of nation-states was not a progressive phase in the evolution of autonomous state structures. Nationalism was the project of traditional elites seeking to eradicate state autonomy in the face of monarchical attempts to impose redistributive and liberal reforms. Throughout the course of absolutism, monarchs had been unable to make state institutions autonomous from dominant groups within society. Attempts to do so precipitated the nationalist movements of the nineteenth century, movements that sought to end the growth of state autonomy. To conceptualize the state as autonomous from social forces is thus to define a disjuncture or discontinuity where, in fact, there is a continuity of social relations.

One of the major tasks confronting international relations theorists, and the task that lies at the heart of the neostructuralist project, is to reconceptualize the relationship between global and local structures and processes in such a way as to capture within a single framework structures or relationships that underlie or form the background of social activity. A major obstacle standing in the way of this endeavor is the notion of state autonomy. A growing number of theorists concerned with analyzing the ways in which autonomous state structures interact with, or operate within, domestic society and/or the international system, have conceived the state as located at the nexus of, acting as a "conduit" between, or in some other way dividing the social totality into internal and external domains. To conceive of the state as autonomous from social forces introduces a sociologically neutral no-man's land between global and local systems, and creates for us the problem of conceptualizing the interaction of what now becomes defined as two separate systems.

This chapter has endeavored to show that, historically, there is no point in time at which the state can be considered as having gained autonomy from social forces. The state grew up within and as part of a larger system of social relations. Social forces limited its power from the start. As a result of the nationalist revolutions and movements of the nineteenth century, state institutions became more embedded in society (but not more representative). The institutions and policies of the nation-states established as a result of these revolutions and movements effectively blocked both the rise to power of new classes and the development of state autonomy. Thus, the state, far from becoming progressively autonomous during the nineteenth and early twentieth centuries, was placed more firmly in the hands of specific class interests.

NOTES

1. Guiseppe Mazzini is perhaps seen as the most liberal-minded amongst those listed. But see, for instance,Guiseppe Mazzini, *Life and Writings of Joseph Mazzini*, Vol. 1, p. 9; Vol. 3, pp. 27, 33; *Fortnightly Review* (April 1877), p. 579. See also Vittorio Alfieri, *Del principe e delle lettere*, 22 vols. (Pisa: 1805–1815), vol. 10, pp. 108–110; Gaetano Salvemini, *Guerra o neutralità*, Milan 1915; and Cesare Battisti, "Il Trentino e l'irredentismo Italiano" (13 January 1915), "Trento, Trieste e il dovere d'Italia" (13 October 1914) in *Scritti politici e sociali*, ed. R. Monteleone, Florence, 1966 edn.; Enrico Corradini, "Per la guerra d'Italia," in *Discorsi politici,* Florence, n.d.

2. The Piedmontese traveler who went to Florence, Rome, or Venice, used to say that he was going to Italy. Cavour knew French better than Italian. A. Graf, *L'Anglomania e l'influsso inglese in Italia nel secolo XVIII* (Turin, 1911), pp. 5–6; cited in Gaudence Megaro, *Vittorio Alfieri: Forerunner of Italian Nationalism* (New York: Columbia University Press, 1930), p. 134.

3. As numerous historians have shown, each phase of the creation of strong states was resisted by most of the European population, and exacted a high cost in death, suffering, loss of rights, and unwilling surrender of land, goods, and labor. See, for instance, Charles Tilly, "Reflections on the History of European

State-Making," in Charles Tilly, ed. *The Formation of National States in Western Europe* (Princeton, N.J.: Princeton University Press, 1975).

4. The linguistic, religious, and educational standardization instituted in the nation-states of northwestern Europe contrasted sharply with the far greater tolerance for linguistic, cultural, and religious diversity that existed in the Ottoman Empire. Under the Turks, conquered populations were often allowed some autonomy in political and cultural affairs. In some cases, where complete conquest had seemed too arduous a task, the self-government left to the subject peoples was very considerable; it included the right to organize themselves into a *natio* or national community, subject only to the sovereign or his representatives, but otherwise standing apart altogether from the national life of the majority people. Out of this principle developed the well-known Turkish millet system, whereby the state acknowledged the existence within itself of communities to whom a different type of law must apply, a concept alien to European thought and practice, since the basis of law in Europe is territorial.

5. Lenin provided the basic formulation: "Throughout the world, the period of the final victory of capitalism over feudalism was linked up with national movements. The economic basis of these movements is that in order to achieve complete victory for commodity production the bourgeoisie must capture the home market, must have politically united territories with a population speaking the same language." "On The Right of Nations to Self-Determination" *Selected Works* (New York: International Publishers, n.d.), vol. 4, pp. 250–293; p. 250. A review of Lenin's views on nationalism is Samad Shaheen, *The Communist Theory of Self-Determination: Its Historical Evolution Up to the October Revolution* (The Hague: W. Van Hoeve, 1956). See also Rosa Luxemburg, *The National Question. Selected Writings of Rosa Luxemburg,* ed. by Horace B. Davis (New York: Monthly Review Press, 1976).

6. Down to 1914 only 6.5 percent of the Hungarian population had votes, and voting was not secret. See Oscar Jásci, *Dissolution of the Hapsburg Monarchy* (Chicago: University of Chicago, 1929), pp. 108, 227.

7. The Mamelukes, purchased slave soldiers in Egypt, eventually gained control over the nominal rulers.

8. In Poland, Bohemia, and Hungary, German colonists were invited by rulers and granted royal charters permitting them to acquire property and to pursue trades under their own German law. The kings of Poland invited masses of Jews from Western Europe, as well as Germans, into Polish territories. Catherine the Great patronized German immigrants and encouraged substantial colonization on the Volga and the Black Sea to offset the power of local Tartar communities. The Hapsburgs recolonized lands reacquired from the Ottomans with Germans and other minorities to inhibit and contain the Magyars. They lured German colonists with free land, free houses, and tax exemptions to the north of the Banat (in the Vojvodina) in 1718. The German immigration that followed totaled 43,000 by 1770; there were nearly 40,000 more by 1787. By 1790, the German immigrants owned more land in the Banat than any other group. John R. Lampe and Marvin R. Jackson, *Balkan Economic History, 1550–1950* (Bloomington: Indiana University Press, 1982), pp. 64–67. Eventually these policies created a middle class nationally different from the surrounding population. In Lithuania and Romania, Jews constituted the main urban class. In Poland, Bohemia, and the Slavonic districts of southeast Austria, the towns were for many centuries exclusively German; all the larger towns of Hungary, including Pest, were essentially German well into the nineteenth century. There were, thus, sharp cultural distinctions between classes in Eastern Europe. Successive waves of conquest had originally left two distinct

classes: one formed by the conquerors—Magyars, Germans, Swedes, Turks, Poles—and the other by the conquered—Czechs, Slovaks, Slovenes, Vlachs, Ruthenes, and White Russians, the Finnish and Lithuanian nations of the Baltic, and the non-Turkish races of the Balkans. (The upper classes of the conquered population tended to assimilate culturally with the conquerors. For instance, when the Poles became the ruling class north of the Carpathians, the nobles of Ruthene origin became Polenized. As a result, there were Polish serfs but no Ruthene nobles.) With the later colonization, there emerged a threefold national and social class structure, with German, Polish, or Jewish colonists supplying the middle, or urban and artisan classes, and in some cases the military. Macartney, *National States and National Minorities*, pp. 82–83.

9. It was the state that imposed differential advantage, preference, or actual monopoly through decisions governing capital allocations, investments, prices and price controls, tax exemptions and deductions, credit, loans, labor drafts, military conscription, rates of interest, wages, forms of law favoring restraint of trade, tariffs, customs duties, access to education, patents, passports and visas, and electoral representation. Without these state policies, "the area of spontaneous and long-lasting monopoly" would have been small compared with "the area of effective competition." "The growth of monopoly since 1870 was everywhere closely associated with the growth of protection. The existence of protective tariffs gives rise to monopolistic obstacles. The existence of monopolistic obstacles gives rise to resistance to free exchange. Resistance to free exchange increases the difficulty of new adaptation. New protection is therefore granted; and the accumulation of obstacles to international trade makes the incidence of change in the remaining parts of the system which are free much more oppressive and productive of sharp disequilibrium" (Robbins 1939, 51, 77, 127–128).

10. For instance, coal mining in Great Britain and in many other countries. The international restriction of tin owes its origin to government support. The attempted restriction of copper had the support of the American government. Potash is the subject of state monopolies in Germany and France. There is no reason to believe that the extraction of mineral resources requires monopoly. The production of iron and bauxite was not subject to monopolistic control.

11. Karl Renner observed that in Austria-Hungary during the nineteenth century, a number of cities changed their nationality, becoming Hungarian or Czech rather then German. German cities, especially Vienna, absorbed an immense influx of nationalities and assimilated them to the German nation. The peasant population is the one that remains national. The peasantry firmly adheres to its nationality as to any tradition, while the city dweller, especially the educated one, assimilates much more easily. Karl Renner, *Der Kampf der osterreichischen Nationen um den staat* (Leipzig and Vienna: Franz Deutike, 1902). Cited in Rosa Luxemburg, *The National Question. Selected Writings by Rosa Luxemburg*. Edited by Horace B. Davis. (New York: Monthly Review Press, 1976), pp. 260, 262.

12. Johann Gottlieb Fichte, *Addresses to the German Nation*, trans. by R. F. Jones and G. H. Turnbull (London: Open Court Publishers, 1922). See, especially, "The General Nature of the New Education" (Second Address), pp. 19–25; and "Description of the New Education" (Third Address), pp. 36–51. The Ninth, Tenth, and Eleventh Addresses are entirely devoted to education, as well. Ernst Moritz Arndt made similar arguments. See *Das deutsche Volkstum* (Niemann und Comp.: Lübeck, 1810), Chapter 5, "On Education," and Chapter 8, "National Literature."

5

Technology and the Logic of World-Systems

Christopher Chase-Dunn

This chapter will examine a set of related problems having to do with actual and possible long-run, large-scale changes in the structure and logic of intersocietal systems. I discuss how technological change has occurred in different modes of accumulation[1] in order to see what is distinctive about the ways in which capitalism changes technology. I ask how technological development is related to power and liberation in the modern world-system and how it has affected movements that have sought to transform capitalism into socialism. How is technological development connected with success in the current system, and how have recent changes in technological style affected the abilities of people to resist or transform power structures? The new international division of labor, global sourcing, and flexible accumulation have undercut some older organizational strategies while creating possibilities for new ones. The spiraling interaction between capitalist development and socialist movements is discussed with these matters in mind. It is my general argument that semiperipheral locations are fertile grounds for innovations that allow for upward mobility within world-systems and/or transformations of the developmental logics of these systems.

Using a very broad definition of technology, I mean techniques of material production, transportation, communications, and organization. This includes the means of production and also technologies of power of the sort discussed by Mann (1986). I follow Collins (1986, 80–85) in stressing the distinction between innovation and implementation, and the importance of social context in the implementation of inventions.

In regard to time scales, most discussions of technology focus on changes that have occurred in the last one or two decades, but this essay considers technological change in a much longer time perspective. Whether change is perceived as fast or slow depends on its comparison to something else. Early humans began making lithic core tools more than two million years ago. Flake tools appeared about 150,000 years ago.

Thus, when we describe technological change as "slow" in the ten thousand years before the first states emerged (about five thousand years ago), we are comparing it to what has happened since then. It was rather "fast" compared to what had gone before.

PRECAPITALIST WORLD-SYSTEMS

The world-systems' perspective is now being applied to the problem of very long-term social change—the twenty-thousand-year "history" during which small-scale networks of nomadic hunter-gatherer bands developed into the modern global political economy (Chase-Dunn and Hall 1991). Early world-systems (intersocietal networks that are important for the reproduction and transformation of everyday life) were rather small because the actions of people in one locale usually had important consequences for other people not very far distant in space. The growth of societal size, population density, and the development of transportation and communications technologies have extended the size of world-system networks for thousands of years, finally culminating in a single, global, intersocietal system that is rather tightly interwound. This perspective allows us the possibility of comparing the structures and reproductive processes of very different kinds of world-systems.

Though this kind of comparative world-systems approach is yet in its infancy, it is useful to make several observations about the way in which technology has been reproduced or transformed in very different kinds of systems. Everybody agrees that capitalism revolutionizes technology, but why does this occur and how was it different in other modes of accumulation?

The world-systems perspective on precapitalist changes in technology and social organization explains how intergroup relations were connected with the patterns of innovation and implementation of new technologies in small-scale systems. In general, it was those groups occupying semimarginal regions who experienced the most severe resource stresses and had the biggest incentives to adopt new technologies (Binford 1968). This is analytically similar in some respects to later patterns of semiperipheral development (Chase-Dunn 1988).

Transformation of modes of accumulation changed the ways in which social processes led to technological change. Competition was always important, but its nature and location changed. Competition within foraging societies was suppressed in favor of a culture of sharing and prestige. Competition between such groups led to technological change as a result of migration into new territories or adaptation to population pressure and environmental degradation. This kind of change was usually accomplished during emergency circumstances. But the selection of new techniques was a fairly democratic matter because there were no hierarchies in place to enforce choices. The normative regulation that was the main guarantor of social order in small-scale societies allowed individuals and households much leeway in decisions about methods of production.

Intergroup interactions in stateless world-systems were competitive, but there is considerable evidence that the level of competition among these egalitarian societies was generally less intense and exploitative than in world-systems composed of more hierarchical societies (Chase-Dunn, Clewett, and Sundahl 1992). Intersocietal exchange took the form of gift-giving rather than true market trade. The "international division of labor" in these systems did involve some specialization in the production of food and raw materials for exchange, but the forces this exerted on groups to alter their subsistence patterns were relatively weak.

The slow rate of technological change (compared to later societies) was primarily because of the slow rate of change in the factors that pushed toward intensification. These factors were the rate of population growth and increasing population pressure (Boserup, 1965), the rise of environmental and social circumscription, the rise of elites who most benefited from increasing intensification, and emerging pressures from competing groups. The "neolithic revolution" (the shift from foraging to horticulture) occurred more or less independently in several different world regions during the last ten millennia. This rate of change may seem slow now, but compared to the length of time it took humans to develop the use of tools and language, it was rather fast.

Things speeded up even more when complex chiefdoms and states emerged. Intensification allowed more people to live on a given amount of land. This made sedentism possible, and further intensification made urbanism possible. The emergence of cities was accompanied by increases in the size and the degree of hierarchy of polities. The division of labor in societies became more complex, and greater amounts of food produced per unit of territory increased the possibilities for some to live on the labor of others. Ruling classes sponsored specialized craft producers and mobilized the development of new productive resources such as canal building and irrigation. The reproduction of class societies added a new dimension to the process of technological development and implementation: technologies of power were an increasingly important element in the struggle between classes and in the competition among states. This new logic of accumulation was legitimated by hierarchical religions.

Core/periphery relations were important structural features of accumulation processes in these early, state-based world-systems, but this worked somewhat differently than in the modern world-system. In Mesopotamia, core city-states needed peripheral raw materials and competed with one another to obtain these. But the ability of these core states to impose stable regimes of unequal exchange was limited by many factors. Some of the most important military technologies were easily adopted by peripheral peoples (such as bronze making). This kind of "technology transfer" limited the ability of core states to exploit the periphery (Kohl 1987).

Nevertheless, competition among core states for control of peripheries was a central factor in determining which core states became preeminent. Technological innovation and implementation (especially in military organization and weaponry) was central to the process by which multicentric interstate systems were brought under the control of more centralized empire-states. A common pattern observed in early state systems in Western Asia, China, and Mesoamerica was the phenomenon of "semiperipheral marcher states," in which younger states on the edges of an old core region were able to conquer the older core states and form a new, larger empire-state (Mann 1986; Collins 1978).

Competing states had to mind costs despite absence (or weakness) of market mechanisms of pricing. Writing was invented for the purpose of record keeping in the first "command economies," the Sumerian temple states. Warfare among these contending city-states became a powerful motive for devoting resources toward the invention of new military techniques. It was not only the effectiveness but the costs of warfare technologies that were important. Other inventions and implementations (e.g., the potter's wheel) allowed much more efficient production. Multicentric interstate systems such as Mesopotamia developed technology more rapidly than centralized empires like Egypt, because the competition between states was a powerful spur behind innovation and implementation (Ekholm and Friedman 1982).

Military competition and control remained the primary mechanism of accumulation for thousands of years despite the vast increase in the size of empires and the growth of market exchange. In addition to building armies and strategic transportation and communications networks, states sponsored large investments in producing and transporting food and other basic resources. Some authors have contended that precapitalist states primarily promoted "extensive" development that was unconcerned with efficiency, while modern capitalist technological change is "intensive" in the sense that it tries to get greater returns from the same amount of effort (e.g., Anderson 1974a). This is often part of a larger argument contrasting the dynamic growth of the Eurocentric world-system with the technological hebetude of older civilizations. Marx's version of this was contained in his concept of the "Asiatic mode of production."

While there is little doubt that technological change is much faster in the capitalist world-system than it was in state-based systems, it is important to remember again that it was much faster in these than it had been in stateless systems. This is because the dynamics of power within and between societies were added to the forces of population pressure as motors of technological change. The technological changes in production that occurred in state-based systems were "efficient" in the sense that they were directed toward producing more from the same amount of land (e.g., irrigation projects) or producing more with the same amount of labor time (e.g., potter's wheels). Though scarcities and tradeoffs were not usually calculated using market prices, they did affect the decisionmaking of elites. The Weberian characterization of precapitalist authorities as "arbitrary" overlooks the economizing that operated in the logic of power and accumulation in these systems.

As class societies emerged, innovation and implementation became intimately connected with the exercise of power, both within and between societies. Competition between contending elite groups and between societies was the main driving force, and means of coercion were the main focus of technological dynamism. Compared to stateless systems, a greater proportion of societal resources were devoted to innovations of new technologies of coercion. Compared to capitalist systems, this is also true. Capitalist systems probably devote a greater *share* of resources to the transformation of productive (i.e., agricultural, industrial) technology than do state-based systems. But this should not be read to mean that state-based systems devoted no resources to the transformation of production. Indeed, kings and emperors often sponsored large investment projects from which they could derive resources with which to compete with contending groups (both internal and external). Empire-states varied considerably in the extent to which they sponsored expansions of material production. Some, like the Aztecs, corresponded to the model of the purely tributary empire extracting resources from conquered territories without intervening in production. Others, like the Inca, carried out extensive projects of road building, terracing, relocating populations, and restructuring agricultural production.

Economies became integrated over larger distances; empires expanded in size and commodified forms of exchange developed. The most commercialized of the agrarian state-based empires (e.g., China and Rome) had important sectors of production for the market, wage-labor, monetary instruments, and commodified land. And yet these remained dominated by the state-based mode of accumulation.

I define capitalism as a mode of accumulation based on the profitable production of commodities for sale in price-setting markets.[2] A commodity is a standardized good produced for sale in a price-setting market. Capitalism also requires that other social goods take the commodity form. Thus wealth should be money, a "universal" medium of exchange that is itself exposed to market forces. Land should be traded as a commodity, and labor power should be bought and sold in a labor market. This definition is an ideal type that has never been found in its pure form in any actually existing society, but societies (and world-systems) differ greatly in the extent to which they approximate this model.

TECHNOLOGY AND CAPITALISM

Capitalism became a dominant mode of accumulation in a large regional system for the first time in Europe in the seventeenth century. There had been earlier capitalist states, especially the maritime city-states operating in the interstices between tributary empires, but they were minor, semiperipheral players within state-based systems that were becoming more and more commercialized. In these systems merchant capitalism— often carried on by semiperipheral city-states—served to integrate larger and larger regions into an international division of labor, but this was primarily based on buying low and selling high.[3] In such a system the tendency for "socially necessary labor time" to transform local techniques is stronger than in marketless exchange systems, but still not so strong as in networks far more devoted to commodity production.

The emergent predominance of capitalism in Europe did not involve the complete replacement of state coercion by market relations but rather the increasing importance of production for the market, to the point where the dynamics of state policy and interstate relations were qualitatively transformed. This occurred because the production and sale of commodities became the most attractive accumulation strategy for those in control of great wealth. Thus, the game of geoeconomics for the first time became more important than the older game of geopolitics.

There is general agreement that capitalism revolutionizes technology much more quickly because it provides strong incentives to producers for producing more efficiently. When price competition is an important determinant of production costs and the final price of a product, an entrepreneur who can produce and sell that product more cheaply will take a larger share of the market. But we know that the conditions of pure price competition are actually somewhat atypical within "real" capitalism. Monopoly and oligopoly are much more often found in both input and final goods markets. And yet, capitalism does indisputably revolutionize technology much faster than earlier modes of accumulation did, and the rate of technological change has itself changed radically over the last four hundred years. Let us examine why.

First, the idea of incentives to producers does operate to a greater extent than it did in earlier systems. Despite numerous nonmarket influences on prices, the operation of market forces is indisputably much greater than in earlier systems. Though the competitive sector of small firms is usually less than half of the economy, it serves as an important source of motivation for individuals and firms. The idea of getting rich by inventing a better mousetrap undoubtedly stimulates innovation even if the big winners on better mousetraps are rarely their inventors.

Monopoly capitalism continues to revolutionize technology because even though market regulation of prices in major inputs or final products is weak, large companies compete for market shares by introducing new products and variations on old ones. This competition through product innovation is a major force behind large expenditures on research and development.

The Weberians see capitalist development as a general process of rationalization and bureaucratization. Capitalism develops forms of calculation such as capital accounting that make it possible to determine much more precisely whether activities are profitable or not. This encourages technological change because it improves the ability to calculate efficiency and to evaluate alternative means of production. But this equates the rather peculiar social, political, and economic institutions that historically have caused industrialization with "rationality," and it relegates claims about injustices that have accompanied these changes to "irrational" or "primordial" concerns about values. Weber and most Weberians assume that rationality works best when it is undertaken by individuals or firms seeking to maximize their own returns. Identifying capitalism with rationality versus equating of collective needs or claims of injustice with irrationality is a much too convenient device to support the conclusion that capitalism is the best of all possible worlds. If collective interests are incalculable and democratic planning is impossible, then the best that can be done is to allow people to vote with their dollars. Never mind that so many have so few of these votes.

The political structure of global capitalism, the interstate system, does not guarantee monopolies at the world-market level. The world market is dynamic and competitive in almost all industries despite the existence of oligopolies within states. States as well as firms are competitors for world-market shares, and states are increasingly becoming major investors in research and development of new technologies to produce goods for the world market.

What is new about this is the direct involvement of states in developing new products for sale. Much older is state sponsorship of military research and development. As Charles Tilly (1990) has so persuasively shown for the European states, states made war and war made states. Military technology has been changing for thousands of years but a geometric increase in the destructiveness of weaponry has accompanied capitalist industrialization. William McNeill (1983) argues that this is because industrialization produces more wealth, thus states have more resources, and so they do what they have always done (arm and make war) but on the larger scale made possible by industrialization. This is true, but we must also understand the ways in which states and the larger system of states have themselves been transformed by capitalism.

Precapitalist interstate systems went through long cycles of centralization and decentralization, which are often described as the rise and fall of empires. Eventually a number of competing states within the core region of a world-system would be conquered by a semiperipheral "rogue power," which would set up a "universal state" (Wilkinson 1988). Such universal states constituted much more centralized polities, and the possibilities for utilizing political power in these to enforce monopolies typically slowed the rate of technological change. These empires eventually disintegrated again into less-centralized interstate or "feudal" systems.

The modern world-system also exhibits a long cycle of political centralization and decentralization, but this differs from the precapitalist systems in important ways. In the modern system this process takes the form of the rise and fall of hegemonic core powers. True empire formation, in the sense of a single state coming to dominate the whole core region, has never occurred. Thus, the multicentric interstate system is preserved through operation of the hegemonic sequence. As in earlier systems, state power is sometimes used to appropriate resources directly (through taxation and tribute), but the most important players in the system—the core states and especially the hegemonic core state—do this least because they use state power primarily to support profitable commodity production.

The politically multicentric structure of the modern world-system is not interrupted by periods of control by a single empire state, and thus the dynamic effects of interstate competition operate more or less continuously on all types of technology (or rather the forces of monopoly are never as constrictive as they are in a system dominated by a single overarching state). This accounts for part of the generally higher rate of technological change, but not for the secular geometric trend within the capitalist world-system. For this we turn to the social transformations wrought by the capitalist mode of accumulation.

Capitalist industrialization has resulted in a number of sociological trends that have greatly increased the rate of technological change, but some of these have been the result of ways in which people have resisted capitalist development as well as the will of capitalists themselves. Mass education is an important structural basis of technological innovation. State expenditures on mass education have developed in response to the needs of capitalists for skilled workers *and* the demands of citizens to acquire marketable skills. The consumerist culture of capitalist societies is a major mechanism for integrating middle classes into the capitalist success story. The expansion of mass consumption is partly the result of the "realization problem," by which capitalists need a demand for the commodities they produce, and partly the outcome of political class struggles, in which certain groups' primary-sector and middle-class workers have obtained higher incomes, especially in core societies.

This kind of income distribution in core countries has spurred technological change in consumer industries as firms compete for market shares through product innovation and built-in obsolescence. Such a technological revolution is only "efficient" (and profitable) as long as environmental costs are externalized, and this depends on maintaining an appropriate political structure. While many of the problems created by this form of consumption are global in extent, the interstate system and the core/periphery hierarchy make coordinated solutions difficult.

Capitalism not only provides the resources for vast core-state expenditures on military technology (and reinforces the structural need for military competition), but it also produces resources to expand technical and scientific pursuits. Such expenditures obviously spur technological innovation and play an important role in competition among core firms and states for shares of the world market. The "Japan Incorporated" model—in which state expenditures on education and science are coordinated with a national industrial policy designed to capture a large share of the future world market for the most profitable commodities—has become the exemplar of rational state capitalism for all.

One of the most important mechanisms by which capitalism reproduces the core/periphery hierarchy is through technological dependency. The development and implementation of new technology by core states and firms is used to extract technological rents from semiperipheral and peripheral producers. The product cycle is a sequence in which new hightech goods are sold for very high prices by their original producers and are produced in core areas. When these products are copied by other producers, or when patents are leased or sold, the price of the product comes down to widen the market, and production moves to regions where labor costs are cheaper, often in peripheral or semiperipheral countries.

Cross-national research on technological dependence—operationalized as foreign control over patents—has demonstrated that it has negative effects on national economic growth and that it mediates the negative effects of penetration by foreign capital investment (Meyer-Fehr 1980; see also Bornschier and Chase-Dunn 1985; 137–140).

TIME-SPACE COMPRESSION

The spatial scale of economic integration has been increasing for thousands of years, but the rate of this increase since World War II has caused many to claim that a new, qualitatively different, global economy has recently emerged. The proportion of daily food and raw materials consumed by the average person on earth that is produced outside of that person's country of residence has greatly increased. Transportation and communications costs have fallen geometrically at the same time that the global population has shot up.

These rapid changes in the scale of economic integration and the precipitous fall of transportation and communications costs are termed "timespace compression" by the Marxist geographer David Harvey. Harvey

(1989, 147) characterizes time-space compression thus: "The time horizons of both private and public decision-making have shrunk, while satellite communications and declining transport costs have made it increasingly possible to spread those decisions immediately over an ever wider and variegated space."

Of course transportation and communications costs have been falling for millennia, but Harvey argues that the recent geometric changes are related to changes since the 1970s in the nature of capitalist accumulation and that these have had important consequences for the culture of capitalism. Harvey adopts the terminology and analytic approach to stages of capitalism employed by those of the "regulation school" who discuss "regimes of accumulation." An accumulation regime is a distinctive constellation of class relations, political institutions, organizational forms of production, and production technologies. This is a recent addition to the literature of stages of capitalism. The accumulation regime approach focuses on the contrast between "Fordism"—the mass production of consumer goods in large factories by large firms using continuous-line methods of production—with "flexible specialization"—the production of customized or small-batch products by small firms integrated through market and subcontracting relations for the global market.

Harvey claims that "flexible accumulation" is much more revolutionary of technology than Fordism was. He contrasts it with the "rigidities of Fordism," stating: "It rests on flexibility with respect to labour processes, labour markets, products, and patterns of consumption. It is characterized by the emergence of entirely new sectors of production, new ways of providing financial services, new markets, and, above all, greatly intensified rates of commercial, technological and organizational innovation" (Harvey 1989, 147).

This new stage of capitalism is alleged to have had big consequences for the relations between capital and labor because it has undercut the basis of Fordist, trade union practices—the organization of craft and industrial unions in large, concentrated factory locations. Harvey is only summarizing the earlier work of others regarding flexible specialization. He contributes a useful discussion of the institutional aspects of capitalism that have *not* changed with the transition and a comparison of the ways in which Fordism and flexible accumulation differently respond to the contradictions of overaccumulation (Harvey 1989, 179–188). The main point of Harvey's book is that flexible accumulation and the associated geometric rise in time-space compression account for the cultural shift from modernism to postmodernity in architecture and art.[4]

My critique of earlier versions of the stages of capitalism approach is found in Chapters 3 and 4 of *Global Formation* (Chase-Dunn 1989), in which I argued that most of what is explained by various specifications of the stages of capitalism can be better comprehended by a model that includes world-system constants, cycles, and secular trends. That book was written, however, before the accumulation regime approach and the contrast between Fordism and flexible specialization became so popular. The discussion below is an extension of the analysis of world-system processes and stages of capitalism.

What Has Really Changed in the World-System?

Recent changes in the international division of labor, shifts of economic and military power, changes in the organizational features of capitalist firms, and the emergence of new technologies have caused social scientists to reassess the options and constraints that operate on developing countries. It is agreed that the significance of these changes for developing countries varies from region to region, but a nearly complete consensus has formed around the notion that insertion into the larger world-economy as a producer of commodities for export is the only viable development path (e.g., Portes and Kinkaid 1989, 495). An objective understanding of the real constraints and options for Third World development in the future requires that we have a clear and true picture of the long-term cycles and trends that continue to operate in the capitalist world-economy.

To know what is new, we must know what is old. Because analysts of social change have primarily focused on national development rather than development of the world-system as a whole, and because the time horizon of development studies is usually rather short, the cyclical processes and secular trends that are apparent when we observe the whole world-system over long periods of time are poorly understood. Both academics and policy analysts repeatedly discover new phenomena and construct theories of the latest stage of development around these. Transnational corporations, "trilateralism," the "new" international division of labor, postindustrialism, flexible accumulation, the end of the Cold War, the decline of the United States—all have been hailed as fundamental changes in the rules of the game. Certainly the players have changed position, but have the rules changed? To answer this question requires a clearly formulated theory of what the old rules were, and an accurate model of the cyclical processes and secular trends in the contemporary world-system.

In *Global Formation* I argued that *there have been no major structural or processual changes* in the world-system in the last few decades. The new phenomena emphasized by many observers are largely predictable continuations of cycles and trends long in operation.[5] In some cases new organizational forms have emerged that represent functional equivalents of older forms, for example, formal colonialism has been replaced by neocolonial institutional structures by which core powers exercise control over peripheral countries. The expansion of transnational corporations continues a long-operating trend toward the internationalization of capital and integration of the world market. Trilateralism, the Group of Seven, the International Monetary Fund (IMF), the World Bank, and others represent a trend toward international political integration that began with the Concert of Europe. The new international division of labor is only the latest reorganization of world production spurred by uneven development, economic cycles, and technological change. The decline of the U.S. and the rise of German-led Europe and Japan are a repetition of the hegemonic sequence: the rise and fall of hegemonic core powers. The current ambivalent movement toward condominium among core states is structurally similar to the period in the last quarter of the nineteenth century in which Great Britain was declining and Germany and the United States were rising (Goldfrank 1983). Postindustrialism and flexible accumulation can be best understood as a recent acceleration of the long-term trends toward increasing capital-intensity and time-space compression. The end of the Cold War, the collapse of the Soviet Union, and marketization in China represent the reintegration of socialist states into the world market, a process that began long ago and that is part of the spiraling interaction between capitalist expansion and socialist movements (Chase-Dunn 1992).

From the point of view of a structuralist approach to the world-system, recent changes are just business-as-usual. The capitalist world-system has undergone vast technological transformations in connection with the Kondratieff cycle for four hundred years (Kleinknecht 1987). The industrial revolution that began in Britain in the middle of the eighteenth century was neither the first nor the last major transformation of production technology, business organization, and labor relations. In each of these industrial revolutions new lead industries emerged based on certain key technological innovations that broadly transformed the economy and provided the basis for increased productivity and profitability. The core country that was able to achieve predominance in these most-profitable lead industries had a good shot at hegemony in the world-system (Thompson 1990). Every "technological style" (Perez 1983, 361) shares certain key features that enable it to form the basis of shifting from a Kondratieff B-phase (stagnation) to a Kondratieff A-phase (renewed expansion). But each technological style also has features unique only to it that transform markets, organization, and labor relations in unique ways.

There is little question that the two new key technologies with the greatest potential for serving as the basis of the next K-wave A-phase are biotechnology and integrated circuits. The question is: What are the unique features of these technologies that might importantly alter the functioning of the world-economy? The accumulation regime arguments about the transition from Fordism to flexible accumulation contend that these new technologies carry with them certain consequences for organizing capitalist firms and labor relations and that these features account for other changes that are occurring.

Is it true, as implied by the flexible-specialization theorists, that small firms constitute a greater proportion of the world economy than they did in the past, and that, therefore, the long-term trend toward the centralization of capital has been reversed? I have not seen any evidence to support this claim. Certainly, the size of the largest production firms and financial institutions (in terms of assets, sales, and employees) has continued to increase. Small firms have long been the most dynamic sector of the capitalist economy, the most likely to undertake risks, and the first to implement new technologies. Is it true that small firms are more dynamic or account for a greater proportion of new jobs than they did before the advent of flexible specialization?

The accumulation-regime theorists have claimed that the degree of competition has increased in the world economy with the rise of flexible specialization. The situation has indeed become much more competitive for some large firms (e.g., U.S. auto manufacturers), but has there really been an overall increase in the degree of competition? And if there has been, is this because of changes associated with flexible specialization? Uneven development has long pressured less-competitive firms out of markets, and this kind of increase in competition has occurred cyclically during shakedowns and economic crises of devalorization. Is the recent apparent increase in competition simply a repeat of the shakedown phase of uneven development, or does it signal something new resulting from flexible accumulation?

A related argument about increasing competition has been made by Ross and Trachte (1990) who claim that capital flight is a new mechanism used by capital to discipline labor in the contemporary stage of global capitalism. Although the ability of firms to engage in global sourcing and flexible location of production and control has been enhanced by new information and transportation technologies, capital flight is *not* a new feature of the struggle between capital and labor. The ability to move production, import new workers, coordinate policy, and escape locations where workers or other groups have won political fights that constrain the maneuverability of capital has been a fundamental aspect of the process of uneven capitalist development for hundreds of years. The spatial scale of mobility has increased with the fall of transportation costs and the speed of coordination has increased with communications and information technology, but these are continuations of trends that have long accompanied the expansion of capitalism.

HEGEMONIC TRANSITION

The decline of U.S. hegemony and the rise of Japan and Germany as challengers for shares of the world market have certainly changed things for particular capitalists and workers. But what has this continuation of the hegemonic sequence changed for the system?

Though we cannot predict who will be the next hegemon—and that determination will undoubtedly be somewhat conjunctural—we can predict that the question of hegemonic succession will again be strongly posed and that conflict over this will likely become strong in the decade of the 2020s. The particularities of the new technologies will affect the abilities of contending states and firms to succeed. Current status regarding biotechnology and integrated circuits will be an important determinant in the contention over who will become the next hegemon, and the potential contenders—German-led Europe, the United States, and Japan—are rather uneven in this regard. Indeed, Volker Bornschier (1992) has argued that Europe is so far behind in the new technological style that it may not be able to catch up.

Several scholars have claimed that a new feature of the current world-system, which demonstrates a qualitative change compared to earlier periods, is the uneven distribution of technology, military power, and cultural legitimacy across the contending core states (e.g., Bornschier 1992). Japan is far ahead in technological superiority, while the U.S. is the unchallenged military power, and Europe (it is argued) has the advantage in global cultural legitimacy. This condition of unevenness in the core, some scholars allege, supports the notion of a new stage of integration among world capitalists, one in which complementarity and economic integration is so great that a period of renewed warfare among core states has been made impossible. The phenomena of trilateralism and the Group of Seven, the coalition supporting the Gulf War against Iraq, and joint ventures between firms from different states are cited as further evidence in support of this "core condominium" vision of the future. This approach implies that the level of competition/conflict has actually decreased—just the opposite of the claim made by the accumulation-regime thinkers.

The current, uneven distribution of military and economic power is certainly a valid observation. The U.S. is the world's policeman more than ever. Germany and Japan, the main economic contenders, have little in the way of military power. First place in world-market power is certainly held by Japan, but the geomilitary basis of this power is the structure of access to raw materials, which is backed up by U.S. armed forces. The "military Keynesianism" version of national industrial "policy," which has been the basis of the U.S. political economy since the Korean War, has been and continues to be costly in terms of economic competitiveness vis à vis Japan and Europe. Essentially, the United States pays the political-military overhead costs for its core competitors. This policy has lost its legitimacy with the demise of the Soviet Union, but the Pentagon and the U.S. military-industrial complex are scrambling to come up with new threats to legitimize the "defense" budget.

If past processes of the world-system that have caused competition among core powers to turn toward conflict during the decline of a former hegemon remain strong in the future, then we should observe a shift toward equalizing the distribution of military and economic power in the next decades—that is, a military buildup by Japan and Europe. If this does not occur, the theorists of global capitalist integration may be correct. If the United States continues to try to maintain global reach based on military predominance, and the competing core economies continue to gain world-market shares from U.S. capital, the pressures of this disparity between economic and military costs and returns are likely to increase.

I agree with those observers who argue that Japan cannot perform the role of hegemon by itself. Some scholars have argued that Japanese culture is inappropriately insular to provide a new basis for hegemonic universalism (e.g., Bornschier 1992). I tend to put less importance on the cultural aspects of hegemony than do others (see *Global Formation,* Chapter 5). The fact that there are more Zen Buddhists in California than in Japan suggests that cultural shortcomings may not be a major obstacle to Japanese hegemony. But Japan does suffer from strategic raw materials' dependencies.

Japanese access to critical energy and raw material resources is geomilitarily dependent on the armed forces of the United States (Friedman and Lebard 1991). Joint ventures and foreign investment work fairly well as long as the world remains peaceful, but in a future period in which core conflicts are more salient, Japanese trade relations and holdings within the blocks of the other hegemonic contenders could easily be abrogated. It is easy to imagine the nationalization of Japanese holdings in Eastern Europe during some future wave of economic nationalism. Who would intervene to prevent such actions? The picture of an economically integrated global economy, in which all property rights are equally enforced, is wishful thinking in the absence of considerable political integration at the global level.

Japan could participate in a serious bid for hegemony by tightly integrating with either China or the United States. Most observers guess that neither of these mergers are likely. If this observation is correct, the Japanese do not have a reasonable potential for hegemony, and they may have the most to lose in a world in which rivalry for hegemony becomes violent. This should make them ardent advocates of world-state formation.

As stated above, the contenders for hegemony will be German-led Europe, the United States, and Japan. The current reorganization of trading and military blocs will likely result in either two or three major international blocs—functional equivalents of earlier colonial empires. Europe, the former Soviet republics, and probably Africa will form one. The U.S and Latin America will form another, either separate from or together with Japan, East Asia, and the Pacific. South Asia will likely be a region of contention (Goldfrank 1991). The interests of Third World countries in this configuration are somewhat complex. To some extent each country will have interests in common with other countries in its bloc and will act to support the bid of its main core partner. But pan–Third World interests, as I have argued elsewhere, will be best served by global-state formation (Chase-Dunn 1990b).

SEMIPERIPHERAL INDUSTRIALIZATION

It is commonly agreed that an important aspect of the new international division of labor is the industrialization that has occurred in many semiperipheral and some peripheral countries. And most agree that this industrialization has differed in very important ways from that which occurred earlier in core countries. Perhaps the most important difference has to do with levels of profitability. The kinds of heavy industry that have moved from the core to the semiperiphery were extremely profitable when they developed within core countries; indeed, many of these were the cutting-edge industries that allowed certain core countries to obtain large shares of world surplus. But industrialization of semiperipheral countries has not led, in most cases, to upward mobility of those same countries in the core/periphery hierarchy. On the contrary, for most of these countries it has been more a matter of running fast in order to stand still.

While some countries have experienced true upward mobility (Taiwan and South Korea), semiperipheral industrialization has not reduced the overall degree of inequality between the core and the semiperiphery because the core has shifted to specialization in new, more-profitable industries. The kinds of heavy industries that the semiperipheral countries attempted to develop with their programs of import substitution and "socialist mobilization" have become less profitable, while a new technological regime has given birth to new lead industries such as computers, robotics, and biotechnology. Comparative evidence indicates that the semiperipheral share of global energy consumption grew in the 1960s and 1970s, while its share of global income did not change (Chase-Dunn 1989, 266). This supports the idea that semiperipheral industrialization has not corresponded to upward mobility in the accumulation of global profits.

Regarding the notion of the transition from Fordism to flexible accumulation, Fordism did not disappear. It simply moved to the semiperiphery. Thus, the labor strategies declared obsolete by the accumulation regime theorists are far from obsolete in the semiperiphery. Indeed, some of the most dynamic labor movements in the world today are in Brazil and Korea.

SEMIPERIPHERAL SOCIALISM

The collapse of state socialism in the Soviet Union and Eastern Europe was the result of a long process of structurally reintegrating these societies into the capitalist world-system (Chase-Dunn 1982, 1992). Their trajectory of opposition and reintegration was analytically similar to other socialist organizations such as trade unions, workers' co-ops, kibbutzim, and socialist parties. The organizational creations of people who resist and seek to transform capitalism spur capital to create new forms and scales of domination. This is part of what drives the expansion of capitalism. And, in turn, the expansion and deepening of capitalism—and its continuing revolutionizing of technology—affect organizational forms created by socialist movements, transforming them and reintegrating them. The threats and opportunities of the larger, expanding capitalist world-economy and its interstate system reintegrate older socialist organizations, but they also create new possibilities for resistance and transformation. I call this the spiral of capitalism and socialism.

Socialist revolutions took state power in the semiperiphery, but they were not successful in implementing autonomous, socialist modes of production. Rather, because of constraints stemming from their underdevelopment and the threats and opportunities emanating from the larger world economy and geopolitical system, they used socialist ideology and state power to mobilize urbanization, accumulation, and industrialization in an effort to catch up with core capitalism. In this effort they were similar in many respects to other semiperipheral states. State firms, import substitution, and protection against core imports are all strategies that both socialist and nonsocialist semiperipheral states have pursued. There have been important differences (Comisso 1986), but the similarities extend to the decisions that were posed around the issue of export promotion. In both socialist and nonsocialist semiperipheral countries class and political struggles occurred over the development path to take. And in almost all the semiperipheral countries, those political forces favoring low wages and profitable production of exports for the world market eventually won out. The only partial exceptions are Cuba, China, and Vietnam.

This outcome has led many observers to conclude that there are no real alternatives to export promotion. The critique of the command economies by laissez-faire economists as inefficient has been accepted by nearly everyone. But the standards of efficiency offered are those of the world market. Hard currency is "real." World prices are the "real" prices. This is the new ideological hegemony, and it is very hegemonic, at least for the present.

What does technology have to do with all this? Capitalism's continued ability to revolutionize technology was an important reason why the communist states became reintegrated into the world market. A critical mass of technocrats and bureaucrats within those states came to see their opportunities in the larger system as enhanced by following the policy of export promotion. They chose this path because they believed their own access to the world market's high technologies and consumer goods could not be satisfied by continuing state socialism. Production by the command economy of the things desired by most workers—food, housing, transportation, health care—was entirely possible. The alleged crisis of the command economy was produced politically by those forces that wanted to engage in export promotion.

The recent, final denouement of the long-term process by which the socialist states became reintegrated into the capitalist world-economy has made it difficult for socialist parties and movements to continue using the old symbols and language. And this has refueled the broad ideological trend toward Reaganism/Thatcherism, deregulation, privatization, attacks on the welfare state, marketization, and glorification of conspicuous consumption that began in the 1980s. I see these ideological developments as different but convergent consequences of the global economic downturn: the Kondratieff B-phase and its effects on capitalists, workers, and the fiscal situation of states. Although these have varied greatly from country to country, and depending on location in the core/periphery hierarchy, the thematic elements in policy and political discourse are strikingly similar across what appear to be radically different situations.

The irony of the ideological victory of neoliberalism is that it has occurred within a context of a capitalist crisis of immense proportions. The objective conditions are growing inequalities, massive irrationalities, and potential global ecological disasters. Under these conditions it would seem a reasonable prediction that the "market mentality" will not hold sway for long. The "yuppie high" has already lost some of its influence in the United States, where growing inequality, economic stagnation, and fiscal crisis have led to a renewal of racial antagonism.

The near-consensus about the severe limits on development options for peripheral and semiperipheral countries is reduced in the ideology of neoliberalism to two alternatives: implement IMF austerity policies and court the transnational firms or become a stagnant backwater. The possibilities for autonomous, balanced development seem to have been sealed off. Only a very few thinkers continue to discuss the idea of national self-reliance and socialism (but see Amin 1990). Even those communist states that have until now resisted marketization and deals with transnational corporations—Cuba and Vietnam—are now trying to preserve the egalitarian aspects of their revolutions while simultaneously inserting themselves into the world market. The most recent Cuban development plans stress joint ventures in tourism and biotechnology, and the language now used by Cuban economists sounds quite close to the discourse of business confidence and comparative advantage. Both the industries and the lingo are not very different from what I hear from the Greater Baltimore Committee, the local "chamber of commerce." The challenge of this kind of insertion for countries like Cuba and Vietnam is how to preserve the great gains of socialist revolution in egalitarian class (and race) relations while becoming exposed to world-market forces. Most observers predict that these experiments will fail and that Cuba and Vietnam will go the way of China, Eastern Europe, and the Soviet Union.

The world-system perspective predicts that semiperipheral countries will continue to be fruitful locations for socialist movements and socialist states. Semiperipheral positions have always been favorable terrain for both upward mobility and challenges to the rules of the game (Chase-Dunn 1990a). Growing industrialization and proletarianization of semiperipheral states will create new possibilities for socialist labor movements and parties (e.g., in Brazil, Mexico, and India). In the next century we can expect that socialist movements will again be able to take state power in semiperipheral states. The new version of "Fordism" creates new possibilities for the organization of industrial unions and socialist parties.

Some of these countries will likely experience revolutions in which socialists take state power, while in others, socialists will come to power through electoral processes. These may do a better job of institutionalizing democratic socialism than the exsocialist semiperipheral states did because they will suffer less from the radical disjuncture between city and country. A major difficulty that undermined majority rule in earlier, semiperipheral socialist revolutions was the very small size of the urban proletariat compared to the rural peasantry. The contemporary semiperipheral states are less unbalanced in this regard.

These new experiments with socialism may also benefit from the renewal and strengthening of transnational socialist networks and organizations working on global problems. The notion of autarkical national development has become increasingly anachronistic, but the alternative need not be capitulation to the power of capitalist core states and corporations.

The new technologies are said to have undermined the labor movement by allowing capital to pit workers in one locale against workers in another. But some of these same technologies can be used by workers to counteract this strategy. The "international" unionism ideology very infrequently was matched by actual collaborative action. But transnational corporations create the structural basis for transnational unions, and the techniques of communication and information processing used by capital can also be used by labor.

The so-called decline of the labor movement has not been primarily because of development of new technologies and organizational forms of capitalist production. Labor unions have been attacked in many countries by both the state and large firms. Welfare provisions, which provide a social floor for wage negotiations and a fall-back for workers who risk struggling with their employers, have been attacked and reduced in the same countries in which the labor movement has declined. Antilabor regimes have occurred during a period of generally slow economic growth. Workers in industries that have lost market shares have been the hardest hit with wage and benefit cutbacks. Buyouts, shutdowns, and "streamlining" have been targeted at strong unions. All these factors account for labor union decline. Laying all these developments at the doorstep of flexible accumulation misses a great deal.

The spiral of capitalism and socialism reintegrates older socialist organizations as functional parts of the expanded and intensified world-system, but it does not make these older forms of organization necessarily obsolete. New trade unions, socialist parties, and socialist states will emerge to challenge the logic of capital. And they will use the very technologies that capital has produced and sold—especially communications technology, computers, and cheap transportation. In an era of global capitalism, trade unions must also be global. The organization of international solidarity among workers has always been difficult and still is, but the new technologies definitely make it less so.

The ideology of globalism and competitiveness has been used to justify restructuring through deregulation and attacks on workers and poor people in some core states, especially the United States and Great Britain. But other core countries have followed a different path. They have maintained welfare-state supports for the poorest people, supported union efforts to retrain redundant employees, and used state power to implement a decent-wage industrial policy, which includes production for the world market. While this may only be enlightened state capitalism instead of socialism, it is a definite improvement over Reagan-Thatcher, welfare-for-the-rich politics.

The ideology of the world market must be countered by the notion of a global society in which problems can be solved cooperatively. The new technologies can play a helpful role in facilitating international communication and organization, which will be the basis on which a more egalitarian and peaceful world-system can be built.

NOTES

1. By "mode of accumulation" I am referring to the deep structural logic by which systems produce, distribute, and develop. The more conventional term that has been used by structuralist Marxists is "mode of production." By using accumulation instead of production, I hope to avert confusion over the issue of "productionism." Nevertheless, much of the literature that uses the "mode of production" terminology (i.e., Amin 1980, 1991; Wolf 1982) is germane to my theoretical approach.

2. A price-setting market is one in which prices are set by the competitive bidding of a large number of buyers and sellers.

3. The exchange of unequals was slow to turn into unequal exchange because most producers were only selling their production surpluses rather than producing primarily for exchange in the larger network.

4. Harvey's discussion of modernism points out that it has always been composed of a dialectic between the eternal and the ephemeral. In this light, postmodernism is just the ephemeral phase that corresponds to the latest acceleration of time-space compression. The identity aspects of postmodern philosophy—the concern for the other and the multiple personalities of the self—are explained by Jonathan Friedman (1983, 1992) as a consequence of the decline of U.S. hegemony.

5. Chapter 2 of *GF* designates a schema of global capitalism that includes four structural *constants*: the interstate system, the core/periphery hierarchy, commodified labor (with greater coercion in the periphery), and commodity production as the most important form of accumulation. There are four systemic *cycles*: the Kondratieff wave, the hegemonic sequence, the war cycle, and an oscillation in the structure of core/periphery relations between relatively freer market trade and relatively more politically constrained exchange. The eight systemic *trends* are territorial and population expansion, expansion and deepening of commodity relations, state-formation, growing size of capitalist firms, the transnationalization of capital, increasing capital intensity of production, proletarianization, and the increasing gap between core and periphery with regard to incomes.

6

States in World-Systems Analysis: Massaging a Creative Tension

Peter J. Taylor

The last two decades have witnessed a remarkable transformation in the progress of the social sciences. From a pattern of separate developments along disciplinary pathways, there has been an abrupt recognition that advances in social knowledge require a multidisciplinary perspective. Nowhere is this change more clearly indicated than in studies of the state and studies of globalization. In their different ways these two massive growth areas of research exposed the poverty of existing disciplinary boundaries.

In this chapter I consider specific relations between these two study areas. Although all the extensive literature emanating from this multidisciplinary research is not covered, I do attempt a comprehensive evaluation of one globalization theory against the main issues arising from the various state theories. The theoretical framework used is Wallerstein's (1979, 1983, 1984) world-systems analysis that studies the capitalist world-economy, which is a hierarchical spatial division of labor (core/semiperiphery/periphery) and a cyclical ordering of capital accumulation (Kondratieff waves, hegemonic cycles). The question asked is which theory, or theories, of the state is used in this world-systems analysis? The answer to this question is not at all straightforward, since various theoretical positions on the state can be found in the world-systems literature.

One obstacle must be addressed as a primary source of misunderstanding about world-systems analysis. After approximately two decades of development, world-systems analysis has come to be generally accepted as a respectable set of social science writings and is usually found in discussions that review contemporary approaches to social science. In the area of state theory and practice, for instance, three recent discussions devote one part of their argument to world-systems analysis (Gill 1988, 38–41; Tilly 1990, 11; Driver 1991, 274–276), but this recognition has a curious twist to it. Despite the demise of disciplinary boundaries, new intellectual barriers are being built. While describing merits and demerits of the approach, these authors manage to "ghettoize" world-systems analysis.

Their brief treatments selectively draw upon the literature to produce a stereotypical, narrowly focused analysis that allows them quite reasonably to discount the "vulgar" world-systems analysis they have created. For instance, one author (Driver 1990) dismisses the relevance of Wallerstein's work on states without referring to the seven chapters on states in Part I of *The Politics of the World-Economy,* which Wallerstein (1984) helpfully entitled *The States and the Interstate System.*

The latter is our starting point here, but the point is that such obstacles are themselves ultimately self-defeating. World-systems analysis is not a monument for worship or demolition but an ongoing, historical social science project available for use. We must utilize "creative tensions" between our alternative social theories (Dear 1986; Taylor 1992). A ghettoized world-systems analysis serves no one; instead, it requires both internal and external stimuli to develop and continue to be useful. One such source of stimuli must undoubtedly be the massive recent researches on state theory, but stimulation in a creative tension should be a two-way street. It is my contention that state theory can benefit as much from this positive confrontation as can world-systems theory, and both theories can be improved through creative engagement with each other without compromising their respective basic assumptions. This essay is offered in proof.

This chapter has four sections. We begin with world-system assumptions that quite literally de-privilege the state. The key point is that political processes viewed through a world-systems perspective are not all located at the level of the state. This is a particular variant of a long-standing minority position in modern political science—explicitly expounded by writers ranging from Duverger (1972) to Walker (1988)—that has attempted to free the idea of politics from dependence on the state. The world-systems contribution to this debate is in proffering an alternative social entity to the state and its society.

In the second part, we reverse this theoretical argument by describing how historically the state did in fact "capture" politics. From this position we devise a "double Janus" model of the state that acts as a vortex in the world-economy, sucking in political power. After this re-privileging of the state, we relate this model to competitive theories about the nature of the state, identifying five basic positions and showing how world-systems analysis uses all five.

The chapter concludes by indicating the implications for state theory of world-systems analysis with its insistence on studying states as part of the interstate system, and on taking a longer historical perspective than do other theories of globalization. Two important contributions of world-systems thinking to state theory are identified: the idea of state maneuverability replaces the controversial "relative autonomy" of states, and the standard accumulation/legitimation balance in state "function" acquires a specific historical interpretation with important implications for the future.

DE-PRIVILEGING THE STATE

World-systems analysis constitutes a theory of social change. It aspires to be a fundamentally new theory, one that overthrows many of our entrenched views on the nature of social change. Hence, it returns to the basic first question: What is the social entity that changes? In our taken-for-granted-world, change occurs in "national societies" that correspond geographically to states—French society, U.S. society, Japanese society, and so on. This state-centric view has been one of the implicit assumptions of conventional social science. World-systems analysis challenges this view of social change by positing the existence of a world system, the capitalist world-economy, that transcends these "state-societies" as the entity through which social change occurs. We cannot understand social change by focusing on the dynamics of any one state-society, because such change can be adequately comprehended only as part of the larger whole. The starting point of world-systems analysis, therefore, is eliminating the privileged position of the state and its associated national society in how we think about social change.

Removing this privilege does not necessarily mean underestimating the role of the state in social change. On the contrary, by overtly recognizing the pervasive influence of the state on our social thinking, world-systems analysis admits its crucial ideological role in influencing social change. The difficulty that other social theorists have in accommodating world-systems analysis to their state-centric studies, as indicated earlier, can be interpreted as an example of this pervasive effect. In this sense, world-systems analysis reveals the insidious influence of the state. But the state is much more than a social mask, of course, so there remains the crucial question of how the state is analyzed in a world-systems framework.

What, then, are the states dealt with in world-systems analysis? At the most general level, they are simply particular examples of social institutions. The capitalist world-economy consists of a myriad of social institutions through which individuals interact with one another in the routine reproduction of the system. Not all types of institutions are equal in significance, of course, and we can identify states as important institutions in the operation of the world-economy. In fact, they are one of four key institutions that Wallerstein (1984) identifies, the others being households, classes, and "peoples." All four are integral to the world-economy; they were created as part of the rise of this system and are continually being reformed as part of its reproduction.

Households are the basic "atoms" of the system and are defined, not in terms of co-residency but by operating a budget and pooling various sources of income, through which their reproduction is organized. Classes are defined in relation to the mode of production and so encompass system-wide economic strata. "Peoples" are more amorphous; as national/

ethnic status groups based upon cultural identities, they may be defined in terms of language, religion, race, or some exclusive mixture of criteria. States, then, are the institutions through which these others are organized. A state is the locus of formal power within the system that sets the rules for others to follow. Each individual is a member of a household, can be located by class, has a cultural identity with his/her people, and will be a citizen of a state.

There are two initial points to make about this quadripartite arrangement. First, each institution has an important historical geography. The forms that households take, for instance, vary greatly over time and space, and the same is conspicuously true of states. This essay concentrates on the core of the world-economy at present or in the recent past. Second, the institutions are closely related in their operations, or as Wallerstein (1984, 36) describes it, "They are indissociably intertwined in complex and contradictory ways." This is the "institutional vortex which is both the product and the moral life of the capitalist world-economy." Let us explore what this means for the state and its politics.

Politics is about power, and power is expressed in and through social institutions. Each institution may be enabling or disenabling depending on the context; individuals are both constrained and provided with opportunities by institutions in the unfolding of power games. Making sense of this complexity begins with identifying different politics in a typology based upon interrelations within the institutional vortex described above. This has been derived in Taylor (1992) and is reproduced here for our argument.

1. There are four *Intrainstitutional politics*:
    (i)   *Intrastate politics* is the most familiar and is usually about competition for government (e.g., the party of the left versus the party of the right).
    (ii)   *Intrapeople politics* varies greatly depending on context but is often concerned with differences in status aims (e.g., devolution versus independence).
    (iii) *Intraclass politics* has been dominated by competitive class strategies of either domination or liberation (e.g., revolution versus reform).
    (iv)   *Intrahousehold politics* is a major realm of patriarchical politics (e.g., career versus family).
2. There are four *Interinstitutional politics*:
    (v)   *Interstate politics* is the substance of international relations research (e.g., peace versus war).
    (vi)   *Interpeople politics* includes aggressive racialism, nationalism, and ethnic conflicts in general (e.g., blacks versus whites in South Africa).

(vii) *Interclass politics* is the classical politics identified in orthodox Marxism (e.g., capital versus labor).

(viii) *Interhousehold politics* involves local competition for survival or consumption (e.g., established hawker versus new
migrant).

3. There are six *Politics between institutions*:

(ix) *State-people politics* has dominated much of twentieth-century
politics through the unattainable ideal of the nation-state (e.g.,
secessionary nationalists versus multinational state).

(x) *State-class politics* has been dominated by the differential incorporation of classes into state politics in the twentieth century (e.g., multinational capital versus state interests).

(xi) *State-household politics* has revolved around rights and welfare issues (e.g., unemployment relief household needs versus
state bureaucratic rule constraints).

(xii) *People-class politics* includes the primary rivalry between nationalists and socialists before 1914 (e.g., international socialism versus particular nationalism).

(xiii) *People-household politics* has been concerned with cultural
issues centering on ideologies of the family (e.g., antiabortion
religion versus household rape victim).

(xiv) *Class-household politics* has included the feminist critique of
socialism for neglecting patriarchy (e.g., high-wage, male,
union labor versus low-wage, part-time, female labor).

By treating each key institution equally in this taxonomy, we have
reached the limits of the world-system argument in depriviledging the state.
Like the other institutions, states appear in just five of the fourteen politics. This position is, of course, quite consistent with those who deplore
the simple equation of politics equals states. Nevertheless, the question
remains why historically the five state-involved politics *have* dominated
the politics of the world-system. Perhaps the time has come to consider re-
privileging the states.

RE-PRIVILEGING THE STATES

In world-systems analysis the states and other institutions are not
treated as "given;" they are created as part of the operation of the world-
economy and are a consequence rather than a cause of the system. But as
a "logical" taxonomy, the fourteen politics above are derived from assum-
ing all four institutions as given. Our conclusions must be supplemented
by a historical description of the variety of modern politics. Undoubtedly,
all fourteen politics have existed and continue to exist in many forms to

constitute the politics of the world-economy. Political parties, whatever their home domain, make their appeals through different combinations of these politics depending on circumstances. But political parties are themselves creatures of states: they are vehicles for access to the state apparatus. Wallerstein's institutional vortex emerges as a very focused nexus of politics in which the states are crucially implicated. Hence, beyond the logical derivation of politics is an unfolding history of creating politics where we can re-privilege the states.

Privileging specific social relations can take several forms. Without re-elevating the state to the basic entity of social change, we will consider the argument for making states primus inter pares in the institutional vortex. This is implicit in some of Wallerstein's (1984, 29) discussion as when, after stating that institutions "create each other," he illustrates the point emphasizing the states: "Classes, ethnic/national groups, and households are defined by the state, through the state, in relation to the state, and in turn create the state, shape the state, and transform the state." In this section I clarify this position by focusing upon the historical development of a particular state form, the nation-state.

Our logical taxonomy of politics through institutions was unconcerned with the historical linkages between institutions. The power of the idea of the nation-state in our modern world illustrates the poverty of our original simple logical argument. "National liberation movements" in the second half of the twentieth century, "national self-determination" in the first half, and the "principle of nationality" in the nineteenth century are all premised on the ideal of state equals nation. The success of this equation can be seen in our language: state control of industry is called "nationalization," world organizations for states have been successively the "League of Nations" and the "United Nations." The idea of merging state and nation and the blurring of their identities in our language are the consequences of a politics set in motion by the upheavals of the late-eighteenth century. Although often thought of as "natural," nation-states are recent political creations and very imperfect ones at that.

For approximately half the existence of the modern world-system, states existed without any necessary reference to "nations." These were the sovereign states confirmed by the Treaties of Westphalia, each of which had its own recognized territory. These states had no particular relation to cultural patterns, their boundaries being set by dynastic legacies and wars. France's promotion of the idea of "natural" state boundaries in the eighteenth century is a classic pre–nation-state strategy justifying French expansion to the Rhine. This contrasts with German state-building a century later promoting the idea of "national" state boundaries to justify incorporating German-speaking peoples along the Rhine into their new state (Pounds 1954).

These states were classic "power containers" as Giddens (1984) terms them. At the simplest level, they are territorial units looking inward on their civil societies and outward to their rivals in the interstate system. We may term this state posture a spatial "Janus" model of the state after the Roman god with two opposite faces, who could look two ways at once. Initially this simply involved using and developing the resources of the territory (soldiers and taxes) to compete in the perennial wars outside of it. This explicit linking of domestic and foreign policy is the essence of mercantilism in the early-modern world-system. These states do not utilize nationalism in the sense of mobilizing the people behind their policies; rather, state power is confirmed and reproduced through a mixture of dynastic loyalty, other traditions of allegiance, coercion and the threat thereof, plus the dearth of alternatives for the mass of the population.

The French Revolution defined an alternative that brought the people as "nation" to the center of the political stage. Nationalism as a radical movement swept through Europe in the first half of the nineteenth century. To existing states this new ideology was dangerous and had to be repressed. Although not antistate per se, it opposed the multinational dynastic states dominating Europe at that time. This ambiguous relation to states allowed the ideology to be de-radicalized in the second half of the nineteenth century, as it was taken over by the states themselves (Billington 1980). This new nationalism from above set about defining new nation-states and, where necessary, converting populations into the correct "people"—witness Russification, germanization, and anglicization.

With the transfer of sovereignty to the people, subjects became citizens, producing an irresistible movement toward more demands on the state. With the extension of the franchise, governments competing for power facilitated unprecedented increases in the state apparatus. Where previously subjects had rarely interacted with their states, citizens now related to them in an increasing number of ways over time. For instance, state education replaced Church and locally supported schools to instill the new nationalism into every child in the land. States became more and more implicated in household budgets as taxes rose and transfer payments through the state became important. The culmination of these processes is the welfare state, whereby the state carries out many of the functions previously done by households. This meant households could be smaller—the nuclear family—and many became the locus for the great expansion in consumption in the second half of the twentieth century. The affluent society and its implications for the nature of the contemporary household can be traced back to the success of nationalism and its "capture" by the state. Other, less-fortunate households have been even more explicitly defined by the state—those dependent on the state through welfare payments. In both cases, contemporary households, in suburb and inner city, are intricately bound to the state.

But what of the third social institution, the classes? In the period up to 1914, nationalism and socialism were generally viewed as competing movements, with the latter wedded to an internationalism that downgraded state politics to a pragmatic status only (Taylor 1987), hence the often-noted point about the neglect of nationalism as a political force in Marxist theory. This view is now being corrected. The key point has been made by Anderson (1983). Nationalism is not like other political "isms"; it is much more fundamental, being similar to religion in its influence on individuals. Whatever the particular processes involved, nationalism undoubtedly gave a sense of identity to the masses whose lives were disrupted by the great economic changes following the industrial revolution. These changes produced what Anderson terms "imagined communities," equivalent to the religious communities of previous periods: in the first half of the seventeenth century millions died for their religious beliefs, and in the first half of the twentieth century millions died for their national beliefs. This powerful ideology is appropriated by states to produce nation-states. It has added a temporal dimension to the territorial state; nations look back to their origins and past golden ages while at the same time using history to project the present into a preferred future success. The idea of the state, its very meaning, is in some sense "deepened" by this process. This is what Nairn (1978) terms the Janus model of nationalism, simultaneously looking backward and forward. This "new Janus" did not replace the initial spatial one but combined with it to define an extremely powerful "double-Janus" model of the modern state. The conclusion, therefore, is that space and time are crucial elements used by states in the world-economy: they look inward and outward through territorial sovereignty and backward and forward through the historical nation.

The immense power of this institutional nexus was illustrated in 1914 when the peace program of the Socialist International was shattered, and worker fought worker under different national flags. Since this time all socialism has been more party than movement, national rather than international (Taylor 1987). Class grievances are now addressed through the state or through frameworks set up by the state. To survive, socialism had to compromise with nationalism, not compete with it. For instance, the "national liberation movements" since 1945 have been simultaneously both nationalist and socialist as they pursued their state-centered politics. We are all "national socialists" now because with the "statization" of nationalism the old power container that was the territorial state accrued to itself the irresistible power of imagined communities called nations. According to Krasner (1989), the social practices that are the state became routinized so that its control over power relations has come to seem natural. The state is so formidable because it combines horizontal breadth, linking into the interstate system, with vertical depth, linking into national history. Individuals through their households, culture, and class are provided with identities that locate them in both the present and the past world through their state. The end result is a social nexus of power called the nation-state that is so much taken for granted that we have trouble even conceiving of alternative ways in which power could be organized across the world (Taylor 1993).

Returning to Wallerstein's institutional vortex, we can see that the state as nation-state has been the vortex drawing power from the other institutions. But what is the purpose of this power-hungry vortex? How should we interpret the political practices that constitute the state? With states re-privileged within a world-systems framework, we now consider other, more-conventional state theories.

STATE THEORY

In the massive literature on state theories, five major clusters of ideas about the state can be identified; for convenience, they are labeled instrumental, structural, managerial, derivational, and ideological. Each set of ideas is very different, and important debates have raged among them. This discussion takes each theoretical position in turn and shows it to be, at least in part, compatible with world-systems analysis. This approach is not a superficial eclecticism because, as we have seen in the de-privileging/re-privileging discussion, our treatment of the state is very distinctive and so may accommodate differences that other social theory cannot. This section demonstrates how each state theory has been used within world-systems analysis, evaluates this use, and relates it to several key debates in the field.

The most straightforward theory of the state is the *instrumentalist*. As social institutions, states are available for use by social groups in their political conflicts. At a general level both classes and nations/ethnic groups have continuously used the state apparatus to attain their political ends. In fact, it is because of this that the very meaning of politics in modern society has been captured by the state, as we have seen. Specifically, states are used to change the balance of power in disputes within its civil society and to project the power of the civil society winners beyond the states' boundaries. An obvious example is in trade policy where protectionism favors some groups within the state at the expense of others and is intended to directly affect foreign producers beyond the state. Our first conclusion, therefore, is that states in world-systems analysis are treated *instrumentally*. Wallerstein (1984 30–33) is explicit on this.

The instrumentalist theory of the state has come to be discredited to some degree as an outcome of the debate between Miliband (1969) and Poulantzas (1969). In contradiction to conventional political science interpretations of the state, Miliband argued for the Marxist case that the state was not neutral in Western society but was an instrument of the ruling capitalist class. He amassed much empirical evidence to show the close social links between the ruling class and the state managers. Poulantzas objected to this mode of inquiry for answering the question whether the state was capitalist. From his Marxist position the state in capitalist society is inherently capitalist, since you cannot logically separate the state from the society in which it exists. Poulantzas's key objection, therefore, was that Miliband's study implies that if empirical evidence is found for dominant noncapitalist influence on the state, then it is no longer a capitalist state even if it exists within a capitalist society. This is unacceptable for Poulantzas because in his structural theory of the state the capitalist nature of the state is not a matter of empirical verification: the state in capitalist society is necessarily capitalist.

Despite its instrumentalist approach to states, world-systems analysis agrees with Poulantzas on this. States and their interstate system are a *necessary* element of the world-system: the existence of multiple polities provides an essential maneuverability for capital. Chase-Dunn (1989) has developed this argument furthest and places the interstate system *within* his definition of capitalism. Hence, Wallerstein (1979) employs a structural theory of the state when he designates the states of the former "Second World" to be fundamentally capitalist. Despite their takeover by Communist parties, they continued to operate within the capitalist world-economy and were thus constrained in their behavior. As part of this capitalist society, they worked within the capitalist rules of the game as vehicles to promote economic development by spreading the law of value, or as Frank (1977) so memorably expressed it: "Capitalists of the world unite, long live transideological enterprise." But these states were poor managers of capital, which was a basic cause of their demise. Our second conclusion, therefore, is that states in world-systems analysis are viewed *structurally*.

This simultaneous adherence to both instrumentalist and structuralist positions on the states is a problem only if we misinterpret the basis of the Miliband-Poulantzas debate. Their differences are over interpretation of the empirical; their common acceptance of the "relative autonomy" of the state shows the similarity of their theoretical positions. Both allow the state autonomy within capitalism and avoid treating it merely as an epiphenomenon of the economic base. But if the state is not an epiphenomenon, then a structural theory must include states as instruments in social conflict. The world-systems position on relative autonomy is very distinctive and will be discussed in the next section.

A second important criticism of the instrumental position comes from the state-centric school's *managerial* theory. These critics argue that the state should always be treated as more than a mere instrument of outside forces. State managers are important actors in the modern world in their own right (Clark and Dear 1984). Block (1977) confronts this issue in his development of a world-systems state theory through a critique of Wallerstein's initial volume (1974) on the modern world-system. He points out that in

Wallerstein's history, states rising in power are explained behaviorally in terms of policies of their state elites, whereas when they decline, structural forces are usually employed to explain the "inevitable" demise. Block corrects this inconsistency by identifying the role of state managers as mediators between the demands of capital and the subordinate classes. They must balance their ultimate dependence on capital for resources against a need to maintain the legitimacy of their state. Thus, state managers will not automatically promote the demands of capital in individual policies, but over the medium term a successful state does require that the aggregate effect of policies should support capital accumulation. The different trajectories of states, therefore, are partly the result of the differential aggregate effects of state managers' behavior in coping with the structural location of their state in an ever-changing world-economy. Our third conclusion, then, which is richly illustrated in Wallerstein's histories (1974, 1980, 1989), is that states in world-systems analysis are more than instruments: their *managers* are themselves important actors in the processes of social change.

What exactly is required of state managers to be broadly supportive of capital? How are the demands of capital translated into policy if the state is relatively autonomous? These questions have been asked by radical critics of state theory who consider the whole idea of relative autonomy fundamentally flawed. Any autonomy conceded to the state will cut off its activities from the fundamental motor of social change found within capitalism itself. These critics, therefore, argue for a *derived* theory of the state based upon the nature of capitalism revealed by Marx (Holloway and Picciotto 1978). As already noted, Chase-Dunn locates the interstate system within his definition of capitalism, so that the derivationist critique is avoided in his formulation. Nevertheless Wallerstein (1984) does derive state policy from the demands of capital within the world-system. States set the rules for control of flows across their boundaries and for social relations within their boundaries. He relates this position to the two basic strategies for increasing profits of individual capitalists and therefore enhancing overall accumulation of capital: either raise commodity prices or lower labor costs. For the former, quasi-monopolies can be created behind tariff walls around one country or larger trading blocs. The importance of this application of state politics is indicated by the fact that, despite the exhortations of liberal economists, the world-economy has never operated as a free-trade system even in its most liberal phases. As to the second strategy, the state in its domestic politics sets the rules of the social relations through which work is organized and wages are decided. It should be no surprise that in most countries of the world, trade unions are coerced with state connivance. Hence, our fourth conclusion is that we can *derive* a strategic role for the state within the world-economy from demands for ceaseless capital accumulation.

Derivation theories of the state are highly susceptible to criticism for their "economism," the sterile "reading off" of noneconomic phenomena from the material base. The derivation above would be open to such criticism if that were the entire world-systems' interpretation of the state. As previously indicated, however, there is more purpose to the state than satisfying the needs of capital. Accumulation must be set alongside legitimation, which brings us to *ideological interpretations* of the state and links into arguments in the previous section concerning the nation-state.

Not all states coerce trade unions, because in one zone of the world-economy, the core, legitimation requirements are as important as accumulation prerogatives. By drawing power into their institutional vortex, states become directly involved in sustaining other social institutions. As a result, they must appear neutral in their relations to the components of their civil society in order to generate loyalty and identity among the population. As we have seen, they have been so successful in this mystification that nation-states seem to most people to be the natural units of politics.

Within the states, despite their neutral stance, imperatives of capital still rank at the top of the political agenda. This is the Gramscian axiom that the ideas of the ruling classes are the ruling ideas of society. Of course, it is not suggested that the noncapitalist sectors, including the state managers, are simply hoodwinked by the capitalists. Whereas all other groups pleading their case in the state arena can accurately have their interests designated as special, only the capitalists can claim to represent a general interest since all other groupings recognize that their ultimate reproduction necessarily depends upon capital's reproduction. Therefore, structuralist arguments about being in a capitalist society relate directly to ideological interpretations of the state.

The fact remains that states are generally viewed as "nation-states" and rarely, outside of state theory, as "capitalist states." Capital and its interests are never presented baldly in economic terms. For instance, despite the hundreds of right-wing political parties throughout the world that promote the interests of capital, not one calls itself the "Capitalist party." Quite simply, capital transcends the states and parties do not; they must translate the particular needs of capital within their state and sell it as policy for the state and its people. In this argument the state acts as an ideological sponge soaking up political conflict between capital and labor that can ultimately be resolved only at the scale of the world-economy. By capturing the politics, any conflict is converted into an issue to be "solved," i.e., evaded, within the state apparatus. In this way the state operates as a scale of ideology separating the local scale of people's experience of capital from the world scale of actual capital realization (Taylor 1981, 1982). Our fifth conclusion is that in world-systems analysis the state has a pivotal *ideological* role separating local experiences from global realities.

These five conclusions may at first seem surprising in the way they interweave what some see as incompatible positions on state theory, but adding a world-systems framework does help locate similarities and develop linkages that are difficult to see without it. There is no doubt that state theory informs world-systems analysis, and the above discussion suggests that benefits work both ways. In the final two sections this creative tension is "massaged" further by focusing on world-systems treatment of key contested areas of state theory: relative autonomy and the accumulation/legitimation relation.

STATES IN A WORLD-SYSTEM

The idea that states are autonomous lies at the heart of their privileged position in politics. Although it is increasingly acknowledged that the world-economy beyond the state impinges on economic sovereignty in particular, the image of every state ultimately controlling its own destiny remains pervasive. This is the basic premise behind the developmentalist models that have dominated thinking about global inequalities in the second half of the twentieth century (Taylor 1989). These models assert that, given the correct policies, all countries could successfully march to their "era of high mass consumption." The practical exposure of the intellectual poverty of such thinking caused by the widening gap between rich and poor has stimulated social science reconsiderations such as world-systems analysis.

From the perspective of world-systems analysis, the key mistake of developmentalism was to confuse the idea of autonomy with maneuverability. Social institutions are not autonomous, they are maneuverable, hence states can be used or managed in attempts to attain certain ends such as development. Whether such ends are achieved depends on much more than the maneuvering, as the discussion of structural theory of the state made clear. But such theories, and those of Poulantzas in particular, persist in considering states to be "relatively autonomous," a position that has left them open to attack. Reforming the structural theory in world-systems terms eliminates this problem.

Scase (1980) clearly stated the need for relative autonomy from a state-centric position. If the world consists of many states, each with its own capitalist economy, then why does this same mode of production produce such a wide variety of state forms? We can pose the situation most simply as a diagram:

States   —   —   —   —   —   —   —

Economies   —   —   —   —   —   —   —

In this world of separate countries each economy has to be related some way to its polity or state: the British economy and the British state, the Japanese economy and the Japanese state, and so on. If the economies are essentially the same, why are their respective states so different? The only answer that can be given is that states must have a large degree of autonomy from their respective economies. This answer is logically necessary but unsatisfactory, for it fundamentally lacks clarity and precision: how autonomous? The answer, however, is not the problem; the problem arises from the question.

This unsatisfactory theoretical result occurs because we assume that multiple states coexist with multiple economies. In world-systems analysis the situation is as follows:

States — — — — — — —

Economies _____

With one economy, the world-economy, the theoretical problem is very different. Each state does not relate to an economy but to a fragment of a larger economy. Given the uneven development of that world-economy, it is hardly surprising that the different fragments are associated with different state forms. Each economy-fragment is different from others, which results in different opportunities and constraints for state maneuverability over time that relate to the different state trajectories we observe in the world-system. In this situation it is unnecessary to postulate any relative autonomy of state from economy.

Removing relative autonomy does not have to produce an absolute-autonomy position of a world-economy that determines all, since the maneuverability of states has already been theorized. Remember, too, that the states themselves have defined the territorial boundaries of each economy-fragment. There is no "causal arrow" with the world-economy simply defining states; the states are constituted of the world-economy as the social institutions that act as a power vortex. As such, they are crucially important in the continual re-forming of the world-economy, while they themselves are forever changing in response to its dynamics.

Changes in the world economy do not come smoothly, because the system is cyclical in nature. State managers, both elected and unelected, must devise policies to cope with these ups and downs as they affect the material resources available to them. For instance, in terms of the long Kondratieff cycles, no government can position its state so that its economy-fragment is autonomous from global trends, but it can aspire to accentuate or ameliorate the general world economic climate in which it operates. This maneuvering is illustrated in the changing policies of governments both over time within one country and comparatively across countries responding to the same world economic situation.

Great Britain's relative decline in the twentieth century illustrates changes over time. Since 1918, British politics has had six distinctive politics, each with its own agenda (Taylor 1991b). Each case represented a "new politics" with agendas that addressed the current world-economy situation and related expectations within civil society. As these were broadly agreed upon by the parties competing for government, the agenda itself was not an election issue. Major parties revised their policies to fit into the parameters of each new politics and then educated the electorate accordingly, hence there were no "critical elections" in the sense of setting new agendas. For instance, Labour's 1945 victory did not mark the beginning of the period of social-democratic consensus since that agenda had already been agreed on by the Conservative-led, wartime coalition government. Similarly, the public-sector austerity politics associated with Mrs. Thatcher did not begin with her 1979 election victory but can be traced to the 1976 "IMF crisis" of the previous Labour government. Basically, when in government, both parties have moved to the left in world-economy Kondratieff upturns and to the right during downturns. For the purists of both sides, Conservative "traitors" are found in the upturn and Labour ones during the downturn. Each shift in agenda represented a political adjustment to fit the changing world economic situation, leaving party politics as a matter of degree within the new agenda.

The 1980s in Great Britain will always be remembered as the years of Thatcherism, but this British political response to the downturn of the world-economy was by no means unique. Most people identify two main domestic-policy packages as the essence of Thatcherism: the severe cutback on public expenditure and the strong legislative attack on trade unions. Comparing government policies in the 1980s, however, presents good cases for arguing that the country whose policies have most curtailed public expenditure is New Zealand and the government that has been most anti-union is in Spain. This comparison shows that the new politics was not a right-left party issue, because these are the policies of the New Zealand Labour party and the Spanish Socialist party. Thatcherism is not a right-wing prescription for making Britain great again, as its rhetoric tries to persuade us; it is the particular British form of a new politics, an agenda of its age that can be found in all states of the core of the world-economy (Taylor 1992).

Although state managers, in responding to the ups and downs of the world-economy, maneuver their states in similar ways, this does not mean that states are powerless institutions tossing in an economic sea. The policies pursued by states are integral to the periodic restructuring of the world-economy. The various new politics complement and reinforce the many "new economics" that are also regularly constructed. For instance, economic orthodoxy succumbed to a "Keynesian revolution" at the same time that a political "social-democratic consensus" was constructing welfare states. The demise of both the economic and political faces of the "postwar settlement" in the 1980s—monetarism and "rolling back the state"—is hardly a coincidence. From a world-systems viewpoint, without the states the restructuring would not be possible.

Finally, it seems appropriate to conclude by referring to one set of interesting literature on the state thus far ignored. Several major political writers (e.g., Deutch 1981; Herz 1976) claim to have identified a "demise" of the states themselves. By this they mean that some of the key functions of the state can no longer be adequately carried out at the geographical scale of the state. They argue that various processes of "globalization" are undermining the validity of the state.

Superficially, the demise of states in the wake of globalization seems similar to our initial argument for de-privileging the state. This is not at all the case and is obvious once the structural theory behind our treatment of the state is remembered. As states are integral to the world-system, a true demise of the states would signal the end of the capitalist world-economy itself. Rather, the functions that states carry out have always changed over time, with new functions being added and old ones discarded. This is true of the recent past as in other periods and does not represent the imminent demise of this key social institution.

But the "demise of the state" literature cannot be dismissed so easily. States are failing to deliver not just any functions but some very crucial ones that go to the heart of "stateness." With the coming of nuclear weapons some argue that states can no longer guarantee their citizens security; Herz (1976) claims they have become as obsolete as the early-modern walled city. In addition, they are failing to combat another basic security issue relating to global ecology (Brown 1990). And they are no longer the appropriate locus for organizing capital accumulation. This latter economic globalization argument is developed here.

Our earlier discussion of state theory noted the dual constraints on the state of capital's accumulation needs and its own legitimation needs vis à vis its citizens. But this accumulation-legitimation contradiction has not always been a feature of states in the modern world-system. As argued above, for about half its existence (in the era of mercantilism) the system operated through territorial states as bases for accumulation but with little or no modern concern for legitimation. All this changed with the invention of nation-states. My speculation is that the era of states based on this contradiction is coming to a close. We will return to a new, simpler form of state based on just one of the duo, this time legitimation, as displayed diagrammatically as:

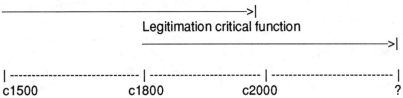

Accumulation critical function

Legitimation critical function

c1500   c1800   c2000   ?

The prediction is, therefore, that the ideological dimension in state theory will become increasingly important for our understanding of states in the world-economy.

The contemporary rise of new nationalisms can be interpreted as reinforcing this conclusion. What this movement represents is a second round of the nationalist attack on multinational states that began after World War I. After 1919, some multinational states were dismantled (Austria-Hungary, the Ottoman Empire), others partially dismantled (United Kingdom, Czarist Russia), and some were created (Yugoslavia, Czechoslovakia). All multinational states are now under threat from "national separatists" again, and more states are becoming multinational (France, Spain). It seems that no state is safe from the threat of national separatists. This is not, however, a general challenge to the state as an institution; rather, the agenda seeks to eliminate particular states that are no longer deemed to meet the nation-state ideal. This process will probably culminate with a substantial increase in the number of states in the interstate system. Two important corollaries of this are: First, state and nation will be made more congruent, thus further facilitating the legitimation of the state; and second, states will be smaller, making them even more vulnerable to economic globalizing processes and less suitable as accumulation bases. The most interesting current example of this disentangling of geographical scales is in Western Europe, where the EC is being converted simultaneously into a single European economic space for accumulation and a "Europe of regions" for legitimation. This geographical-scale resolution to the accumulation-legitimation contradiction—nation-states in economic blocs—is likely to be repeated across the globe.

If we are moving into a new era of the state in the world-economy, then obviously the creations of the last era become problematic. This must be true of the power vortex, the nation-state. As economic sovereignty is reduced, can the state retain its "natural" political attraction? It seems to me that households and classes have a new opportunity to be de-nationalized and build alternative politics. States, however purely national they may become, will be much less able to mask the reality of the world-economy that determines their citizens' life-chances. Hence, it should come as no surprise that the "demise" of states is paralleled by the rise of new, nonstate social movements—antinuclear peace, feminist, green—that define fundamentally new politics for this final political era of the modern world-system (Walker 1988). And so our argument has come full circle. The state *is* being de-privileged, not theoretically as described in the first section, but much more fundamentally through these political practices.

7

Capitalist Development
and the Nation-State
K. P. Moseley[1]

A concern with the "wealth of nations," central to classical political economy, has been dramatically extended to new sets of countries, issues, and interpretive frameworks over the past forty-five years. The resulting theories are variously connected to the other great movements of the period: conflict between the socialist and capitalist blocs, the creation and disaggregation of the Third World, and the ongoing transnationalization of production and exchange. It is no doubt a measure of the latter trend that, apart from disputes over different political options and development "paths," the analytic status of the nation-state—conventionally assumed to be the principal subject and object of the development process—has itself been brought into question. Classes and capital, markets and modes, operative on various "internal" and "external" planes, are among the alternative sources of determination that have been put forward. Even in the most nominalist perspective, however, nations remain an unavoidable empirical concern and a major terrain for the various forces at work.

This paper will look again at these issues, surveying the debates concerning the initial rise of capitalism in Europe, on the one hand, and the more halting development process in the Third World, on the other. This section, confined to issues that cut across historical periods, introduces three major positions on the nation-development issue: world-system, Marxist-structuralist, and state-centered views. Later, in the contemporary context, these categories will be partly reorganized around contrasting "nationalist" and "globalist" camps. Our interest will be confined to critical theories, more or less Marxist in inspiration, that view capitalism in historical and relativist terms. And it is their debates with each other, rather than with liberal/capitalist views, that will be the focus here.

At least in sociology, the leading development theory over the past twenty years has been the world-system approach. Inspired by Andre Gunder Frank, elaborated by Immanuel Wallerstein, with the critical support of such diverse scholars as Samir Amin and Christopher Chase-Dunn, it has inspired a major reappraisal of world history over the past five-hundred years. Despite increasing internal diversity, it retains traces of its initial preoccupation: to attack and destroy the then-hegemonic liberal-functionalist schools (see Frank 1967; Foster-Carter 1974; Wallerstein 1979; Peet 1991). What we will call "underdevelopment theory," which posited a zero-sum relationship between development in the advanced and less-developed countries (LDCs), was an extreme (and now disputed) version of this trend. Two more-or-less methodological innovations, however, have been widely accepted. Moving from a focus on groups and processes within countries, it became de rigueur to take the global context more systematically into account. And, as opposed to the typologies and "stages" favored by earlier theorists, there was a shift to a resolutely historical perspective. Together with a Marxian preoccupation with economic phenomena, the new paradigm entailed a substantive focus on the capitalist world economy, while the temporal frame for modern developments was pushed back to the fifteenth or sixteenth century. Uneven development, and thus international inequality—in state strength, productive base, and surplus appropriation—would be expected features of the system as a whole. Beyond these general formulations, extensive differences remain, one of the most fundamental being the relative weight assigned to classes, markets, or the states. In the "strong" version of the world-system perspective, the world market and the global accumulation process play a clearly determinant role. For Frank and Wallerstein, production for that market is the essential feature of capitalism (Frank 1969; Wallerstein 1979, 15–16). Beyond a certain threshold of commercial involvement, all units, regardless of their internal structuring, are capitalist. Indeed,

> the development of the capitalist world-economy has involved the creation of all the major institutions of the modern world: classes, ethnic/national groups, households—and the "states." All of these structures postdate, not antedate capitalism; all are consequence, not cause (Wallerstein 1984, 29).

A key distinction in Wallerstein's model is between world empires, in which economic processes are politically constrained, and world economies, predicated on a plurality of states. Given the uneven advance of commodification and proletarianization, the states fall into a three-tiered hierarchy: the periphery, semiperiphery, and core. Political fragmentation and structural heterogeneity are both functional for the system itself, the former assuring the free play of capitalist interests, the latter, new zones of expansion and low-cost labor and supplies. These arrangements, strategically reinforced by differences in state power, ensure a flow of surplus from the periphery (where commodities and labor are less rewarded) to the core (1984, 13 ff.).

States may well attempt to improve their global standing, but this is conditioned by their productive capacity relative to world market demand. State strength itself, Wallerstein argued, should be primarily explained

> in terms of the structural role a country plays in the world-economy. . . . To be sure, the initial eligibility for a particular role is often decided by an accidental edge a particular country has . . . located in part in past history, in part in current geography. But once this relatively minor accident is given, it is the operations of the world-market forces which accentuate the differences, institutionalize them, and make them impossible to surmount over the short run (1979, 21).

At the same time, states are used by dominant classes against both labor within and competitors without. Thus, although classes objectively emerge at the world-system level, they are generally effective only at the level of the states. The strength of the state, in turn, is closely related to that of its own particular segment of the bourgeoisie (1980, 747).

All this, of course, is a far cry from traditional Marxism, a rupture decried by those who would continue to give a privileged place to class structure and conflict in the analysis of change. Marxist structuralists, in particular, have been interested less in national development than in "modes of production," considered on a fairly abstract plane. Variation in social relations of production and forms of appropriation of surplus are the major focus here. Relative to the world-system approach, two major propositions have been put forward. The first, following from a traditional definition of capitalism in terms of the appropriation of surplus value from wage labor, is simply that precapitalist (or at least noncapitalist) modes persist, even in the era of the world market and imperialism. Second, trade, by itself, "is not at the *origin* of a dynamic of development because trade cannot determine the transformation of class relations of production" (Brenner 1977, 38); rather, it is the "historically specific class structures of production and surplus extraction, themselves the product of determinations beyond the market," that produce here, development, and there, stagnation or decline (Brenner 1977, 91). Capitalist development (itself divided into distinct historical phases) is thus conditioned by the varying incorporation/resistance/dissolution of precapitalist modes (see, e.g., Rey 1973; Foster-Carter 1978; Taylor 1979; Wolf 1982; Peet 1991).

Although structuralists attribute at least a relative autonomy to the state, they have often neglected it empirically—distracted, no doubt, by the antinationalist bent of their own development-critique. This brings us to a third perspective on the nation-development theme, expressed more by a congeries of scholars than a school but sharing a concern for the holistic analysis of the Marxian tradition, with stress on the importance of the political instance and the state. Among the structuralists, Perry Anderson (1974a) stands out as one of the few who has turned his attention to not only the state but to international politics; his important historical work will be discussed later in this paper. The Marxist-Leninist tradition, with its emphasis on imperialism and national struggles, is another source of state-centered work. This provides a major thread in Samir Amin's writing (1980), which also straddles the world-system and structuralist schools; it has been further elaborated by Abdel-Malek (1979, 1981), who argues for the "primacy of the political," above all, the nation-state, the "fundamental matrix" of social structuration and change.

Another effort to "bring the state back in" (Evans et al. 1985) has occurred in American sociology, aimed not only against the class-centered analysis of Marxism but the "economic reductionism" of the world-system school (Skoçpol 1979, 22). States, Skoçpol argues, are

> organizations geared to maintain control of home territories and populations and to undertake . . . military competition with other states in the international system. The international states system as a transnational structure of military competition was not originally created by capitalism. Throughout modern world history, it represents an analytically autonomous level of transnational reality *interdependent* . . . with world capitalism, but not reducible to it.

It follows that

> as long as nation-states and their competition remain important realities, it is best (at least for analyzing phenomena that centrally involve states) to employ the state/society as the basic unit of analysis (1979, 22).

This analytic autonomy extends to the relationship with classes, with which the state may actually compete for control over resources, policies, and personnel. Anderson, while giving greater weight to structural determinants, would agree: states "seal the basic shifts in the relations of production, so long as classes subsist" (1974, 11). All the authors in this category, finally, agree on the importance of geopolitics—patterns of interstate relations that, more or less independently of the world economy, act back on the power, behavior, and structuring of the states themselves.

Each of these different schools of thought seems unduly marked by its polemics with previously dominant points of view. Certainly, we should not be forced to choose between the "*true* autonomy" of the states, as opposed to the "*absolute* causal primacy" of socioeconomic factors as Skoçpol (1985, 6, 347; my emphasis) has proposed. The structuralists, on the other hand, have tended to neglect the effects of larger state structures and/or networks of exchange on the spheres of production and class. As for world-system theory, there is a double irony: that it should be criticized for being too "nationalist," and (as that complaint reflects), that its explicit theorizing and its substantive content should often be so much at odds. The intended thrust is to transcend national societies as units of analysis; in fact, there are few general theories that put nations so much in the fore. What is achieved, rather, is the transformation of our understanding of nations through placing them in a world-historical perspective in which *inter*national and *trans*national processes take pride of place.

It seems fruitful, then, to at least re-problematize the mutual relations between world economy, classes, state system, and states. Indeed, this is a central thrust of a new generation of critical theorists, emerging more or less alongside or in dialogue with world-system views. These include interpreters of the "new international division of labor" (NIDL) and the "new comparative political economy" school (see Corbridge 1986; Evans and Stephens 1988a,b; So 1990; cf. Chase-Dunn 1989). Generally, there is renewed concern with the interface of economics and politics, with cross-national variations, and with the ways in which "the world political economy both shapes and is shaped by the historical trajectories of development within individual nation-states (Evans and Stephens 1988b, 725). In a similar spirit, we will look again at some of the connections, historical and contemporary, of capitalist development and the nation-states.

THE RISE OF CAPITALISM

From the sixteenth to the eighteenth centuries, the modern world took form—out of a crucible of geopolitical rivalry, worldwide commerce, and the crystallization of the national states. Although the rise of capitalism has been a subject of perennial discussion, the possible impact of the states has been long ignored. The classic antinomy, elaborated in the course of the Dobb-Sweezy debates a generation ago, was that of the relative weight of trade versus class relation, a polarity resurrected in the more recent divergence between Brenner and Wallerstein. For Wallerstein (1974, 1990), the modern world system is predicated on an international division of labor, including variant forms of production and labor control. These different class structures, he argues, were dictated by market conditions, assured "the kind of flow of surplus which enabled the capitalist system to come into being" (1974, 87), and were "necessarily redefined" in capitalist terms (1974, 92).

For many scholars, particularly those of a more classical Marxist persuasion, the early modern world looks very different. For Banaji, for instance, the capitalism of the sixteenth and seventeenth centuries was, if anything, financial and commercial in character; a world market "based on the capitalist *mode of production*" was still three centuries away (1980, 510). In an early paper aimed against the "neo-Smithian" bent of the Frank/Wallerstein school, Brenner (1977; also Aston and Philpin 1985) took an even stronger line. Differences in development, in his treatment, seem entirely rooted in class relations. Only with the emergence of free wage-labor, as in England, could trade have a dynamic effect, improvements in productivity occur, or capitalist rationality prevail. Neither absolute forms of exploitation, as in Poland, peasant smallholding, as in France, nor surplus transfers, in whatever direction, could have such effects.

Brenner's own formulation, centered on the inner teleology of autarchic productive modes, must be treated with reserve. Brenner may have underestimated the impact of grain exports, for instance (Denemark and Thomas 1988), as well as the pressures that might be brought to bear by other states. This stands in sharp contrast not only to Wallerstein's emphasis on international politics, but to Perry Anderson's brilliant reanalysis of the early modern period, *Lineages of the Absolutist State* (1974a). Both authors emphasize the revival and development of the centralized state, the political fragmentation that helped liberate commercial/capitalist growth, and the interstate competition that provided additional stimulus and often, along with fiscal considerations, political support as well.

What were the origins of the European state system, however, and to what extent did it play an independent role as far as capitalism was concerned? For Wallerstein, the interstate system, "evolved as the political superstructure of the capitalist world-economy" (1984, 50):

> The nation-state itself was formed long ago as a by-product and servant of capital, whose existence and accumulation had already been "international" from its inception, before the nation-state was born (1978, 251).

While noting the medieval *origins* of the European states, Wallerstein emphasizes the *consolidation* of the state system only in the late sixteenth century, by which time capitalist interests were powerful enough to defeat such imperial attempts as mounted by the Hapsburgs (1974, 31–32, 36, 184 ff.; 1984, 50). The weight of the evidence, however, seems to favor the relative anteriority of the state system, the roots of which have been traced back as far as the eleventh century (cf. Mann 1986, Chaps. 12–13; Zolberg 1981, 260–261, 277). The national and other "particularizing tendencies," moreover, that Phillips and Wallerstein attribute to capitalist development (1980, 7), can be linked to feudalism just as well (Anderson 1974a, 43 ff., 411; also see Robinson 1983, 9, 19). Finally, not only Christianity but even the institutional heritage of antiquity may have helped create the cultural commonalities permitting a single state system to emerge (Anderson 1974a, 428).

Wallerstein (1990, 35 ff.) has recently rejected such "civilizational" interpretations in favor of the conjunctural one of sheer feudal collapse. As his own treatment suggests, however, and as others have argued, the political dispersion and inner fragmentation of feudalism seem to have had a positive impact on capitalist growth, something that was perhaps only hastened by the fourteenth-century decline. The weakness of the state gave an unusually large leeway to private property and trade (Wallerstein 1990, 46, 54–56; Mann 1986, 399, 504; Baechler 1976), the towns and the merchant class held exceptional economic leverage (cf. Anderson 1974a, 22, 422–424; Fine 1978, 89–91), and the contractual nature of feudal obligations facilitated the monetarization of both labor and property arrangements, and a fairly painless "articulation" with capitalism. In this very particular urban/rural context, commercial expansion could have an extraordinarily dynamic effect (Amin 1976, 31–36; 1977, 51–53; Rey 1973, 37 ff.; cf. Anderson 1974a, 420, 450–455; Mann 1986, 409–412; Brenner 1977, 76–79).

Capitalist growth was further "overdetermined," one might say, by the incessant and ever more costly competition between the states. Wallerstein is absolutely correct in insisting on the "failure of empire" as a condition of continuing development, a point made long ago by Weber (cited in Chase-Dunn 1989, 135–136) on which there is considerable consensus. The raison d'être of state activities, however, remains ambiguous. For Wallerstein, of course, the interstate system is an "expression" of capitalist development (1990, 26), its boundaries "more or less synonymous" (1980, 371) with those of the world economy, and its operations dominated by "capitalists" even before the latter could take political control at the level of the states.

For Anderson, on the other hand, the state system is distinctly political and military in character, completed with the spread of absolutist structures to Eastern Europe and lacking any unified economic counterpart in the early modern era. If Holland and England were "capitalist" by the eighteenth century, the absolutist state otherwise functioned as "a redeployed . . . apparatus of feudal domination," protecting a "threatened nobility" against the peasantry and urban bourgeoisie (1974a, 18, 22–23). In the East, the state developed in response to foreign pressures, even "in advance of the relations of production on which it was founded" (1974a, 208–209). The "second serfdom" in the East, in other words—attributed by Brenner to endogenous class forces, by Wallerstein to the response to world-market demand—is seen by Anderson as at least partly a creation "from above," at the initiative of the state.

Chase-Dunn (1989, 141 ff.), reviewing these debates, has tried to refute any notion of the "independence" of the state system vis à vis capitalist accumulation and exchange. It remains difficult, however, to give up this notion, at least in relative and analytic terms. One problem is the non-coincidence of the boundaries between the commercial and political systems: there is general agreement, for instance, that the Ottoman state was not part of the European world economy, although it was central to the European balance of power (cf. Zolberg 1981, 263–264). A related issue is the salience of the Renaissance states' military dimension: "conquest, not commerce," Anderson (1974a, 197) argues, was their primary goal. He may well underestimate the commercial factor, as Chase-Dunn (1989, 139–40, 144) suggests. On the other hand, there is considerable evidence for the formative impact of warfare on the very process of capitalist growth. War, as Tilly argues (1975, 21 ff., 72–76; 1985), required that states develop not only their coercive and bureaucratic capacities, but their fiscal and economic base. This helps explain both the "predatory mercantilism" (Anderson 1974a, 37) of the states and their accommodating, even protective attitude toward capitalist activities and interest groups (Mann 1986, 426 ff.; Anderson 1974a, 47, 428–429). More directly, the early "arms race" set off a cumulative interplay of commercialized procurement, capitalist production, and technical innovation, superbly documented by McNeill (1983, Chap. 3).

Finally, there is the issue of the determinants, indicators, and effects of relative "state strength." Wallerstein argues that different roles in the international division of labor (or different degrees of "productive efficiency," the favored formulation in the second volume of his work) "led to different class structures which led to different politics" (1974, 157) and to differences in power. Critics have decried this "reduction" of state strength to market position (Skoçpol 1979; Zolberg 1981; cf. Chase-Dunn 1989, 146 ff.), pointing to various anomalies (e.g., powerful noncore states, such as Sweden). In practice, Wallerstein is sensitive to the reciprocal links between power and economic status; this is particularly clear in the semiperiphery (Wallerstein 1974, 356; 1980, 113–114, 197), where state policies may set the course toward development or decline. As Brenner notes (1977, 64), this opens the way to a major shift in argument. There is a tendency, however, to restrict this sort of analysis to less "efficient" countries, where state autonomy from dominant classes might be positive for economic growth; conversely, as Garst (1985) suggests, state activism may be less necessary or functional in the core. This sort of dichotomy seems unsatisfactory. Wallerstein emphasizes, for instance, as late as the nineteenth century, the importance of "politico-military victories" and defensive strength in the relative industrial development of different European powers (1989, 112–113, 125; also McNeill 1983, 210–213; cf. Chase-Dunn 1989, 159–162). Conversely, the disadvantages of inadequate state autonomy and activism are revealed particularly clearly in periods of core decline (Evans 1985, 210 ff.; Chase-Dunn 1989, 147–148), first evidenced in classic form by the Dutch.

We might now rethink some of the questions that Wallerstein so aptly posed concerning the early modern period. "Why," he asks, "should capitalism, a phenomenon that knew no frontiers, have been sustained by the development of strong states?" (1974, 67). His answer, which is essentially that it was functional for capital, might now be reversed; capitalism flourished—at least initially—because it served the purposes of the states in a highly competitive setting that was still predominantly precapitalist in character. It was thus, as Kiernan put it, "less the creator than the creation of the modern state" (cited in Robinson 1983, 29), despite its eventual displacement of the traditional ruling classes it had been designed to serve. Without them, however, a cumulative process of "development," a process eventually canonized as world-historical ideology and goal, could not have been conceived.

Recognition of the autonomy and strength of the state, in its own right, allows different answers to two other questions as well. Why, Wallerstein asks, did efforts at empire fail? He argues that it was not in the interests of nationally based capitalist groups. Rather, it is more plausible that the principles of territorial sovereignty and balance of power, by-products of feudalism more than of the Hapsburg defeat, were already firmly installed, embodied in a plurality of strong state machineries that, collectively, could simply not be subdued by force of arms.

Why, finally, were some areas "incorporated" to the world economy, and others not, or only much later on? Rather than the volume and nature of foreign trade, as Wallerstein suggests, the military and administrative capacities of states seem especially critical. Thus, it was not because they were "external" to the world economy that Russia, for instance, or the Ottomans, retained strong states, but the reverse; similarly, East Asia was external not because of its luxury trade, but because, unlike the New World, it was distant and difficult to conquer (cf. Wallerstein 1974, 313, 325 ff.; 1980, 273–274).

It remains that Wallerstein's overall conception of the capitalist world economy, which highlights both unitary and fragmentary trends, the "antinomy" of economics and polity (Wallerstein 1979, 272–273), and the importance of commerce as a stimulus of change, provides an indispensable framework of analysis. The transition, however, was long and uneven, the system never complete, and its effectiveness remained structurally and spatially variable (cf. Worseley 1980, 302 ff.). At the same time, the state system spread steadily outside Europe, spurred on by core imperialism and, in the long run, by colonial rule. As the strategic importance of "development" became clear, new cohorts of semiperipheral states entered into the drive for economic growth, with top-down policy initiatives and military pressures, again, playing important roles. Even in the most revolutionary cases, moreover, and despite the universalistic thrust of European culture and capitalism, the result was to reinforce the nationality principle and state power. As Robinson notes (1983, 9), capitalism "never achieved the coherence of structure and organization which had been [its] promise," and ethnonational particularisms pervade the countries, the working classes, and the bourgeoisie. These competing forces, crisscrossed by other structural forms and cultural themes, continue to have their trajectories outside the West.

DEVELOPMENT AND
UNDERDEVELOPMENT OUTSIDE THE WEST

For the European consciousness, the "backwardness" of the non-Western world was generally taken to be an "initial condition" that would, in principle, be overcome. The distinctively *exogenous* character of capitalism outside the West, however, was recognized, as was—in critical writing, at least—the destruction and exploitation that "development" might entail. A more radical possibility, suggested in the work of Lenin and Trotsky, was that the capitalist phase might simply be bypassed.

Such notions were reinforced by the October Revolution, which took on the "bourgeois tasks" of national development with unprecedented zeal. Outside the West, socialism began to be propagated along national as well as class-based lines, aided by the increasing ideological allure of "development" and "catching up." By the 1950s, East and West were running neck and neck to promote their respective brands of development in the emergent/renascent South, which itself acquired a certain unity in the spirit of Bandung.

Development theory has flourished since World War II, but, as Sunkel (1979, 19) notes, the boom has been "in stark contrast to the crisis of the development process itself." The disappointments of successive "development decades" have been compounded by worldwide contraction and indebtedness, while the three great blocs have fallen into disarray. These trends are linked with, and partly defy, the increasing objective unity of the world economy, which has entered an authentically "transnational" phase (Sunkel and Fuenzalida 1979). They have also contributed to a pronounced theoretical malaise, one no longer confined to the liberal/modernization schools. The crisis "in Marxism as an explanatory model, as well as . . . in socialism as a . . . movement," was noted by radical critics (Amin et al. 1982, 238) almost a decade ago. This crisis rests less on capitalist success than on the limitations displayed by state-led alternatives as well, meanwhile, the condition of most of the world's poor remains untransformed.

Whether "national development" is even desirable—in the sense of being indefinitely feasible, or as an emancipatory goal—is an issue that is beginning to be voiced. Generally, however, debate continues to center on *achieving* development and on the relative efficacy of states and markets in this regard. This antinomy, which had become explicit at least by the time of Adam Smith, was magnified by the ideological splits that developed after 1917. Thus, in addition to the broad analytic groupings identified earlier, treatments of contemporary development are strongly divided on prescriptive grounds. "Nationalists" and "globalists" make up two major camps here, each containing various socialist/Marxist strands (cf. Edwards 1985; Harris 1986, 18–25). World-system theory is also divided.

Its dependency and underdevelopment wings, along with Latin American structuralism and neo-Marxist theories of imperialism, fall into the nationalist camp, while the Wallersteinian school proper takes a more globalist stance.

The structuralist school of economics has various historical links to Latin America, particularly the theory and practice of import substitution industrialization (ISI) as it developed in the wake of the Depression. This problematic was extended by dependency theorists (e.g., Furtado 1964), who pointed to structural problems such as class polarization and backward agrarian sectors that could constrain the pace of change. Structuralists have also been concerned, however, with national variations, the impact of politics and policies, and strategies of reform (e.g., Cardoso and Faletto 1979; Szentes 1976; Sunkel and Fuenzalida 1979).

The state is equally central to the Marxist analysis of imperialism, focused on phases in the global expansion of capitalism and on international inequalities in political and economic power. The Leninist camp, while emphasizing the revolutionary potential of the East, pointed to the varying forms that "progressive" change might take, ranging from socialist (based on some combination of "popular" forces) to capitalist (under the aegis of a "national" as opposed to "comprador" bourgeoisie) (see, e.g., Amin 1976, 1990; Willoughby 1986; McEwan and Tabb 1989).

The radical dependency or "underdevelopment" school, drawing from Marxist economists such as Baran and Emmanuel, takes an even dimmer view of most Third World states and bourgeoisie (So 1990, 91 ff.). This line of thought, represented particularly by Frank and Amin, constitutes a radical break with traditional Marxism, which never imagined that capitalism, despite its attendant horrors, could act as an impediment to economic change. Although Amin dates this blockage only to the late 1800s, Frank (1978b, 171), like Wallerstein, has traced such constraints to the inception of the capitalist world economy five centuries ago. "Unequal exchange," the transfer of "surplus" from low-wage to high-wage countries in the course of international trade (Emmanuel 1972), is postulated as a key mechanism in this respect.[2] Despite changes in form, less-developed economies will remain confined to less-profitable activities within the international division of labor, and an autonomous dynamic of growth is ruled out. A solution would be significant disengagement from the world system and a reorganization of the economy along autocentric and more or less socialist lines (see Amin 1990).

World-system and dependency theories, given their common roots and shared framework of economic analysis, are often treated as variants of a single perspective (but cf. So 1990). There are critical differences, however, concerning national development and political strategies, particularly in prospective terms. Most central here is not only Wallerstein's concept of the semiperiphery, which remains a zone of considerable mobility, but his even-handed skepticism concerning the possibilities for radical change for *any* country within the present world system (1979, 49 ff.). Thus, neither "imperialism" nor "underdevelopment" figure significantly in his discourse, not because he doubts their significance but, on the contrary, because he doubts they can be eliminated by national-level revolution or reform.

It is this pessimism, expressed even more unequivocally by Marxists of the more internationalist/Trotskyist sort (e.g., Harris 1983, 1986; Chaliand 1978), that distinguishes the "globalist" perspective as defined here. This does not entail neglect of the state, whose developmental role is actually emphasized—both historically (see, e.g., Wallerstein 1983; Harris 1983) and with respect to the contemporary semiperiphery (Wallerstein 1985, 35; Arrighi and Drangel 1986, 27–28; also Chase-Dunn 1989, 210 ff.).[3] Cases of mobility, however, do not necessarily imply any rupture with capitalism. Aggressive state capitalism ("seizing the chance") or even "development by invitation," in collaboration with foreign capital, provide alternative routes to growth (Wallerstein 1979). Even radical nationalist and socialist movements, with their shared aspiration to de-linking, tend to reconnect to the larger system after taking state power (Wallerstein 1991).

Harris reaches similar conclusions but on rather different grounds. The "real world" (1983, 14), as with Wallerstein, is the global economy, but it reflects an integration that has approached completion only since World War II. The states, meanwhile, pursue disruptive, coercive logics of their own. *National* development, in fact—launched by core rivalries and now forced on LDCs—is not an outcome of markets but, "invariably," of the competition of states. Such development, while not progressive in political terms, expresses an authentic expansion of capital, possible in principle wherever conditions are ripe. World-system theorists are more dour. National development is "pernicious," since erstwhile radical movements are co-opted to "catching up"; (Wallerstein 1988, 2022); it is "illusory," since it "will never be achieved, even in a partial way, by most countries" (1991, 97). In any case, the core-periphery hierarchy is reproduced, in fact intensified, with gains by one country matched by losses elsewhere (Arrighi and Drangel 1986; Chase-Dunn 1989, Chaps. 10, 11).

A first round of debate on these points occurred in the 1970s, when the joint world-system/underdevelopment approach was targeted by critics from more "classical" Marxist schools (e.g., Bernstein 1979; Phillips 1977). Underdevelopment theory, particularly, was reproached for its "stagnationist" thrust, the notion that capitalism is necessarily thwarted outside the core. Warren (1973, 1980) drew attention to the growth of industry, for instance, while various forms of "dependent development," with the state playing important collaborative and regulatory roles, were signaled by Cardoso and Faletto (1979; also, Evans 1979). The world-system perspective, in the meantime, was reproached for its functionalist bent, a tendency to interpret virtually all phenomena as reinforcing capital in the end. Marxist structuralists pointed, rather, to the variable resistance to capital manifested by feudal and other precapitalist modes (Laclau 1977; Rey 1971, 1973; Lacoste 1976, 261 ff.; Amin 1976, Chap. 2). The "historical structuralists" (e.g., Cardoso) and Leninists, on the other hand, emphasized the progressive possibilities of certain class alliances, policies, and states.

In the wake of the "Third World euphoria" (Chaliand 1978, xv) of the 1960s, however, the split between anti-imperialists and antinationalists reemerged. At one pole, Abdel-Malek (1981, 13), for instance, advocated the "nationalitarian project," centered on a revival of state power and a "reconquest of identity" from the West. At the other were orthodox Marxists who rejected the "entire framework of 'dependency theory'" as un-Marxist, nationalist, and bourgeois (Banaji 1980, 518; also, Bernstein 1979; Gulap 1981).

The new regimes, moreover—even where communism was in power —were found to conceal new structures of accumulation and class control (Chaliand 1978; Harris 1986, 170 ff.). World-system theorists, too, began to see the socialist states as doing little more than pursuing mercantilist objectives—the "everyday bourgeois capitalist theory and practice of 'national development'" (Frank, in Amin et al. 1982, 149)—by other means.

The prospects for new "national capitals" in the LDCs, on the other hand, seemed to have improved. By the 1980s, a "new international division of labor" (NIDL) was observed, reflecting deindustrialization in the core and the rise of another generation of "newly industrializing countries" (NICs), with East Asian exporters in the lead. These trends encouraged a revival of both neoclassical economics and neoclassical Marxism, and a correlative decline of Keynesian, structuralist, and underdevelopment views. Few agree, however, on what has been achieved. Harris (1986), along with a number of Marxist geographers (cf. Corbridge 1986), sees the rise of a "global manufacturing system" constraining core and NICs alike —and featuring significant new centers of production and accumulation outside the West.

World-system theory, on the other hand, seems determined to minimize the changes underway. The pioneering work in this vein (Frobel et al. 1980), argued that the NIDL was *not* "the result of positive decisions taken by . . . governments or companies," but an "innovation of capital itself," in response to the emergence of world markets for labor and production sites (1980, 12, 46). The industrial relocation involved, mainly to low-wage enclaves and under the aegis of foreign firms, might damage the core economies but yields few compensating benefits for local hosts. Wallerstein, similarly, insists that these are relatively uncompetitive activities (1991, 102), and, like Frank (1980; cf. Corbridge 1986, 177 ff.), Arrighi and Drangel (1986, 56), and Amin (1990), sees little in (semi)peripheral industrialization that could threaten the hierarchy of the world economy overall.

In fact, however, there is immense variation in the scope and organization of Third World industrialization, in contrast to which Frobel's version of the NIDL seems something of a caricature (see e.g., Gereffi and Wyman 1990; Deyo 1987). Tariff barriers, import substitution, capital-intensive production, local ownership, and relatively high-wage "Fordist" regimes, inter alia, remain important, often in combination or alternation with more open/dependent strategies (see Gereffi 1989, 514 ff; Senghaas 1988). As opposed to any overweening logic of capital, Lipietz (1987, 99) argues, the NIDL actually has a "random" character, reflecting the relative autonomy of national economies, the mediating role of local social structures, and "the myriad strategies" of companies and states.

Although free-market partisans attempted to claim the East Asian success as their own, the NICs have actually stimulated a new wave of interest in the "developmental state" (cf. White 1984; Evans 1989). Following the Japanese prototype, development is associated with "entrepreneurial state intervention" and an "active state industrial policy" (Evans and Stephens 1988, 750, 755); South Korea and Taiwan provide model cases of such "bureaucratic authoritarian industrializing regimes" (BAIRs), fusing "state and economic power in pursuit of comparative advantage in world markets" (Cumings 1987, 71, 75). State intervention is now seen to be central not only to various phases of ISI but to liberalization and export promotion as well (cf. Haggard and Cheng 1987, 102; Haggard and Moon 1983; Gereffi 1990, 17–22). Successful collaboration with foreign capital, as suggested earlier by the Latin American case, has also been connected with state strength (see So 1990, 144 ff.; Deyo 1987, 237–238).

As the converse of the above, inadequate economic performance might be simply interpreted in terms of inadequate autonomy or state strength. The *problèmatique* of failure, however, has generated a whole battery of analytic notions of its own. This is particularly the case as regards Africa, where a bevy of political scientists have resuscitated notions originally applied to early modern (e.g., "absolutist," "patrimonial," and "predatory"), or feudal (e.g., "prebendal") European states (see Callaghy 1990; Sandbrook 1985). The shared imagery here is of a state so permeated by personalistic relations, on the one hand, and redistributive pressures, on the other, that the accumulation process, bureaucratic performance, and even the legal order are undermined.[4]

If state capacities vary so sharply, however, or if an interventionist state produces development here, stagnation and disarray there, further qualifications are required. This tends to shift the analysis back a step to historical and local specificities, on the one hand, and on the other, to the grand systemic determinants that the "statist" analysts wanted to escape (cf. Skoçpol 1985). Most commonly evoked is class structure, the conventional association of strong states with hegemonic industrial-capitalist classes, for instance (e.g., Chase-Dunn 1989, 114; 238–241). The "developmental state," however, has been linked to a certain *autonomy* from domestic interest groups, as well as to the technical and ideological capacities of state elites, qualities pronounced in the East Asian cases (see Deyo 1987). More subtly, Evans (1989, 569, 575) points to the importance of "embedded autonomy," dense linkages between the state and private capital that encourage "a project of accumulation," its effective implementation, and the emergence of strong "national capitalist classes" in the longer term.

In "predatory" states, on the other hand, exemplified by Zaire, both internal discipline and organized external constituencies are weak (Evans 1989, 569–571; cf. Ziemann and Lanzendorfer 1977). Indeed, the "politics of survival" (Migdal 1988), based on manipulation of patronage and ethnoregional cleavages, may further weaken the formal economy and the state. The literature on populist/socialist regimes also points to the problem of inadequate social moorings, in this case more the absence of a structured working class than of a bourgeoisie (see Roxborough 1979; Marton 1978; Amin 1990, 140, 152 ff.)[5] In Latin America, however, more-pronounced class formation and class conflict have tended to result in stalemate or authoritarian, conservative regimes.

It is in Asia, in fact, that we find the most successful cases outside Europe of not only capitalism but communism, in either case constructed on a peasant base, state tradition, and national identity of great historic depth (Abdel-Malek 1983, 2–3, 5; 1981, 64, 178–181; Amin 1980, 174 ff.). This sort of contrast takes us beyond classes to the *longue durée* of precapitalist trade and state formation, civilizations, and modes, but we have few generalizations here. The role of Confucianism, for instance, in East Asian success has been long debated; one might point instead to intervening factors, such as cultural distance from Europe (Dore 1990, 358 ff.) or the geopolitics of the postwar years, or ask why the equally ancient traditions of the Arab world have not had similar effects.

In any case, there is little agreement about where the Third World will go from here. For Harris (1986), the transnationalization of production means that attempts at independent national development simply no longer work. For Amin, on the contrary, it is independent *capitalist* development that is now, more than ever, ruled out. With some possible East Asian exceptions, only "dependent industrialization" and "compradorization" (1990, 138 ff.) are in store. Globalists may accept that "development *is* dependent development" (Friedman 1982, 19); for "anti-imperialist socialists," de-linking is still required. For analytic purposes, an emphasis on the relative and contingent character of dependence (Lipietz 1986, 55, 67; Senghaas 1988) seems more useful, along with an acknowledgement of the limited prospects for more NICs, still less for more revolutionary breakaways, in the near to medium term. In the meantime, the periphery remains, wracked by debt crisis, natural calamities, and "downward spirals" of decay (Sandbrook 1985); indeed, since the 1980s, theses of immiseration have taken on new life.

Five hundred years ago the European expansion began, and was completed and consolidated only at the turn of the last century. In light of that long ascent, the period of uncontested hegemony was brief, and the postwar dismantling of empire extraordinarily condensed. Disappointments with many of the new regimes, however, along with the rising transnationalization of capital and production, has sparked a counteroffensive against nationalist perspectives, particularly, perhaps, those that "expropriated the concepts of the left" (Harris 1986, 183). Underdevelopment theory has been badly damaged by this critique. The same should not be said, however, of the (historical-)structuralist school. With due respect to Harris, dependent development that relies on adaptation to the market is really not so new, nor are the vulnerabilities it entails. Conversely, a certain degree of national economic autonomy and integration remains vital, clearly, for the long-term prospects of most countries (see e.g., Senghaas 1988; Bienefeld and Godfry 1982).

In any case, the state remains critical, and—contrary to world-system theory—this activism may not be so concentrated in the semiperiphery as one might think. Indeed, virtually all countries seem continuously and obsessively engaged in adjustments to at least maintain their competitive position, with the exception, perhaps, of some "drifter states" (Dore 1990, 358) at the bottom and a few capital-exporting hegemons at the top. As we have argued, moreover, the states seem to have played a particularly formative role in the genesis of the world economy itself. And today, also, there is reason to believe that the competition of states, as well as of companies, drives the system on. "Whoever fails to increase his power, must decrease it, if others increase theirs," as Fichte said long ago (cited in Davis 1978, 44). This "Hobbesian" character of the world system, the need for "increased capabilities in the international arena," compels states to mobilize resources and extend internal control (Migdal 1988, 23, 24).

World-system theory, which accommodates so much and hopes for so little in the short to medium term, has survived relatively well, partly because of a skillful blend of what ultimately may be contradictory elements: Leninist/nationalist perspectives on the global economy and Marxist/globalist perspectives on the states. One argument is indisputable: constraints operate on even the most powerful or radical regimes, each of which must "observe certain limits," none of which "is free to transform processes within its boundaries as it sees fit" (Wallerstein 1984, 51–52). A second line of argument—the functional necessity and subordination of the multistate system in the world economy and, thus, its *pro*systemic effects—is more debatable. Apart from the methodological problems (functionalism, teleology, and so on), it also collides with the historical/empirical evidence at a number of points (when states perform in unexpectedly controlling, suboptimal, or idiosyncratic ways).

At least for heuristic purposes, it seems advisable to unpack the world-system construct, restoring the analytic autonomy of capitalism and the states. The ongoing analysis of imperialism provides rich resources for work along these lines, stressing geopolitics, distinctive historical phases in capitalist development, and the problematic character of states in class/economic terms (e.g., Willoughby 1986; see also Chase-Dunn 1989, 235–237; McEwan and Tabb 1989). Lipietz (1987) points to the national accumulation regimes and "modes of regulation" that exist alongside and mediate global ones; Zeitlin, similarly, refers to the "class relations within nations that shape the global relations between them" (cited in So 1990, 223; emphasis dropped) and that filter the local impact of such foreign affairs.

The "new comparative political economy" (Evans and Stephens 1988a,b; Koo 1984) has incorporated similar ideas. The focus here is on cross-national analysis in the context of *two* world systems, oriented respectively to global capital accumulation and to geopolitical competition between the states. As with Lipietz (1987), the "contingent character" and structural mediation of international factors (Evans and Stephens 1988b, 725) is emphasized. Similar themes appear in the "second structuralist" perspective proposed by Palan (1992a, 1992c) and Gills. This approach, however, also has a distinct nominalist cast, positing the primacy of national-level social processes and groups as opposed to both the "first structuralism" of world-system theory and the traditional realist conception of the state(s).

There are also issues of evaluation and strategy. Interstate competition spurs on capitalist expansion, to be sure. But if one retains a "hard" dependency perspective—of a capitalist system battening on international superexploitation and unequal exchange—why should increases in local appropriation, reducing flows to the core, not be considered "*anti*systemic"? And if raising Third World wages can be recommended in this context (Wallerstein 1988, 2022–2033), why not increasing shares to Third World capital or states? Local capital is often *not* integrated to transnational capital, after all, and the latter *can* be made to suffer, as suggested by the crisis now afflicting Great Britain and the United States. This decline may reflect, indeed, the "normal entropy of monopolistic advantage within capitalism" (Wallerstein 1991, 53). The specific mechanism, however, is the competition emanating not only from the EC and Japan but from the industrializing South (cf. Corbridge 1986, 199–200). Moreover, if one admits the relative autonomy of the interstate system—if that system is not merely a mechanism of surplus extraction but one of political domination in its own right—then nationalism, "statism," and even subimperialism on the periphery, whether socialist or not, take on more antisystemic hues (Arrighi 1982, 90, 94 ff.; Abdel-Malek 1981, 1983; Worseley 1980, 315 ff.).

In sum, while world-system theorists insist that the core-periphery hierarchy is virtually impossible to change, the buildup of productive, financial, and military capacity in the semiperiphery over the past generation is unmistakable from other points of view. From a Marxist perspective, of course, the long-term issue is "not the consolidation of the state and the fulfillment of 'autonomous capitalism,' but how to supercede them" (Cardoso and Faletto 1979, xxiii–xxiv). In the meantime, the unhappy process of national development, including development of the state itself, remains imperative for virtually all regimes. Such developmentalism is thus hardly "defunct" in practical terms (cf. Wallerstein 1988, 1991), although it does seem to be losing its radical allure. But if class struggles still seem tied to national terrains, there are two trends towards the transnationalization of politics that should be mentioned. One is the growing significance of multilateral organizations, such as the World Bank and the IMF, a trend remarkably neglected in the theoretical literature. Another is the growing attention given by these sorts of institutions, along with various national elites, to the dual threat of world poverty and environmental decline.

Wallerstein's multiplex critique of developmentalism contains several additional strands that may help guide us forward. One is to demonstrate the centrality of development in the panoply of European Enlightenment values, and how such strange bedfellows as Leninism, national liberation, and Wilsonian democracy have drawn from this common source . . . and thus enhanced the state (1991, 5 ff., 96). What is more significant, in our view, is the hint, at least, of an effort to demystify not only national development, but development *tout court*. This ties in to the problematic of "civilizations," and the specific problem of Eurocentrism, both recurrent Wallersteinian themes (e.g., 1983, 97 ff.). Abdel-Malek's notion of the "civilizational project," the articulation of endogenous traditions outside (and against) the West, has been a seminal influence here (1981, 189; 1983, 5–6; also Taylor 1979, 265 ff.). The fundamental tension between developmental and productivist values, however, and the stability, (re)distribution, and satisfy strategies more favored in non-Western/precapitalist traditions, is something often glossed over in these accounts (cf. Moseley 1992).

Developmentalist values are also being questioned on more-practical grounds because of growing awareness that the system simply cannot continue to expand as in the past. As Wallerstein (1991, 132) notes, the "last redoubts of partial non-involvement in the world-economy" are now under threat. The problem here, however, is not only social polarization but actual extermination of hitherto isolated populations; not only the approaching asymptote of capitalist commodification but the approaching limits of the environment in terms of resource depletion, pollution, and so on (cf. 1988, 2020, 2022; 1991, 82–83, 101, 132); In addition to declining room for maneuver and adjustment, this threatens the sheer physical base required for reproduction of the industrial mode, something at least as fatal as the cultural breakdown and immiseration that are also underway.

All this is still given little attention in development theory, where neo-Marxists, like neoliberals, may make some ritual bows to "sustainable development," but actually seem to still believe in indefinite growth—if only we can get the institutions right. In fact, it may be environmental crisis that will generate the next wave of pressures to bring markets under control, pressures that may issue both from antisystemic movements and, preemptively, from above. In any case, "workerist" radicals, nationalists, and Greens might all agree, for somewhat different reasons, on the key problem: the nexus of an "ungovernable world market" and interstate competition. They might agree, too, on at least one aspect of the solution: that "to control capital, the State needs to extend its power to encompass the world" (Harris 1983, 261, 237).

NOTES

1. A version of this paper was first presented at a United Nations University Symposium, HSDP-SCA series, Colchester, England, 1984. I am grateful to Anouar Abdel-Malek, the organizer, and to the UNU for its support. A revision was presented at the meetings of the American Sociological Association, Washington, D.C., 11–15 August 1990.

2. In Frank's recent work, this reasoning, centered on centralized intersocietal flows of surplus, has been pushed back to much earlier "historical world-systems."

3. Whether such activism is particularly associated with "B" phases of economic contraction and hegemonic decline is still a matter of debate.

4. This sort of perspective has been linked to fierce policy disputes between partisans of the market, led by the World Bank and IMF, and defenders of state-led development, drawn from the radical intelligentsia and OAU. Ironically, the neo-liberals have found themselves faced with "using the state to change policy in a less statist direction" (Nelson 1990, 358; cf. Sandbrook 1985, 153 ff.), requiring, in fact, a new spate of "capacity-building," now a specific program-focus at the Bank.

5. "Real" socialist revolutions, moreover, have consolidated themselves as much on the basis of national feeling as of class. It might be fair to say that socialist regimes appear not only in the wrong places (poor), for the wrong (national) reasons, on the wrong (petit bourgeois/peasant) class base, but all this to pursue the wrong (accumulationist, developmental) goals (cf. Abdel-Malek 1979, 11). Of course, there *is* nothing wrong with all this, apart from the discrepancies with Marxist theory . . . and our hopes.

8

A World-Economy Interpretation
of East–West European Politics
Andre Gunder Frank

> The most important lesson of the East German voting is this: Economics
> is more important than nationalism or ideology. East Germans behaved
> like any "normal" democratic electorate: They voted their pocketbooks
> . . . not so much "Deutschland über alles" as "Deutsche Mark über alles."
> —Josef Joffe
> foreign editor of *Süddeutsche Zeitung*
> in *New York Times,* March 22, 1990

> The more important point is that life goes its own direction, without
> heeding the legislators' provisions.
> —Tadeusz Kowalik (1991)
> *Privatization and Social Participation:*
> *The Polish Case*

This chapter[1] brings a world-economic interpretation to bear on selected
historical and contemporary facets of European politics and policy, as well
as its culture and ethnicity. Economic circumstances and motives behind
political policy and cultural, ethnic, or national[ist] behavior are frequently
neglected or explicitly denied, and *world* economic ones all the more so.
Instead, most opinions from left to right—and curiously, the free marke-
teers especially—subscribe de facto to the Maoist ideology of "politics in
command." Ironically, like Mao, they put their faith in the power of ideology itself.

Opinion leaders rely on the media, education, religion, and other vehicles of popular culture and ideology to promote or prevent the real-world
changes they seek. People in the street reward or blame the government
"in power" for economic and other changes over which the government
has scarce, if any, control and lend their vote or other support to the political, national, or ethnic "opposition" and its ideologies if things go wrong.

Yet, as will be argued, most of the favorable and unfavorable changes
—and even the ideological and popular responses themselves—are rooted

in worldwide economic developments that existing or prospective politics, ideology, or culture ironically have little or no *power* to change. Indeed, if deliberate policy accomplishes anything at all, it usually reinforces the economically underlying trend and achieves, at best, the opposite of what was intended. An important reason for this limitation is that political power and policy is locally, nationally, or, at most, imperially confined; but it is up against *world*wide economic forces, which are beyond any-one's control. This thesis is argued here with regard to selected events and policies in the history, contemporary life, and relations of Eastern and Western Europe, which are usually (mis)accounted for and promoted pri-marily in terms of local and European politics, policy, culture, national-ism, ethnicity, or, in short, of ideology.

Any "objective" review of economic policy in Europe and elsewhere belies, instead, the three most widespread myths about such policy: (1) That policy is based on economic theory or political ideology; (2) that it is the initiating motor force of events; and (3) that it is largely effective in converting intentions into reality. None of these widely believed claims is borne out by experience. Economic policy both in Eastern and Western Europe and elsewhere is largely independent of political ideology and pre-cedes the economic theory, which is then adduced, invented, or exhumed only to lend support to policies whose primary impulse under the circum-stances is expediency.

Therefore, it is hardly ever the case that policies are the cause of events. Instead, most policies are only belated responses to events and trends, which they then reinforce. Per contra and as an illustration of the more usual inter-pretation, *The European Economy: Growth and Crisis* claims that

> if a theme does emerge from this book, it is that economic policies were important in shaping Europe's post-war history and had, on the whole, beneficial effects. Thus, the use of demand management policies con-tributed to the dampening of cycles and to the acceleration of economic growth. Policy intervention to improve external performance . . . had sig-nificant effects (Boltho, ed. 1982, 3).

None of these themes or claims corresponds to reality, certainly not since the onset of the world economic crisis in the mid-1960s and, least of all, in the 1980s after the book was written. Nonetheless, every semester's issue of the OECD *Economic Outlook* and the daily press repeats essen-tially the same message, which is routinely disconfirmed by the OECD's own statistics.

In particular, these economic policies in Western Europe (and also in Eastern Europe, which Boltho did not even consider, and of course in the United States and the Soviet Union as well) did *not* on the whole have beneficial effects, and they did *not* dampen the economic cycle, acceler-ate economic growth, or improve external performance. Instead, these economic policies almost invariably did the opposite: they amplified the economic cycle, reduced economic growth, and worsened external performance. That is, they were pro-cyclical and had consequences that were very different from, if not largely opposite to, those that were supposedly intended. In Western Europe these consequences were perhaps most visible in Britain, which during Prime Minister Thatcher's tenure deindustrialized more and faster than ever before. Higher inflation and a lower pound sterling relative to its European neighbors were at the root of her "nationalist," "ideological" resistance to European union and that, in turn, of her eventual downfall. However, excepting perhaps Germany among major economies, other economic policy in other European countries also militated against their growth and external performance, so much so that "Eurosclerosis" became a popular buzzword in the late 1980s (for a critique, see Ellman 1987).

The U.S. political-economic arms-race policy under President Reagan did have the intention, and indeed the consequence, of obliging the Soviet Union to spend itself into bankruptcy and suffer defeat in the Cold War. Probably unintended, however, were some further consequences: One is that the U.S. economy spent and borrowed itself into near bankruptcy as well. It is kept afloat only by the bailout of continued inflows of capital from Europe and Japan, which won the Cold War. This capital support, also from the Third World through its debt service, was not available, however, to the USSR. Thus, the latter not only had to cry uncle but even to end the Cold War altogether. This turn of events, however, unexpectedly (and unintentionally?) deprived the United States of its favorite enemy and de facto subimperial junior partner (Wallerstein 1991). Thereby it also dissolved the principal glue that held the common opposition to the Soviet Union together in the U.S. alliance with its de jure junior partners in Japan and Western Europe. Perhaps these threatened to become more independent, at least before the Gulf War (temporarily?) brought them back into line (Frank 1991c). Another unintended consequence of U.S. policy and Gorbachev's response to events in his country was that the Soviet Union not only went bankrupt, but it has also been breaking up completely. As a result, fears spread in the U.S. and Europe that Soviet nuclear armaments would proliferate and fall into uncontrollable and irresponsible hands. Reagan's vice president and successor then had to do all he could, at least politically, to keep Gorbachev in power and the Soviet structure in one piece—but it was not enough. What bitter irony!

If economic policy had beneficial and intended effects in Eastern Europe and the Soviet Union, we would have to suppose that their regimes really wanted to pave their road to hell with good intentions. The world economic crisis opened the way: The regimes first sought unsuccessfully to keep the economic wolf from the door and subsequently accelerated their own downfall by accepting and imposing policies that aggravated the cycle, halted and reversed economic growth, and ruined their external performance. The momentous economic and political changes of perestroika and glasnost in the Soviet Union and Eastern Europe and therewith the end of the Cold War did not simply emerge, like Pallas Athene out of Zeus, from the head of Mikhail Gorbachev. He said himself that they were "inevitable." As (economic) necessity is the mother of (political) invention, had Gorbachev not existed, he would have had to be invented. His pragmatic praxis outpaced and overturned ideological preconceptions, including his own and those of his opponents at home and abroad. The exigencies of the world economy generated all manner of pragmatic praxis and political ironies in the 1970s and 1980s. Moreover, these pragmatic reforms started in the most open and affected economies of Eastern Europe and were perforce transferred to the relatively more independent Soviet Union only later.

In particular, it was the world economic crisis that spelled the doom of the socialist economies, much more than their socialist-planning "command economy," which is now almost universally blamed for the same. Not unlike the "Third World" economies of Latin America and Africa, the "Second World" economies of the USSR and Eastern Europe were unable to bear the pace of accelerated competition in the world economy during this period of crisis. Like every previous one, this economic crisis forces one and all to restructure economically and to realign politically. It is true that economic command organization and political bureaucracy were instrumental in depriving economies in Eastern Europe and the Soviet Union of the flexibility necessary for adaptation to the world economic crisis and the technological revolution and restructuring, which that same crisis engendered elsewhere. Many Third World "market" economies, however, and sectors in the industrial world and especially the United States also failed. In the meantime, Japan Inc. and the East Asian NICs relied on important state political-economic commands to promote their technological advance and adjustment.

WORLD-ECONOMY AND
EAST-WEST EUROPEAN DIVISIONS IN HISTORY

The rise of Europe or of the West itself is mostly ascribed Eurocentrically to features of European politics and civilization. Martin Bernal (1987) and Samir Amin (1988) have recently challenged this almost universal view in their *Black Athena* and *Eurocentrism*, respectively. Bernal argues that "European" Greece had African cultural roots, and Amin emphasizes the Mediterranean roots of European development. Both authors' alternative to Eurocentrism is certainly welcome; however, both limit their critiques and alternatives largely to culture, civilization, or ideology.

The transition from feudalism to capitalism in Europe as the basis of its expansion in the world has been debated endlessly, among others in the Dobb-Sweezy-Takahashi debate (Hilton 1976) and the *Brenner Debate* (Ashton and Philpin 1985). Dobb (Hilton 1976), Brenner (Ashton and Philpin 1985), Anderson (1974) and most others argued that certain *political* features of feudalism and absolutism *in Europe* gave way to those of capitalism. Sweezy and, more recently, Wallerstein (1974) argue per contra for the determinant economic factor of foreign trade *in or of Europe*. That is, all of these authors see only European political or economic factors. None of these authors or their co-debaters, took account of Europe's place in the world economy *Before European Hegemony*, as Janet Abu-Lughod (1989) entitled her book. She describes a "Thirteenth Century World System," of which Europe was but a marginal outpost before "the fall of the East preceded the rise of the West." McNeill (1964) and Stavrianos (1970) writing on *The Rise of the West* and *The World to 1550: A Global History*, respectively, Hodgson (1974) and Lombard (1975) on Islam, Gernet (1982) on China, and more recently Wilkinson (1987) writing on "Central Civilization" are important precursors for an interpretation that sees the economic and political development of Europe not so much in its own Eurocentric terms as through the westward shift of the economic center of gravity in a worldwide division of labor, and consequently of political hegemony within the world economy/system as a whole (Frank 1990c, 1991a,b; Gills and Frank 1990–1991, 1992; Frank and Gills 1992, 1993). The "discovery" of America in 1492 is then seen as an event in the long economic cycle and expansion of the whole world economy (Blaut 1977, 1992; Frank 1992b,c). This world economic reinterpretation of the rise of Europe and the West also challenges the scientific validity of the "Transitional Ideological Modes: Feudalism, Capitalism, Socialism" (Frank 1991b), to which we will return in discussing more contemporary events below.

Max Weber's ([1904–1905] 1958) famous *The Protestant Ethic and the Spirit of Capitalism* ascribed the development of capitalism in the North/West and its supposed failure to develop in the South to differences in religion. R. H. Tawney (1945), using the reverse causation, argued in his *Religion and the Rise of Capitalism* that the development of capitalism underlay that of religion. Either way, if capitalism developed in Europe at all, it started in Catholic Italy, Spain, and Portugal, who were in commercial contact with Muslims and others in the "East"; and it became dominant in the European Northwest only later. Indeed, the decline of the South (including the Muslim Ottoman empire) and rise of the North/West began in the seventeenth century, and it was certainly due more to the seventeenth-century world economic crisis than to any supposed cultural differences (Frank 1978a). Moreover, the subsequent failure of capitalist *development* in most of the Americas, Asia, and Africa, as well as in Eastern

Europe, and its success in the North American Northeast cannot be accounted for by cultural or religious differences among the colonizers, but must be ascribed to economic colonization itself and to the economic roles of the colonies in the development of the world economy (Frank 1978b).

The division of Europe into a more-developed "West" and a less- or underdeveloped "East," as well as a "Central Europe" both geographically and economically in-between, also stems at least from the sixteenth century—or the ninth. The dividing line has run remarkably close to the Elbe River and "Iron Curtain" of the forty years following World War II for a long time. "It is as if Stalin, Churchill and Roosevelt had studied carefully the *status quo* of the age of Charlemagne on the 1130th anniversary of his death" (Szücs 1983, 133). Moreover, "the old Roman *limes* would show up on Europe's morphological map, thus presaging right from the start the birth of a 'Central Europe' within the notion of the 'West'" (ibid.).

The fifteenth-seventeenth century division of Europe into East and West has been the subject of a long debate, with a line-up similar to the above-cited "transition" debate: Dobb (Hilton 1976), Anderson (1974), and Brenner (Ashton and Philpin 1985), et al., saw political differences, especially in the strength of the state, between East and West. Others emphasized cultural or ideological distinctions. Sweezy (Hilton 1976), Wallerstein (1974), Frank (1978a), and Denemark (1988, 1991) have been in the minority of those who ascribe greater and underlying importance to the regions' different roles and places in the system of international trade. Curiously, in this debate, also about the reasons for the "second serfdom" in Eastern Europe, these authors derive contrary interpretations from the same primary sources such as Kula (1976) and other Central–East European writers.

However that may be, Western Europe was already exporting manufactures and Eastern Europe agricultural and mineral raw materials in the sixteenth-century expansion. Moreover, Western Europe used its access to the gold and silver of the Americas to pay for its imports from—and economically to colonize—the East, in Europe and beyond. Later and until World War I,

> the whole history of the Hapsburg state was an attempt to balance the unbalanceable while being squeezed somewhere between the two extremes of East-Central Europe. The only consequent structural element in that formula . . . [was] the setting up by the Hapsburgs of a diminished—"East-Central European"—copy on an "imperial scale" of the division of labour drawn up by the nascent "world economy" on a larger scale. . . . The Hapsburgs had no chances in the Western sector of the world economy either. So the House of Hapsburg settled down to a division of labour between West (industrial) and East (agricultural) through the economic structure within its own, East-Central European, political framework. . . . In the "Hapsburg division of labour," Hungary was cast in the

East's role [with its hinterland, and Austria governing Bohemia in the West's] (Szücs 1983, 172, 173).

POLITICAL ECONOMIC IRONIES IN EUROPE

This apparently long-standing economic structural and therewith political and cultural division of Europe has been perpetuated to this day— and promises to continue for some time to come. This historical and contemporary economic reality appears ironical only in terms of the more common political and cultural interpretations of the divisions in and of Europe and the now excessively optimistic aspirations of many of its inhabitants. The irony is that many of the "Second World" East Europeans who sought to join the "First World" West will find themselves in the "Third World" South instead. The difference between economic reality and political and ideological aspirations is at least triply ironic.

The first irony is not really so except in reference to present ideals: It is that historically Eastern Europe, albeit culturally European, was never economically developed like Western Europe. Therefore, its people have little historical claim to become West European now. Only a portion of the eastern sector of Germany, the Bohemian and Moravian sections of former Czechoslovakia, and, in some sense, part of Hungary, Slovenia, and maybe part of Croatia in former Yugoslavia in Central Europe, plus perhaps the Soviet Baltic republics, were historically similar to Western Europe.

The second long-term economic irony is that forty years of the politics and ideology of "socialist development," literally not to mention the "development of socialism," seems not to have changed the economic positions of these regions, neither relative to each other, nor relative to Western Europe. Eastern Europe did narrow the gap with Western Europe in the 1960s. The gap narrowed a bit more or at least was maintained in the 1970s by virtue of recessionary, lower growth rates in the West, which fed Western loans to the East and allowed Eastern borrowing from the West. The gap quickly widened again, however, with the onset of the debt crisis in the East and long cyclical recovery with technological advance in the West during the 1980s. Thus, over the entire postwar period taken as a whole, the East-West gap and the relative positions within the East changed but little.

Indeed, there is some question of whether these forty years even have changed much the internal class structure. If any change of position or class structure occurred, it was mostly the decline of Bohemia, Moravia, Hungary, Slovenia, and perhaps the Baltics in Central and "socialist" Europe relative to the rise of parts of Spain, Italy, and Greece in "capitalist" Southern Europe. Industrialization, of course, modified the class structure everywhere in Europe, but apparently not more, and perhaps less, in the

East than in the West and South. Therefore, only the above-mentioned regions in Central Europe now have a fighting chance to recover their historical positions in Europe, and that in competition with Southern Europe. Public opinion in Southern Europe already indicates great awareness of this threat, while that of Central and Eastern Europe still appears unaware of the problem (Hofbauer and Komlosy 1991).

The third irony, therefore, is that the same present-day political and ideological changes in Eastern Europe through which its people aspire to join the First World in Western Europe now threaten instead to place Eastern Europe economically in the Third World—again, for that is where it was before. Poland has already been Latin Americanized. The earlier, dependent agriculture—and only temporarily, oil—export economy par excellence of Romania will be lucky and thankful if it can even regain that position, for it now competes with Bulgaria, which developed agribusiness for export during the socialist regime.

The same problem obtains a fortiori in the former Soviet Union. A few parts of Russia and the Ukraine were westernized by Peter the Great and industrialized by him, Witte, and Stalin. But most of the former Soviet Union, at best, still is a Third World economy, like Brazil, India, and China, which also have industrial capacities, especially in military hardware. The Transcaucasian and Central Asian regions, which have now broken off from old Russia, are not even likely to be Latin Americanized, but rather economically more Africanized or, in the worst case, politically Lebanonized. The same sad fate befell former Yugoslavia, whether it remains one or, more likely, becomes several.

Many of these regions now face the serious prospect, like Africa, of being marginalized out of the admittedly exploitative international division of labor. Their natural resources have been squeezed dry like a lemon for the benefit of industrial development farther north, and now the regions and their peoples can be discarded. That is the political position, for instance, represented by Russian President Boris Yeltsin. The southern inhabitants' wrath at having so long been exploited in the past and demanding its cessation for the future is understandable. So is the appeal to (or discovery of) "traditional" ethnic and national identity and interethnic strife in response to aggravated economic deprivation, such as 30 percent unemployment in parts of Central Asia. Political "independence" and interethnic strife in Central Asia or Central Africa, however, now can afford them little economic benefit in the future. On the contrary, the erection of politically motivated ethnic and other barriers to economic interchange, and even exploitation, threatens to convert them again, separately and altogether, into backwaters of history. (However, the "Centrality of Central Asia" was a fact of history for millennia before the world's present North-South arrangement took shape after the sixteenth century) (Frank 1992a).

The other irony, of course, is that it was not so much the now universally faulted and rejected ideological socialism or political planning that is responsible for Eastern Europe's backwardness relative to Western Europe, but rather the historical economic differences and relations between the two parts of Europe. Indeed, the revolutions of 1989 in Eastern Europe were not so much responses to supposed *differences* between East and West economic and political policies. The revolutions were more the consequences of the *similarities* of economic policy in the East to those in the West and especially those in the South, that is, in Latin America, Africa, and parts of Asia.

WORLD ECONOMIC CRISIS
AND POLICY IN EAST AND WEST EUROPE

The world economic crisis expanded and deepened in Eastern Europe and the Soviet Union. The economic crisis and related economic factors contributed materially to the desire and ability of social (and also ethnic/nationalist) movements to mobilize so many people at this time for such far-reaching political ends. The decade of the 1980s, and half of the 1970s, is now called "the period of stagnation" in the Soviet Union; it generated accelerating economic crisis and absolute deterioration of living standards in most of Eastern Europe, as also in Latin America, Africa, and some other parts of the world (see Frank 1988). Significantly, especially in Eastern Europe, this period also saw an important deterioration and retrocession in its relative competitive standing and standards of living relative to Western Europe and even to the newly industrializing countries (NICs) in East Asia.

In the 1970s, the same export/import-led growth strategies were adopted by Communist party-led governments in the East (Poland, Romania, Hungary) and military dictatorships in the South (Argentina, Brazil, Chile). Thus, neither differences in political ideology nor in economic system were sufficient to spell significantly different political-economic policy responses to the world economic crisis. The same economic strategies with reliance on foreign debt then generated the same debt crisis within the crisis, which began significantly in Poland in 1981, before the more-usual dating in Argentina and Mexico in 1982.

Then in the 1980s, the same debt-service policies on the IMF model were adopted and implemented by Communist party-led governments in the East (Poland, Hungary, Romania, Yugoslavia) and by military dictatorships, other authoritarian governments, and their successor democratic governments in the South (Argentina, Brazil, Mexico, Philippines). There were variations on the theme of debt service, but it is difficult to correlate, let alone explain, them by reference to the political color or ideologies of regimes or governments: The most stellar pupil of the IMF was Nicolae Ceaucescu in Romania, who actually reduced the debt until the lights went out, first for his people and then for himself. In Peru, on the other hand, the newly elected President Alan Garcia defied the IMF and announced he would limit debt service to no more than 10 percent of export earnings. Actually, they were less than that before he assumed office; then they rose to more than 10 percent under his presidency. Real income fell by about half, and the novelist Vargas Llosa sought the presidency after moving from the political center-left to the extreme right. But what does that mean, if anything? Alberto Fujimori won the presidential election by opposing Vargas Llosa's economic program, and then turned around and applied the very same policies in what became popularly known as "Fujishock."

Communist General Jaruselski in Poland and the populist Sandinistas in Nicaragua also implemented IMF-style "adjustment" and "conditionality" on their people. Both did so without the benefit of pressure from the IMF, since Poland was not a member and Nicaragua had no access to it. In Nicaragua, there was "condicionalidad sin fondo," that is, conditionality without the Fund and without any bottom or end to the Sisyphus policy. Hungary had the most-reformed economy and the most-liberal political policy still led by a Communist party in the Warsaw Pact. Yet, Hungary paid off the early 1980s principal of its debt three times over—and meanwhile doubled the amount still owed! That is more than Poland or Brazil or Mexico, which on the average paid off the amount of debt owed only once or twice, while at the same time increasing its total two times. No matter, the Solidarnosc government that replaced General Jaruselski and the Communist party in Poland benefited from IMF membership and imposed even more-severe economic sacrifices on its population than its predecessors. In Hungary's first free election, all parties promised to follow the IMF prescriptions after the election.

Moreover, the Western IMF and its policies were the "secret weapon" and "de facto ally" of the opposition groups. They are now in power or making their bid for it, thanks primarily to the economic and secondarily the political crisis engendered by the implementation of these austerity "adjustment" policies with IMF support. So now there is not only no economic but also no political alternative to further austerity policies, which are tied to IMF and other Western advice and conditions.

The political irony is that "really existing socialism" failed not least because of the unsuccessful implementation of import/export-led growth models and IMF-style austerity policies in the East. Yet "really existing capitalism" pursued the same models and policies in the South and also failed. Nobody in the West or East says so, however, and nobody in the South any longer has a plausible "socialist alternative" to offer. Why was there a "change of system" in (part of) the East in the face of failure, but none in the South in the face of the same failure? Jeanne Kirkpatrick was wrong when she said that "totalitarian" countries in the East don't change, while "authoritarian" ones in the West do. Actually, it is arguable whether in either case there was any "change of system" or an "end of history" (Frank 1990b).

These same economic policies, however, were not limited to the East and the South. Similar economic policies were also implemented in the West and almost universally in Western Europe. Public opinion on both the right and the left usually attributes this economic policy to the ideology of Reaganism or Thatcherism and its followers elsewhere. This opinion is, at best, based on short memories and/or a misreading of recent history. In fact, the abandonment of Keynesian policy and its replacement by monetarism and supply-side economics began in 1976 under the Labour government of James Callaghan in Britain and was followed in the United States by Democratic President Jimmy Carter in 1977. Both did so halfway through their terms of government in response to the growing world economic crisis and against their previous electoral promises and still-continuing political ideologies. Callaghan changed policy in 1976, ostensibly to get a $3.9 billion loan, the conditions for which were set by Carter's secretary of the treasury. An official later admitted, however, that his British Treasury wanted to change policy anyway and used the IMF conditionality as a justification (Frank 1980). However that may be, Reagan's and Thatcher's economic policies were only the logical extensions into the 1980s of the monetarist/supply-side economic policy, that had already been instituted by their Democratic and Labour predecessors. Reaganomics and Thatcherism were not the basis but rather the ideological, "fig-leaf" justification for economic policies that were implemented for previous and other economic reasons. The real economic reasons and their ideological beclouding were long since analyzed by Frank (1980, 1981b, 1984–1987, 1986).

Support for this economic interpretation of policy formation is widely available in the review of political-economic policy by other governments in Western Europe, which did not share the ideologies—or electoral promises—of Reagan and Thatcher but faced the same imperatives of the world economic crisis. The self-same economic policies were implemented—with the support of their loyal Communist party opposition, if any—by the Social Democratic and "socialist" governments of Schmidt in Germany, Vranitsky in Austria, Den Uyl in the Netherlands, Mitterrand in France, Gonzalez in Spain, Soares in Portugal, Craxi in Italy, and others elsewhere. Their Christian Democratic and other conservative party predecessors, successors, and alliance partners also pursued the same political-economic policies. The clearest case of this independence of economic policy from political ideology was the U-turn in Mitterrand's economic policy from Keynesianism to liberalism/conservatism after the French balance of payments became unsustainable in the world recession of 1981. The same dissociation is also illustrated by the continuity in French economic policy since then, regardless of which political party has supplied the prime minister or economic ministers (Frank 1980, 1984–1987).

As noted, the East European NICs and the USSR pursued export economic strategies of promotion no less than others, only with less success. Both the external and thereby the internal economy of the Soviet Union was particularly hard hit by the decline since 1981 of the prices of gold, oil, and gas, which accounted for over 90 percent of its exports. The deepening economic crisis in the economies of Eastern Europe also affected the Soviet Union. It was dependent on them for imports of essential manufactures from Eastern Europe produced with technology that they, in turn, had to import—but increasingly could not—from Western Europe.

In the 1970s, the countries of Eastern Europe (and socialist countries everywhere) switched from ISI import substitution to "import-led growth." They then sought to fuel their growth by importing technology and capital from the West, which they intended to pay for by exporting the derivative manufactures back to the West and the world market. Actually, this import-led growth strategy of exporting manufactures to import technology by the East European NICs was only the supply constraint/scarcity economy version of the self-same "export-led growth" strategy. That strategy was to import technology in order to export manufactures, and it was followed by the demand-constrained surplus economies of the East Asian and South American NICs.

In the 1980s, however, the East European NICs, like ones in South America and Africa, lost their capacity to compete in export markets. As for all dependent, developing economies, by far their most-important supply constraint was and remains that of hard currency/dollar foreign exchange. For that reason also, the East Europeans continued and tried to step up their intra-COMECON trade with each other and the Soviet Union, which was not paid for in dollars. Therefore, as we will note below, the dollarization of ex-COMECON trade in the 1990s would all but dry up this intraregional trade without permitting any extraregional replacement, because dollarization could only exacerbate this most-critical foreign-exchange supply constraint.

This foreign-exchange supply constraint was both cause for—and then the effect of—missing the high-tech train; it left all the East European economies standing on a side track in the 1980s. If the East European equivalent of NICs had become, indeed even remained, more competitive in the world market than the East Asian NICs, they would have had no revolution of 1989, Fukuyama's and our own celebration of democracy notwithstanding (Frank 1990a,b). Now their failure is universally attributed to socialism, and Eastern Europe now shares the Reaganomic and Thatcherist belief in the "magic of the market" as the sure-fire alternative.

Freeing the market and market freedom are now seen as the solution to all problems on the way to paradise, when in fact, in the short run, it can only deprive them of the only partial protection they had before. Greater inequalities of income and mushrooming unemployment are regarded as "small" costs. Moreover, few are willing to consider the real costs of privatizing or reconverting East European economies and particularly their military sectors, which accounted for perhaps 25 to 50 percent of goods production but have since lost many of their export markets (personal communication from Andras Brody [1990] in Budapest, based on his input-output calculations).

It is simply not true, therefore, to suppose or claim that Eastern Europe or even the Soviet Union were in a separate "system," which did them in. On the contrary, what did them in was their participation in the *same* world economic system with everybody else. Nor did they have any other choice! Or so I have argued already in 1972 and 1976 (Frank 1977, 1980, 1981b).

Perhaps the biggest irony is that the resulting "transition from socialism to capitalism" is taking place just when another severe recession in the world economy is helping to pull Eastern Europe and the former Soviet Union even deeper into depression. Therefore, the celebrations of the revolution of 1989, as liberation in the East and victory in the West, may be premature. Marketization—through perestroika and glasnost in the Soviet Union and privatization and democracy in Eastern Europe—was supposed to offer their peoples some of the benefits (although also some of the costs and discipline) of Western freedom of the "market" equals "democracy." East Europeans sought to become like West Europeans, and the Soviet people sought at least to join Western civilization. The transition would be unsettling, and better or worse domestic policy could smooth or roughen the transition. Many people hoped, and some still do, that the more that old ideological ways are rejected and replaced with Reaganomic and Thatcherist ideology and practice, the better the policy and faster and smoother the transition will be.

The short-term economic irony, however, is that the transition is accelerating economic decline in the East, at least in part because this transition is being promoted at the worst possible time. The world economy fell into severe recession again in the West, which exacerbates the difficulties of transition in the East. In 1990, production declined an average of 20 percent and spelled severe depression and galloping inflation in the East. In 1991, that decline was by some 20 percent in both and for the same amount in 1992, for a decline by half since the "revolution" began. This inflation is measured in terms of the national currencies, however, which become worthless. Accordingly, these economies are being "dollarized" or "D-markized." Therefore, the real market value of their properties and goods is suffering a classical and severe deflation in terms of these world currencies. (Ironically, the dollar is increasingly valued only in the socialist or ex-socialist East and the underdeveloping South, while it is declining in value on the world market.)

Unemployment is ravaging the population in the East, which has no unemployment insurance because previously the old ideology and full employment made it unnecessary, and now the new ideology and bankruptcy make it impossible. In Germany, politically accelerated unification deepened the depression and aggravated unemployment, which has rapidly risen to several million in the East. Ironically also, unification was accelerated to avoid mass migration from the bankrupt East. Yet, unification so accelerated the East's bankruptcy and unemployment that it promoted even more westward migration, to which we return below.

Thus, the policies of accelerated economic integration and marketization of the East are again more effect than cause; and insofar as they cause anything, their effects are rather the opposite of those supposedly intended. Perhaps more significantly still, the industrial economies of the West, in Europe and elsewhere, are increasingly able to transfer a major part of the costs of adjusting to the world economic crisis to the Second World East, as they already have to the Third World South. In so doing, the "second" world is also being "Third-Worldized." This is where deliberate policy does come in, however. It is most dramatically visible in West German colonialization of the former DDR, which is reminiscent of the carpetbaggers who went from North to South after the confederate defeat in the U.S. Civil War. The West is systematically eliminating real and potential competition from the East by forcing even economically sound enterprises into financial bankruptcy and/or buying them up at artificially lowered, bargain-basement prices (Schneider 1990). The interminable missions of "expert advice" and IMF policies that already depressed economies in the South and East in the 1980s now are even more legion in the East and only promote this bankruptcy further. They counsel "getting the prices right" by increasing the prices of all commodities, including those of basic consumer goods, to Western "world" levels—but excluding the price of wage-labor!

Unfortunately also, ideologically promoted privatization is no remedy for the ills of Central/Eastern Europe, any more than stabilization and privatization policy have been in Latin America and elsewhere. Indeed, during the present worldwide recession, these privatization policies can only socialize and aggravate poverty further. The current privatization craze is just as economically irrational and politically ideological as was the earlier nationalization craze. It makes very little difference whether an enterprise is owned privately or publicly, for all have to compete with each other on equal terms in the world market. The only exceptions to this rule are public enterprises that are subsidized by the state budget and private enterprises that are also subsidized from the state budget and/or are otherwise bailed out "in the public interest." Well-known examples in the United States are Detroit's Chrysler Corporation; Chicago's Continental Bank and Trust Company (at the time, the eighth-largest U.S. bank); the Ohio, Maryland, California, and Texas savings and loans; and even New York City. But this protection of the public interest is not supposed to be extended to the poor, Second and Third World countries.

Moreover, in the market, public and private enterprises both can make equally good and bad investments and other management decisions. In the 1970s, (public) British Steel overinvested badly, and (private) US Steel underinvested badly. In the 1980s, both closed down steel mills over the public objections of labor, as did the private steel industry in Germany under a Christian Democratic government and the public steel industry in France under a Socialist government. In Eastern Europe as well, whether investment decisions are good or bad is not determined by whether they are made publicly or privately. Indeed, the German [public!] Treuhandanstaldt, which is in charge of privatizing public firms, has been making disastrous (dis)investment decisions in the East to serve big private-business interests in the West (Schneider 1990). Privatizing public enterprises now at bargain-basement share prices that double next week on the national stock exchange is just as fraudulent a practice as nationalizing loss-making enterprises and paying for them above market value, or nationalizing profitable enterprises with little or no indemnification. This "now you see it, now you don't" game is all the more egregious in the case of enterprises in the East and the South that are now privatized and bought up with devalued domestic currency purchased (or swapped for debt) by foreign companies or joint ventures with foreign exchange from abroad. In sum, the privatization debate is a sham; it is far less about productive efficiency than about distributive (in)justice.

The breakup of the Soviet Union and East European privatization are destroying old forms of economic organization before, and much faster than, they are replacing them with new ones. In particular, the Soviet Union made the serious mistake of starting perestroika where it is most difficult: in industry and trade instead of in agriculture. The Chinese model of beginning privatization on the land, even if the Soviet Union had relatively less agriculture and peasant enterprise, could have increased food supplies to the cities and built up political capital for Gorbachev. Both the USSR and especially Eastern Europe began by marketizing the industrial and commercial state monopolies and permitting them large measures of private monopoly power instead. The result was, of course, that they raised prices to consumers and intermediaries. At the same time, the state ran the money-printing presses faster and faster to cover its growing deficits, including those generated by higher purchase prices from and support subsidies to these enterprises. The inevitable result was a breakdown of the supply system and runaway inflation. Instead of serving the consumer—not to mention the worker—better, liberalization ironically brought the economy to a screeching halt.

Therefore, the medium-term economic irony is that domestic economic and political liberalization and the breakdown or abolition of COMECON are breaking up the only still-available international economic foundation of East-East trade. Eastern and Central Europe are dependent in various ways on fuel and other raw materials from the former Soviet Union. This dependence is physically based on the already-installed network of oil and gas pipelines and railways. A further bitter irony is that Iraq had agreed to pay off its own large debts to several East European countries by supplying them with oil—until the UN embargo and then the Gulf War left Eastern Europe high and dry and with temporarily tripled import prices for oil, to boot. The dependence on the former USSR is also economic, since these countries cannot import and pay for fuel from elsewhere. They cannot do so as long as they are dependent, in turn, on manufacturing exports to the former Soviet Union and to each other, which they cannot sell in the West because they are not competitive there. The East also has difficulty selling them in the South, because the West and East Asia increasingly outcompete it there and must take away some of its market share to compensate for domestic and export markets lost to the new recession. Moreover, especially under French pressure, the EC is reluctant to reduce its tariff barriers to imports from the East.

The conversion of East European and Soviet trade from transferable-accounting rubles to hard-cash dollars can only exacerbate the problem of their mutual economic dependence. The medium-term economic result can only be that the short-term domestic economic depression and unemployment in each country is exacerbated by the international decline of its export markets elsewhere in the region and the impossibility of replacing them by export markets in the West and South. East German industry, of course, lost all of its export markets in the East once it adopted and required payment in the strong D-mark. It was particularly dependent on these exports to the East after its capacity to export to the West was all but eliminated by heightened competition and lagging technology during the 1980s. It is no wonder that the export-dependent economy of East Germany is in depression. Dollarization and regionalization among republics within the former Soviet Union and Yugoslavia and elsewhere extend the same problem inside these "countries." Again, the new ideology and politics is also replacing the old international economic organization before it can be replaced by another new one. Therefore, another economic irony is that, after cancellation of its foreign debt, the next best assistance Eastern Europe could get from the West would be a fund of convertible currencies to maintain the existing international trade network among its countries and with the former Soviet Union until it can be replaced by more multilateral East-West trade in the long run.

The talk of supposed new, Western economic "aid" to the East is no more than a smokescreen for continued real exploitation through the debt-service flow of funds from the increasingly impoverished East into the coffers of Western banks. The former Romanian ambassador, Silviu Brucan, estimates that the total debt of over $150 billion generates an annual flow of $10–15 billion, which is more than the entire capital of the European Bank of Reconstruction and Development. Indeed, the *International Herald Tribune* (October 15, 1991), reported an annual payment of $11 billion on a debt of $70 billion from the Soviet Union alone. The controversial reduction of the Polish debt by half is the quid pro quo for starting to pay interest on the remaining half after paying *no* interest on the whole debt!

The ultimate consequences of these policies are dubious at best. In the long run, the accelerated incorporation of Eastern Europe and parts of the former Soviet Union into a European economic zone or bloc may help Western Europe weather the world economic crisis by strengthening its ability to compete against the Japanese-led East Asian and the U.S.-led American regions. The very regionalization and possible bloc formation of the world economy is itself a consequence of the same world economic crisis (Frank 1981b, 1986, 1988). While talking multilateralism at GATT and elsewhere, de facto economic trends and de jure political-economic policies have promoted the regionalization of the world economy as the result of heightened competition during this—as also in the previous—world economic crisis. The EC and its policies for a regional market after 1992 are only its most institutionalized expression. In *The European Challenge* (Frank 1983–1984) I argued that, notwithstanding any supposed ideological obstacles, the EC could and should be extended de facto to include Eastern Europe, even if the latter is and would continue to be dependent on Western Europe. That process is now in full swing, and the elimination of ideological obstacles thereto is more its effect than its cause.

In this regard, it is useful to remember that, as already noted, economic colonization of Eastern Europe by its neighbors in the West has a centuries-long history. In the previous world economic crisis, economic, not to mention political, colonization of Eastern Europe by Germany—and the infamous payment with German harmonicas for Eastern raw materials—was in full swing in the 1930s and early 1940s. Moreover, German ambitions were not confined to the East nor to political domination in the West. In 1944, German big businesses, some of which still survive with the same name, published advertisements about the postwar European economic union they then foresaw under German management (*Illustrierte Zeitung* 1944). The same year, an Austrian by the name of Kurt Waldheim submitted his Ph.D. dissertation about the German ideologist Konstatin Franz (1817–1891), in the conclusion of which he wrote approvingly of the marvelous cooperation of all European peoples under the leadership of the Reich. . . . To accomplish this, is the national calling of Germany. . . . Germany alone has the inner spirit and world position to put this idea into practice and to make it universal. . . . Through the regeneration of the East, Western Europe will regenerate itself; and through the domination of these countries, it will regain its erstwhile position in the world. Otherwise, it will lose its previous importance ever more to North America . . . and on the other side to Russia (Waldheim 1944, 90, 94, translated by AGF).

The European Coal and Steel Community and its successor European Economic Community may well have been conceived by its spiritual and political fathers like Schuman and Monnet for the admirable political purpose of forestalling yet another European war launched from German soil. Nonetheless, it takes little reflection to see that there is also a longer historical precedent and economic rationale for the EC and the prospects of its de facto, if not de jure, eastward extension during the present world economic crisis. Moreover, it is again under German leadership and still to the chagrin of the French, British, and Americans. Le plus ça change, le plus ça reste le même?

In the medium run, parts of Central Europe (East Germany, Bohemia, Hungary, Slovenia) may well be incorporated into the "Common European Home," but in a dependent position at the back of the ground floor where they will compete with the other recently incorporated parts of Southern Europe. Other parts of Eastern Europe (in Poland, Romania, Bulgaria, Serbia, perhaps Slovakia) will more probably be relegated to the basement, where they are likely to be less "Europeanized" than "Latin Americanized," or even to suffer "Lebanonization." Poland is already experiencing Latin Americanization; and Kosovo, Transylvania, and the Transcaucasus are already threatened with Lebanonization.

PRESENT ECONOMIC CONSTRAINTS
OF FUTURE POLITICAL PROSPECTS

The short- and medium-term prospects, however, are beclouded by the accelerated impoverishment of Central and Eastern Europe and the former Soviet Union, first by the world economic crisis and then by political-economic policies that further aggravate its regional effects. At least four dangerous and mutually related consequences already loom before Europe and also in the West, especially with another recession in the world economy and Europe in the early 1990s (1) accelerated migration from East and South to West; (2) radical-right political gains; (3) ethnic and nationalist strife and conflict; and (4) the breakdown of existing territorial states and outright war among their successors. Each of these is often (mis)interpreted in its own terms on cultural, ideological, or political grounds. Yet all of them are not only intimately related to each other, but they all also ultimately derive from the world economic crisis and the unintended consequences of ill-considered policies to confront that crisis.

The truth of this world economic interpretation is most easily seen and accepted with regard to migration. Poor, jobless people see no future for themselves in the East and South and become economic migrants to the West. Moreover, economic deprivation fuels political and ethnic repression and thereby creates political refugees as well. Additionally, migration has a sort of domino/chain effect. People from the former Soviet Union seek work and black-market business deals in Poland and elsewhere in Eastern Europe. To do so, they also take advantage of policy-induced differences in exchange rates. Poles and Romanians (not to mention oppressed minorities like Gypsies) invade the new and old German states and Western Europe, while consumers from the latter take advantage of their hard currency to buy out the former. East Germans commute or migrate to West Germany. Some, like the "Germans" from Romania and Khazakstan, jump over several links of the chain in one fell swoop. The number of migrants who threaten to invade Western Europe are variously estimated to range from several hundred thousand to several tens of millions. National parliaments and EC institutions are already preparing to wall in the rich to protect them from the poor. A wag has suggested, perhaps not as a joke, that "the Wall" should be rebuilt—twice as high!

Existing migrants and the threat of more to come have already unleashed a wave of radical right-wing responses. Skinheads, neo-Nazis, and even the U.S. Ku Klux Klan proliferate, particularly in the ex-DDR/new German states, but also elsewhere. They have launched ever-more-physical attacks against refugees, migrants, foreigners, "blacks," and others. Bystanders applaud them—and vote radical right. All complain that "these people or animals"—foreigners, Jews, Gypsies—are taking housing and jobs. The complainants are apparently oblivious to the economic crisis and policy causes that underlie both their own plight and that of those they blame and victimize. In Central and Eastern Europe and the old USSR, as well as in Western Europe, political sentiment and organization has been swinging ever further to the right and often to the radical right. In Western Europe political parties of the center and the left are shifting further to the right, and the West is also threatened by infection through the dangerous new radical-rightist virus from the East. Even without it, the Republicans in Germany and Le Pen's National Front in France are gaining votes and elected representatives.

Ironically, one of the short-term victims of this political-economic process are the very civil-society social movements that brought on the transformation and democratization of Eastern Europe in the first place (for an analysis of their historical and contemporary importance, see

Fuentes and Frank 1989, Frank and Fuentes 1990), but of course only in a sociopolitical economic environment prepared by the deepening economic crisis (as recounted in Frank 1990a). Progressive social movements and their organizations with "Forum" names in several countries have everywhere been bypassed in the rush to organize new political parties through which to reorganize the state. Symbolically, in Czechoslovakia two of the leaders of Civic Forum in civil society, Vaclav Havel and Jiri Dienstbier, became president and foreign minister instead. The new leader of the (split) Civic Forum, Economics Minister Vaclav Klaus, pushed ultra-right-wing, free-marketeer Thatcherist views and policies. No doubt, this ideological reliance on the "free" market will fail to address the real problems in the economy and will sharpen economic, social, and political polarization. That, in turn, will again generate new social movements; however, then they will threaten to become fascistoid populist and chauvinist ones instead. The lessons of how the previous world economic crisis promoted Nazism, Fascism, and military dictatorships in Central, Southern, and Eastern Europe seem to be insufficiently remembered.

The course and (mis)management of the economic crisis generated shifts in positions of dominance, or privilege, and dependency, or exploitation, among countries, sectors, and different social, including gender, and ethnic groups within the Soviet Union and Eastern Europe. All of these economic changes and pressures generated or fueled social discontent, demands, and mobilization, which are expressed through enlivened social and ethnic/nationalist movements—with a variety of similarities and differences among them. It is well known that economically based resentment is fed by the loss of "accustomed" absolute standards of living, as a whole or in particular items, *and* by related relative shifts in economic welfare among population groups. Most economic crises are polarizing, further enriching (relatively if not also absolutely) the better off and further impoverishing (both relatively and absolutely) those who were already worse off, including especially women.

Therefore, it is remarkable that the increasingly virulent and violent nationalist and ethnic tensions and conflicts in Eastern Europe and the former Soviet Union are scarcely attributed to their underlying causes in the economic crisis. This is the case not only among the emotionally involved, direct participants in these ethnic/nationalist movements, but surprisingly also for most dispassionate outside observers. The former appeal to some real and even more imagined "essentialist" ethnic and national tradition and oppression. The media at home and abroad dutifully reproduce and play up these ethnic and nationalist differences and conflicts. Even authoritative academic observers, however, refer only to political and cultural causes for the recent increase in ethnic/nationalist strife. Thus, in a collection of analyses of this strife by Professors Dahrendorf, Jackson, Llobera, Gellner, and Hobsbawm, all of whom have written important books on the subject, there is not one explicit mention of the underlying economic causes (*El Pais*, October 10, 1991, Supplement). For instance, Hobsbawm details four reasons: (1) the collapse of the communist system has reopened the wounds of World War I; (2) the massive population movements of the past forty years generate xenophobia; (3) ethnic identity is easier to understand than complicated social and political programs; and (4) most important, the disintegration of an old regime renders social relations unstable, increases insecurity, and converts ethnic membership into the only sure thing (ibid., 8). There is no mention of the fact that increased and unequal economic deprivation is surely as significant a destabilizer and generator of interethnic tensions as the disintegration of the social relations of the old regime, not to mention that the former was also responsible for the latter.

The breakdown of existing territorial but multiethnic/national states and armed conflict, including war, between them, as in former Yugoslavia and the Transcaucasus, must also be traced to their underlying economic causes. If economic times had remained good, people in these regions and states would not have mobilized around previously existing and newly fueled ethnic and nationalist differences and grievances. Specifically, if the economic crisis had not hit Yugoslavia so deeply and differentially—and concretely, if differential economic deprivation had not been severely aggravated by servicing the foreign debt—Croatian and Serbian neighbors and families would still be living together peacefully despite their interethnic savagery during World War II. The Slovenian and Croatian desire to separate from Yugoslavia is not derived so much from their Catholic religion or Western culture as from their contributions to the federal budget, managed by Belgrade, of hard-earned and scarce foreign exchange. The chauvinistic appeals to "Greater" Serbia and the protection of Serbian minorities from a "fascist" government in Croatia leave the oil wells, refineries, and other economic assets, as well the Adriatic ports on Croatian soil, without mention but not out of account for the Serbs. They covet them in exchange for loss of the former's economic contributions to the Serbian standard of living. If that had not declined, albeit unequally, for almost all Yugoslavs, the economically best-placed regions would not now dream of economic salvation by trying to join Western Europe and the EC on their own. In reality, of course, Western Europe offers no such easy road to salvation to any region or state in Central and Eastern Europe. From a historical perspective, however, perhaps it is neither accidental nor surprising that the strongest foreign support for Slovenian and, to a lesser extent, Croatian independence has come from Austria and Germany, who have historic and apparently future interests still in the region. This support seems to outweigh their fear that the Yugoslavian nationalist virus and belligerent example may spread elsewhere in the Balkans. The Balkans threaten to become "balkanized" more than ever before. Tragically, first, it is balkanized regional independence and then interethnic/state and civil war—with its physical destruction and economic dislocation—that impoverish the people all the more so. Mutatis mutandis, the same economic imperatives and corresponding political-cultural consequences are also operative in the former USSR.

Finally, all four economically based processes feed on and reinforce each other. The economic crisis generates migration, rightist politics, ultranationalism and ethnic strife, and finally war, both separately and in combination. Then, separatist nationalism and migration generate radical-right populist appeal, which in turn threatens war, and that, in turn, creates more of all the above. Appeals for EC, WEU, NATO, and CSCE political intervention, such as that orchestrated in The Hague in October 1991, are too little and too late, if appropriate at all.

If Western Europe had wanted to prevent the long-foreseeable strife and war in Yugoslavia and its possible extension elsewhere, it could and should have intervened long ago to defuse it by offering a solution to the debt crisis. If the West still wishes to forestall worse to come elsewhere in Eastern Europe and the ex–Soviet Union, timely economic measures, including *both* the controverted false alternatives of effective deepening and widening of the EC, would be necessary instead of more ideological platitudes and political jockeying, as I have argued under the title, "World Debt, the European Challenge and 1992" (Frank 1989). The renewed world economic recession of the early 1990s, however, renders any such economic measures more difficult and less likely—and the sham ideological and political substitutes less difficult and all the more likely.

Some questions do remain open but not necessarily to political and, much less, ideological answers. How will economic depression and political chaos in the East of Europe, including the former USSR, affect the West? Will they force more and faster European union or place obstacles in its way, or both? Will they and this process strengthen or weaken Europe against its rivals in the U.S. and Asia? Will the well-intentioned policies of European integration lead to further disunity in Europe—in a future political-economic irony?

By almost universal agreement politics, policy, and ideology are once again still supposed to be in command and offer the answers. Historical and contemporary evidence, however, as well as this chapter, suggest that, especially in a world economy in crisis, these factors and answers are really beyond sectarian ideological guidance, let alone national political control.

NOTE

1. This chapter was written in 1990 when the Soviet Union was collapsing. It anticipates many of the recent developments of the post-Soviet, post-communist

situation in Europe correctly, as events have borne out many of the predictions contained in the chapter.

An earlier version of this essay was published as "Economic Ironies in Europe: A World Economic Interpretation of East-West European Politics" in UNESCO's *International Social Science Journal* 131 (February 1992). The author is grateful to the editors (Barry Gills and Ronen Palan) and to Andrea Komlosy and Hannes Hofbauer for help with the present version.

9

The Reich Resurrected?
Continuity and Change in
German Expansion

Kees van der Pijl

This chapter draws on work in progress at the University of Amsterdam. The approach taken understands contemporary international relations as the arena in which social forces are engaged in the pursuit of profit, power, or social protection. States, as well as national, regional, or world economies, may be viewed as *structures* in which these social forces assume a particular, historic form and combine therefore into concrete configurations (see, for instance, Lipietz in this volume—*the Editors*).

While state structures may at times achieve an autonomy from these social forces to the extent that they effectively act as if constituting a single social force themselves, it is still inappropriate to regard states as independent social actors. This is true even more so in the twentieth century. The development of capital as the dominant organizing principle of social production and exchange has made state borders increasingly permeable.

From a transnational approach sensitive to the dynamics of capital, it is useful to distinguish between a liberal capitalist "heartland" and its immediate periphery. During the (prewar) phase of capitalist development in which the scale of operations of the dominant industries roughly coincided with the territorial dimensions of the major states, the "national interest" served as a frame of reference guiding and legitimating the rule of a capitalist class (what we term a "concept of control"). But this is no longer so. In the case of Germany, following the defeat of Nazi rule, the dominant classes regrouped under the aegis of the "Free World." The national interest became subordinated in the wider North Atlantic framework of capital accumulation and Cold War confrontation.

The question posed in this chapter is whether today, the Federal Republic of Germany (viewed as the postwar structure for bourgeois rule), following the absorption of the defunct German Democratic Republic, is breaking loose from its Atlantic moorings to fall back to a national interest frame for guiding the internationalization of capital under state auspices (the "Fourth Reich" thesis); or whether the West German social formation has been integrated into Western economic and normative structures to such an extent that the return to a German *Alleingang* is unlikely. The answer, necessarily provisional, is that a spill-back to prewar patterns of power politics is not to be expected given the degree of internationalization of capital and the autonomization of civil society from the state that is characteristic of advanced capitalist society. The authoritarian tradition, however, has continued to play a role and is clearly operative in handling the incorporation of the GDR. Also, where Germany makes its influence felt on the borderline between the integrated heartland and its periphery, particular continuities with the past may be detected that can be qualified as structural.

THE GLOBAL STRUCTURE OF INTERNATIONAL RELATIONS

To define the historic evolution of the German states and social formations, we must analyze the ways in which state and society have been articulated in the course of the development of the global political economy. (Neo)realism cannot help us here since it abstracts from social contexts of politics altogether (Keohane 1986). But the zonal differentiation of the world economy into center, semiperiphery, and periphery (Wallerstein 1974, 1983) in turn requires a new "critique of political economy" in the sense of an analysis that looks for historical and social processes underlying the apparent economic-structural logic.

The modern state/society configuration developed on the basis of the transformation of tributary agriculture into mobile wealth and the separation of people from their means of existence (*original accumulation*). As merchant capital on the fringes of agricultural society, and subsequently, as industrial capital organizing a productive and reproductive world of its own, mobile wealth becomes subject to a dynamic of capital accumulation and expansion into its environment. The conditions under which this process got underway, the corollary processes of class formation, and the crystallization of state forms right from the beginning have been mediated by international relations. England and France here represent the original ideal-types.

In sixteenth- and seventeenth-century England, original accumulation was accomplished largely by means of exploiting overseas mercantile opportunities. Over more than a century, the landed population was gradually "set free" and ushered into the emerging factory system that, in turn, supplied the export manufactures for English trade. The aristocracy and the bourgeoisie concluded what Lefebvre (1976: II, 35) calls "a historic compromise . . . , minimising the role of the state." In France, on the other hand, original accumulation was primarily accomplished by intensifying tributary patterns of exploitation of the peasants. Here "the *state* exercises its continuous pressure, economic . . . and extra-economic . . . , on the countryside" (ibid., 36; cf. Moore 1966).

It is my contention that international relations between England and France, both of which were rival centers that grew out of the feudal mosaic and each engaged in overseas colonization (North America, India), determined the structure of social development, not only for France but for the entire European continent as well. The English social formation generated the liberal pattern of accumulation and the "Lockean heartland" of the world economy, whereas the French social formation became the model for nationalist or "Hobbesian" patterns of accumulation.

After the Puritan Revolution terminated royal absolutism and was itself circumscribed by a constitutional monarchy, the English state could recede into the background. Creating the circumstances for capital to be reproduced in a context of regular accumulation implied subordinating the state to civil society. This was the society of property-owning citizens to which Locke addressed his recommendations.

Locke never contemplated a friendly or benevolent state: its task was to defend property rights, both against the propertyless and in the dealings of property owners among themselves. Otherwise it was supposed to leave society to its own workings, that is, regular capital accumulation ("regular" referring also to the Dickensian underworld of the early industrial revolution). Child labor for three-year-olds and up, and slavery overseas, were as much part of the recommendations of the *Two Treatises of Government* as were representative democracy, or the sanctity of property, contract, and individual civil rights (Lasslet 1965). "Hence the paradox," writes E. P. Thompson, "of a bloody penal code alongside a *liberal* and, at times, meticulous administration and interpretation of the laws" (Thompson 1968, 87).

In France, and henceforth in all industrializing continental countries, the social forces controlling the state could not allow civil society a comparable degree of freedom if they were simultaneously to hold their own in the confrontation with England. Here we see the first instance of what Gramsci (1971) later called (with reference to the French Revolution's effect on Central Europe) the phenomenon of *passive revolution*. In a passive revolution, the social group controlling the existing order seeks to anticipate and emulate the changes that have already transpired in the more advanced social formation it confronts in the international arena. It does so by absorbing the forces of a real revolution in the prevailing structures. Thus, the cardinals and Louis XIV manipulated modernizing elements such as the (Huguenot) Protestants rather than being swept away by them like Charles I. Meanwhile, Colbertism sought to achieve, by state intervention mainly, what the industrial revolution was accomplishing in the context of early liberalism (more or less) by the free interplay of social forces—once the Lockean state following the Glorious Revolution receded into the background.

In seventeenth-century France, "The impulse towards establishing the bases of a modern society, i.e., a unified state and even some of the habits of precision and obedience, came much more from the royal bureaucracy than from the bourgeoisie," writes Moore (1977, 57). A bourgeoisie, or a working class for that matter, remained undeveloped and dependent on state encouragement, protection, and interest articulation; while the very structure of rule remained tied to the state as such.

The English-speaking bourgeoisie settled overseas in the context of an initially informal empire (pushing the French out of North America and South Asia from the late eighteenth century on). Class formation that developed as a *transnational process* linking the British Isles to the settler colonies eventually organized in the Commonwealth. The Commonwealth, its historian writes, functioned "as a system of interlinked groups, organizations and societies within the greater community" which hence "was able to avoid in very large measure the growth of rigidities and compartmentalization in its political, economic and social structure" (Hall 1971, 106). Informal rule, flexibility in dealing with domestic and foreign challenges, and, underpinning it all, centrality in the global profit-distribution process based on the near-monopolization of global resources, henceforth became the hallmark of the Anglo-Saxon legacy in global politics. This process has to be understood in terms of its contradictions, that is, as a development marked by conflict and sharp departures from any apparently evolutionary pattern.

Thus, the settler colonies first broke away from Britain through a war of independence in the case of the United States, and by consensual autonomy for Canada, Australia, and New Zealand, while Britain continued to expand and annex elsewhere. Devolution and empire building came together again in South Africa on the threshold of the twentieth century (Gallagher and Robinson 1967). Only then, the return to the loose association of the Commonwealth (1911) began, and in the case of the United States, its gradual rise to hegemony over and within the English-speaking world. Meanwhile, the passive revolution in France, overtaken in 1789 by Jacobin revolution, resumed and, overtaken again in 1848 by the advance of the bourgeoisie, left the country midway between the English-speaking, Lockean heartland of the global political economy and the latecomer states who embarked on passive revolutions in the later nineteenth century. These states, of which Prussia/Germany is our interest here (the others were Japan and Italy), shared a number of characteristics with the earlier French state/society configuration that we may sum up as general characteristics of a *Hobbesian state*. We will briefly comment on each of these to define the structural traits of historic Germany that Atlantic integration began to replace after the war.

1. *The heterogeneity and relative backwardness of society is compensated for by a Hobbesian state.* The unequal development of the German

social formation failed to produce a civil society capable of self-regulation in the manner of English-speaking society. Hence the necessity for a strong state. The confrontation with the British Empire and, on the continent, with France and later Russia, contributed to the hypertrophy of the state by the workings of international relations. When Germany was unified in the Franco-Prussian War, the coexistence of an advanced industrial sector with a backward countryside produced the characteristics of the German social formation often mistaken for its progressiveness, such as "organized capitalism." Organized capitalism in reality reflected "an historical configuration of the development of underdevelopment within an already existing hegemonic world market" (Spohn and Bodemann 1989, 78–79).

2. The reverse side of the first item, *civil society is confiscated by the state.* The salience of the state in the process of passive revolution tends to turn the incipient classes of the bourgeois order into parts of the feudal-absolutist state, into estates of an ascriptive hierarchy. The identity between ruling and governing class in a single *state class* (Cox 1987; Fernández 1988), is one of the key phenomena of the Hobbesian state, from seventeenth-century France to twentieth-century state socialism. (State) corporatism, in the sense of a pattern of relations between the various incipient classes and sectors of the modern economy imposed by the state on society, constitutes the social counterpart to "organized capitalism."

Just as Protestantism had been an autonomous force in England (or Holland) but was subject to state manipulation in Richelieu's France, so the nineteenth-century labor movement was dealt with primarily in the context of civil society in the Anglo-Saxon world, but was repressed or manipulated (as in Bismarck's "Socialist Law" of 1878) in Prussia/Germany. Also, working-class strategy was state-oriented to begin with, epitomized by Lassalle and the Gotha program. Although manifesting a persistent tendency toward repression, the Hobbesian state may also pursue compensating social welfare policies. The interventionist state, Gramsci (1971, 262) writes, is "connected on the one hand with tendencies supporting protection and economic nationalism, and on the other with the attempt to force a particular state personnel . . . to take on the 'protection' of the working classes against the excesses of capitalism."

Here, too, the lineage of "enlightened authoritarianism" or "repressive welfare statism" of the Hobbesian state can be traced to the present day— in Germany, but sometimes paradoxically, also in the other historical concretizations of the *Leviathan,* including twentieth-century state socialism.

3. The rigidities inherent in the Hobbesian confiscation of society and its sharp demarcation from the Lockean heartland *foster economic and cultural autarky in relation to liberal capitalist society, interacting with war.* The failure to accommodate aspirations for structural change in the domestic context has informed the wars of the imperialist period as much as rivalries over spheres of influence did. The outbreak of revolutions in their

wake (from the Paris Commune to the Chinese Revolution) must also be understood in this light. The attack on Germany by Napoleon III that ushered in Prussia/Germany as the dominant European power; Prussia's own previous war of 1866; and its invasion of France in reaction to French aggression, all served to channel domestic discontent into aggression abroad (Alff 1976, 17).

World War I, too, from the perspective of the Central Powers that started it, reflected the incapacity to deal with domestic and international changes (Schmitt and Vedeler 1984, 18–20; Alff 1976, 17). War stifled reform and subsumed those informal transnational relations in civil society, such as existed, under national power politics, as in the case of Belgium and Germany (Alff 1976, 121) or France and Germany (Girault 1975, 215–217). All along, values alien to the Prussian/German "heroic" tradition were rejected, whether commercial (as associated with England or with the Jews) or sexual (vis à vis the French), providing a vicious undercurrent to relations with the more-developed foreign world.

INTEGRATING WEST GERMANY
INTO THE LOCKEAN HEARTLAND

From the above, it would follow that the integration of Germany into the "West," that is, into the Lockean universe originally developed around England and the British Commonwealth, and the United States, can be gauged from three relatively concrete developments: (1) the modernization of society and relaxation of state control; (2) the differentiation of the state class into ruling and governing class and the evolution of class relations in a context of self-regulating civil society; and (3) the insertion of German civil society into the Atlantic normative structure and into informal networks of transnational elite consultation. We will discuss each of these briefly with regard to the Federal Republic.

Structural Changes: Devolution of Authority

Following the collapse of Nazi rule, military occupation and division placed West Germany in the trust of the Atlantic victors and France. The failure of the July 20 plot in 1944—in which the East German landowner class played a key part—the loss of East Prussia, and the partition itself worked to enhance the power of that part—of the country where the ideas of the French Revolution had had their greatest impact.

The newly established Christian Democratic Union (CDU) in this phase became the medium by which the devolution of authority from a Hobbesian Leviathan to a less-authoritarian state was to be achieved. Built around a small core of Catholic postwar planners in Rhineland and Westphalia who, on the basis of traditional adversity to Prussian methods, advocated rule by class compromise, the incipient CDU was soon reinforced by liberal economists like Erhard. Still, the hand of the occupation authorities had to help the authors of the federal constitution to block attempts by the Rhine/Ruhr interests to resurrect a prewar, authoritarian-type of state (Spohn and Bodemann 1989, 94).

Adenauer, who concentrated power in the chancellor's office with its circle of advisers and was until 1955 his own minister of foreign affairs, took the Federal Republic halfway to the Lockean pattern. As a German political scientist puts it, the CDU under its first chancellor

adapted the political thinking of the older conservatism (which was state-oriented and, in principle, remote from or even hostile to political parties) to the emerging "late capitalist" class society of a new type . . . ,

thus guiding the German upper classes

one-half to three-quarters of a step away from "German exceptionalism" into the direction of the Western parliamentary systems, without copying their political model *completely* (Leggewie 1989, 299).

Around the mid-1950s, this process was clearly interrupted. With the relative contraction of American involvement, conservative trends resurfaced in Europe. Anglo-French neoimperialism, culminating at Suez, was matched by a resurgence of the Hobbesian legacy in the Federal Republic. In 1956, a trend toward reasserting German sovereignty also in military matters (since 1955, in the context of NATO) spilled over to the question of German access to nuclear weapons under the new Minister of Defense, Franz-Josef Strauss (Hellema 1984, 91–93).

When the Liberals lost their government positions in the same period, and the CDU, with Strauss's CSU in Bavaria (plus a small nationalist party), formed a government on their own in 1957, it looked for a time as if the CDU-CSU, like its Italian counterpart or the Japanese LDP, would become a monopolistic state party. The danger of returning to a Hobbesian pattern was averted, however, first by a new U.S. Atlantic "offensive" launched under Kennedy, which mobilized the outward-looking forces in the West German and European class structure; and second, by the first postwar recession that followed this episode, which ushered in the "Grand Coalition" of CDU and SPD formed in 1966 (Abendroth 1981, 337).

Let us here briefly note that the German constitution, by prescribing a federal format to the new state, was an important departure from traditional authoritarianism. It took almost two decades before federalism was secure, however. Initially, the absence of a developed, bourgeois political culture transpired in the political role of the constitution represented by the obligation of political parties to constitutionality (*Verfassungstreuepflicht*, Art. 21). On this basis the Communist party KPD could be outlawed in 1956 (Ladeur 1981, 118–119). The Constitutional Court also had to defend federalism when the government sought to recapture authority in matters of education by appealing to Hitler's Concordat with the Vatican (*Reichskonkordaturteil* 1957).

Here, too, the Atlantic opening of the early sixties and the political opening through the Grand Coalition following it fostered a socialization of constitutional practice away from the Hobbesian pattern. In the 1960s, a degree of self-regulation of society was introduced by allowing the constitution to be interpreted by a process of dynamic bargaining. Not a supposed "will" of the constitution was to be discovered, but a concretization of its underlying (but not static) basic values, *Grundwerte*, in the light of the prevailing social consensus. Legal memoranda (*Gutachten*) served the purpose of attuning court policy with a shifting interpretation of normalcy (Ladeur 1981, 126–127).

The Emancipation of Civil Society from the State

As indicated, the termination of the trend to one-party rule cannot be understood if not placed in the broader North Atlantic context. The last gasp of Adenauer-style CDU rule was the treaty with France of January 1962, one week after the French veto on British EEC membership. Within a few months, important representatives of the German capitalist class made vocal their protest over Adenauer's endorsement of Gaullist "Euronationalism," signaling their preference for Atlantic partnership (Bowie 1963, 61).

Already in 1957, the future President Kennedy in a seminal article in *Foreign Affairs* had written that "American policy [had] let itself be lashed too tightly to a single German government and party." Rather, the U.S. should look more to the rising SPD, and Kennedy warned against a conservative equation of the SPD with the GDR, current in U.S. government circles. "In all of Europe," Kennedy wrote, "a new generation is coming to power, and it is dangerous to become alienated from them" (Kennedy 1957, 50).

Willy Brandt would become the standard-bearer of this new generation in West German politics. Nicknamed the "leader of the American faction" from his early days in Berlin onward (Brandt 1990, 29), Brandt was instrumental in transforming his party in line with the deradicalization consummated in most Northern European Socialist parties between 1958 and 1962. The counterpoint to stagnant CDU rule, the Bad Godesberg program, marked the emancipation of the rising "cadre class" of managers and technicians (Bihr 1989) from the authoritarian patterns of German "organized capitalism," and their orientation to the particular mixture of state intervention and liberalism, or *corporate liberalism*, which guided postwar Euro-Atlantic integration. The Erhard interlude of 1963 to 1966, reflecting the free-trade aspect of the actual Kennedy period rather than the underlying social changes the future president had pointed to in 1957, was terminated in 1966 by the Grand Coalition of CDU and SPD. Brandt in the ensuing years grafted Kennedy's imaginative idealism and dynamic, Wilsonian approach to the contest with socialism onto the ambition to restore Germany's centrality in Europe. Therefore, he should not be seen as representing the comprador element in the German class structure, but rather in relation to its most self-conscious, forward-looking elements. Abandoning the sterile power realism informing the Hallstein doctrine, Brandt aimed at shifting the terrain of struggle with Soviet socialism from the interstate level to the level of rival social models competing peacefully. The *Ostpolitik*, while departing from the 1950s Cold War context by its underlying strategy of "change through rapprochement," was a way of attuning the ambitions of German capital to the conduct of what Gramsci would call a "war of position" against Soviet influence in Eastern Europe. The attraction posed by an autonomous, civil Western Europe rather than a Europe subordinated to the U.S. in the Cold War, in Brandt's view, was decisive. His appreciation of De Gaulle as a "European" was based on this equation (Brandt 1990, 67; Braunmühl 1973, 90).

The backdrop to these shifts in policy were the autonomization of the capitalist class from the state, the rise of the technical and managerial cadre element in production, and the tendential subordination of the West German state to a Euro-Atlantic civil society and its informal networks of consultative, planning, and quasi-state structures. In this context, the ruling class could assume a more independent and flexible position while broadening its social base. Paradoxically, Brandt's rise to power was accompanied by the enhanced salience of the representatives of German capital in government. As a German business journal commented at the time, "The entry of the managerial elite into the Bonn power apparatus only began when the Social Democrats assumed power" (quoted in Simon 1976, 171). Access to state power acquired a new quality, now that "the state has increasingly turned into a mediator between the various industrial interests, in contrast to its previous initiating and controlling functions" (Spohn and Bodemann 1989, 87).

The rise of the managerial and technical element from the late 1950s on was accompanied by a steady decline of the old middle class of self-employed, a stratum often named a mainstay of German authoritarianism in the past. In a comparative study covering the EC and North American countries, Thomas Hagelstange notes that the self-employed, nonemployer middle class in the West German social structure declined from a share of 15 to 5. 8 percent between 1961 and 1982, while the independent employers declined from 12. 6 in 1960 to 8. 6 in 1982 (Hagelstange 1988, 212).

Thus, the Federal Republic almost caught up with the U.S. and the U.K. in terms of eliminating class structures typical of early capitalist development (ibid.; and Spohn and Bodemann 1989, 84, Table 4. 1, and 85, Table 4. 2).

Much less than in the case of the English-speaking heartland or the other EC countries, newly available labor power was absorbed by the service sector. With the highest share of active people engaged in the secondary sector (Hagelstange 1988, 216), the overall social structure of West Germany is highly skewed to an industrial profile setting it apart from the "financial" profile of the other major capitalist states. This is also corroborated by the pattern of profit distribution among functional fractions of capital, as can be gauged from Table 9.1.

Table 9.1   Cash Flow[a] of Financial Corporations as a Percentage of Cash Flow of Non-Financial Corporations. Germany versus U.K./U.S.A. and Japan

Year	West Germany	U.S.A.	U.K.	Japan
1972	34	81	46	63
1980	55	118	146	107
1988	49[b]	128	112[b]	138

Source: OECD, *National Accounts 1972–1984* (Paris) 1986, Vol. II, country tables; *National Accounts 1976–1988*.
a. Cash flow defined as total current receipts.
b. 1987.

It is this prominence of industrial capital and employment that has continued to set West German society apart from the other North Atlantic countries. Also, the centrality to German capital of capital-labor compromise in production has tended to soften the impact of neoliberalism compared to the remaining Atlantic heartland (Van der Wurff 1993). Here the corporatist tradition interacts with functional prequisities of an industrial export economy. But like the capitalist and cadre classes, the trade unions have effectively emancipated themselves from state tutelage. The massive September 1969 strike may be seen as the breaking point terminating "about two decades of centrally directed and controlled trade union activities" set off by the self-organization of the strikers (Müller-Jentsch 1979, 42).

Transnational Integration and Normative Structure

Germany's position as a latecomer rival to established Anglo-Saxon liberal imperialism long condemned its bankers and industrialists to either inscribe their strategies for capital internationalization into Germany's war plans (Fischer 1984; Opitz 1977) or expand surreptitiously, by means of cloaking and other clandestine techniques (Aalders and Wiebes 1990). After World War II, the West German economy initially developed as an "over-industrialized" exporter of mainly investment goods, in a bilateral constellation with "under-industrialized" France (Schlupp 1979, 19).

The Grand Coalition presided over West Germany's transition to Keynesianism as well as over the rapid internationalization of its economy belatedly geared to mass production (Piore and Sabel 1984, 147–149, 185, Table 7.2; see also Huffschmid 1975). In spite of this time lag and an initial lack of overall foreign investment strategy, German capital by the mid-1980s was established as one pole of the "Triad" of the global political economy and well integrated into the world structure of capital interpenetration (Ohmae 1985; Tolchin and Tolchin 1989).

In terms of normative structure, there was a corresponding shift in attitudes. "Within the broader strata of the capitalist class, in the middle classes and the *Bürgertum*, Christian-conservative and liberal-democratic attitudes began to be articulated. These blocked any return to the old authoritarian-conservative pattern of class formation" (Spohn and Bodemann 1989, 95). In general, the German bourgeoisie accommodated easily to the Christian-social, consensual political culture of the emerging mass consumer society (Leggewie 1989, 299). The outlawing of the KPD in 1956 and the Godesberg transition of the SPD in 1959 had the effect of closing the channels of articulating working-class militancy, thus reinforcing the "center" of politics.

This center was capable of absorbing the shock of the workers' and students' movement of the late 1960s, which contributed so decisively to bringing the SPD into the forefront as the medium of social equilibration, and in this sense helped Brandt to power. Although Brandt with his 1972 *Berufsverbote* decree reproduced the tradition of having the state assume a role in class struggles, it must also be noted that in the CDU, the advocates of a hard-line toward the extraparliamentary opposition never won the upper hand. The moderate approach of Helmut Kohl, who in the early 1970s transformed the CDU from a party of notables into a mass party, all along prevailed over the revanchist line favored by many of the newly won adherents after 1969, who wanted a militant opposition to the *Ostpolitik* and the Brandt reforms. It fell to Strauss and his CSU, as well as the neo-Nazi NPD, to accommodate this sentiment, thus condemning it to a minority role ultimately confirmed in Strauss's defeat as the CDU/CSU chancellor candidate in the 1980 general elections.

Authoritarian nationalism more particularly seems to have ceded to the *calculating attitude toward the state* that is typical of the Lockean configuration of state and civil society (Charlier 1990, 183), which may be summarized by the dictum, "Don't ask what you can do for your country but what your country can do for you." In hindsight, the social upheavals of the 1960s may paradoxically have represented the watershed in this development toward a Lockean political culture.

The actual integration of German economic statesmen into transnational consultative and policy-planning networks was lagging as long as German capital expanded only under state auspices or undercover. With North Atlantic integration, this has changed, although a "fractional" difference seems to persist. Historically, the German capitalist class can be divided into a fraction committed to head-on rivalry with Anglo-Saxon capital, and a usually less-powerful fraction willing to settle for the role of junior partner. Thus, in the 1920s and 1930s, a loose coalition of the Dresdner Bank (with the subsequently absorbed Danat Bank), Thyssen steel, and AEG, on the coattails of U.S. ascendancy in world politics, aligned into an "American fraction," partly because of the many American participations in these corporations as well. The Deutsche Bank (including the subsequently absorbed Diskontogesellschaft) connected a group composed of IG Farben and Siemens, both strongholds of the independent orientation, and a number of steel and engineering companies (Mannesmann, Hoesch, Haniel, Klöckner). Between and within the two combinations there were many overlaps and contradictions. In IG Farben, for instance, both the more-enlightened Middle European and the ultranationalist tendency were present (Gossweiler 1975; Stegmann 1976).

Yet after World War II, this tendential dividing line between a fraction supporting the primacy of the U.S. (Dresdner Bank, AEG, Thyssen) and a tendency preferring to deal with the United States on a more equal basis (the Deutsche Bank group) remained operative. The 1954 "Declaration of Atlantic Unity" in Germany was an initiative of Kurt Birrenbach of Thyssen, and many other examples could be mentioned also, in terms of geographical spread of foreign affiliates. The historical dimension is pertinent here, too, in the sense of the earlier forms of capital (like merchant capital) and industry (like textiles) often gravitating to the Dresdner Bank coalition, and the industries that arrived on the scene later—"high-tech" in their own days—often in the Deutsche Bank orbit (Van der Pijl 1984, 162–163, 266–267). Internally, the combinations remained interlocked around these two centers, also when in the course of the 1970s, the two banks became more central in the international network of banks and industry: Dresdner Bank with AEG, Thyssen, Volkswagen, and Metallgesellschaft; Deutsche Bank with Hoesch, BASF, Siemens, and Bosch (Fennema 1982, 146 and passim).

Typically, we find Thyssen as a major foreign player in U.S. politics (through the political action committee of its subsidiary, Budd Co., cf. Tolchin and Tolchin 1989, 269). But the Dresdner Bank combination also was most visibly present in transnational bodies such as the Bilderberg Conferences or the Trilateral Commission. In this latter, most prestigious of transnational private elite groups (Gill 1991), the Dresdner Bank network clearly dominated the scene. This is shown in Table 9.2.

Table 9.2   German Company–Related Membership of the Trilateral Commission, 1973–1980, Dresdner Bank Network/Other

Dresdner Bank Network	
K. Birrenbach	(Thyssen)
H. G. Sohl	(Thyssen, Dresdner Bank)
H. K. Jannott	(Münch. Rückversicherung, Dresdner Bank)
O. Wolff v. Amerongen	(Otto Wolff, Exxon)
L. Huber	(Bayerische Landesbank Girozentrale)
Count Lambsdorff	(Victoria Lebensversich)
Other/Unidentified	
F. Dietz and H. Hartwig	(German Association of Wholesale and Foreign Trade)
A. Münchmeyer	(Bank Schröder, Münchmeyer, Hengst)
F. A. Neuman	(Neuman Eschweiler metal mnf.)

Sources: Names in Sklar 1980, 121–122; links in Fennema 1982, 146; Ziegler et al., 1985, 108)

In the course of the 1980s, the already-stronger Deutsche Bank further outdistanced the competition. In 1985, its profits were equal to those of the Dresdner and third-ranking Commerzbank combined, while strategic acquisitions dramatically reinforced the bank's international position, such as the takeover of Morgan Grenfell that turned the Deutsche Bank by one stroke into one of the decisive players in the City of London (*Financial Times*, 20 November 1986; F. Clairmonte in *Le Monde Diplomatique*, April 1990, 15). The industrial interests of the Deutsche Bank group also surged ahead. The Deutsche Bank's key industrial holding, the 29 percent-owned Daimler group, in the 1980s branched out into aerospace and electronics. This included the acquisition of AEG, traditionally linked to the Dresdner Bank (*Newsweek*, 28 October 1985). In 1986, Deutsche Bank took over Libya's share in Fiat, making it the second-largest shareholder after Agnelli.

If we may judge from the decline of forces historically associated with the transnational Atlantic elite network, and the further rise of the Deutsche Bank in the center of German economic sovereignty, a trend toward relative disengagement seems underway. Objectively, the assassination of two of the more Western-oriented personalities in the Deutsche Bank group, the bank's CEO, Alfred Herrhausen, and Detlev Rohwedder, CEO of Hoesch, reinforced this trend. Both men had played a key role in the reunification of Germany: Herrhausen as Kohl's adviser and Rohwedder as president of the *Treuhandanstalt* (charged with privatizing the GDR economy).

When the latest Bilderberg conference was held in La Toja in Spain in May 1989, only four German participants were present amidst the cream of the Atlantic capitalist class and European royalty—two parliamentarians, journalist Theo Sommer, and Otto Wolff von Amerongen—although the agenda included discussion of a roll-back strategy in Eastern Europe in which German capital, again with the Deutsche Bank up front, is the main player economically (Bilderberg 1989).

The direct presence of German economic statesmen in Moscow and other East European capitals apparently has drastically reduced the need for consultation with the Western partners on these matters, even among the traditional Atlanticist elements in the German ruling class.

This brings us to the final part of our chapter, the question of whether —following the eclipse of German authoritarianism, the emancipation of civil society from the state, and the apparent integration into Western society—a new, reunified Germany will remain faithful to its new Lockean identity.

CONTRADICTIONS OF GERMAN MODERNITY

In this concluding section, we will concentrate on two areas in which, in our view, the heritage of the Hobbesian relation between state and society is still or again pertinent in the new Germany. One is the authoritarian handling of dissent by the state, and the potential "Europeanization" of this German approach; the other is the continuing interplay between foreign economic expansion and the projection of state power abroad. The factor identified above, however, as the mediating one between the dimensions of authoritarianism and aggressive foreign policy—the relation of civil society to the state—has evolved toward a Lockean pattern. This would imply that these regressive tendencies *can* be challenged and remedied within the German context.

Resurgent Authoritarianism

In 1968, the emancipation of civil society from the state and of the Federal Republic from allied occupation obtained a counterpoint in the Emergency Laws (*Notstandgesetze*) enacted by the Grand Coalition. By itself, the preparation for a state of emergency reflected not an ingrained authoritarianism of German society but the need to provide the state with the means to intervene if the capacity of self-regulating civil society to maintain bourgeois rule would fail—providing hegemony with "the armour of coercion" (Gramsci 1971, 263). The introduction of *Berufsverbote* legislation of 1972, however, set in motion a creeping process of enhancing state security's freedom of maneuver and a corresponding encroachment on civil rights (Mayer 1979, 390).

Brandt, consistently under fire for supposed leniency to radicalism, in 1974 was ousted by secret-service machinations (Brandt 1990, 312–313) and replaced by his right-wing rival in the party, Helmut Schmidt. Terrorism by RAF urban guerrillas and a continuous increase of state security powers fueled a neoconservative appreciation that instead of Brandt's adage of "risking *more* democracy," a *reduction* of democratic rights by reinforcing state prerogatives was in order, a recommendation also made in a 1975 report of the Trilateral Commission in response to a supposed "crisis of governability" (Gill 1991, 199). Following the assassination of employers' chief Hanns Martin Schleyer and the German raid to end the hijack of a Lufthansa plane at the Mogadishu airport in autumn 1977, SPD Minister of Justice Vogel affirmed that

> our people have had in these weeks a new and stronger feeling about the relation of a single individual toward the state. . . . The people, especially younger people, . . . learned that the state, in order to uphold its functions and protect life, may also demand services and sacrifices (Interview in *Newsweek,* 21 November 1977).

Although actual terrorism rapidly subsided and the RAF was defeated, the repressive apparatus continued to operate as a means of intimidation and stifling dissent. Under paragraph 129a of the West German Penal Code, the *Bundeskriminalamt* (BKA), by reference to suspected membership of a terrorist organization, penetrates leftist circles in order to map their membership into a "sociogram of resistance." Copying addresses from the notebooks of lawyers has become routine. This particular investigative purpose, rather than the actual application of justice, has characterized BKA activity in the Federal Republic. From 1982 to 1987, only 5 to 10 percent of the cases under paragraph 129a were concluded by a final verdict (guilty or not guilty), compared to 44 percent of regular criminal cases. In the 1970s, 70 percent of the cases under paragraph 129a were based not on actual terrorist acts, but on "support," which usually meant having made particular statements—a trend that in the 1980s was even reinforced (Gössner 1989, 403–404).

All along, the German response to the challenge of the left was accompanied by a "European" dimension. The Berne Club of heads of security services in 1971; an informal working party of the heads of antiterror services from the EC countries, plus Austria and Switzerland, in 1974; and, at a later date, the Vienna Club of ministers of internal affairs of the Federal Republic, Austria, Switzerland, France, and Italy, provided an infrastructure to a surveillance system on a European scale (Klerks 1989, 171). Interpol, in the 1970s, also became active in matters concerning terrorism and set up a committee on crimes of violence in 1983, headed by a representative of the Pinochet regime in Chile. He was succeeded by the then-head of the BKA, Boge, later in the decade. Interpol channels were used for the aggressive surveillance of the left by German police, which extended to obtaining information on family members of RAF witch-hunt victims abroad (ibid., 162–163).

In 1976, the EC inaugurated the so-called TREVI discussions, initially at top civil-servant level and subsequently upgraded to ministerial level, with a data bank for surveillance of suspected persons and organizations. The EC in the same year introduced the practice of screening its seven thousand civil servants in Brussels on possible Communist links (Kade 1980, 128). In 1986, frequency of the TREVI meetings was intensified, and non-EC, NATO countries (U.S., Canada, Norway, Turkey) and neutral states (Sweden, Yugoslavia, Morocco) also participated, thus connecting the European intelligence network to the long-standing *UKUSA* network of the U.S., Britain, Canada, Australia, and New Zealand (Richelson and Ball 1990). At the TREVI conference in London, also in 1986, it was decided that persons "supporting terrorism" would henceforth be included as a TREVI area of concern (Klerks 1989, 166–167). This has to be considered an extension of West German practice to the European level and constitutes an important encroachment of civil rights, especially in light of the 1977 European Convention on the Suppression of Terrorism, which largely suspends the rule that no one can be extradited on account of a political offense. A strict definition of terrorism is lacking in this treaty, which opens the way to generalizing the West German idea that all political actions outside parliamentary channels are terrorist acts, including "support for terrorism." The infrastructure of police surveillance was given its most recent extension when, in 1985, the Schengen Agreement was concluded between West Germany, France, and the Benelux countries. Ratification of this contested treaty was caught up in the turmoil of Eastern European events, however, and its application cannot be as yet be evaluated (Klerks 1989, 175, 179).

The full weight of the West German surveillance apparatus landed on the defunct GDR once it was clear that the Communist leadership abandoned by the USSR was not planning to resort to force. In fact, strong elements in the GDR Ministry for State Security (MfS, popularly abbreviated to *Stasi*) had made a belated attempt to align the GDR with a reformism like Gorbachev's. Following reunification, GDR state-security archives were placed under a West German commission and access to them granted to the West German intelligence services and the counterespionage service, *Bundesnachrichtendienst* (BND). Some East German politicians (De Maizière, Böhme) were forced out of politics by press leaks concerning former Stasi association, but the files on some key personalities with recorded contacts in Western intelligence circles miraculously disappeared (*De Volkskrant*, 28 November 1991; 8 February 1992; *Manifest* 13 February 1992).

The use of the Stasi connection (which was not a simple matter and often concerned people who, by voluntarily informing the Stasi on their own activities, sought to prevent *being* informed on) to eradicate anything reminiscent of the former GDR—be it in the universities, in sports, or elsewhere—and to harass the Communist party–turned–PDS is continuing at the time of this writing. On a different level, the case against former Stasi minister, Erich Mielke, charged with having been involved in the killing of two policemen in street fighting in *1931*, for which Gestapo files must provide the evidence, testifies to the fragility of the state of law in Germany.

It may well be that the frontal attack on the GDR legacy has exacerbated the state of anomie among the young for which violence against foreigners provides an outlet; at any rate, if German prosecutors and judges proceed to build their cases on evidence from the near–civil war preceding the Nazi seizure of power and on actual Nazi documents, the resurgence of neo-Nazism among segments of German youth should not come as a surprise.

To this must be added the existence of right-wing and ultraright, transnational networks providing infrastructure to the surge of neo-Nazi or militant conservative forces. These networks often interlock with the international intelligence and antiterror structures referred to above. Thus, the militant conservative *Pinay Circle* brought together the late Franz-Josef Strauss and men like Alexandre de Marenches of the French counterespionage service, SDECE (which collaborated with the BND in obtaining information on Brandt); former CIA head and architect of the *Gladio* network, William Colby; as well as South African and Swiss secret service chiefs and assorted right-wing politicians. The Gladio network in West Germany was a BND operation (Müller 1991; *Lobster* 17, November 1988, 14–15; Brandt 1990, 326). Actual neo-Nazi connections also show a pronounced link to France, connecting the colonial rightists of Algérie Française into the Latin American network of old German Nazis protected by the CIA (*Lobster* 12, Autumn 1986, 11–12). Recent ideological influences such as Alain de Benoist's "Gramscian" construction of an integral neo-Nazi doctrine have also found their way from France to West Germany (De Benoist 1983).

On the whole, the German response to the students' and workers' movement of the 1960s and early 1970s has assumed formidable proportions in which lingering Nazi and militant conservative trends have been allowed to proliferate and surface in the vastly expanded repressive apparatus. Although strong bulwarks of genuine liberalism persist, the malign neglect with which West Germans regard the humiliation of the East is not encouraging.

Two Orientations in German Expansion

The integration of West Germany into the Lockean heartland of developed capitalism has allowed German capital to expand into the integrated zone freely. Outside this zone, however, the aspect of undercover penetration persists, and so does economic expansion by the projection of state power.

The effects of integration are clearly visible in the case of Spain. Whereas in the 1930s, German economic expansion (aimed in particular at critical raw-material deposits) still was part of Nazi involvement in the Spanish Civil War (Bougoüin and Lenoir 1938), in the early 1970s German capital was part of the general inflow of foreign capital into both the Spanish and Portuguese economies. The emancipation of civil society from the state in West Germany and, at a distance of several decades, in the Iberian countries, indeed was a continuous process in which social democracy played a vanguard role.

Upon his ouster from the chancellorship in 1974, Willy Brandt assumed the key role in this process. First, the attempt by the French Socialists to woo the South European Socialists—supposedly to the left of the North European "Social Democrats,"—away from their West German sponsors in 1975–1976, was defeated by the SPD. In April 1976, common working groups of the PS and the SPD were formed on issues such as European policy, economic and social policy, and development policy. This programmatic cooperation not only undermined the *Programme Commun* of the PS with the French Communists, but also put out potentially anti-German brushfires such as the formation of a committee of French Socialists concerned with "civil rights in the Federal Republic" (Günsche and Lantermann 1977, 145).

With German and French capital taking turns as second-largest investor in Portugal and Spain in the 1970s (behind the U.S., Deubner 1982, 64–65), more than mere prestige was involved in deciding who would be the privileged interlocutor of the ascendant Iberian Social Democrats. In fact, the SPD had effectively groomed the new South European leadership already from 1973–1974 onwards (Bourdin 1979, 130). Both Gonzales and Soares became Brandt's lieutenants in the revamped Socialist International, of which Brandt assumed the presidency in 1976. These links complemented the penetration by German capital. The takeover of SEAT by Volkswagen between 1986 and 1990 (with a 2.7 billion–mark subsidy by the Gonzales government) was the crowning achievement (*NRC-Handelsblad*, 22 February 1986). Since the SPD's Friedrich Ebert Foundation, through which support for sister parties is channeled abroad, is 80 percent government-funded, and the Spanish Socialist leadership is very close to the most dynamic segments of the business community (Holman 1989, 98), the number of mediating links between the state and private interests is still surprisingly low. Yet the bottom line is that German capital and Spanish and German social democracy all have become emancipated from state control and operate in the context of a transnational civil society, which in the 1970s had come to include all Mediterranean European countries (Holman 1987).

An entirely different pattern prevails in German activities outside the Lockean heartland. Here the tradition of cloaking and undercover penetration lingers on. This was the case in German involvement in the nuclear program of South Africa, but also in various other weapons' development programs in Africa. The OTRAG missile firm, with a 6 million–mark subsidy from the Brandt government, leased a province in northeast Shaba in Zaïre to build cheap missiles for potential Third World clients. To prevent a planned law against the export of missile components from Germany, it set up a subsidiary in France (*Le Monde*, 5 July 1978). The Imhausen Chemie affair, in which Germany was accused by U.S. journalists—amidst intense transatlantic rivalries in the trade field—of building a Libyan gas warfare production site at Rabta, was a sign of U.S. dissatisfaction with Germany's strategy in Europe and its continuing involvement in weapons development on foreign soil.

But whereas in the example of Spain, the imbrication of economic expansion with German diplomacy has been abandoned for structural reasons, in Eastern Europe the situation is still compromised by the legacy of violent German expansion. Against the backdrop of a massive drive of German capital into the disintegrating world of state socialism (L. Carroué in *Le Monde Diplomatique*, January 1992, 12–13), the case of Yugoslavia is particularly disconcerting.

In Yugoslavia, German expansion in the 1930s also was linked with taking sides in a civil war (Sohn–Rethel 1975, 126). But unlike Spain, Yugoslavia has not meanwhile been integrated into the Lockean heartland, at least not intact. As in the 1930s, Serbian nationalism has exacerbated differences between the nationalities, but German support for Croatian separatism has been a critical factor in their explosion. Milovan Djilas, upon the declaration of independence by Slovenia and Croatia, accused Austria and Germany of kindling civil war (interview in *De Volkskrant*, 11 July 1991). The two republics represent the most modern, export-oriented parts of Yugoslavia, and their ambition is obviously to be integrated into a larger West European whole (Palan 1991, 120). This ambition was reciprocated by Austria, where national politicians openly contemplated the reincorporation of Slovenia (until 1918, part, like Croatia, of the Dual Monarchy), and by West Germany. The West German press, notably the business-oriented *Frankfurter Allgemeine*, continuously harped on support for Slovenian and Croatian independence and declared Serbia "outside civilization" when federal troops restored control of the Yugoslav-Italian border upon the unilateral secession (Reuter et al. 1991). Meanwhile, the German and Croatian governments established a direct link through top aides to Chancellor Kohl and President Tudjman in August 1991 (Heinrich 1991, 1450).

Even apart from arms and aid pouring into Croatia (also through Hungary), this may have encouraged the Croatian leadership to defy federal authorities where it otherwise would have had to negotiate. With civil war raging, Germany then proceeded to break the EC ranks and openly declared support for Slovenian and Croatian secession (*De Volkskrant*, 24 December 1991). Meanwhile, the EC (which still in July censured German support for secession) has let itself be swayed 180 degrees and has invited all Yugoslav republics to apply for EC recognition. This policy has not only contributed to the tragic events in Bosnia-Herzegovina and may ignite further tension in Macedonia, but is pregnant with the gravest consequences for the entire Balkan region.

Germany's integration into the Lockean heartland must be considered secure even if the Atlantic bond is being loosened in the process of German emancipation from postwar Allied tutelage. The emancipation of civil society from the state must be judged as irreversible, but this is not the same as democracy. The incorporation of the former GDR illustrates that the two may even be each other's opposites. Yet whatever regressive and explosive tendencies may surface in the current restoration of German sovereign power in Europe, the new configuration of state and society makes it possible to combat these in the context of a democratic struggle.

NOTE

An earlier version of this chapter was presented at meetings in Amsterdam, Sheffield, and Newcastle between October and December 1990. I owe a debt to participants in these discussions, especially to Professor Kurt Tudyka. I also thank an anonymous reviewer for critical comments.

10

Swedish Social Democracy and the World Market

Lawrence Wilde

For decades the Swedish model of welfare corporatism provided full employment, comprehensive social provision, and nationally agreed-upon wage settlements—it was widely regarded as the pinnacle of social-democratic achievement. The Swedish Social Democratic party (SAP) was in government for all but six years between 1932 and 1991, and even when a center-right coalition assumed governmental power, from 1976 to 1982, the social-democratic institutions of society were left untouched. While the rest of the capitalist world accepted mass unemployment as a necessary tool of economic management in the 1980s, Sweden maintained the best trade-off between unemployment and inflation of all the European states (*The Economist,* September 21–27, 1991), and its living standards were among the highest in the world. It gave the appearance of holding a position of relative autonomy in the world economy for much of the 1980s, preserving many of its corporatist processes and defying the trend toward laissez-faire economic policies. In September 1991, however, after two years of economic difficulties, the SAP lost the general election and was replaced in government by a right-wing bloc led by Carl Bildt, leader of the Conservatives. Less than 38 percent of the vote went to the SAP, its lowest level of support since 1928. The new government pledged to drive down public expenditure and greatly reduce state intervention in the economy. Mass unemployment returned for the first time since the 1930s and very substantial public-spending cuts were announced in September 1992 (*The Economist,* September 26–October 2, 1992) and January 1993 (McIvor, 1993). It appears that the strongest social democracy in the world has succumbed to the inexorable logic of the capitalist world market.

When recent political and economic developments are considered, it is hard to believe that little over a decade ago a number of writers argued that the Swedish model of welfare capitalism provided a sound basis for the development of full-fledged socialism. Their arguments resurrected the Marxist tradition of "gradual transformation" associated with the Second

189

International and in particular with Karl Kautsky. They centered largely on the significance of the wage-earner funds scheme in gradually transferring the ownership of the means of production to the workers. In Sweden, it was argued, a combination of factors made possible a peaceful transformation to socialism. In support of this, Walter Korpi supplied detailed empirical research findings on the organization and attitudes of the Swedish working class in *The Working Class Under Welfare Capitalism* (1978) and *The Democratic Class Struggle* (1983), and several large-scale empirical studies were also cited in *Beyond Welfare Capitalism* (1981) by Ulf Himmelstrand, Goran Ahrne, Leif Lundberg, and Lars Lundberg. The transitional potential of Sweden was also enthusiastically espoused in *The Transition from Capitalism to Socialism* (1979) by the American socialist John Stephens. Why were these powerful arguments rendered chimerical? This chapter will focus on three interrelated factors that combined to undermine the Swedish model: the breakdown of class solidarity, the economic and political pressures on the interventionist state, and, above all, developments in the world economy. This last point is decisive because the first two factors are explicable only in relation to it, and it is this power that must be confronted in any attempt to restore the social-democratic goals of full employment and social security, let alone to advance the proposition of the transition to socialism.

THE SWEDISH MODEL

The SAP first entered government in 1932 after winning over 40 percent of the vote. The continued strength of electoral support, the high level of unionization and party membership, and the fragmentation of the right helped the Social Democrats to fashion a society committed to the welfare of all its citizens and the prosperity of its industries, seeing the goals of efficiency and equality as complementary rather than contradictory (Milner 1989). The foundations of the corporatist model were laid in the 1938 Saltsjobaden agreement between the blue-collar labor organization (the LO) and the employers' Federation of Swedish Industries (the SAF). The state played a guiding role, claiming the power to steer the economy while at the same time leaving industry in private ownership. If the British Labor Government of 1945 nationalized but did not plan, the Swedish Social Democrats built a consensus on planning without nationalization.

The economic strategy on which the success story of the 1960s and 1970s was based was designed by two labor economists, Gosta Rehn and Rudolf Meidner. Profits were to be squeezed by high wage settlements gained through collective bargaining, and the likelihood of high inflation was to be averted by high indirect taxes to dampen down demand and finance a high level of social provision. "Solidaristic bargaining" ensured that all workers received commensurate increases, which would put small or relatively inefficient firms under great pressure. In order to combat the potential increase in unemployment, an active labor-market policy was adopted, including retraining programs and other attempts to increase mobility of labor, as well as job-creation schemes (Dahlberg and Tuijman, 1991). As well as helping to promote an affluent and egalitarian society, the Social Democrats encouraged the most efficient sectors of Swedish industry to innovate and expand. The success of the model was greatly aided by the long postwar boom and the low level of defense expenditure, which flowed from the country's neutrality. This "left corporatist" model was strong enough to cushion Sweden from the worst effects of the international crisis that set in after 1974, and the strength of the consensus embodied in this strategy was shown during the "bourgeois" coalition from 1976 to 1982. Indeed, this government reaffirmed the state's responsibility for employment protection by nationalizing more industries than all of its SAP predecessors (Pontusson 1984, 84). As we shall see, however, the model was placed under severe strain from the mid-1980s onward in the face of the "free" market pressures emanating from changes in the world economy.

Although the model was envied by the moderate majority in the executives of social-democratic parties elsewhere in Western Europe, by the mid-1960s some Swedish socialists considered that the welfare state compromise was unnecessarily generous to capitalist interests. Two related issues were viewed with concern by left-wing socialists and trade unionists. The first was the LO's perception of excessive profits among the richest companies caused by the self-limiting wage increases that formed part of the solidaristic bargaining system. The second was the workers' lack of power in decisionmaking at enterprise level. The general thrust toward greater power for organized labor was manifested in the adoption of a new industrial policy by the SAP in 1957, instituting a state investment bank, an industrial ministry, regional and sectoral planning, a state holding company, and public (state) representation on the boards of large corporations. An element of worker participation was introduced in 1971, when it was decided that there would be two workers' representatives on the boards of companies employing over one hundred workers. In 1974, the employers' absolute right to hire and fire labor without consultation ended, a policy that had been accepted under the 1938 agreement. In 1976, a Co-Determination Act required management to initiate negotiations with unions on any proposed changes (Elder 1988, 157–158; Hamilton 1989, chap. 10).

The great issue that shattered the peace between capital and labor was the "wage-earner funds'" proposal, first put forward by Rudolf Meidner within the LO in 1975 and adopted as official LO policy the following year (Himmelstrand 1981, chap. 19; Korpi 1983, 233–236). When the proposal was finally put before the SAP for adoption in 1978, it declared that firms with more than five hundred employees would be obliged to issue shares every year to wage-earner funds, the shares representing 20 percent of their profits. The funds, set up on a regional basis, would appoint shareholders' representatives (from the unions and local labor representative bodies) to the boards of enterprises. It was estimated that with average profits of 15 percent, it would take twenty-five years for labor to achieve majority voting rights in a company (Himmelstrand 1981, 266).

THE TRANSITION THEORISTS

Let us consider the arguments that suggested the Swedish model could act as a stepping-stone to the achievement of socialism. These arguments should be seen in the context of the collapse of the postwar boom and the need to offer a left alternative to the Keynesian measures that had helped to sustain it. Similar "left turns" were witnessed in Britain (the Labour party's 1973 program), and in France (the common program of the PS and PCF). Korpi reasoned that the immense strength of the organized working class in Sweden had tilted the balance between capital and labor decisively in favor of the latter. In adopting the practice of solidaristic wage bargaining, the Swedish labor movement focused power at its center (the LO and also the TCO, the white-collar workers' federation) rather than with individual unions (Korpi 1978, 231). The strong links with the Social Democrats and the willingness of members to vote for the SAP and to join it in large numbers had produced a situation in which labor was well positioned to win the "democratic class struggle." The wage-earner funds' debate was considered to be a landmark battle in the broader struggle between capital and labor. The demands were premised on the view that excess profits were being made partly as a result of the solidaristic bargaining process. The funds' proposals maintained the principle of solidarity, extended real powers to the collective worker, and implied a foreseeable qualitative change in the ownership of the means of production (Korpi 1978, chap. 11; Korpi 1983, 232–236). Korpi was aware that this would put the unions in a difficult dual role as representatives of the employees and owners of the firms, and he recognized that the unions' own democratic structures would come under careful scrutiny. He urged the fullest possible intraunion democracy and also advocated universal and equal suffrage in the elections to the boards administering the funds, thereby giving a voice to the unwaged (Korpi 1983, 234–235). At the time Korpi wrote his two books, it was not clear which way the SAP would move on the funds. Korpi recognized that the SAP faced a choice of historic significance, and he called on the leadership to formulate a "provisional utopia" and demonstrate a way of moving toward its attainment.

In reasserting a form of gradualist Marxism, Korpi explicitly rejected both Leninist and neocorporatist interpretations of the role of organized labor. Leninism rejected parliamentarianism as an effective means of change, while corporatism minimized the significance of political competition, emphasizing agreements between the "big" actors in all major decisionmaking (Korpi 1983, 4). In Korpi's view, decisive struggles *were* fought out politically, but a "key part" of these struggles was generated by conflicts of interest in the sphere of production (Korpi 1983, 208). In view of the significance given to the political struggle, it is not surprising that both Korpi and Himmelstrand paid particular attention to the reasons for the 1976 defeat of the SAP. The message they conveyed, supported by an abundance of survey findings, suggested that a more left-wing stance would have found a receptive audience. Like Korpi, Himmelstrand rejected the idea that social democracy had forged a permanent integration of the working class into capitalism (Himmelstrand 1981, 23–24), and he followed the view that the Swedish working class had engaged in a number of stages of development that had opened up the possibility of a transition to socialism (Himmelstrand 1981, chaps. 21, 22). The situation in the late 1970s and early 1980s posed critical problems for the SAP, for the end of the postwar boom exposed the contradiction between the increasingly social character of productive forces and the private character of the relations of production, and this was bound to limit the possibility of compromise between class interests. The strategy to push for economic democracy as the "next stage" was closer to Marx's thinking than was the Leninist model, according to Himmelstrand (309), and the danger that it would place excessive power in the hands of union technocrats had to be countered by the widespread democratization of all elements of society (207, 312–315).

Stephens was also impressed with the level and strength of organized labor in Sweden and the consequent potential for the transition to socialism. He distinguished between the welfare statism common to most advanced capitalist countries after World War II and "production politics," which relocated the question of ownership and control of the means of production to the center of political debate, as it did in Sweden in the late 1970s. He described three conditions for the development of production politics: first, ruling without petty-bourgeois coalitions; second, a high level of white-collar unionization; and third, a long period of government by the socialists (Stephens 1989, 197–198). Sweden was the only country that came close to achieving all three conditions. For Stephens the wage-earner funds provided a more subtle and effective method of transition than nationalization, the "brilliance" of the policy turning on the combination of progressive socialization without compensation and the provision of new sources of investment. As the need for capital investment appeared likely to be a major problem in all capitalist countries in the 1980s, it was a practical answer to the problem of renewed accumulation (Stephens 1979, 205).

FROM COMPROMISE TO DEFEAT

The response from business and the right-wing parties was predictably hostile, for the proposed funds posed a direct threat to the existing relations of production. The former president of Volvo and recent chairman of the SAF, Gunnar Johansson, described the proposition as "an attempt to introduce a socialistic economy by the back door," and complained that the funds would result in "one actor dominating the whole stockmarket" (Johansson 1991). Inside the Social Democratic party many were afraid that the proposal would break the consensus that had hitherto been beneficial to the working class, and they blamed this new radicalism for the election defeat of 1976. Korpi maintained that the SAP's insistence on maintaining its nuclear energy program was the main reason for the defeat (Korpi 1978, 330–331), but there can be no doubt that the opposition was galvanized by the funds issue and that they were able to count on the vociferous support of the majority of the press (Korpi 1983, 219). The 1978 conference of the SAP decided to defer the matter for consideration by the 1981 conference, at which the original idea was considerably diluted. Although the SAP returned to power under Olof Palme in 1982, the unions were by then adopting a more defensive posture, and the forces of the right maintained their staunch opposition, organizing protest marches in 1983.

The 1983 law set up five regional employee investment funds, financed by a payroll tax and a 20 percent profits' tax on larger firms (Milner 1989, 135). Each fund was authorized to own no more than 8 percent of a firm's shares, but as five funds were created, it was possible for the collective workers to obtain an important stake in some enterprises. The funds ceased to receive profit shares from 1990, however, relieving the long-term threat to the ownership of Swedish capital. The enactment of the legislation in 1984 triggered the suspension of centralized bargaining, for the employers' federation, the SAF, refused to cooperate with the government, despite attempts by Prime Minister Palme to persuade them that the workers required some incentive to secure their moderation (Walters 1987, 70). The weakening of centralized bargaining, hitherto dominated by the LO and the SAF, had in fact already begun with the decision of the employers in metal (cars and engineering) to insist on separate bargaining in 1983 (Lash 1985; Mahon 1991, 305). A return to less-rigid central bargaining occurred in 1985 (Rehn and Viklund 1991, 318), however, and in that year renewal funds were set up, which increased union power. These funds were financed by a tax of 10 percent of profits exceeding a certain level, but they remained in the Central Bank without earning interest until unions and management agreed on their use for training and research and development (Rehn and Viklund 1990, 309–310).

The SAP governments in the 1980s sought to protect the high levels of welfare provision and relatively full employment while at the same time preserving competitiveness of the economy (Therborn 1991, 117–118). The pressure of maintaining international competitiveness led the SAP to engage in a number of departures from its established principles of steeply progressive taxation and cheap public services (Sainsbury 1991). In response to business pressure, the SAP government cut public expenditure as a percentage of gross national product from 67 percent in 1982 to approximately 50 percent in 1991 (Kelman 1991). The central wage-bargaining system was weakened by the more-affluent firms paying out wage supplements through profit-sharing schemes and allocating bonuses to individuals (Mahon 1991, 305–306). Finally, in 1990, the SAF disbanded its central negotiating secretariat, a symbolic withdrawal from the old consensual framework.

Although the SAP retained political power in the elections of 1985 under Palme and 1988 under his successor, Ingvar Carlsson, the level of support dropped on each occasion as the economy became more difficult to manage. Partially as a result of the dilution of the solidaristic bargaining system, industrial unrest grew and inflation increased to 7 percent by 1990. Unemployment grew, from 1.4 percent in 1989 to 3.1 percent in the summer of 1991, but this was still a remarkably low figure compared with Sweden's competitors. Growth remained at less than 2 percent per annum throughout the 1980s, lower than the average for the West European economies. Inflation pressures led to the introduction of austerity measures in January and October 1990, involving cuts in welfare provision, public-sector job losses, and the privatization of electricity and telecommunications (Vulliamy 1990). Sweden's competitors had been able to limit or cut public expenditure in a number of fields, and the prospect of a large "peace dividend" in the NATO countries resulting from the end of the Cold War added to the pressure. Sweden remained tied to comparatively high levels of public expenditure, and 40 percent of the work force was employed in the public sector compared with less than 25 percent in the EC by the end of the 1980s (Vulliamy 1990). As if to acknowledge the impossibility of preserving Sweden's relative autonomy, the Social Democrats applied for membership in the European Community in the summer of 1991.

As for the wage-earner funds, the preelection proposal by the SAP government was for the five funds to be merged with five general-pension funds, the five new funds to be allowed to hold a combined 25 percent of votes in a listed firm. The opposition parties immediately denounced the new funds proposal as a threat to the private ownership of industry (Reuters March 15, 1991). The employers' association proposed a five-year plan that comprised the familiar canon of neoliberal political economy: privatization, marketization of health care and child care, privatization of insurance and pensions, sale of council-controlled housing, introduction of education vouchers, and, of course, abolition of the wage-earner funds

(*Financial Times,* November 8, 1990). The stated aims were "to break the pattern of economic stagnation and to reestablish Sweden as a nation of growth and enterprise, with a strong and expanding economy" (Brodin 1992, 20). Almost immediately, the dismantling of the Swedish model commenced (Kay 1992), but the depth of the recession that hit the economy meant that the government felt obliged to seek the cooperation of the SAP in September 1992, in order to cut the huge budget deficit. Although this produced big cuts in public expenditure, the SAP was at least able to secure the continuation of the wealth tax (*The Economist,* September 26–October 2, 1992, 47). This cooperation was withdrawn, however, when further massive cuts were announced in the 1993 budget, and the right continued to press for lower taxes and the running down of the welfare system (McIvor, January 12, 1993).

WHAT WENT WRONG?

The Swedish "transition" theorists have been criticized on a number of counts, and with the benefit of hindsight we can identify three major, interrelated areas in which they overestimated the strength and radical potential of Swedish socialism. The first area centers on the nature of class consciousness and organization, the second concerns the relative neglect of the role of the state, and finally and crucially was the failure to anticipate the constraints imposed by the operation of the international economy.

Korpi, Himmelstrand, and Stephens all argued that high levels of unionization and party membership should be taken as an indication that the working class was actively class conscious, and Korpi and Himmelstrand provided survey findings to support this. They tended to underestimate the tendencies that weaken class homogeneity (Pierson 1986, 122–123). From the outset the idea of the wage-earner funds was associated with the major manual-workers' federation, the LO, and was premised on the strength of labor and the SAP in the corporatist compromise. In common with all advanced industrial countries in the 1980s, the numerical strength of the manual-worker unions fell in comparison with the white-collar unions (Lash 1985, 224–228), and certain sectors of the LO became very hostile to public-sector workers who were regarded as living off the productive workers and holding back their just rewards (see Svenson 1991). The verdict of Rehn and Viklund was damning:

> The unions in private industry—mainly the Metalworkers' Union—from having been the leaders of social reform inside the labor movement now appear as more self-centred and "red-necked." They play no role in the uphill fight for equal opportunity between the sexes which many consider the most important issue on the labor market: they have come to accept employer proposals for higher wage differentials; and they have joined

the liberal criticism of the public sector, using a rather tough language against their fellow workers (Rehn and Viklund 1990, 324).

The unions have found it difficult to respond positively to the demands of feminists and environmentalists, as one might expect from powerful entrenched bureaucracies facing new challenges (Micheletti 1991). Although the SAP adopted a sympathetic posture toward environmentalism at its 1987 congress (Therborn 1991, 117–118), at the 1990 congress it was decided that it would be too costly to move to the speedy decommissioning of nuclear power stations. This dismayed Green opinion, although the Swedish people as a whole were evenly divided on the issue (Sainsbury 1991, 51).

The divisions between the different groups in society may have been difficult to anticipate a decade ago, but it was then not hard to see that support for the left had not increased with the size of the "broad" working class. After achieving over 50 percent of the vote in the 1968 elections, the SAP lost support in three successive elections, and although the share of the vote showed a small revival during the period of the bourgeois coalition, it further declined in 1985 and 1988, when the Greens entered Parliament with 5.5 percent of the vote and the left-party Communists retained a 5 percent share. In 1991, the Left party polled 4.5 percent, but the combined vote of the socialist bloc was only 42.1 percent, while the Greens (3.4 percent) lost the representation they had gained in 1987. The surprising success of the right-wing, populist New Democracy party (6.7 percent) and the neoliberal Christian Democrats (7 percent) revealed the extent to which the election represented an "antibureaucratic" turn, which was prompted by the skillful propaganda of the bourgeois parties linking Swedish statism with the collapsed bureaucratic socialism of Eastern Europe. In order for an important initiative like the wage-earner funds proposals to command popular support, it was essential to link them to a wider democratic movement, particularly in the areas of the environment and the position of women in society. Both Korpi and Himmelstrand recognized the danger of placing too much power in the hands of the labor bureaucracy, but they did not anticipate the extent to which such "labor power" was vulnerable to the ideological onslaught of neoliberalism, presented by propaganda units financed by the SAF (Micheletti 1991, 155).

The second factor to be considered is the role of the state. Pontusson pointed out that the state was limited in its capacity to nationalize private property by the terms of the Swedish model (Pontusson 1984, 87). The cooperation of the employers was premised on the inviolability of their ownership rights, and once they were threatened, the consensus was bound to be broken. In that sense the historical compromise stemming from 1938 contained an important obstacle to effecting a transition to socialism. In Sweden, the state apparatus was thoroughly permeated by supporters of the SAP, but it was also thoroughly tied to the idea of consensus, which many considered to be under threat from the wage-earner funds proposals. It was also obliged to facilitate the most-advantageous conditions for capital accumulation, irrespective of its ideological disposition, as withdrawal from the world market was unthinkable. Faced with an intense international struggle for profitability, the Swedish state came under great pressure to dance to the employers' tune. Even when the state apparatus is not itself dominated by conservative forces, it is obliged to act in the interests of those who control the levers of economic power, for its own power as a state would be undermined by economic failure. This has been identified by Claus Offe as the "institutional self-interest of the state" (Offe 1984, 120). Nor were the "internal" practices of the state immune from the pressures of international post-Fordism. In areas where highly skilled civil servants might be tempted to move to the private sector, they were offered large salary increases (Mahon 1991, 305–306). The final point in relation to the state could not have been anticipated by the writers in question, and that involves the collapse of Soviet communism. Although social democracy can claim to have been consistently opposed to communism, the two arms of the world socialist movement shared a commitment to the power of the centralized state to deliver the goods in terms of economic growth and social welfare. Swedish social democracy suffered by this association, which enabled the right to convince many voters that increased state power was a threat to liberty.

Moving on to consider the effects of the increased internationalization of the Swedish economy, we find that this was largely ignored by the transition theorists. They did not anticipate likely effects on the class struggle of changes in the accumulation process flowing from the downturn in growth experienced since 1974 (Pontusson 1984). The Swedish economy is one of the most open of the advanced industrialized nations. An index of openness (ratio of exports to GNP multiplied by 100) indicates that Sweden's openness increased from 22 in 1965 to 35 in 1985, compared with average world figures of 24.9 in 1965 to 29.1 in 1985. In the space of twenty years the economy moved from being less open than average to being considerably more open than average. The Swedish economy in 1985 was relatively more "international" than West Germany (33), the United Kingdom (29), France (25), Japan (15), and the United States (7) (Husted and Melvin 1990, 7). An important factor in this increased significance of trade was the establishment of the free-trade agreement between the European Free Trade Association (including Sweden) and the European Community in 1973. In particular, this encouraged the big Swedish firms to establish plants elsewhere in Europe (Hansson 1992, 594). As the importance of exports increased, so did the power of the exporters, and Johansson, former president of Volvo and 1991 president of the SAF, pointed out that SAF members contributed more than 95 percent of

Swedish export value (Johannson 1991). Volvo alone accounted for 12 percent of Sweden's exports and employed 6 percent of the country's manufacturing work force by the late 1980s (Milner 1989, 145). Saab, the "other" motor manufacturer, highlighted the extent of international competition when it was taken over by the U.S.-based giant, General Motors. It is not surprising that big exporters in Sweden, such as Volvo, Electrolux, Ericson, and SKF, have wrought favorable concessions from government at central and local levels, with or without the approval of the SAF, a process described by Rehn and Viklund as "almost blackmail" (Rehn and Viklund 1990, 321). However much the state intervened to maintain investment with schemes such as the wage-earner funds and the renewal funds, the ultimate power to invest rested with management, and the possibility of shifting operations to countries with lower taxation and more flexible bargaining arrangements placed an enormous constraint on the SAP government. Two major firms, Tetra Pak and IKEA, moved their headquarters out of the country (Kelman 1991). The relative lack of attention given by the transition theorists to the effects of increased Swedish integration into the world economy may have been due to the exceptional strength of the labor movement in Sweden, and in Scandinavia in general. At the time they were writing, the Social Democratic party was also in government in Germany. This strength was quickly dissipated, however, and with the advantage of hindsight the lack of an international political-economy perspective was the greatest weakness of the writers in question.

THE END OF THE NATIONAL ROAD

The resounding defeat of the left in Sweden points to the immense difficulty of defending a social-democrat state in a world economy that has become increasingly open, and in which high unemployment, high differentials, and flexible pay-bargaining are perceived by capitalists to be prerequisites for competitiveness. The experiences of the socialist governments that have ruled in France and Spain for much of the past decade offer further evidence of the difficulty of managing social democracy in one country. It must be remembered, however, that when key criteria for judging economic performance are applied to the record of Sweden under the SAP between 1982 and 1991, it was more impressive than most other European countries. As well as low unemployment and low inflation, the high budget deficit of 1982 was turned into a surplus by 1988 (Sainsbury 1991, 38–39). The active labor-market policies were widely admired (*The Economist,* September 21–27, 1991, 65). Clearly, this record did not impress the Swedish people in 1991, but it will be looked upon more favorably in the light of the abysmal economic record of the Bildt government in its first eighteen months. It is now obvious that neoliberal measures taken to ensure short-term profitability are not only damaging to the social fabric of the individual countries but are exacerbating the structural contradictions of the world economy.

There are few indications, however, that the failure of neoliberal policy automatically produces a substantial shift in support back to social democracy, and there is clearly a need for parties of the left to develop policies that can foster a new basis for social solidarity. In Sweden, this solidarity was led by a strong, blue-collar trade union movement, the driving force behind the wage-earner funds' policy, but the pursuit of narrowly perceived group interest fostered divisiveness in the 1980s. If there is to be a renewed feeling of common interest among a majority of the electorate, it will have to embrace different priorities and accommodate tensions in the demands from various sectors. The right was able to take advantage of these tensions between industrial workers, public-sector workers, feminists, and environmentalists, and even between nationalists and internationalists, in a climate of doubt about the continued relevance of the highly interventionist Swedish model. The economic debacle that has occurred since the SAP lost power will persuade some that the past was really not so bad, but a return to the past is not possible. The formulation of full-employment policies that can be implemented without producing capital flight would require a broad consensus involving the Left party and the Greens as well as the SAP.

If the accelerated internationalization of capital has placed enormous limits on the potential of redistributive strategies in Sweden, despite its strong social-democratic political culture, it may well be asked if there is any space for a renewal of the socialist project. In theory, at least, the proposed expansion of the European Community to include Sweden, Austria, and Finland implies a strengthening of the social-democratic element in a powerful European federal state. The size and strength of such a state could enable social-democratic policies to overcome the pressures that have so far prevailed at the level of the nation-state, and such a state could aspire to a hegemonic position from which to contribute to the reordering of the world economy via coordinated restructuring of financial and trade relations. The socialist group became the largest in the European Parliament after the elections of 1989, and the formation of a European Socialist party was announced in 1992 to help promote policy cohesion. In political and economic terms, however, the internationalization of labor lags well behind the internationalization of capital. The Social Charter and the Action Program stemming from the party's organization are both circumspect on the issues of workers' information and participation in decision-making, and although the European Parliament has been more forthright in its demands for information and participation guarantees, there is nothing approaching the radical nature of wage-earner funds (Hughes 1991). The looseness of the political unit suggested by the Maastricht agreements denies legislative power to the European Parliament and discourages a large federal budget that could be used for redistributive purposes. The possibility of realizing schemes such as the wage-earner funds and the renewal funds on a European-wide basis is therefore clearly distant, despite their great merits. Nevertheless, building a new international social solidarity is a prerequisite for the emergence of a new radical and pluralist socialism, now that all illusions in "national roads" have been shattered.

11

The International Origins of
South Korea's Export Orientation
Barry Gills

This chapter illustrates the utility of a neostructuralist IPE analysis to explain fundamental transformations on the level of a single nation-state. Hitherto, the origin of South Korea's export orientation has most often been explained by endogenous factors, for instance a "crisis of import substitution" or the outcome of astute but idiosyncratic leadership decisions after the military coup d'état of May 16, 1961. I will argue that the evidence supporting these conventional explanations of the emergence of South Korea's export orientation is far from convincing or satisfactory.

An alternative explanation should analyze the transformation of the state and the economic development strategy in South Korea within the specific domestic, regional, and global conjunctural situation of the late 1950s and early 1960s. This unique conjuncture both required and allowed the emergence of a select group of East Asian NICs in the world economy and its hegemonic power structure at that specific moment in time. This transformation was therefore much larger than South Korea alone and reflected a convergence of interests that directly encompassed economic, social, and political forces in the U.S., Japan, Korea, and Taiwan. That is, rather than the outcome of national policy decisions on their own merit, a *structural opportunity* was made available to South Korea at a certain time and for specific reasons. This structural opportunity was part of a larger reorganization expressing many convergent interests. In the final analysis, the neostructuralist approach may provide a much more satisfactory explanation for the emergence of the export orientation in South Korea than a state-centric approach. It also undermines the ideologically motivated argument that there was ever, or is now, any true "model" of development in South Korea that could be universally emulated by other Third World countries.

STATE-CENTRISM VERSUS AN IPE PERSPECTIVE

Two basic approaches can be taken to study the role of a particular state in economic development: the "state-centric" approach and the "international political economy" (IPE) approach. The state-centric approach takes a single state as the unit of analysis. Often, however, it adopts the assumptions of an abstract evolutionary model of development and thus suffers from a danger of imposing an ahistorical universalism. The IPE approach takes the wider international system as at least the framework if not the unit of analysis, but its tendency to eschew abstract evolutionary models of national development can lead to imposing an historicist perspective on particular outcomes.

Two sets of factors must be considered in conjunction with the choice of approach above. First, is the often-presumed internal/external dichotomy and second is the issue of whether to adopt a "productionist" or an "exchange" bias. The state-centric approach privileges internal factors and a productionist bias in its explanations of change. The broad IPE approach privileges external factors and an exchange bias. What follows is an attempt to demonstrate from a concrete case study the greater utility of an IPE approach over a state-centric one even to explain transformations within a single nation-state.

State-centric analyses have affinity with the realist paradigm in international relations, i.e., the common emphasis on the overriding "struggle for power among sovereign nations." The alternative is a more-holistic, world-historical, sociological paradigm of international *change*. Its premise is that all states and societies dynamically undergo restructuring by participating in the world system. In this restructuration there is a codetermination between agency and structure and, likewise, between internal and external structures and agencies. The question arises: Should the global arena be conceived of as an ontologically distinct realm, with actors, structures, trends, and dynamics of its own that affect conditions both between states and within them? If the answer is yes, then the world of IPE, or alternatively the world system, is not merely the sum of its parts nor is it merely a matter of balance of power, polarity, hegemonic stability, or rivalry, as realists would have us believe. I will argue that for any "part" of the world system, participation in the global political economy is the governing process of transformation.

A neostructuralist IPE perspective attempts to bridge the gap between state-centrism and IPE approaches. In this case, the real affinity is with the IPE approach, which is a framework through which to analyze a nation-state's specific time-bound responses to stimuli from the international arena, while both levels, domestic and global, are viewed as being mutually engaged in transformative processes. Between global structures and domestic ones there is on-going interpenetration, transformation, and restructuring.

In this chapter I will briefly review the general characteristics of the state's role in South Korea's economic development, primarily relying on existing state-centric analyses. Most of the existing literature on South Korea's political economy attempts to explain how policy choices inside

Korea resulted in subsequent export success and economic growth and development (Amsden 1989, 1990; Clark and Chan 1990; Wade 1990; White 1988; Jones 1980; Wade and Kim 1977).

In contrast to this approach, I will show that the decisive transformation in South Korea, as in Taiwan, occurred *before* and *outside* the "national" decision to adopt the export strategy. This decisive moment can be found in the regional/global reorganization of production and trade, in which both the U.S. and Japan played central roles and by which certain East Asian NICs, including South Korea, were provided with a unique structural opportunity to industrialize. No new empirical research was undertaken or new facts discovered in order to defend this argument. Rather, well-known facts from existing sources have been assembled and interpreted in a new framework.

STATE-CENTRIC ANALYSES OF
SOUTH KOREAN ECONOMIC DEVELOPMENT

In this section I present a composite sketch of the main features of the South Korean state's role in economic development. Most studies of the economic development of South Korea stress the importance of the strong state, state capacity, or autonomy in creating economic growth (Amsden 1989, 1990; Cotton 1992; Haggard and Cheng 1987; Haggard and Moon 1983; Johnson 1982, 1987; Wade 1988, 1990; White 1988; Kim 1989; Deyo 1987). There is widespread recognition that in this case the (relative) autonomy of the state was a key factor shaping the political economy of South Korea and explaining its outcomes. State autonomy in Korea was derived from its historical class composition and social structure (Hamilton 1984, 1986), a situation that arose primarily in the transition to capitalism by state-led means. In Korea, this process occurred under Japanese colonial rule, during which the imposition of a strong colonial state had the effect of virtually eliminating the old ruling class, leaving only a compromised fraction to survive with Japanese support. But Japanese rule also created a new proletariat and an industrial infrastructure.

After liberation from Japanese colonial rule in 1945, the surviving Korean landowner class was further weakened by land reform undertaken under U.S. auspices. This period of transformation was dominated by national division and the requirements of an emergent U.S. hegemonic sphere in Northeast Asia (Kolko and Kolko 1972; Bix 1974). The postcolonial South Korean state inherited both a weak national bourgeoisie and politically excluded labor. Guided by U.S. anticommunist preoccupations, the new counterrevolutionary South Korean state reinforced both of these conditions. Labor was politically excluded in both South Korea and Taiwan throughout the period of "miracle" growth that began in the 1960s (Deyo 1989).

Sustained only by massive U.S. assistance, South Korea went through a fairly brief period of postwar import substitution during which social forces resistant to the state remained weak. The result was that by 1958, ten years after the Republic of Korea was established under U.S. and UN tutelage, the state was still very autonomous vis à vis any countervailing class/sectoral/civil-society interests. This historical autonomy was reinforced when a military regime was established after the coup in 1961.

The historical conditions that gave rise to such an exceptionally strong autonomous state in South Korea must therefore be sought in the characteristics of two successive hegemonic orders in the region, i.e., the Japanese and the American. Comparison of this East Asian history with Latin American history is very instructive and has occupied considerable scholarly attention (Hart-Landsberg 1987; Cumings 1989; Evans 1987; Gereffi and Wyman 1989; Barrett and Chin 1987; Haggard 1986, 1990).

In Latin America, agrarian oligarchies have in general been much stronger and more historically entrenched. The Latin American period of ISI (import substitution industrialization) was generally longer and much deeper. The national bourgeoisie have been larger and more entrenched, while labor has not been so effectively excluded from the state. Thus countervailing institutional power by both labor and capital to the state has been much more pronounced in Latin America than in South Korea or Taiwan.

Also important is the different hegemonic influence in Latin America. Political, strategic, and economic goals of hegemonic powers differ, and even the goals of the same hegemon and the means used to achieve them may differ from one region to another. For instance, the U.S. pursued goals in East Asia different from those it pursued in Latin America and used different methods to reach them. The anticommunism of Latin American regimes has not been directed primarily externally but rather internally, thus facilitating a ruling coalition between the landed oligarchy and the military while allowing penetration by foreign capital. In East Asia, externally oriented anticommunism had very different domestic results. It facilitated the elimination of the landed oligarchy and the emergence of an autonomous state class with more leverage over foreign capital. In Latin America, there has been no engine of investment, and especially industrialization, comparable to that of Japan in East Asia. This is true to such an extent that, in fact, East Asian industrialization cannot be separated from the industrial and financial rise of Japanese capital (Nester 1990).

The historical outcome in South Korea produced a state with the capacity to discipline all classes and class fractions, including finance (via nationalization of banking and credit) and industrial capital (via "guided capitalism"), resulting in blocking the articulation of other class and sectoral interests in the political sphere. All particular interests were subordinated to the general interests of the state, the ruling party, and the state-class. The development of civil society was stunted by the overdevelopment of the apparatus of police repression. This effectively excluded real political challenges to the state and the ruling coalition. Within the state, military intelligence and the KCIA guarded the ruling circle against the threat of counter–coups d'état. Labor was controlled either through repression or experiments with corporatism, depending on the period (Deyo 1989; Ogle 1990). Populism, however, was conspicuous by its absence. The peasantry was controlled by comprehensive programs such as the New Village movement and became an electoral bulwark of the ruling party in parliamentarily overrepresented, rural electoral constituencies. Even foreign capital was regulated to a remarkable degree by this strong South Korean state for a certain period. For instance, there were initially very strict controls on foreign direct investment. Until the end of 1978, only one-quarter of FDI in manufacturing was 100 percent foreign-owned, while nearly two-thirds of FDI had at least 50 percent Korean ownership.

The strength of the South Korean state was reflected in its implementation of economic planning. The keystone of this was "executive dominance," by which the office of the president directly supervised planning coordination and implementation. The "pilot organization" common to so-called "capitalist developmental states" (Johnson 1982, 1987) was also present in the form of the Economic Planning Board. This presidential-EPB combination gave the state extensive powers throughout the economy. The state also issued directives to the banking system that determined the credit allocation to firms, thus decisively influencing corporate investment decisions. A substantial public sector of large parastatals produced a mixed economy, which was always a combination of import-substitution and export-orientation strategies after the stabilization policy of the early 1960s. That is to say, there was never a "pure" export orientation in the South Korean domestic economic structure; however, there was not a true national bourgeoisie in the ISI sector, which was dominated by parastatals directly managed by the military state-class.

In terms of external orientation and trade policy, the South Korean state was decidedly (neo)mercantilist (Haggard and Moon 1983; Nestor 1990). This neomercantilism is not simply a matter of tariffs or import restrictions, which are in fact ritually defended as having always been "liberal." More to the point, it is a matter of how the domestic structure of the economy serves international trade goals. Thus, this type of neomercantilism entails the concentration of corporate ownership in the Jaebol (the large, family-owned corporate groups that dominate the Korean economic structure), as well as the domestic system of credit allocation, the retail system, the system of export incentives, and marketing support through the general trading companies and the import-export bank. In South Korea, an alliance between the state and national capital—in which the state was the senior partner—predominated and not a state-MNC alliance, where the state is usually a junior partner. Between 1963–1985 some $42 billion in foreign capital was imported into South Korea, but FDI by foreign MNCs was less than 10 percent of that total. In general, the South Korean state firmly backed its own national firms in the unending quest to achieve market share and international competitiveness.

Perhaps above all, the South Korean state's role in economic development was decisive through successfully directing the sequentialization of industrialization via "market conforming principles" (Johnson 1982, 1987). The preconditions for subsequent success in sequentialized industrialization were domestically established in the stabilization program of 1964. The prescriptions favored by neoclassical liberal economists (Adelman 1969) prevailed, with sweeping reform of incentives, lowering of protection, liberalization of the exchange rate regime to "realistic" levels (to ensure international competitiveness), and so on. This preparatory stage led to a phase of accelerated investment in labor-intensive, light manufacturing. This was the period of the first and second five-year plans. Key sectors in this export-led boom were textiles, apparel, shoes, and other light manufactures. Historically, this was a period of unprecedented growth in world trade as a proportion of world production.

The labor-intensive, light manufacturing model supposedly experienced a crisis starting about 1969 (Kim 1989) that led to the third phase: heavy and chemical industrialization (HCI). This was the period of the third and fourth five-year plans, which overwhelmingly prioritized capital-intensive heavy industries such as petrochemicals, iron and steel, heavy construction, and engineering. So intense was the rate of investment in these sectors that almost overnight, by the end of 1979, HCI exports exceeded textiles and apparel, and shoes by 38 percent to 35 percent respectively.

This period culminated in genuine economic crisis in 1978–1980. Massive foreign borrowing to finance investment in HCI, overconcentration of the economic structure by the Jaebol—with resultant serious structural imbalances and overheating in the economy—political repression under the draconian emergency measures of the "Yushin" dictatorship, and the effects of recession in the world economy all combined to bring a drastic economic bust in Korea. The Park regime collapsed in late 1979, as social unrest exploded during the recession. There was a 5 percent contraction in GNP in 1980.

The crisis produced a political and economic reorganization aided by the U.S. and Japan, both of whom agreed it was best to put Humpty-Dumpty back together again. The new strategy in the fourth phase was "low-energy consumption and high technology," with accelerated liberalization and internationalization of the economy from 1980 onward. HCI was drastically restructured, but Korea retained some of the gains in iron and steel, shipbuilding, and construction achieved in the preceding period. The new emphasis in sequential industrialization strategy was in automobiles, electronics, and high technology. All of these required a higher research and development expenditure, a new science and technology policy, and more autonomy for capital vis à vis the state class. This strategy of continued upward mobility in the context of increasingly difficult competition presents South Korea with a "structural squeeze" between the rising NICs of Southeast Asia and mainland China and the existing advanced industrial powers (Bello and Rosenfeld 1990).

THE INTERNATIONAL POLITICAL ECONOMY APPROACH

Very few scholars have attempted to interpret transformation in South Korea from a broad IPE perspective (Koo 1987). Probably the most interesting attempt (to date) to analyze large-scale transformations in the Northeast Asian region as a whole is Bruce Cumings's impressive essay, "The Origins and Development of the Northeast Asian Political Economy: Industrial Sectors, Product Cycles, and Political Consequences" (Cumings 1987). His thesis is that the region underwent a Japan-led pattern of upward mobility in the world system. This occurred in "successive waves of industrial competition" along the outlines of the "flying geese" model as propounded by Kaname Akamatsu in the 1930s.

According to Cumings, Japan's classic sequentialized industrialization pattern occurred in three broad phases. In the first phase, beginning in the 1880s, labor-intensive manufactures dominated, with textiles as the leading sector. In the second phase, beginning in the 1930s, capital-intensive investment predominated, and the leading sectors were steel, chemicals, armaments, and finally autos. The third phase began in the mid-1960s on the basis of knowledge-intensive investment. The leading sectors in this "low-energy, high-technology" phase are electronics, computers, silicon chips, and communications equipment.

In Japan's case, each sequential phase of investment has been marked by state protection of nascent industries, adoption of foreign technologies, comparative advantage derived from labor costs, technological innovation, and the advantage of "lateness" in world time. Cumings examines not merely Japan but the dynamic of the Northeast Asian regional political economy seen as a whole. He argues that:

Time-series curves for imports, import substitution for the domestic market, and subsequent exports of given products tend to form a pattern like wild geese flying in ranks. The cycle in given industries—textiles, steel, automobiles, light electronics—of origin, rise, apogee, and decline—has not simply been marked, but often mastered, in Japan; in each industrial life cycle there is also an appropriate jumping off place; that is, a point at which it pays to let others make the product or at least provide the labor. Taiwan and Korea have historically been receptacles for declining Japanese industries. . . . *A country by country approach is incapable of*

*accounting for the remarkably similar trajectories of Korea and Taiwan
. . . ; understanding of the Northeast Asian political economy can only
emerge from an approach that posits the systematic interaction of each
country with the others, and of the region with the world at large.* Rapid
upward mobility in the world economy has occurred, through the product
cycle and other means, within the context of two hegemonic systems
[Japanese and American] (emphasis added above) (Cumings 1987, 45–47).

Cumings's framework, combining the overall regional industrialization pattern, the dynamics of the world economy, the changing nuances of
hegemonic influence, and the domestic responses by national states is
much to be applauded. His emphasis on product cycles and industrial off-
loading (at the presumed appropriate jumping-off point), however, is un-
comfortably mechanistic. It virtually ignores the fact that both Korea and
Taiwan also compete with Japan, even in industrial sectors that Japan
wishes to retain. Its virtue is that it analyzes the "rise" of the entire region
and recognizes the central role of sequentialization of industrialization and
Japan's unique position in leading the overall pattern of development.

THE INTERNATIONAL ORIGINS
OF THE SOUTH KOREAN EXPORT ORIENTATION

In the early postwar period just after the defeat of Japan, U.S. strate-
gic imperatives were overriding in comparison to immediate economic in-
terests. The U.S. needed to stabilize its newly won hegemonic sphere in
Northeast Asia, and this required establishing stable client governments. In
Korea, this was particularly difficult given the fact that the U.S. held what
amounted to a territorial enclave on hostile territory. The climate of the
Asian continent was revolutionary, and this included the Korean peninsula.
The U.S. wanted to contain the Soviet Union, China (after 1949), and
North Korea and chose South Korea as its "bulwark against communism"
in the region, actually a buffer state for its vital interests in Japan (Kolko
and Kolko 1972).

The United States devised the division of the Korean peninsula in
1945 and proceeded to establish a military government in South Korea.
The extent of U.S. commitment to the new state it helped create was neither certain nor consistent at first, but proved to be very great indeed in the
course of the Korean War. After the war, the U.S. embraced its client with
massive economic and military assistance to the South Korean government. This hegemonic influence determined the character of South Korea's
economic strategy at the time.

South Korea, being overwhelmingly dependent on U.S. grants to
sustain its import-dependent economy (there were virtually no exports in
that period), developed a type of pre-Marcos "crony capitalism." A few

businesses with connections to the ruling Liberal party and President Rhee were favored, while national budgetary resources flowed disproportionately to the police, the military, and the bureaucracy, with some state investment going to basic infrastructure. From 1955 to 1958, U.S. aid paid for some 70 percent of all South Korean imports. In this period, it is very clear how the domestic structure was transformed in accordance with the requirements of the global. That this "model" was a direct product of external circumstances is made even clearer by the abruptness with which it was later abandoned when external circumstances changed again.

From 1958 onward, a decisive shift in U.S. policy precipitated far-reaching transformation in the state's role in economic development in Korea. In general, U.S. policy goals shifted to a preference for assistance in the form of loans instead of grants, the rapid reintegration of the Korean economy with that of Japan, and a stabilization policy to be followed by export promotion and economic planning. From that time, the United States increased its bilateral pressure on the South Korean government to adopt these guidelines (Haggard 1990, Woo 1991). When President Syngman Rhee was overthrown in the "student revolution" of 1960, Washington welcomed the news and warmly supported the new government led by the Democratic party. This new government proceeded to adopt most of the U.S. guidelines. When the military coup took place in May 1961, the new military government likewise adopted these same guidelines, that is, the coup did not bring about a sudden change in fundamental economic policies but continued virtually the same policies as its immediate democratic predecessor.

An influential study of the economic and social modernization of South Korea (Mason et al. 1980) concluded that the United States "dictated" reform of the grant-dependent, import-substitution strategy in both the Republic of Korea and the Republic of China (Taiwan). It is extremely important to note that the shift away from ISI to export orientation in both Korea and Taiwan occurred at approximately the same time. Both Korea and Taiwan made this shift under bilateral U.S. political pressure and via bilateral economic cooperation with Japan. In Taiwan the Nineteen-Point Reform, which included such basic stabilization measures as monetary, fiscal, and tariff reform, was promulgated in 1960. In South Korea, the decisive shift of policy also happened in the early 1960s. After the military coup in 1961, concrete measures were established such as devaluation (to cheapen exports), lowering of tariffs (especially on imports destined to contribute to exports), tax exemptions, and state guarantees for FDI and on foreign loans. Between 1963 and 1964, South Korea extended the preparatory phase with measures such as accelerated depreciation allowances, discounts and subsidies, and discriminatory privileges for successful exporters. From 1965 on, free export zones (EPZs) were established in Taiwan (e.g., at Kaohsiung, December 1966) and in South Korea (e.g, at

Masan). Both Taiwan and South Korea established "pilot organizations" for macroeconomic planning within this same period in the early 1960s (the Economic Planning Board in 1961 in Korea; the Council on International Economic Cooperation and Development in 1963 in Taiwan). U.S. bilateral pressure on Taiwan to shift away from U.S. aid–dependent ISI was intense from 1958 onward, following new, congressional aid guidelines that stressed "self-sustaining growth," privatization, and reduction of U.S. assistance (Kim 1989, 370).

The case of Taiwan is instructive because it is so parallel to Korea's. The U.S. deployed its existing and considerable influence over Taiwanese economic policymaking, together with the threat of aid cuts and promises of other aid, to achieve its ends (Jacoby 1966). The external pressure to adopt export-oriented industrialization caused a rift within the ruling circle in Taiwan. There was considerable resistance to the export orientation by a coalition of the party bureaucracy, the military, and the large state sector of ISI industries. Private business was ambivalent on the matter as "Commercial and industrial concerns shared an interest in liberalization of controls on raw materials imports and foreign exchange, *but they did not see exports as a solution to market saturation, and appeared to favour cartelization, restriction of investment and state aid to troubled sectors*" (Kim 1989, 371; emphasis added).

The hard-line traditionalists of the party, bureaucracy, and the military feared too much privatization of industry. Privatization was a political risk since it might mean increased power for private business elites vis à vis the state. Privatization also threatened the entrenched interests of the managerial fraction of the ruling coalition who controlled public enterprises.

Though Taiwan bent to U.S. pressure and accepted the EOI strategy on offer, the evidence clearly indicates this was not the natural or preferred choice. In the event, the regime compromised with traditionalist interests by continuing to finance very high levels of defense spending, while promoting exports in the early 1960s, via cartelization of key industrial sectors such as textiles, paper, iron and steel, rubber goods, and cement. Beginning in 1961, USAID commissioned Stanford Research Institute to prepare feasibility studies on the future establishment of new industrial sectors in Taiwan, especially petrochemicals, synthetic fibers, and electronics, to be undertaken in the form of direct foreign investment into Taiwan. These studies influenced future industrial policy and foreign investment, particularly by the United States. As the Taiwanese opening progressed in the 1960s, a nascent "division of labor" emerged whereby Japan concentrated investment in the EPZs in light manufactures for export, such as textiles and electronics, and the U.S. concentrated on chemicals and machinery. The degree of state involvement in industry was so high, however, that only the electronics sector was actually dominated by direct foreign investors.

THE TRIANGULAR PATTERN
OF INDUSTRIAL RESTRUCTURING

These parallel developments in Korea and Taiwan are not sufficient in themselves to explain the emergence of the export orientation. It is necessary to look at a triangular relationship among the United States, Japan, and the peripheral states of East Asia in order to understand the transformation as a whole.

First, it is important to note that the U.S. was experiencing economic recession and dollar problems in 1958; indeed, its action toward South Korea at the time has been explained by reference to the "declining condition of the American economy." According to Chong-sik Lee, "US trade suffered deficits in 1958 and 1959 to such an extent that international concern was aroused about the strength of the dollar. The US government responded by adopting a fiscal retrenchment policy in 1959 and calling on European countries *and Japan* to share the burden of aiding underdeveloped countries. The US continued to reduce its economic aid to South Korea and urged closer cooperation between Japan and South Korea" (Lee 1985, 44, emphasis added). According to another author, "The fact that Washington's balance-of-payments problem became chronic from 1958 onward was an important incentive behind its desire to subordinate South Korea to Japan" (Bix 1974, 206). It was precisely in this period that the Bretton Woods system first became fully operational, in which the dollar was the anchor in a system of fixed exchange rates. Economic recovery in Europe and Japan put new strains upon the U.S. trade balance and the international position of the dollar.

Indeed, as argued above, the crucial transition in economic development strategy in South Korea did not come with the imposition of a military junta in 1961, but occurred earlier under the democratic government of Prime Minister Chang Myun. Even earlier, the Rhee regime had been moving inexorably toward the agenda demanded by the U.S. and other influential external forces between 1958–1960. Chang Myun's government almost immediately sought to improve relations with Japan, a cornerstone of U.S. policy but long obstructed by Rhee. Chang Myun sent Pak Hung-sik, a Korean businessman with ties to Japanese interests dating back to the colonial period, to see Cabinet Secretary Ohira Masayoshi in Japan to discuss a new relationship between the two countries. The Chang government referred to the establishment of a "Korean-Japanese economic cooperation system."

The first five-year plan as promulgated by the Chang government for the period 1962–1966 anticipated considerable Japanese aid and loans to Korea, i.e., extensive economic reintegration with the Japanese economic system. It must be appreciated how politically sensitive was this issue of economic reintegration into the Japanese sphere in the Korean postliberation environment. After decades of harsh oppression and thorough economic subordination, Koreans retained a great fear of becoming resubordinated to Japan. For Rhee, anti-Japanese patriotism was one of his strongest domestic cards in a regime that otherwise seriously lacked popular support.

Chang Myun's government also envisaged a shift from ISI to EOI (export-oriented industrialization). This was originally conceived, however, as a drive to sell primary products such as minerals, timber, marine resources, and agricultural surplus in order to earn foreign exchange, a trade strategy very typical in the Third World. To a considerable extent it reflected the economic interests of the social class then predominating in the ruling Democratic party, i.e., the remaining landed class. It is this element of EOI that most changed with the advent of the military to state power in 1961. The alliance of the landed class and the national bourgeoisie that formed the ruling coalition in 1960 was too weak politically to hold state power in the face of military opposition and without real popular support.[1] The new military state-class had no particular economic interests to protect and was free to promote general national economic development goals by the best means available.

In Japan, influential elites viewed the military coup of May 16, 1961, by General Park as a blessing in disguise. Former Prime Minister Kishi and his faction were the foremost representatives of this viewpoint inside the ruling Liberal Democratic party. Kishi had been a central figure in preparations for developing a U.S.-Japan military-industrial complex during the talks begun in April 1959, on revision of the 1951 U.S.-Japan Mutual Security Treaty (Bix 1974, 206). The logic behind Kishi's support for the coup was that he preferred to see a system of strong "executive dominance" in South Korea that the advent of Park provided. This new Korean regime would actually increase Japan's leverage over Korean society as a whole, i.e., over the Korean nation, which was adamantly opposed to close economic relations with Japan. Kishi and his supporters correctly anticipated that only a dictatorship in Korea would be capable of containing popular resistance to normalization of relations with Japan, whereas a civilian democratic regime would be overcome by such opposition. The Kishi line likewise maintained that given the background of the new leaders in Korea—their former close ties to Japan—this would enable Japan to rachet down the "price" demanded by Korea for normalization, i.e., its "compensation" claims for the colonial past.

Kishi's influence is thought to have been considerable in persuading not only his own government, but that of the Kennedy administration in the United States, that the new military junta in Korea should be supported. The Kennedy administration was hesitant to accept the overthrow of the democratic regime. General Park himself was personally suspect because of certain questions about his activities as a younger man. His brother had been active in military rebellions against the fledgling Republic of Korea by left-wing officers and troops in 1948. U.S. support for the new military regime was quickly consolidated, however, in the Kennedy–Ikeda communique of June 22, 1961.

The new Korean military regime was led by a graduate of a Japanese imperial military academy who had served as an officer in the Japanese imperial army. General Park immediately reinitiated serious bilateral negotiations with Japan on normalization of relations and economic reintegration. The head of the new Economic Planning Board, Kim Yu-t'aek, held talks with Japanese Foreign Minister Kosaka. The Japanese were able in these talks to reduce an initial Korean demand for $2 billion in compensatory sweeteners down to $800 million. At one point Kosaka had suggested a mere $50 million. The head and founder of the new Korean Central Intelligence Agency, Kim Jong-pil, also held talks with Foreign Minister Ohira in October–November 1962, on the matter of money. In the Kim Jong-pil–Ohira Masayoshi memorandum of November 12, 1962, South Korea acquiesced to Japanese demands that Korea's so-called "property and claims rights" (i.e., reparation and compensation claims for damage inflicted during the colonial period) be abandoned in favor of the blanket, euphemistic Japanese concept of "economic cooperation" (Bix 1974, 188).

These talks also provided a forum for establishing a new network of interelite relations between Korean political and economic figures and their Japanese counterparts. From 1961, the Korean Businessmen's Association, representing the interests of Korean capital, like their Japanese counterparts, lobbied hard for normalization of relations and "economic cooperation" with Japan. General Park and his entourage in the military junta, and later in the government of the Third Republic after 1963, had both public and personal interests in normalization. Total political and private kickbacks in the 1965 agreement are believed to have been approximately 8 percent of the total amount of $800 million. Subsequent Korea-Japan deals were typically marked by insider arrangements that relied heavily on the unseen plutocratic network of Korean and Japanese elites established between 1961–1963.

Public opposition in Korea to these talks and the prospect of a national sellout to Japan was so intense that in 1964, martial law was proclaimed in South Korea in order to quell dissent over the impending Korea-Japan normalization agreement. In the course of this crisis the regime felt it expedient to temporarily exile Kim Jong-pil in 1963 and again in 1964. Kishi's analysis that only a strong military hand at the helm in Korea could ensure passage of the treaty seems accurate in retrospect.

In Japan, as mentioned above, business leaders pushed hard for normalization with Korea, and they did so in a particular context. Japan urgently required a periphery in Asia in which to expand. After total defeat in World War II, Japan had been forced to reorganize its economic structure. It became an appendage of the dollar zone, the yen not yet convertible, and was quickly transformed into a "huge captive market" for American goods (Halliday and McCormack 1973, 3), while U.S. corporations and banks asserted themselves in key sectors of the Japanese economy (Bix 1974, 190–191). Joseph Dodge oversaw an extension of the "reverse course" policy through new efforts to stimulate Japanese industrial expansion even at the cost of furthering reconcentration of its industry, i.e., resurrection and rehabilitation of the *zaibatsu*. The United States established a counterpart fund with a special account for Japan; through this means it was able to "guide" Japanese economic development by channeling Japanese tax funds into the reemerging military-industrial complex, particularly useful during the Korean War (1950–1953), which was a bonanza for Japanese industry. Such a counterpart fund was later established by the Japanese in relation to Korea after normalization, as discussed below.

During the occupation period Japan took two-thirds of its imports from the U.S., but the U.S. took less than a quarter of Japan's exports. This bilateral trade imbalance had to be ameliorated somehow. In the mid-1950s, John Foster Dulles promoted a triangular trade arrangement involving the U.S., Japan, and resource-rich Southeast Asian countries. The intention of this program was apparently to facilitate Japanese economic expansion by targeting the nearby Asian periphery and to fill Japan's yawning dollar gap. The U.S. provided dollars for Southeast Asian countries to use to purchase goods from Japan. In return the U.S. offered Southeast Asian participants certain trading privileges in the U.S. market. In global terms its investment in Southeast Asia was relatively weak, thus leaving ample room for Japanese expansion. Again, strategic imperatives seem to have determined overall economic and political policy on the part of the United States. The U.S. also wanted Japanese economic expansion into the Southeast Asian periphery as a means of containing communist expansion in the area (Halliday and McCormack 1973, 15).

The Japanese expansion into Southeast Asia was greatly accelerated by the advent of the Vietnam War and the huge influx of U.S. aid funds into Vietnam in the mid-1960s. These aid funds to Vietnam were used to finance imports from Japan until 1970, when this was prohibited under new measures to protect the dollar. In the period from 1966 to 1969, Japanese investment in and credits extended to Southeast Asia dwarfed all other regions by comparison, coming to a total of almost $1.7 billion. Japan was able to partly fill its dollar gap on the strength of its trade surplus with Southeast Asia in the 1960s. Its trade surplus with the region increased from half a billion U.S. dollars in 1960, to almost $2 billion in 1970 (Halliday and McCormack 1973, 54).

It was in the context of President Johnson's sudden expansion of the U.S. war effort in Vietnam that a regional economic reorganization was finally consolidated. U.S. pressure was brought to bear on Korea and Japan, under the watchful eye of Dean Rusk, to rapidly conclude their prolonged normalization talks.

Korea urgently needed Japanese capital to finance its ambitious five-year plan. U.S. procurement contracts for the Vietnam War and the dispatch of Korean armed forces to South Vietnam and their dollar remittances were another key source of capitalization. The U.S., for its part, ensured further support for its war effort in Vietnam, while simultaneously "sharing the burden" with Japan of economically sustaining its Korean army-in-waiting.

Japan had achieved the world's highest rate of growth in exports and GNP by the beginning of the 1960s. By 1961, however, the Japanese economic juggernaut was beginning to experience certain difficulties as a result of such rapid expansion. Inflation reappeared, reaching 7.6 percent in 1963. The Bank of Japan responded with tighter monetary policy, which, as could be expected, had a deflationary impact on economic growth. The rate of growth dropped by practically two-thirds from 1961 to 1965. A serious business crisis existed by 1964–1965, which was reflected in an alarming bankruptcy rate, particularly affecting small and medium enterprises. Bankruptcies reached record postwar levels in 1965, with the collapse of Sanyo Special Steel Corporation causing a particular stir. Therefore, "Clearly, apart from political and security perspectives, Japanese businesses needed the expanded South Korean market" (Lee 1985, 53).

Thus, economic reintegration between the Japanese and Korean economies was viewed by influential business elites in recession-hit Japan as one avenue to stimulate recovery and recoup profits. This view coincided with renewed urgency on the part of the United States government, in the context of escalation of the Vietnam War and its massive outlay of funds, to reduce its dollar-aid commitments to South Korea, the economy of which was still heavily dependent on U.S. assistance.

In the normalization treaty of 1965, Japan provided some $800 million in grants and credits to Korea, most of which were payable in annual installments over a ten-year period beginning in 1965. Japanese aid money was used to purchase imports from Japan, with Japan having the right to designate which commodities should be purchased. The returns on subsequent sale of these goods were placed into a yen counterpart fund, to be channeled to such sectors as the military-industrial complex. This enabled ailing industries in Japan to off-load unsaleable domestic surplus production onto the Korean market, while recouping some profit. The new economic relationship also opened the door to Japanese direct investment and joint ventures, such as the giant Pohang Iron and Steel complex agreed to in 1969. Japan rapidly became South Korea's largest trade partner. From the outset of the relationship until the present, Korea has run a structural trade deficit with Japan. Thus, the Japanese benefit from this "second opening" of Korea (the first being by Japanese gunboat "diplomacy" in

1876) has been very substantial, despite appearances of acting primarily as a donor. As Lee puts it, "The marriage of South Korean labor to foreign capital and technology was to propel South Korea's economy. Japanese exports to South Korea began to rise at a phenomenal rate once the political issues were settled. . . . South Korean trade was enormously profitable to Japanese businessmen" (Lee 1985, 56).

Parallel to Japan's expansionary drive into Korea was a similar and similarly motivated expansion into Taiwan. As argued above, the developments in Korea and Taiwan during this period should be understood not merely as coincidence or parallel trajectories but as part of a much-larger regional and global reorganization of production and trade with U.S., Japanese, and also European interests at the center.[2]

In the period up to 1958, United States policy toward both South Korea and Taiwan was driven by the necessity to stabilize these regimes as anticommunist bulwarks in a partitioned Asia. By 1958, however, the U.S. was much more confident that the armed forces of the two regimes were adequate to this task. To ensure this, the U.S. had poured military assistance into both and—very important—by 1958, it had prepared the ground for introducing nuclear weapons to both clients. This was achieved through the May 7, 1957, agreement with Taiwan on the Matador tactical missile and through unilateral abrogation of subpargraph 13d, article two, of the Korean Armistice Agreement, which had prohibited military escalation on the peninsula and allowed for inspections at five ports by the Neutral Nations Supervisory Commission. U.S. nuclear defense sealed the "security" risk and made possible a dramatic shift of aid policy as discussed earlier.

U.S. aid to Taiwan was heavy in the early postwar period. Between 1951 and 1965, economic aid accounted for approximately 34 percent of total gross investment in Taiwan's economy (Jacoby 1966, 38). This aid ended in 1965, and thereafter Japan accelerated direct investment in Taiwan, which was already well established. With typical foresight, the very first yen loan to Taiwan focused on construction of infrastructure that would facilitate future industrial relocation.

The adjustments of the mid-1960s between Japan and both Korea and Taiwan were the precursors of a new phase at the end of that decade. Japan now actively sought to relocate large-scale heavy industries to these countries and take advantage of the EPZ opportunities to reap higher profits from relocating light manufacturing to areas with low labor costs. This economic onslaught also brought new forms of Japanese political influence in South Korea (Chang 1985). Industrial restructuring was also due partly to Japan's perceived need to relocate polluting industries abroad and partly to Cumings's product-cycle jumping-off point. In particular, iron and steel, shipbuilding, petrochemicals, and oil refining were targeted for relocation in that period. The overall regional pattern thus finally came to full fruition in the second half of the 1960s, precisely the same period when the Korean and the Taiwanese "miracles" first impinged on world consciousness.

CONCLUSION

From the foregoing analysis it is clear that the origin of the export-orientation strategy of industrialization adopted by both South Korea and Taiwan in the early 1960s resulted from the convergence of particular national, regional, and global interests. These interests were economic, political, and also strategic. The world economy was arriving at a new stage of organization at the end of the 1950s, with European and Japanese economic recovery accomplished and the Bretton Woods system becoming fully operational. The U.S. decided that its basic strategic objectives in Northeast Asia had been achieved, i.e., the stability of allied regimes, and therefore desired to reduce direct subsidy to these clients and so also reduce pressures on the dollar. Recession and trade imbalances in both the U.S. and Japanese economies played a key role in the emergence of a wider regional agenda for the industrial restructuring of Asia and the Pacific in the 1960s. MNCs were able to realize their expansionary impulse in the Asian periphery, which was targeted for a special production role in the new international division of labor. Export-oriented industrialization in East Asian NICs was facilitated by the readiness of foreign capital to invest in production and the receptivity of advanced-country markets, particularly that of the U.S., in the context of rapidly growing world trade. In both Korea and Taiwan the state-class remained unquestionably hegemonic in the domestic sphere vis à vis both private and foreign capital despite the shift to EOI. The U.S. hegemonic sphere was strengthened overall by this industrialization, as both Korea and Taiwan became more self-sustaining military and economic powers and Japan found new outlets for expansion.

The conclusion to be drawn is that EOI, far from being a "model" that a national state adopted or did not adopt, was a product of a conjuncture and its specific structural opportunities, hegemonic influences, and convergent (elite) interests. This analysis can be applied not only to the international origins of the EOI in East Asia but equally to subsequent adjustments that were synchronized throughout much of the region. Though outside the scope of this chapter, such synchronized, parallel adjustments to EOI occurred in the early to mid-1970s. Both Taiwan and South Korea reverted to an ISI emphasis, though both turned ISI heavy industries toward future export opportunities. This adjustment occurred in the context of the collapse of the Bretton Woods system, the U.S. defeat in Vietnam, détente with China and the Soviet Union, the oil crisis, and the onset of global recession. Yet another major adjustment to EOI occurred at the end of the 1970s and on into the 1980s. This parallel adjustment stressed internationalization of the economy, liberalization, and the low-energy, high-technology strategy for industrial upward mobility in the international division of labor.

During the second half of the 1980s, both South Korea and Taiwan came under renewed, heavy bilateral pressures from the United States over economic issues. In the post–Cold War order the U.S. prioritized its own direct economic interests over strategic goals. Therefore it is far less tolerant of the large trade surpluses accumulated by the East Asian NICs than was previously the case. The U.S. used its influence to attempt to reduce its trade deficit with Asia. In the 1990s, both South Korea and Taiwan became not only more "open economies" but also bowed to mounting pressure, both domestic and external, for at least formal democratization. Both have become major exporters of capital in the region in the past several years and, taken together, present a serious rival even to Japan's export of capital in Asia.

Several important implications can be drawn from the preceding analysis for general IPE approaches and for development theory. First, the findings point to the conclusion that states, particularly in the Third World, do not "choose" an economic development strategy so much as they adopt one thrust upon them by circumstances largely beyond their control, or, at most, they exploit a structural opportunity. The "choice" of the strategy is largely "directed" by globally powerful external forces.

Conversely, by implication, if global power holders (e.g., transnational capital, MNCs, or hegemonic governments) choose to obstruct, block, or ignore a Third World country's economic strategy, it is far less likely to succeed, and perhaps such opposition would even make it impossible to succeed. In one sense, the "magnifying glass" of global forces, especially capital and technology, must first be directed on a Third World country in order for it to subsequently "rise" to the occasion. Without this magnifying glass that facilitates industrialization, no Third World country is likely to become a "miracle." Such structural opportunities are *not on offer* for more than a select few Third World countries and then only at very specific moments.

The magnifying glass moves around the globe, according to its own logic, and not that of the national development of states in the Third World. The most "fortunate" are those that can successfully exploit an opportunity for upward mobility when it becomes available. The East Asian NICs and particularly South Korea and Taiwan exploited their structural opportunity very well indeed, not least because of their extremely "autonomous" state power domestically. Those Third World regimes that actually defy global power holders rather than accept their designated role, such as Vietnam, Cuba, or Iran after the Islamic revolution, are severely penalized for doing so.

Thus, the much-discussed, analyzed, and lauded "model" of the East Asian NICs' industrialization is not necessarily replicable by any other present regime in the Third World. The idea that success depends merely on the adoption of the "right" policies that exist objectively on their own intrinsic merits wherever applied is extraordinarily misleading. Such an idea, nevertheless, has much currency within the context of the old order's collapse in the former USSR, Eastern Europe, and Central Asia. Actual experience with the EOI in Latin America and especially Africa in the last decade, however, gives far less cause for optimism.

The evidence suggests that the industrialization and rapid upward mobility of states such as South Korea and Taiwan was exceptional, in that it was not the "natural" choice of either political or business elites in Korea or Taiwan at the time of its adoption. On the contrary, EOI was the creation of external forces. Even the concrete form of policymaking was not domestically created. Rather, it roughly followed the existing Japanese practices on economic planning and sequentialized industrialization that were available for emulation, and the overall vision and facilitation for a regional restructuring fostered by economic experts in the U.S. and key global agencies like the IMF and the World Bank. The model did not have to be and certainly was not domestically "invented," but only adopted. There is much evidence to support the contention that in both Korea and Taiwan foreign experts were extremely influential in guiding these governments toward the new model in the late 1950s and early 1960s, including lending crucial technical expertise.

This adoption of EOI was exceptional in that it reflected a unique conjuncture and a special convergence of interests not necessarily present in other cases. The hegemonic influences in this case were crucial to the transformative processes and cannot be considered to be universally available for all. In fact, expansion of the East Asian industrial core itself is very exceptional as a process in this century, and no other region has experienced a similar trajectory of growth in the same period. It is therefore foolish to expect Latin America, Africa, the Middle East, South Asia, Central Asia, the former USSR, or Eastern Europe to follow the East Asian pattern successfully. In the context of a world crisis in which even the advanced states' industries face ferocious competition in a limited world market, the prospect of so many NICs joining the fray is outright ludicrous.

The final analytical conclusion must be that state-centric approaches to analyzing national economic development are patently insufficient to explain the patterns of political-economy transformation we observe. Above all else, it is the "opportunity structure" of the global political economy that is the central determinant of development possibilities. Within this opportunity structure of the global political economy, it is foremost the historical conjuncture that is the key dimension of the transformative process and not domestic crisis or national strategy.[3]

This case illustrates that the governing transformative processes affecting states are at the level of the international political economy and not the level of endogenous factors. In the case of Northeast Asia the historical sequencing of industrialization as a regional process and the hegemonic sequence have been the principal processes conditioning the states' structure of opportunities. National social formations and state formation clearly play an important role in creating specific historical trajectories, but are not on their own sufficient explanations of divergence in different national development trajectories. In this case, the legacy of the relative autonomy of the state that resulted from Japanese colonialism and the specific character of the postwar U.S.-imposed geopolitical framework are central factors in any explanation of national development. The importance of the historical rise of Japan as an industrial capitalist core zone in the region is likewise a factor that should never be underestimated.

Domestic structures and global structures do interpenetrate, but in the case of peripheral or weak states it is the domestic that responds to the global more than the other way around. In this case, national development is clearly subsumed within regional and world development patterns.

NOTES

1. This analysis of the class base of economic strategy in 1960 on the part of the Democratic party arose in the course of discussions with Ronen Palan, to whom I am indebted for this point.

2. This global reorganization is often referred to as the so-called "new international division of labor" that emerged from the 1960s. Its principal feature is the globalization of production under the auspices of mobile capital controlled by MNCs operating for a world market.

3. A previous version of this paper was presented at St. Antony's College, Oxford, February 21, 1992, in the seminar series, "The Political Economy of Korean Development."

12

The Infrastructure of the Infrastructure? Toward "Embedded Financial Orthodoxy" in the International Political Economy

Philip G. Cerny

FINANCIAL GLOBALIZATION AND THE STATE: APPROACHES AND DEBATES

In the 1980s, many states modified the system of regulating their financial markets, including both banks and securities markets. The dynamic behind these changes, which often transcend traditional political cleavages, was a complicated blend of several different but interrelated political and economic factors. In the first place, there was an ideological backlash against government interventionism in general. This became the most salient feature of right-wing politics, especially Thatcherism in Britain and Reaganomics in the United States. Second, a widespread perception had already developed in the 1970s that the welfare state and Keynesian demand management had reached a plateau of effectiveness and were leading to a vicious circle of stagnation and inflation. This perception was shared by significant elements of the left as well as the right. Finally, states had to deal with growing pressures from more complex and volatile international capital flows and the increasing impossibility of insulating national economies at both macroeconomic and microeconomic levels. In this context, governments attempted to experiment with a variety of measures intended to improve their competitive advantage in a relatively open world—the "competition state" (Cerny 1990, chap. 8).

The importance of these changes for the international political economy cannot be overemphasized. Finance has often been thought of as the "life blood" of the physical economy. Today, with the coming of the information technology revolution and what the French call the "dematerialization" of financial instruments—the shift from physical share and bond certificates, for instance, to entries in a centralized computer system—finance is coming to have some characteristics of the nervous system as well. It incarnates the fungibility of capital at its most abstract. It is, in the last analysis, the embodiment of capital accumulation and of the fundamental, indispensable process of exchange that enables markets to exist in the first place and to function in the real world. It is "the infrastructure of the infrastructure." In the contemporary world, this is more true than ever. An international financial system of some kind, linking and cutting across the national capitalist economies of the world, has always been a basic feature of capitalism per se. Today, however, the globalization of finance brings with it the prospect of a genuinely global capitalist economy, with all of its problems and prospects.

But, as Karl Polanyi pointed out (Polanyi 1944), the creation of a capitalist market economy—and of the financial system needed to sustain it—does not happen by itself. It is a political act, in two interlocking ways. First, the capitalist market is only one dimension or model of social organization in general. For the market to become the dominant organizing structure of a society, it must be instituted and guaranteed through *politics*—either imposed in an authoritative way or embodied in some kind of collective process. Second, certain necessary prerequisites for the organizing and working of stable and efficient markets in themselves require the backing of the state. These include: the establishment, within a circumscribed *territory*, of clearly defined and enforceable *property rights*; common *standards of value* such as weights and measures; a *currency* for exchange and accumulation; a system of *contracts*; a *legal system* to enforce the above; and a *state apparatus* to manage the above and to sanction predators.

In modern times, these things have been provided by nation-states. International law has been customary and weak in its application to specific cases, and international economic regimes are themselves primarily the creatures of states. In this context, it is a common postulate of international relations that transnational markets are brittle structures unless backed by a powerful state or supported by a group of states acting in concert (Underhill 1991). According to neorealist "hegemonic stability theory," the modern transnational, capitalist market system of the nineteenth and twentieth centuries was constructed and maintained predominately under the aegis of one power, first Britain and later the United States. In both cases, moreover, the limitations of that same hegemony were manifest in the system itself—embodied in the profound tension between specific national interests, on the one hand, and the imperatives of the international marketplace, on the other. In particular, growing conflicts between the national interests of the hegemonic state, on the one hand, and the conditions necessary for international economic stability and efficiency, on the other—conflicts intensified by the hegemon's relative economic decline—undermined the financial stability and economic efficiency of the international marketplace (Mann and Hobson, forthcoming).

The logic of hegemonic stability theory (which is in reality a hegemonic *instability* theory), however, depends on the continuing structural predominance of the state—and therefore upon the absence of a suprastate financial structure that can perform at the *trans*national level the same kind of systemic political functions the state has traditionally performed *inter*nationally, so to speak. Nevertheless, a transnational financial structure of some sort does exist, as Susan Strange (1988) has argued. But to what extent does it possess structural autonomy? In other words, how far do actors within the transnational financial structure have the capacity to act independently of constraints from other structures? Can they use the resources available to them to pursue autonomous organizational goals, bypassing the constraints embedded in the state and/or the states system?

Several approaches have emerged that focus on the transnationalization of the global economy in general. Analysts like Robert Cox and Stephen Gill, who stress the structural autonomy of capital, see the emergence of a world production and financial structure as creating a new, Gramscian global hegemony. This new, transnationalized structure of capital transcends and shapes state action—much as national capital shaped development in an earlier era, creating the conditions for the ascendancy of the nation-state itself. In this context, the contradictions of capital will play themselves out at the global level rather than within and between autonomous states. In contrast to the neo-Gramscians, a range of monetarist, neoclassical, and supply-side economists regard the retreat of the state in the Reagan-Thatcher era as the harbinger of a more-efficient allocation of resources at the global level. This will lead to the emergence of a market system with a higher equilibrium, free from the distortions of state intervention (McKenzie and Lee 1991). Yet another interpretation comes from a "liberal social democratic" perspective, such as that developed by Robert Reich. Reich, too, foresees a fundamental shift in the role of the state, with much greater transnational constraints on economic intervention. He regards the space still controlled by the state, however, as not merely significant but crucial in a democratic society (Reich 1991). My own argument is that the very concept of the national interest is expanding to embrace the transnational dimension in new ways: the so-called competition state is itself obliged by the imperatives of global competition to expand transnationalization (Cerny 1990).

Across the analytical spectrum, then, is a realization that globalization is a qualitatively new phase. In some ways it replaces or transcends the nation-state; in other ways it entwines or assimilates the state itself. Only neorealists hold out by using the catch-all concept of "regimes" to keep the state in the driver's seat at the transnational level. But what has been remarkable in the specifically financial arena since the breakdown of the Bretton Woods system in 1971, has been the absence of any stable, state-based "regime"—an absence manifest in the way the system of floating exchange rates itself has worked. The controversy over the transnationalization of finance therefore revolves around several questions: How far has the process gone? What has been its wider impact on the world economy? And how does it actually work?

With regard to the first question, I argue that financial globalization has become irreversible. States can no longer control their own domestic financial systems as they learned to do in the 1930s. Furthermore, without either a hegemonic or a genuinely transnational regime to regulate it, the transnational financial structure is actually driving the wider economic globalization process. With regard to the second question, I argue that financial globalization severely restricts economic policy in increasingly complex ways, making it more and more difficult for states to follow an autonomous path driven by domestic (democratic?) economic goals. This is as true for the First World, with its financial bubbles and panics, as for the Third World, with its debt crisis. This also has serious consequences for the working of the global economy, which leads into my response to the third question. Tensions are growing between financial globalization— rooted in the abstractness and fungibility of financial transactions and power in the information technology age—and the requirements of production and trade. Even *within* the financial arena, a tension exists between different financial markets. Both kinds of tensions will characterize the international political economy for the foreseeable future. In this situation, not only will financial markets dominate production and trade, *but within the financial sector itself, the most abstract of "dematerialized" financial markets—those most concerned with the pure trading of complex financial instruments and therefore most detached from productive investment—will predominate.*

What will this mean in substantive terms for the real economy and for the political structure of financial power? It may mean, as the authors of *Quicksilver Capital* argue, a renewed surge of stable growth in the world economy. Or it may mean, as I argue, a new *embedded financial orthodoxy*. "Embedded financial orthodoxy" means that economic production and exchange is shaped first and foremost by financial and monetary imperatives. Like several earlier eras of monetary primacy such as the 1920s, a system characterized by embedded financial orthodoxy is prone to unstable cycles of boom and slump, the use of blunt instruments like interest rates rather than Keynesian fine tuning, and calls for monetary stability before all else (including, but not limited to, permanently prioritizing anti-inflationary policy). The predominant climate is austerity, although that austerity is punctuated by financial bubbles and panics that disrupt the efficient working of the real economy.

Keynes warned that financial markets drain resources from the real economy, and Eric Helleiner (1993) has argued that the strength of the postwar world economy (under U.S. hegemony) stemmed not from financial openness and the liberalization of financial markets, but from the strict *control* of international finance under the Bretton Woods system. In the current environment, however, effective financial regulation at a transnational level has yet to materialize, and its prospects look dim. Interstate cooperation was seen as a potential solution during the 1980s, but such regimes have not been particularly effective except in narrow (and contentious) areas such as the 1988 Basle Accord on bank capital adequacy, to which we shall return later. The recent abdication of the Group of Seven (G7) in the face of economic chaos in the former Soviet Union is also significant here. And although a move toward regional trading zones has been widely anticipated, it will probably be a piecemeal affair and not likely to constitute a serious, countervailing power structure to globalizing finance.

A new hegemony seems unlikely, too. Japan has been seriously handicapped in its pursuit of a wider financial role by the collapse of the "bubble economy" since 1989, and the recent crisis of the exchange rate mechanism (ERM) suggests that European financial hegemony is not likely to emerge. Nor is it likely, finally, that the politics of global finance will prove sufficiently coherent to ensure either financial market stability or a positive synergy with the wider growth of the "real economy." Whether this is the beginning of an epoch of crisis, a transition to some more closely structured world politico-financial order, or just an extended phase of "muddling through" is impossible to say at this stage. I consider, however, that the last of these is the most likely outcome of the new era of "embedded financial orthodoxy" in "the infrastructure of the infrastructure."

FINANCIAL GLOBALIZATION, THE NATION-STATE, AND THE WORLD ORDER

Since the first "financial revolution" of the late eighteenth and early nineteenth centuries, government intervention in the operation of financial markets has been driven by the imperatives of the nation-state and the state-based international system. The first imperative was to consolidate and expand the state apparatus. This required secure sources of capital for the state itself, especially during periods of fiscal crisis and, most spectacularly, in times of war (Ingham 1985; Sassier and de Witt 1985). To this end, governments have supported and guaranteed both domestic banking systems and, more sporadically, securities markets. This analysis differs from the standard explanation given by economists for the emergence of financial markets: that "whatever the location, they were formed in response to an increase in the number of people anxious to dispose of some sort of financial asset and of buyers prepared to put their savings into them" (Thomas 1989, 1). In contrast, even today, government demand for finance—especially to cover growing budget deficits—is still a major factor in the expansion as well as the regulation of markets, as has been argued for U.S., Japanese (Feldman 1986, Horne 1985) and French (Cerny 1989a) deregulation in the 1980s.[1]

The second imperative has been economic competition *between* nation-states. The objectives of expanding national wealth and promoting new production and consumption processes has always been a central concern of governments. To this end, states have pursued several lines of policy. They have (1) provided direct finance to industry through subsidy, procurement, and public ownership; (2) attempted to direct private sources of finance to targeted sectors; (3) manipulated monetary and fiscal levers; and (4) frequently supported the development of so-called "finance capital" or "organized capitalism," especially in the era of corporate integration typical of the "second industrial revolution" from the late nineteenth to the mid-twentieth centuries (Rothwell and Zegveld 1981; Zysman 1983; Reich 1983; Johnson 1982). National systems of regulation have consisted of policy measures and enforcement structures that represent different balances between the above approaches. These systems have also been shaped by disparities between states: by differences in endogenous state capacity; by the structural distinctiveness of particular national economies; and by the degree of vulnerability of each national economy to transnational market forces and other pressures.

Essentially, two competing models of capitalism have emerged from this process: relatively open, market-driven systems, and relatively closed, state- or corporate-driven systems (Cerny 1988). The first model has tended to be characterized by what has been called "arms-length" financial systems (Zysman 1983), combining active financial markets and a diversified banking system providing relatively short-term credit with a view to financial returns per se. The second type has tended to be characterized by financial systems that give a greater developmental role to long-term debt rather than to equity or short-term debt, and that integrate industrial and financial decisionmaking under the aegis of structured linkages between the state apparatus, the banks and financial markets, and the corporate networks. It is argued that modern capitalism's spread has been through the hegemony or "leading" position during key phases of its development of those states characterized by arms-length financial systems—especially Britain in the nineteenth century and the United States since World War II (Madison 1982).

In other words, the form international capitalism has taken has first and foremost been a consequence of the predominance of economies with arms-length financial systems and not merely of the productive power of the leading economy. Such systems are more compatible with the anarchic nature of international relations, because government influence on them is indirect rather than direct. The stability of the production and trading system under the gold standard, for example, was guaranteed by the dominance of London as a financial center (rather than by Britain as the industrial "workshop of the world"), by the willingness of the British state to back up its financial institutions, and by the willingness of British individuals and institutions to export capital (Ingham 1985). Similarly, the stability of the post–World War II era was guaranteed by U.S. support for the Bretton Woods system and the dollar-exchange standard, along with a willingness to alleviate the postwar dollar shortage (Gardner 1980; Block 1977). Nevertheless, had the Axis powers not been defeated—and the Soviet, centrally planned model not been "contained"—state-dominated financial systems might well have eclipsed arms-length systems despite inherent impediments to transnationalization.[2]

In both types of systems, however, the dominant pattern for regulating financial markets involved the national government protecting domestically based institutions. Finance was widely seen as a vital strategic industry, too important, especially in the context of postwar macroeconomic management, to be left to the market alone. In Britain and the United States, despite different mixes of statutory supervision and "self-regulation," financial regulation developed incrementally, generally as the result of market failures and exogenous shocks. The U.S. framework, from establishment of the Federal Reserve System in 1913 to the post-Depression reforms, was a particularly ad hoc structure, reflecting the fragmented sovereignty of U.S. bureaucracy (Cerny, forthcoming). In both cases, the main principle of regulation was *compartmentalization*. To prevent endogenous market failure, this involved the separation of different kinds of financial "markets" in order to prevent failure in one from creating a chain reaction through the others, as had happened in 1929. In the United States, commercial banks were prevented from dealing in securities; in Britain, stockbrokers were prevented from trading on their own account, while "jobbers" (market-makers) were prohibited from trading directly with the public.

In the context of the Keynesian welfare state, too, government intervention established a set of buffer mechanisms to prevent exogenous shocks from setting off domestic chain reactions: interest-rate control and other monetary policy instruments, exchange-rate stabilization, lender-of-last-resort facilities, and the like. The operation of these mechanisms ultimately depended on the capacity of transnational regimes and the financial strength of the international "hegemon" to underwrite the liquidity and stability of the system. Wider financial stability, in turn, made it possible for governments to "fine tune" national economies in order to maintain the economic expansion necessary to manipulate the levers of the welfare state. Supporting an increasing flow of credit to the economy enabled capitalist economies to go beyond the bounds of fixed capital and physical monetary reserves, expanding the production system in a way compatible with greater openness and interdependence in production and trade.

Indeed, the post–World War II expansion of the welfare state depended on maintaining financial regulatory mechanisms that had developed earlier in reaction to the breakdown of the pre–World War I international financial structure. It still depended on protecting and guaranteeing the nationally based financial systems that had originated in the first financial revolution and had been "recaptured" by the state from international high finance in the 1930s. This became much more difficult in the postwar environment, however, for those very systems were increasingly being called upon to perform transnational tasks in the rapidly expanding world of international integration of production and trade during the "Long Boom." Against this background, the "second financial revolution" of the 1980s is widely attributed to structural tension between the internationalization of finance and the continuing national basis for financial regulation. The chief consequence of this tension at the state level, financial "deregulation," is fundamentally a response to the inadequacy of nationally based regulatory systems to deal with the consequences of financial globalization.

These trends raise a number of issues for the analyst. It is important, first, to examine whether this new transnational financial structure is likely to work well as a financial system: (a) will it lead to a more- or a less-efficient allocation of capital in the world economy, promoting or constraining economic growth, trade, etc.?;[3] and (b) will it be an endogenously stable or unstable system, given the increasing volume and volatility of capital flows and the destabilizing effect that similar flows have had on previous international financial arrangements? At this point in time, competing interpretations have emerged and the debate is very much open. For example, were recent crashes—the October 1987 worldwide stock market crash, the mini-crash of October 1989, the Tokyo crash of 1990—indicators of underlying destabilization or merely sharp "corrections" of price levels that have since allowed the markets to consolidate without interrupting long-term growth? The onset of recession since 1989 has also been linked with financial deregulation, particularly in the U.S. and the U.K. These more technical questions will not be dealt with here, although the basic shape of the new structure, and some of the more central hypotheses about its functioning, will have significant consequences for the other issues dealt with in this paper.

A second issue is to look for explanations of change. An understanding of the different factors that have shaped the new financial system is crucial not only for an analysis of the actual responses of different states, but also for an awareness of the possibilities for and limitations on state actions in the future—especially in terms of the potential for transnational financial regulation. The third issue, therefore, is the wider one of the future of financial regulation in particular, and its relationship with state economic intervention in general. This question is of critical significance as transnational structures increasingly constrain the activities of states and, more specifically, the cluster of activities making up the postwar welfare state. Particular focus will be on the process of "regulatory arbitrage." It will be argued that although states corresponding to the competition-state model may be better able to manage and exploit shifts in competitive advantage than those that do not, in the long run the power of all states to manage their economic affairs will be structurally constrained by the development of the integrated, 24-hour global financial marketplace.

Several factors stemming from financial transnationalization have altered not only the scope but also the substance of government economic intervention. It is by now well known that growing transnational constraints have undermined Keynesian demand management policies through their effects on capital flows, the exchange rate, and the like. Monetary policy has become the principal instrument of macroeconomic control. Yet at the same time, these "exogenous" constraints have increasingly meant that monetary policy instruments have themselves become blunted. To work, they must "overshoot," reinforcing boom-slump cycles. The consequence is that governments, even where they seem to be able to live beyond their means (as in the United States), increasingly measure their performance according to criteria acceptable to the financial markets. They must be seen as "strong" or "sound" if they are to retain the confidence of the transnational financial community. Rather than a system of "embedded liberalism" (Ruggie 1982), what we have today is one of "embedded financial orthodoxy," which sets an international "bottom line" for government economic intervention more broadly.

Globalization is thus a two-edged sword. Without the crystallization of transnational linkages at key times, the various forms of deregulation and re-regulation that governments have promoted in recent years—decompartmentalization, disintermediation/securitization, financial innovation, and so on (Cerny 1993)—would not have been able to take off; each would have been stunted in its development. There have been several key mechanisms of globalization: the emergence of virtually unregulatable competition for lending via the Euromarkets; the breakdown of Bretton Woods and the explosion of international currency flows after 1971 (much exacerbated by the subsequent oil shocks); inflation and the fiscal crisis of the state in the 1970s, followed by deflationary monetary policies; the Third World debt crisis; "competitive deregulation" or "competition in laxity" between states; the emergence of new institutional structures in the financial sector itself; and the development of electronics and information technology, which make financial markets far more flexible and therefore difficult to control.

It must be pointed out, however, that the end result of these processes is not an evenly "integrated, global 24-hour financial marketplace," as media images would have it. Of course, gross financial exchange transactions, estimated at $60–70 trillion a year in the mid-1980s, dwarf exchanges of goods and services, which then totaled around $4 trillion; and gross capital exchanges between the United States, Europe, and Japan (excluding intra-European exchanges) grew at an average annual rate of 54 percent per year between 1980 and 1986, while trade grew at an average 8 percent per year over the same period. But, as research by international management consultant McKinsey pointed out, the development of transnational financial market structures has been very uneven, leading to "the emergence of distinct world markets for each type of instrument . . . depending closely on the complex nature of the risks which determine the price of each instrument in different countries" (Giry-Deloison and Masson 1988, 725–729). Therefore, although the major trends are still toward global integration, some markets are highly globalized, some still essentially national despite some transnational inroads, and others a more complex mixture.

For example, in currency and short-term capital markets, instruments are relatively simple, forward markets liquid, and information about the main price signal, interest rates, easy to obtain. Analysts have also noted a long-term convergence of interest rates, when controlled for inflation expectations (Fukao and Hanazaki 1987). In this context, technological developments make complex arbitrage profitable with low transaction costs from minimal spreads; price changes have an immediate impact across markets. It is easy to see why the move to floating exchange rates provided a lever for internationalization. In partial contrast, risk assessments are far more complex in bond markets, especially private-sector bond markets, which are more integrated at the level of primary markets, where interest-rate levels and ratings provide more-comparable international price signals than in secondary markets. Nevertheless, it was the role played by the Euromarkets in broadening price signals transnationally in this sector that provided the main linkage between transnational capital flows, securitization, and the process of regulatory arbitrage, which undermined compartmentalization. Finally, share markets are still relatively national, although there has been some globalization in secondary markets for purposes of portfolio diversification. There have been few genuinely international issues, however, despite a gradual growth in Euroequities and an increasing tendency to offer a proportion of shares or a rights issue in foreign markets (Giry-Deloison and Masson 1987). The main impact of the 1987 stock market crash, in fact, was on the share markets, where it led to a process of "coming home": a trend toward investors preferring to buy domestic shares again.

Most share markets have been stagnant compared to their performance before the crash, but they have not fallen further and indeed have touched on or surpassed pre-crash highs in certain cases. Despite the continuing recession in the United States and the United Kingdom, U.S. equities climbed strongly well into 1992. The Japanese market, however, has undergone a fundamental downward correction of about 60 percent. Bond markets, which signaled the onset of the 1987 crash, benefited from a "flight to quality" and from government support. The main impact of the 1987 crash on state/financial market relations was probably the decision taken informally by G7 finance ministers to increase liquidity to the markets after the crash. Currency and short-term capital markets were relatively healthy until the September 1992 ERM crisis. Financial market structures have proved remarkably resilient, and state action has in general reinforced or even initiated patterns of restructuring—a trend continuing today. Although there are significant differences in the restructuring process from state to state, governments in all the major financial powers have decompartmentalized their financial markets, gone along with disintermediation and securitization, and supported or even forced the pace of financial innovation. States have thus had to cope with the same globalizing trends, but this common situation is multilayered and uneven, and states have differential endogenous capacities to deal with the different layers.

GLOBALIZATION AND THE PROBLEM OF HEGEMONY

The globalization of finance, however, does not merely constrain the role of the nation-state per se. Financial power—and the capacity and will of both state and private-sector actors to use that power—has been at the core of the structure of the international system, especially the issue of international hegemony, since the modern state system emerged in the nineteenth century. If we look at the history of British and U.S. hegemony, however, and at the decline and failure of those hegemonies—including the long interregnum during much of the first half of the twentieth century—what we see is a situation in which the most crucial factor is not so much broad economic power, nor cultural dominance, nor military power—as important as those are—but financial power (Barkin 1992). The crucial element of financial power is a stable, guaranteed, international payments system. Without such a system, trade decays into mercantilism and protectionism. As a result, culture and knowledge become inward-looking and suspicious of the foreign, while military power becomes zero-sum and predatory rather than balancing or stabilizing.

The key to British hegemony was not British balance-of-power diplomacy on the European continent (with due respect to Henry Kissinger),[4] the expansion of the empire, the navy, nor even the industrial revolution, but the maintenance of the gold standard. Furthermore, this was, it must be emphasized, not because it constituted a central policy aim of the British state as such. The gold standard emerged from, and developed through, deeply embedded networks linking the treasury, the Bank of England, and the City of London (the center of Britain's financial services industry). British financial institutions were concerned chiefly with financing trade (as well as financing the state itself). During the nineteenth century this increasingly meant financing trade between third (non-British) parties. The other main role of the City was to direct British investment capital abroad, mainly to the empire and to the U.S. (Ingham 1985). If there was any hegemonic "power nexus" in the nineteenth-century international system, this manifested itself not in the British state per se, but in a transnational network of high finance with the City of London at its core (Polanyi 1944). The British state continued to play a critical supporting role for the gold standard system until it was fatally weakened in World War I, despite the long decline of British hegemony (Silverman 1982). Nevertheless, it was finance, not force, that had been the basis of the *pax britannica*.

Perhaps the most influential work in the development of the hegemonic stability school deals with the interregnum between the *pax britannica* and the *pax americana*, the period between the two world wars. Economic historian Charles P. Kindleberger argues that the root cause of the economic overheating of the 1920s and the Great Depression of the 1930s, which in turn reinforced the global trend toward more virulent and totalitarian forms of autarchy, was the lack of not a military or diplomatic hegemon in the world system, but a financial hegemon (Kindelberger 1973).[5] In the 1920s, several closely intertwined factors were symptomatic of the wider disease of the epoch: the volatility of financial flows between Europe and the United States; the lack of an international consensus on certain structurally significant financial issues (especially German reparations); and the political inability of the United States to go beyond just patching up cracks in the gold standard at a time when the latter was undermining the economic and social health of the major powers. With the Great Depression came the collapse of world trade and the final demise of the gold standard system, but the Roosevelt administration took several years to fully shift from domestic planning and corporatism to free trade. By the outbreak of World War II and the subsequent formulation of U.S. economic war aims, however, that shift would be virtually complete (Gardner 1971; Penrose 1953).

Indeed, there arose a consensus among American elites (Ikenberry 1992) that a new world order was required, in which U.S. structural leadership—hegemony—would be required to guarantee free trade. And the key to that new world order had to be, first and foremost, a new international financial system to replace the defunct gold standard. Since the mid-1930s and the tying of the dollar to gold, the slow recovery of world trade had come to depend on a de facto dollar standard. This would be the linchpin of the new system agreed at Bretton Woods in 1944. By fixing the exchange rates of member states of the International Monetary Fund (the new, U.S.-backed, international lender of last resort) to the dollar, the world would once again have a stable and guaranteed financial system. This was to be a free-trade system, but not a free-market system entirely. Indeed, the mechanisms of Bretton Woods rested on an apparent paradox:

in order to promote trade liberalization, finance would have to be controlled. U.S. hegemony in the postwar period may have been made possible by its military victory over the Axis, but the world's dollar shortage was what gave the United States the leverage to impose a new financial system to stabilize Western economies and thereby to guarantee the peace, or so U.S. elites believed. Bretton Woods, however—like the gold standard—had built-in tensions that would eventually undermine it; these came to the fore in the 1960s. Chronic balance-of-payments deficits, followed by chronic trade deficits, reflected the U.S.'s decreasing competitiveness. Outflows of its capital were not being repatriated from abroad but they made their way to the expanding Euromarkets in London, where they could escape domestic regulatory controls. The "dollar shortage" had turned into a "dollar overhang."

The dollar overhang had drawbacks for both the United States and its increasingly dynamic European and Japanese competitors. On the one hand, these countries put the United States under pressure to devalue the dollar against gold in order to counterbalance the U.S.'s own external deficits. On the other hand, this pressure from outside seemed to U.S. policymakers to threaten the Bretton Woods system as a whole by undermining the dollar's guarantee of stability—as well as undermining the ability of the United States to conduct an autonomous economic policy. They resisted by demanding the revaluation of competitors' currencies instead (ignoring the potentially deflationary effects of this approach for the wider international economy). Stalemate between the Nixon administration and America's major trading partners led to the abandonment of Bretton Woods itself and the move to a system of floating exchange rates. In effect, the international financial system was transformed by the back door. The former financial hegemon was no longer able to guarantee the system by itself; neither could it exploit its eroded political capital to persuade its partners and rivals to restructure the system around its preferred options.[6] International finance had been based since World War II on attempting to restrict and control financial markets in order (paradoxically) to liberalize trade. What would the sudden liberalization (Cohen calls it "privatization"; Cohen 1986, 70) of the cornerstone of this system, the foreign exchange market, mean for the role that finance would come to play in the future? What would be its impact on trade? And how would this new role for finance intersect with the wider power structure of the international system?

The development of the international financial system since 1971—and its impact on the wider world order—has been interpreted in three contrasting ways. From one perspective, U.S. hegemony still exists, but it is of a much more complex and subtle kind, which Susan Strange calls "structural power." In this context, the floating exchange rate system was not so much adopted by default as imposed on the world by the U.S.—whether by conscious intent or inadvertently, through a "non-decision"

(Strange 1986). Indeed, the structurally dominant position of the United States in the world financial system was seen, despite ostensible U.S. withdrawal, to continue to confer on the U.S. a quasi-Gramscian hegemony, based on its "structural power," even if it no longer possessed the realist kind, based on "relational power" (Gill 1986; Helleiner 1992). But was this a usable form of power, which would contribute to developing a more efficient, market-based system, or was it just the power to cause disorder by default?

From a second perspective, the move to floating rates marked the end of real U.S. hegemony and signaled the advent of a more volatile world order. In this emerging order (or disorder), stability would have to be continually negotiated among several major economic powers, especially Japan and Germany, as well as the United States. The form this new disorder might take is contested. To some, escalating neomercantilism in trade, especially in the form of the non-tariff barriers, is likely to mirror an analogous trend in finance, reinforcing the tendency for the multilateral liberal system to be undermined at its heart in the monetary sphere. For others, however, partial agreements to avoid crises, such as the Plaza and Louvre Accords in the mid-1980s, could lead to more cooperative habits of interstate behavior in the longer term.

A third interpretation, however, is that the dramatic expansion of financial flows resulting from the floating exchange rate regime would make international financial markets into autonomous, transnational structures. In the future, the "24-hour global financial marketplace" would increasingly constrain and shape state behavior, imposing upon monetary policy, fiscal policy, and trade policy a much greater "market discipline."[7] Proponents of this view are also divided. Would this new market discipline lead to future economic growth and a more efficient allocation of resources, as monetarist and supply-side economists would contend? Or, conversely, would it impose a new "embedded financial orthodoxy" on states, producing either long-term rigidity and stagnation or more volatile boom-and-bust cycles? The empirical focus of that debate, discussed below, has been deregulation and its implications for the state, especially the United States.

The issue of deregulation has raised questions that go beyond both neorealist hegemonic stability theory and the Gramscian notion of hegemony, to raise again the question of the nature of collective action. Each of these versions of hegemony, in different ways, sees interstate competition and cooperation as the dominant mode of international interaction and system structuring.[8] Such an interstate system, however, must ultimately depend for its effective operation upon what I have elsewhere called the "decisional capacity" of state apparatuses (Cerny 1989b). States are not just hierarchical objects that behave like solid, billiard-ball-type units. They are real historical entities, composed of complex patterns of conflict and coalition building, mediated through institutional structures, socio-political cleavages, and competition of economic interests. By the same token, the international system is not merely a configuration of unitary states, but a complex congeries of states and other, cross-cutting structures (Cerny 1993). Within this context, the role of finance is twofold. It has always constituted both a cross-cutting, transnational structure *and* a crucial element of state building and state power. Although particular states may have played hegemonic roles in the modern era, their hegemony has itself been rooted in structured coalitions of state and private-sector actors able to marshal financial and other resources in the wider, world financial order. The gold standard and the Bretton Woods system represented the intersection of private financial power, the power of state actors and apparatuses (internally as well as externally), and the state or condition of the transnational financial structure.

Holding together this complex hegemonic "crossroads" in each case was a decisionmaking network mediated through the "Janus-faced" state. State *structures* provided crucial linkages between different groups of domestic and international private and state actors. At one level, provisions of the law—a key attribute of "state-ness"—provided both the operational rules for this process and the basis for its legitimacy. At the same time, the good faith and credit of the state—and the influence of its financial apparatuses such as treasuries, central banks, and others—provided more tangible guarantees of material solidity. Furthermore, the state's diplomatic apparatus coordinated international political negotiations. Of course, the state's military power also was always present in both the *pax britannica* and the *pax americana*. But the glue holding this complex system of finance and hegemony together was not the state as a supreme hierarchical unit per se, but the very character of the state's complex structure, including the decisionmaking processes of which the state was itself composed. The key independent variable was in effect the decisional capacity of the state—the capacity of state actors to organize their own efforts, marshal the state's resources and coordinate them with private resources, and manipulate the international environment in a coherent, consistent, and goal-directed fashion.

DEREGULATION AND U.S. DECLINE

At this point in the analysis, two quite distinct but cross-cutting factors come to the fore. On the one hand, the process of financial deregulation becomes a critical focus of policymaking. On the other hand, the problematic character of decisionmaking in the American state itself—what I have called its tendency to "Madisonian entropy"—reemerges as a critical element in foreign economic policy as well as in the domestic policy arena. The first factor is deregulation. Deregulation became crucial because a policy based on deregulation dovetails rather too neatly with key constraints present in both (a) the entropic domestic political process, and (b) the anarchic character of the international system. The breakdown of U.S. postwar financial hegemony has been seen by Strange as the result of key "non-decisions" taken against the background of the decreasing competitiveness of the domestic U.S. financial structure, both public and private, with the rise of Europe and Japan. But the shift to floating rates also had a wider rationale—deregulation—and deregulation was proactively supported by both monetarist economists and certain politicians for the very reason that it was intended to obviate state control of the foreign exchange markets.

Such financial deregulation can be seen from two perspectives: positively, as a transfer of responsibility for the allocation of financial resources to more efficient financial markets; or negatively, as an abdication of responsibility for managing the international financial system. The real strength of deregulation as a policy option, however, is that it can play both of these roles at the same time. Deregulation, both in the financial arena and in more general terms, can appear to be a nonpolicy. It involves, ostensibly at least, the simple removal of regulations.[9] On the domestic level as well as the international, therefore, it can attract an alliance of strange bedfellows. It does not appear to require agreement on the direct, authoritative distribution or redistribution of resources; this is, in theory at least, left to the market. On the other hand, unlike the multilateral decisionmaking processes embodied in the IMF or the GATT, the decision to deregulate can be a unilateral one. This was a crucial advantage in an international system where consensus—in this case, around the Bretton Woods system—was breaking down. Deregulation, then, is a policy option that is possible to pursue in an anarchical international system in which exists what public-choice theorists call an "empty core": the systematic lack of sufficient, shared preferences from which a collectively agreed outcome can emerge. It represents a noncooperative equilibrium in policy terms. These twin facets of deregulation—the apparent absence of the necessity for actors to agree on substantive alternatives and the fact that it can be decided upon unilaterally—are crucial for understanding the development of the post–Bretton Woods international financial system.

One of the most important issues in the study of the international financial system is the "collective action problem." In the trade arena, multilateral action has been seen as necessary and vital for the maintenance of an open, liberal, world trading order. Unilateral action, in contrast, has been seen as having by its very nature a neomercantilist "closure" effect. Many international political economists, influenced by the emphasis in the discipline upon international trade, assume that the same dynamic is at work in finance. In the financial arena, however, the converse would seem to be the rule. Multilateral action is necessary to *control* financial flows in an open world; abstract money would simply flow around and through most national-level controls. Furthermore, a central tenet of the Keynesian approach, which lay behind the Bretton Woods system, was that open and unregulated international financial markets (a) have an inherent tendency to be volatile and destabilizing (as in Keynes's analysis of the 1920s), and (b) they would drain funds from industrial investment and trade; such markets both undermine the virtuous circle of open trade and crowd out production.

Therefore, multilateral control of financial flows—which the Bretton Woods system was supposed to achieve through fixed-but-flexible exchange rates (the "adjustable peg")—is an a priori necessity for maintaining a virtuous circle of free trade and production growth. Worldwide economic growth via free trade requires a closed, not an open, international financial regime. *Unilateral action, in contrast, has the effect of "opening" the world financial system.* What I call the "widening circle of deregulation" reflects an interactive series of unilateral actions by states to deregulate first limited, but later more sweeping, classes of financial markets, institutions, and transactions. The collective action problem as developed in trade-oriented analysis must therefore be stood on its head in the financial field.

But by the 1970s, not only were financial markets that were free from postwar controls supposed to become far more efficient allocators of capital than the Bretton Woods regime had ever been, but deregulation was intended to remove the state from the financial decisionmaking process in general. Indeed, the widening circle of deregulation touched off by the collapse of Bretton Woods[10] has undermined the decisional capacity of far more unitary, "strategic" states than the United States (Cerny 1989a; Loriaux 1991). Deregulation, then, was the reaction of the American state to the problems it was experiencing in maintaining its financial—and therefore its political—hegemony. But deregulation, by its very nature, entailed the next turn of the screw. For deregulation is meant to transfer decisionmaking responsibility from the state to the market. From now on, the United States would be less able than ever to act in a neorealist "state-like" fashion; the parameters of state decisionmaking would be increasingly set by transnational financial markets.

At the same time, the second factor mentioned above comes into play: the complex decisional structure of the American state itself. It might be argued that its decisional capacity has always been inherently fragile, the consequence of its institutional structure: the system of "checks and balances" embodied in the separation of powers and federalism. In a series of issue-areas either directly concerned with or otherwise relevant to foreign policy and the U.S. role in world affairs, the American "state" is divided, stalemated, entropic. Entropic states are peculiarly vulnerable in international affairs; French foreign and economic policy weakness under the Third Republic has been attributed to France's "stalemate society" of the epoch (Hoffman 1963; Duroselle 1963). Furthermore, my own analysis of U.S. "political entropy" in foreign economic policy is complementary to analyses of U.S. politics that have focused on weaknesses in the policymaking process on a range of domestic issues (Lowi 1969).

Against this background, what is surprising is not that the United States has lost financial hegemony, but that it ever gained it in the first place—a situation that can be explained by the special circumstances of the postwar period. By the late 1960s and early 1970s, however, those conditions no longer prevailed. A new set of circumstances—external deficits, a renewed conservatism in domestic economic policy, the Vietnam War, détente with the Soviet Union, the competitive economic challenge from the U.S.'s political allies (soon to be exacerbated by the mid-1970s' slump), and the collapse of Bretton Woods—led to a search for alternatives to a foreign economic policy that had lost its central rationale. In this situation, the U.S. was no longer in *political* control of the capitalist world economy, but U.S. elites—politicians, bureaucrats, and businesspeople—still had enough de facto structural power to impose deregulation. This approach quickly became the focus of a new domestic consensus.

The inspiration for deregulation came from the floating exchange rate system, but its impact was much wider. It cut across issue-areas and party lines (Derthick and Quirk 1985). Right and left to some extent shared a diagnosis of the slump and its symptom of "stagflation," an analysis that stressed the failure of Keynesianism and the "fiscal crisis of the state" (O'Connor 1973). Against this background, the end of Bretton Woods led to the revival of long-standing claims by internationally oriented sectors of the U.S. financial community for deregulating financial markets and banking. Subsequent deregulatory decisions were spread across five different administrations—those of Nixon, Ford, Carter, Reagan, and Bush—and cut across the executive branch, Congress, and a range of regulatory bodies. They concerned not only finance, of course, but also, in a somewhat more politically salient fashion, trucking, airlines, communications, and, eventually, under the Reagan administration, a range of social policies as well.

In finance, they included not only the end of Bretton Woods and the move to floating exchange rates, but also abolition of minimum commissions for securities trading ("May Day," 1975), lifting of a range of interest-rate controls, deregulation of money markets (the Depository Institutions Deregulation and Monetary Control Act, 1980), deregulation of savings and loan institutions (the Garn–St. Germain Act, 1982), and a variety of other measures including ones designed to attract foreign funds (and also increasingly footloose U.S. funds), which had previously preferred the unregulated Euromarkets. Together, these measures have had the effect of removing barriers erected mainly in the New Deal period between distinct kinds of financial markets. Decompartmentalization has permitted banks,

brokers, and market-makers to engage in arbitrage between different financial markets at home and abroad in order to get the highest rate of return on
their capital. This, in turn, led to a wave of financial innovation that is still
continuing. The resulting structural changes in financial markets are the
focus of the intense debates indicated earlier, debates about the role of
worldwide financial deregulation in provoking the long recession that began
in 1989 and the austerity policies associated with it.

THE DILEMMAS OF RE-REGULATION
IN A POST-HEGEMONIC WORLD

In this environment, the substance of the political and economic debate has shifted from deregulation per se to "re-regulation." Re-regulation
can mean several different things, and elsewhere I have distinguished between two types of re-regulation (Cerny 1991). The first type (Type I re-
regulation) is inextricably intertwined with deregulation itself, especially
drafting and implementing new "deregulating regulations." These new regulations are intended precisely to promote and reinforce market-oriented
behavior. This is very different from the traditional conception of regulation as controlling or constraining markets according to authoritative, nonmarket criteria, i.e., taking activities out of the marketplace. The second
type (Type II re-regulation), in contrast, involves new, authoritative mar-
ket-constraining measures to prevent both old and new kinds of market
failure, i.e., to control and counteract perverse, unintended consequences
that may have been caused by the original deregulation. Neither of these
types of re-regulation is wholly incompatible with deregulation. Indeed,
Type I is by definition necessary for deregulation itself to proceed. Type II
usually does not involve a wholesale return to authoritative, market-con-
straining regulatory patterns, but tends to be part of a mixed package of
proposals including both (a) further, specific deregulatory (Type I) measures intended to make deregulation itself more effective, and (b) market-
constraining (Type II) measures designed in theory both to offset the kinds
of unintended consequences revealed by earlier experience and to anticipate further drawbacks.

For the most part, deregulation of financial markets has had the intended effect of permitting and speeding up the further integration of U.S.
financial markets into what Strange has called the "transnational financial
structure." To that extent, therefore, further national-level re-regulation
has become much more difficult. The genie is out of the bottle. This situation could be described as one of "level-shift." This level-shift has two
kinds of consequences. In the first place, the level of the problem itself has
shifted. U.S. banks and financial markets (and those of other countries) are
not merely "interdependent" but *structurally interlocking*. There are direct

linkages between international financial markets (markets for securities of various kinds[11] and for banking services) and domestic markets. Arbitrage between these markets can, in theory, take place in a variety of different centers in a range of different countries, in effect, on a twenty-four-hour basis, if the players are determined and knowledgeable enough—and if they have the necessary resources to participate in the game.[12]

In this context, the most effective form of re-regulation might be to evolve new multilateral mechanisms or to breathe new life into old ones (Ruggie 1992). This "new multilateralism" might in theory be achieved in two distinct ways: either by developing more effective forms of *intergovernmental* cooperation, or by establishing and/or reinforcing more autonomous *transnational* regimes.[13] In other words, the very process of regulation itself, whether defined as deregulation or re-regulation, must become more internationalized and/or transnationalized. The problem is that international regimes are easy to prescribe but hard to establish and to make work effectively. This is, above all, for the simple reason that, as realist theory has emphasized, there is no overall transnational or supranational state, nor even any latent equivalent; the international system is anarchic. In effect, therefore, unless there is a cumulative and simultaneous mobilization of different states' perceptions of their shared national interests—in a fundamentally *additive* rather than hierarchical process—even well-established regimes are likely not only to lack clout but also to be rudderless and fragile in practice. Although some progress has been made in managing exchange rates (the Plaza and Louvre Accords of 1985–1986) and agreeing re common, capital, adequacy standards for banks (and probably soon for securities firms as well—Waters 1992), these mechanisms are very limited. They are circumscribed in at least two ways: in terms of their specific technical content (e.g., capital adequacy standards, however important, are only one regulatory tool with limited application); and in terms of their operational feasibility (attempts by central banks to manage exchange rates are highly dependent upon conjunctural market conditions).

The first critical ramification of level-shift, therefore, is that although international-level regulatory solutions may be potentially the most effective response to such problems as volatility and market failure, among others, in internationalized financial markets, such solutions are unlikely to come forth to the extent necessary to deal with the legacy of deregulation. Therefore, although U.S. administrations have been able in some international negotiations to overcome the bureaucratic and legislative turf battles that have paralyzed domestic re-regulatory politics, the most important resulting agreement—the 1988 Basle Accord on bank capital adequacy ratios—represents only a limited success.

The success lies in the fact that an apparently workable, intergovernmental agreement was reached on a significant aspect of prudential regulation and that it is actually being implemented, despite setbacks.[14] The limitations, however, are twofold. First, capital adequacy is only one ingredient in effective prudential regulation, as we have already noted. Indeed, some argue that agreement on ratios, however important in themselves, might become a substitute for wider regulation, preventing more-effective action. Second, the adoption of strict capital adequacy standards may have perverse consequences, causing banks to retrench and reduce lending in order to bolster capital ratios. In this way they are said to be contributing to the "credit crunch" typical of the recent recession. Finally, the process of adjustment to the new standards has been problematic and may be in danger of breaking down. Thus the Basle Accord may demonstrate just how far the deregulation and internationalization of financial markets in practice constrain the action of even more effective and strategically placed state policymakers. Further multilateral steps are proving more difficult to achieve. The lesson of the agreement on capital adequacy does demonstrate, nonetheless, that such steps are not impossible. But it also indicates that future projects are likely to require certain conditions to be successful.

Four such conditions can be identified from a look at the Basle case. First, an effective *international coalition* must be formed in such a way that no major state can impose a blocking veto.[15] Second, the substance of any agreement must be limited enough in scope that it can be treated as a *technical issue* and dealt with by experts away from the political limelight. Politicization, whether at an intranational or an international level, might well prove to be an insuperable barrier, if not always to the conclusion of any specific agreement, then to its effective implementation. The third condition—in fact a corollary of the second—is that state actors charged with undertaking (a) the negotiation and (b) the implementation of such an agreement need to have the *legal and political autonomy and discretion* to carry out these tasks without having to engage in turf battles or competitive politicking at a party or interest-group level.[16] In effect, the open and competitive U.S. political system has to behave as if it were a more autonomous, cohesive, "state-like" bureaucratic apparatus both internally and externally—a tall order in the normal run of events. The fourth and final condition translates the first three onto the economic plane. This is quite simply that the form of regulation agreed upon must be effectively *enforceable*: it must not be vulnerable to being undermined by normal market activities or by the standard avoidance tactics the private sector will inevitably apply.

The success of the Basle negotiations depended upon (a) the capacity of the Federal Reserve to take an effective lead role; (b) the deference with which the Fed was treated by U.S. bureaucrats and politicians on this issue; and (c) the ability of national regulators to ensure compliance by the private sector (Kapstein 1992). Compared to the setting up or even the collapse of the Bretton Woods system, however, this episode may turn out to be the exception that proves the rule. It may reflect the limits of U.S. financial power, not the resurrection of hegemony or the emergence of new forms of cooperation. The problem itself is no longer one of U.S. financial hegemony—or, indeed, of any state's "hegemony" as such. The question is about the nature of the "transnational financial structure," where the actions of bureaucrats and politicians take place in a much more complex setting than that of the state or even of the states system. These actors' own "second structural" linkages, not those of the state as a unit, define the new playing field and a whole new set of even more complex and intractable policy conflicts and turf struggles. Shifting the problem to the transnational level, therefore, does not hold out the promise of broadly based transnational solutions.

A second critical ramification of the level-shift entailed by financial deregulation and internationalization is its impact on domestic political processes. This effectively involves "whipsawing" the state between increased system entropy and a growing demand for political action. That demand takes two forms. On the one hand, liberal-democratic political systems are based on the assumption that political officials are accountable for the outcomes of policy decisions. Politicians, in turn, are expected to pursue policies that prevent financial crises and market failures. When crisis and market failure occur in open political systems with widespread access for individuals and groups to a range of state actors at different governmental levels—especially in the United States with its constitutional separation of powers and federalism—re-regulation at the domestic level becomes a salient political issue. Politicians must at least address the issue and may attempt to seize the opportunity to propose domestic-level solutions, even if such solutions are unlikely to be operationally feasible because of international constraints. On the other hand, whatever the real possibilities for preventive action (given international constraints), the state must deal with the domestic *consequences* of financial deregulation. This may mean pursuing unpopular and damaging monetary policies in order to prop up exchange rates or even bailing out the banking system itself with taxpayers' money—the "socialization" of banking.[17]

Just as level-shift imposes new demands for autonomous, cohesive, state-like policy action upon the political process, that process in effect becomes less capable of operating in a transnationally effective way. Against this background, the most likely outcome for the United States, and increasingly for other countries too, will be to exacerbate the vicious circle of political entropy. The more that political activity of a re-regulatory kind is generated, the less the state will be able even to process those demands, much less to convert them into policies and to implement them effectively. The search for cures can speed the spread of the disease. Whatever decisional capacity the state may once have possessed is further eroded.

This, I would argue, is what has happened with regard to the decline of U.S. postwar financial hegemony. Financial deregulation after the collapse of Bretton Woods may have indicated that the U.S. still possessed considerable structural power at that time, but the consequences of that deregulation, especially given the unusually fragmented nature of the U.S. state, has led to the rapid erosion of what remained of its hegemony—financial *and* economic. Indeed, combined with the fiscal and monetary policies of the Reagan/Bush era, it has made the U.S. dependent on foreign capital: First came the inflows of foreign capital to finance the federal budget deficit; then the slide in the mid-1980s from being the world's largest creditor nation to being the largest debtor; and finally going cap-in-hand to Germany, Saudi Arabia, and Japan to finance its participation in the Gulf War.

The erosion of U.S. financial power has had significant consequences well beyond the financial arena. On the one hand, U.S. influence in non-financial issue-areas at the international level has been undermined; on the other, its capacity to control its own domestic economy has been reduced. The same can, of course, be said for other countries as well—even for Japan, as the recent bursting of the Japanese "financial bubble" and slow-down in growth there demonstrates. With the erosion of U.S. financial hegemony, however, the need for transnational re-regulation has grown, while the limits prevailing at that level have become more evident. Constraints on domestic re-regulation are more obvious, too, as that process runs into the sand. Together, these trends highlight (and further exacerbate) entropic tendencies in the U.S. (i.e., "gridlock"), which is even more striking from an international perspective. Growing interpenetration of the global political economy demands that states play a more coherent role in organizing and manipulating their potential "competitive advantages."[18] This is the imperative of the competition state, and it poses questions for the U.S. political system itself (Cerny 1994).

TOWARD EMBEDDED FINANCIAL ORTHODOXY

Financial market deregulation and re-regulation, in their various guises, constitute a major developmental trend not only in the global economy but also in world politics. Regulatory arbitrage, market expansion, and the development of the competition state in a more-open world have been among the key factors leading to the emergence of an uneven but real 24-hour global financial marketplace. Globalization and deregulation have affected different states (and different market structures) in distinct ways, but they have constrained the actions of policymakers everywhere. Market change is inextricably intertwined with political change, and political change in response to transnationalized economic structures and pressures alters the nature of politics itself. States are like lumbering giants—vastly powerful when roused, but often easy to circumvent or to disable with a hundred random blows from different directions (or a few well-aimed stones from a slingshot), causing it to topple over in a dazed condition. This is especially apt, given that real states are not true Leviathans but unevenly developed structures, riddled with both obstacles and loopholes. Globalized, diversified, and active financial markets in an open world are especially difficult for states to regulate effectively; and yet markets also depend on states, in the absence of strong transnational regimes, to guarantee their structures, prevent market failures, and carry out a range of other tasks that can vary widely from state to state.

Attempts to cope by reforming regulatory systems have been subverted by a major shift of power, albeit of a very diffuse kind, away from states to financial market structures themselves. Furthermore, all governments have found also that their capacity to intervene in the domestic economy has been radically altered, reducing the capacity of the state to pursue demanding economic strategies and frustrating the kind of market interventions they do adopt. Finally, state actors have all found themselves having to pursue financial policies that entwine state structures even more closely in transnational financial structures—even though this allows all states to some extent, and some states more than others, to manipulate those structures to their own competitive advantage. The interaction of financial market structures and states has done more than production, trade, or international regimes to undermine the Keynesian welfare state and impose the norms of the competition state, while at the same time narrowing the parameters of competition still further. In this context, the competition state itself has become the main vehicle, the preeminent carrier, of "embedded financial orthodoxy."

The role of the United States is especially problematic in this context. Its incapacity to act as a competition state paradoxically opened the door to embedded financial orthodoxy, by setting off a vicious circle of unilateral deregulatory decisions. The result is that the U.S. is incapable of taking action to counteract the competitive advantages possessed by more strategic states and to re-regulate its own financial regulatory system in a competitive direction. But it is not the U.S. alone that has been forced to toe the line of austerity, deflation, and stagnation. The crisis of the European exchange rate mechanism implies that, in Margaret Thatcher's phrase, "You can't buck the markets" in this deregulated era. Even Japan, whose banks and securities firms came to dominate the world in the 1980s, is finding in the 1990s that its financial bubble has burst, leading to stagnation in the real economy. Is this a new haute finance, or a new quasi-anarchy in the deregulated financial markets? Can the real global economy ever begin to recover when this kind of short-termism rules? The key question is whether we have reached the end of Polanyi's "Great Transformation," or whether the politics of financial market regulation might also shift, however unevenly or equivocally, to the transnational level. More than that, however, this complex, interlocking relationship among states, financial markets, and the international political economy indicates that international relations do not so much involve the simple juxtaposition of an "anarchical" international system and a "hierarchical" state, but instead underscore the multilevel, plurilateral, polyarchical nature of the contemporary world order.

NOTES

1. Although British deregulation took place mainly in the context of a reducing deficit, a significant proportion of this reduction resulted from the sale of state assets in the markets through the privatization process, which was in turn a major element in the expansion of U.K. financial markets in the mid-1980s.

2. In the 1930s, of course, the autarchic/bureaucratic model—not only in its German, Japanese, and Soviet versions but also in trends visible in more-open economies affected by protectionism (Britain and France, for example) and in the less-developed world (Brazil, Argentina)—seemed to be on the way to dominance; only war defeated it, and U.S. political dominance of the economic reconstruction process in the West played a major role in ensuring that shattered capitalist economies did not close up again.

3. The relationship between the financial system and the "real economy" is a key issue for economists. "Keynes's subtle point [in Chapter 12 of the *General Theory*] was that *inefficient* financial markets are necessary for the efficient working of the rest of the economy. The argument starts with Adam Smith's 'invisible hand': if people seek to maximize their own welfare, social welfare will be maximized as a consequence. In pursuit of personal gain individuals will be motivated to 'invest in better mousetraps' and otherwise satisfy and improve the lot of their fellow citizens. However, financial markets distort incentives. Once a developed system of financial markets exists, by far the best method of getting rich is likely to be in finance. Hence financial markets will be overdeveloped and other industries neglected. Both British and American firms have echoed this by complaining that an excessive proportion of highly skilled and/or trained labor goes into finance. Moreover, many forms of finance are 'rent-seeking' rather than 'wealth-creating,' to use the terminology of the ultra pro-marketeer Buchanan—i.e., no-one else gains as a consequence of the individual's profit (share dealing being one of the examples he cites)" (see Gowland 1989).

4. Kissinger (1957) is in the mainstream of international historians when he attributes the relative stability of post-Napoleonic international politics to Britain's role as a military and political "balancer of power" in Europe.

5. While it might be argued that Kindleberger is looking (analytically speaking) for an *economic* hegemon in the wider sense, his analysis seems to me to define the bottom line of hegemony in *financial* terms.

6. The first of these was the establishment of "special drawing rights" backed by the International Monetary Fund (although a limited version of SDRs was set up); the second was the Smithsonian System, based on a moveable "basket" of currencies rather than gold. (The latter, agreed in 1971, collapsed almost immediately; however, an analogous system was later adopted as the basis of the exchange rate mechanism of the European Monetary System.)

7. "Simply put, . . . a country can have at most two of the following three conditions: a fixed exchange rate, monetary policy autonomy, and capital mobility" (Frieden 1991).

8. The Gramscian approach, however, has, in effect, two levels of operation. On the one hand, the heart of the analysis lies in the crystallization of a transnational capitalist ruling class. On the other hand, the *political* action of this class—the way it develops and sustains its hegemony—must still be carried out through the existing mechanisms of the states system (in the absence of a supranational authority), although this, in turn, puts emphasis on a more subtle structural (rather than a simple relational) conception of how state power actually manifests itself in practice.

9. This is, of course, a contested view of what deregulation actually entails. For a critique of the notion that deregulation is a simple removal of regulations, see Cerny 1991.

10. It is often argued that the collapse of Bretton Woods was not the beginning of the process; that is usually attributed to the chronic U.S. balance-of-payments deficits after 1958 and the rapid expansion of the unregulated Euromarkets to recycle exiled dollars. The shift to floating exchange rates is nonetheless generally thought to have led to a crucial acceleration and expansion of the deregulation process by removing the main regulatory obstacle to market-induced, international capital flows.

11. Although it is widely accepted that, for example, government debt markets (especially secondary markets for shorter-term treasury bills) are the most integrated, and equity markets the least; probably the most rapidly integrating markets are those for financial derivatives such as stock market index futures, while insurance markets may be the next major deregulatory battleground.

12. A critical debate is taking place as to whether the technological and institutional attributes of globalized financial markets (computerization in particular) are characterized by sufficiently large economies of scale and transaction-cost economies that they will be structurally dominated only by the largest players, i.e., whether they will look more like the "airline reservation system model" of oligopoly control, or whether they will correspond to what might be called the "personal computer model" of easy market access and entry.

13. "Intergovernmental cooperation" is defined as involving *states* and *state actors* as the main participants; this is the most viable process dealing with issues at an international level according to realist interpretations. The notion of "transnational regimes" brings into the game—without necessarily leaving out state actors—a range of other significant actors, primarily those holding positions in bodies that have some level of structural autonomy (in terms of independent rules and resources) from states. These bodies range from public international organizations themselves, especially so-called "supranational institutions," to private entities such as large firms, financial markets, and cross-national pressure groups.

14. This is widely regarded as the case with the Basle Accord, in which the Federal Reserve chaired by Paul Volcker took a strong lead in its negotiation (conversation with Dr. Wolfgang Reinicke of the Brookings Institution, September 1991; cf. Kapstein 1992).

15. Kapstein (1992) argues that the alliance between the Fed and the Bank of England was strong enough to impose its approach on a somewhat divided group of central bankers from other states.

16. What Cohen (1986, 248 ff.) calls "policy coherence asymmetry" can be even more negative in its effects at an international level than at the domestic level.

17. As is well known, the cost to "the American taxpayer" of bailing out failed savings and loan institutions alone has been estimated at $300–500 billion over several years. For a wider critique of the "socialization" of finance, see Grant 1992.

18. For the concept of "competitive advantage"—and the contrast between it and the more traditional notion of "comparative advantage"—see John Zysman and Laura Tyson, eds. (1983).

Bibliography

Aalders, G., and C. Wiebes. 1990. *Zaken doen tot elke prijs*. The Hague: SDU. English ed. forthcoming. *The Art of Cloaking*. Oxford and New York: Berg.

Abdel-Malek, Anouar. 1979. "The Primacy of the Political." Paper presented at 4th Round Table symposium on "Socialism in the World," 1–5 October, at Couvat, Yugoslavia.

———. 1981. *Social Dialectics*. Vol. 2, *Nation and Revolution*. Albany: State University of New York Press.

———. 1983. "The Nation as Crucible." Typescript.

Abendroth, W. 1981. "11 Thesen zur politische Funktion und zur Perspecktive des Kampfes für die Erhaltung des demokratischen Verfassungsrechts in der Bundesrepublik Deutschland." In Abendroth et al., *Ordnungsmacht? Über das Verhältnis von Legalität, Konsens und Herrschaft*. Frankfurt: EVA.

Abu-Lughod, Janet L. 1989. *Before European Hegemony: The World System A.D. 1250–1350*. New York: Oxford University Press.

Adelman, Irma. 1969. *Practical Approaches to Development Planning: Korea's Second Five Year Plan*. Baltimore, Md.: Johns Hopkins University Press.

Aglietta, Michel. 1976. *Regulation et crises du capitalisme*. Paris: Calmann-Levy.

———. 1979. *A Theory of Capitalist Regulation: The US Experience*. London: NLB.

Ake, Claude. 1982. *Social Science as Imperialism: The Theory of Political Development*. 2d ed. Ibadan: Ibadan University Press.

Alff, W. 1976. *Materialien zum Kontinuitätsproblem der deutschen Geschichte*. Frankfurt: Suhrkamp.

Almond, Gabriel A. 1988. "Separate Tables: Schools and Sects in Political Science." *PS: Political Science & Politics* 21 (Fall): 828–842.

———. 1990. *A Discipline Divided: Schools and Sects in Political Science*. Beverly Hills, Calif.: Sage Publications.

Amin, Samir. 1976. *Unequal Development*. New York: Monthly Review Press.

———. 1977. "Capitalism and Ground Rent." In S. Amin, *Imperialism and Unequal Development*. Sussex: Harvester Press.

———. 1980. *Class and Nation*. New York: Monthly Review Press.

———. 1982. "Crisis, Nationalism, and Socialism." In Amin et al., *Dynamics of Global Culture*. London: Macmillan.

———. 1988. *L'eurocentrisme. Critique d'une ideologie*. Paris: Anthropos.

———. 1990. *Delinking*. London: Zed Books.

———. 1991. "The Ancient World-Systems Versus the Modern Capitalist World-System." *Review* 14 (3): 349–385.

Amin, Samir, Giovanni Arrighi, Andre Gunder Frank, and Immanuel Wallerstein. 1982. *Dynamics of Global Crisis.* London: Macmillan.

Amsden, Alice H. 1989. *Asia's Next Giant: South Korea and Late Industrialization.* Oxford: Oxford University Press.

———. 1990. "Third World Industrialization: 'Global Fordism' or a New Model?" *New Left Review* 182, July/August: 5–31.

Amnsbury, Clifton. 1979. "Patron-Client Structure in Modern World Organization" in Seaton S. Lee and Henri J. M. Claessen, eds., *Political Anthropology: The State of the Art.* The Hague: Mouton.

Anderson, B. 1983. *Imagined Communities.* London: Verso.

Anderson, Frank M. 1904. *The Constitutions and Other Select Documents Illustrative of the History of France, 1789–1901.* Minneapolis: H. W. Wilson.

Anderson, Perry. 1974a. *Lineages of the Absolutist State.* London: New Left Books.

———. 1974b. *Passages from Antiquity.* London: Verso.

Aoki, M. 1984. *Learning by Doing vs. the Bounded-Rational Control: An Approach to US–Japan Comparison of Industrial Organization.* CEPR Publication 53, Stanford University. Mimeo.

Apter, David E. 1987. *Rethinking Development: Modernization, Dependency, and Postmodern Politics.* Beverly Hills, Calif.: Sage Publications.

Arrighi, Giovanni. 1982. "A Crisis of Hegemony." In Amin, et al., *Dynamics of Global Crisis.* London: Macmillan.

Arrighi, Giovanni, and Jessica Drangel. 1986. "The Stratification of the World-Economy: An Exploration of the Semi-Peripheral Zone." *Review* 10 (Summer): 9–74.

Aston, T. H., and C. H. E. Philpin, eds. 1985. *The Brenner Debate: Agrarian Class Structure and Economic Development in Pre-Industrial Europe.* Cambridge: Cambridge University Press.

Auster, Richard D. and Morris Silver. 1979. *The State as a Firm: Economic Forces in Political Development.* Boston: Martin Nijhoff.

Badie, Bertrand, and Pierre Birnbaum. 1982. *The Sociology of the State.* Trans. Arthur Goldhammer. Chicago: University of Chicago Press.

Baechler, Jean. 1975. *The Origins of Capitalism.* New York: St. Martin's Press.

Banaji, Jairus. 1980. "Gunder Frank in Retreat?" *Journal of Peasant Studies* 3 (4):508–521.

Barkin, Samuel. 1992. "Financial Dominance and Economic Leadership." Paper presented to the Annual Meeting of the American Political Science Association, 3–6 September, Chicago.

Barrett, Richard E. and Soomi Chin. 1987. "Export-oriented Industrializing States in the Capitalist World System: Similarities and Differences," in Frederic Deyo, ed. *The Political Economy of the New Asian Industrialism,* Ithaca: Cornell University Press.

Barzun, Jacques. 1932. *The French Race: Theories of Its Origins and Their Social and Political Implications Prior to the Revolution.* Columbia University Studies in History, Economics and Public Law no. 375. New York.

Beetham, David. 1974. *Max Weber and the Theory of Modern Politics.* London: Allen and Unwin.

Bello, Walden and Stephanie Rosenfeld. 1990. *Dragons in Distress: Asia's Miracle Economies in Crisis.* San Francisco: Institute for Food and Development Policy.

Benseler, Frank. 1980. "On the History of Systems Thinking in Sociology," in Frank Benseler, Peter Heji, and Wolfram K. Kock, eds., *Autopoiesis,*

Communication, and Society: The Theory of Autopoietic System in the Social Sciences. Frankfurt: Campus Verlag.

Berend, Iván T., and György Ránki. *Economic Development in East-Central Europe in the 19th and 20th Centuries.* New York: Columbia University Press.

Bernal, Martin. 1987. *Black Athena: The Afroasiatic Roots of Classical Civilization.* New Brunswick, N.J.: Rutgers University Press.

Bernstein, Henry. 1979. "Sociology of Underdevelopment vs. Sociology of Development" In *Development Theory: Four Critical Studies,* ed. David Lehmann. London: Cass.

Bienefeld, Manfred, and Martin Godfrey, eds. 1982. *The Struggle for Development.* New York: Wiley.

Bihr, A. 1989. *Entre bourgeiosie et proletariat: L'encadrement capitaliste.* Paris: l'Harmattan.

Bilderberg. 1989. Papers presented at the Thirty-Seventh Bilderberg Meeting. May 12, 13, and 14, La Toja, Spain.

Billington, J. H. 1980. *Fire in the Minds of Men.* London: Temple Smith.

Binford, Lewis R. 1968. "Post-Pleistocene Adaptations." In *New Perspectives in Archeology,* eds. Sally R. Binford and Lewis R. Binford. Chicago: Aldine.

Bix, Herbert. 1974. "Japan and South Korea in America's Asia Policy" in Frank Baldwin, *Without Parallel.* New York: Pantheon Books.

Blaut, J. 1977. "Where Was Capitalism Born?" In *Radical Geography,* ed. R. Peet. Chicago: Maasoufa Press.

———. 1992. "Fourteen Ninety-Two." *Political Geography* 11 (July).

Block, Fred L. 1977. *The Origins of International Economic Disorder.* Berkeley and Los Angeles: University of California Press.

———. 1978. "Marxist Theories of the State in World-Systems Analysis." in *Social Change in the Capitalist World-Economy,* ed. B. H. Kaplan. Beverly Hills: Sage Publishing.

Bodin, Jean. [1576] 1986. *Les Six Livres de la Republique.* Paris: Fayard.

Boltho, Andrea, ed. 1982. *The European Economy: Growth and Crisis.* Oxford: Oxford University Press.

Bornschier, Volker. 1992. "The European Community's Uprising: Grasping Toward Hegemony or Therapy Against National Decline in the World Political Economy." Paper presented at the First European Conference of Sociology, August 26–29, Vienna.

Bornschier, Volker, and Christopher Chase-Dunn. 1985. *Transnational Corporations and Underdevelopment.* New York: Praeger.

Boserup, Esther. 1965. *The Conditions of Agricultural Growth.* Chicago: Aldine.

Bougoüin, E., and P. Lenoir. 1938. *La finance internationale et la guerre d'Espagne.* Paris: Centre d'Etudes de 'Paix.

Bordieu, P. 1978. *Questions de la sociologie.* Paris: Minuit.

Bourdin, N. 1979. "L'internationale socialiste, stratégie du recours?" In J.-D. Poulain, et al., *La social-démocratie au présent.* Paris: Ed. Sociales.

Bowie, R. R. 1973. "Tensions Within the Alliance." *Foreign Affairs* 42 (1 October).

Boyer, R. and J. Mistral. 1978. *Accumulation, inflation et crise.* Extended ed. 1983. Paris: P.U.F.

Bradby, Barbara. 1975. "The Destruction of Natural Economy." *Economy and Society* 4: 127–61.

Brandt, W. 1990. *Herinneringen.* Utrecht and Antwerp: Veen.

Braudel, Fernand. 1979. *The Perspective of the World: Civilization and Capitalism, 15th–18th Century.* Vol. 3. Trans. Sian Reynolds. New York: Harper & Row.

Brenner, Robert. 1977. "The Origins of Capitalist Development: A Critique of Neo-Smithian Marxism." *New Left Review* 104 (July–August):25–92.

Brodin, Eric. 1992. "Collapse of the Swedish Myth." *Economic Affairs,* 12.

Bruford, W. H. 1970. "The Organisation and Rise of Prussia." In *The New Cambridge Modern History.* Vol. 5, *The Old Regime.* Cambridge: Cambridge University Press.

Brym, R. J. 1989. "Canada." In T. B. Bottomore, eds. and Robert Brym. *The Capitalist Class: An International Study,* New York: New York University Press.

Bunker, Stephen, and Dennis O'Hearn. 1991. "Strategies of Rising Hegemons for Securing Access to Raw Materials: A Comparison of Japan and the United States." Paper presented at the Annual Spring Conference on the Political Economy of the World-System, March 30, University of Hawaii.

Callaghy, Thomas M. 1990. "Lost Between State and Market: The Politics of Economic Adjustment in Ghana, Zambia, and Nigeria." In *Economic Crisis and Policy Choice: The Politics of Adjustment in the Third World,* ed. Joan M. Nelson. Princeton, N.J.: Princeton University Press.

Caporaso, James A., ed. 1989. *The Elusive State: International and Comparative Perspectives.* Beverly Hills, Calif.: Sage Publications.

Cardoso, Fernando Herique, and Enzo Faletto. 1979. *Dependency and Development in Latin America.* Berkeley: University of California Press.

Cerny, Philip G. 1988. "Modernization and the Fifth Republic." In *France and Modernization,* ed. John Gaffney. Aldershot: Avebury/Gower.

———. 1989a. "The 'Little Big Bang' in Paris: Financial Market Deregulation in a *dirigiste* System." *European Journal of Political Research* 17 (March): 169–192.

———. 1989b. "Political Entropy and American Decline." *Millennium: Journal of International Studies* 88 (Spring):47–63.

———. 1990. *The Changing Architecture of Politics: Structure, Agency, and the Future of the State.* London and Newbury Park, Calif.: Sage Publications.

———. 1991. *The Politics of Transnational Regulation: Deregulation or Reregulation?* Special issue of the *European Journal of Political Research* 19 (March/April).

———.1992. "Plurilateralism: Functional Conflict and Complex Stability in the Emerging World Order." Paper presented to the Annual Meeting of the International Studies Association, 31 March–4 April, Atlanta.

———. 1993. "Global Finance and Governmental Gridlock: Political Entropy and the Decline of American Financial Power." In *The Politics of Relative Decline,* eds. Richard Maidment and James A. Thurber. Oxford and New York: Polity Press and Basil Blackwell.

———. "The Re-regulation of Financial Markets in a More Open World." In *The Political Economy of International Finance,* ed. P. Cerny. Cheltenham, Glos., and Brookfield, Vt.: Edward Elgar. In press.

Chaliand, Gerard. 1978. *Revolutions in the Third World.* Middlesex: Penguin.

Chang, Dal-joong. 1985. *Economic Control and Political Authoritarianism: The Role of Japanese Corporations in Korean Politics 1965–1979.* Seoul: Sogang University Press.

Charlier, M. 1990. "Deutschland, schwierig Vaterland." *Blätter für deutsche und internationale Politik* 2.

Chase-Dunn, Christopher, ed. 1982. *Socialist States in the World-System.* Beverly Hills, Calif.: Sage Publications.

———. 1988. "Comparing World-Systems: Towards a Theory of Semiperipheral Development." *Comparative Civilizations Review* 19 (Fall):39–66.

―――. 1989. *Global Formation: Structures of the World Economy.* Oxford: Basil Blackwell.

―――. 1990a. "Resistance to Imperialism: Semiperipheral Actors." *Review* 13 (Winter):1–31.

―――. 1990b. "World State Formation: Historical Processes and Emergent Necessity." *Political Geography Quarterly* 9 (April):108–130.

―――. 1992. "The Spiral of Capitalism and Socialism." In *Research in Social Movements, Conflicts and Change,* ed. Louis F. Kriesberg. Vol. 14. Greenwich, Conn.: JAI Press.

Chase-Dunn, Christopher, Edward Clewett, and Elaine Sundahl. 1992. "A Very Small World-System in Northern California: the Wintu and Their Neighbors." Paper presented at the Annual Meetings of the Society for American Archaeology, April 23, Pittsburgh.

Chase-Dunn, Christopher, and Thomas D. Hall. 1991. *Core/Periphery Relations in Precapitalist Worlds.* Boulder, Colo.: Westview.

―――. *Rise and Demise: The Transformation of World-Systems.* Boulder, Colo.: Westview. In press.

Chilicote, Ronald H. 1981. *Theories of Comparative Politics: The Search for a Paradigm.* Boulder, Colo.: Westview Press.

Claessen, Henri J. M., and Peter Skalnik. 1978. *The Early State.* The Hague: Mouton.

Clark, C. and S. Chan, eds. 1990. "The East Asian Development Model" *International Studies Notes,* Special Issue.

Clark, G. L. and M. Dear. 1984. *State Apparatus.* Boston: Allen & Unwin.

Clark, J. C. D. 1985. *English Society, 1688–1832.* New York: Columbia University Press.

―――. 1986. *Revolution and Rebellion: State and Society in England in the Seventeenth and Eighteenth Centuries.* New York: Cambridge University Press.

Clarke, Simon. 1988. *Keynesianism, Monetarism and the Crisis of the State.* London: Edward Elgar.

Coates, Ken. 1990. "Towards a European Socialist Party?" *European Labour Forum* 2.

―――. 1991. "Towards a European Socialist Party." *European Labour Forum* 5.

Cobban, Alfred. 1971. *The Social Interpretation of the French Revolution.* Cambridge: Cambridge University Press.

Cohen, Benjamin J. 1986. *In Whose Interest? International Banking and American Foreign Policy.* New Haven, Conn.: Yale University Press for the Council on Foreign Relations.

Cole, Kenneth C. 1948. "The Theory of the State as a Sovereign Juristic Person." *The American Political Science Review.*

Collins, Randall. 1978. "Some Principles of Long-term Social Change: The Territorial Power of States." In *Research in Social Movements, Conflicts and Change,* ed. Louis F. Kriesberg. Vol. 1. Greenwich, Conn.: JAI Press.

―――. 1986. "A Theory of Technology." In R. Collins, *Weberian Sociological Theory.* Cambridge: Cambridge University Press.

Comisso, Ellen. 1986. "State Structures and Political Processes Outside the CMEA. A Comparison." In *Power, Purpose and Collective Choice,* eds. Ellen Comisso and Laura D. Tyson. Ithaca: Cornell University Press.

Connor, Walker. 1973. "The Politics of Ethnonationalism." *Journal of International Affairs* 27:1.

Corbridge, Stuart. 1986. *Capitalist World Development: A Critique of Radical Development Geography.* London: Macmillan.

Coriat, B. 1984. *La robotique.* Paris: La Découerte.

Cotton, James. 1992. "Understanding the State in South Korea: Bureaucratic-Authoritarian or State Autonomy Theory?" *Comparative Political Studies* 24 (January):512–531.

Cox, R. W. 1987. *Production, Power, and World Order. Social Forces in the Making of History.* New York: Columbia University Press.

Crouch, Colin, 1986. "Sharing Public Space." In *States in History*, ed. John A. Hall. Oxford: Basil Blackwell.

Cullen, L. M. 1968. *Anglo-Irish Trade 1660–1800.* Manchester: University of Manchester Press.

Cumings, Bruce. 1987. "The Origins and Development of the Northeast Asian Political Economy." In *The Political Economy of the New Asian Industrialism*, ed. Frederic C. Deyo. Ithaca, N.Y.: Cornell University Press.

———. 1989. "The Abortive Abertura: South Korea in the Light of Latin American Experience." *New Left Review* 173 (January-February).

Dahlberg, Ake, and Albert Tuijman. 1991. "Development of Human Resources in Internal Labour Markets: Implications for Swedish Labour Market Policy." *Economic and Industrial Democracy* 12.

Dahrendorf, Ralf. 1967. *Society and Democracy in Germany.* Garden City, N.Y.: Doubleday.

Dankert, P., and A. Kooyman, eds. 1989. *Europe Without Frontiers.* London: Mansell.

Davis, Horace B. 1978. *Towards a Marxist Theory of Nationalism.* New York: Monthly Review Press.

Davison, Roderic. 1973. *Reform in the Ottoman Empire, 1956–1876.* New York: Gordian Press.

Dawson, Philip. 1972. *Provincial Magistrates and Revolutionary Politics in France, 1789–1795.* Cambridge, Mass.: Harvard University Press.

Dear, M. 1986. "Theory and Object in Political Geography." *Political Geography Quarterly* 5: 295–297.

De Benoist, A. 1983. *Aus rechter Sicht.* Tübingen: Grabert. 2 vols. [orig. *Vue de droite*, 1977].

Delorme, R., and C. Andre. 1983. *L'etat et l'economie.* Paris: Seuil.

Dendrinos. 1992. *The Dynamics of Cities: Ecological Deteminism, Dualism and Chaos.* London: Routledge.

Denemark, Robert. 1988. "The Brenner-Wallerstein Debate." *International Studies Quarterly* 32:47–65.

———. 1991. "Core-Periphery Trade: The Debate over the Nature of the Link and Its Lessons." Paper presented at the International Studies Association annual meetings, Vancouver, Canada.

Derthick, Martha, and Paul Quirk. *The Politics of Deregulation.* Washington, D.C.: Brookings Institution.

Deubner, C. 1982. *Das Auslandskapital in der iberischen Industrie. Entwicklungsaussischen auf dem Wege in die Europäische Gemeinschaft und die Option einer luso-spanischen Kooperation,* Ebenhausen: Stiftung Wissenschaft und Politik.

Deutch, K. W. 1981. "The Crisis of the State." *Government Opposition* 16, 331–343.

Deyo, Frederic C., ed. 1987. *The Political Economy of the New Asian Industrialism.* Ithaca, N.Y.: Cornell University Press.

Deyo, Frederic C. 1989. *Beneath the Miracle: Labor Subordination in the New Asian Industrialism.* Berkeley and Los Angeles: University of California Press.

Djordjevic, Dimitrije, and Stephen Fisher-Galati. 1981. *The Balkan Revolutionary Tradition.* New York: Columbia University Press.

Dore, Ronald. 1990. "Reflections on Culture and Social Change." In *Manufacturing Miracles. Paths of Industrialization in Latin America and East Asia,* eds. Gary Gereffi and Donald L. Wyman. Princeton, N.J.: Princeton University Press.

Dos Santos, T. 1970. "The Structure of Dependence" in C. K. Wilber, ed., *The Political Economy of Development and Underdevelopment,* New York: Random House.

Downing, Brian M. 1992. *The Military Revolution and Political Change in Early Modern Europe.* Princeton, N.J.: Princeton University Press.

Driver, F. 1991. "Political Geography and State Formation." *Progress in Human Geography* 15, 268–280.

Dumont, Alain. 1990. "Technology, Competitiveness and Cooperation in Europe." In *The Technical Challenges and Opportunities of a United Europe,* ed. Michael S. Steinberg. London: Pinter.

Dunleavy, Patrick, and Brendan O'Leary. 1987. *Theories of the State: Politics of Liberal Democracy.* London: Macmillan.

Duroselle, Jean-Baptiste. 1963. "Changes in French Foreign Policy Since 1958." In Hoffman, et al., *In Search of France.* Cambridge, Mass.: Harvard University Press.

Duvall, R., S. Jackson, B. Russett, D. Snidall, and D. Sylvan. 1981. "A Formal Mode of 'Dependencia' Theory: Structure and Measurement." In *From National Development to Global Community,* ed. R. Merritt and B. Russett. London: Allen & Unwin.

Duverger, M. 1972. *The Study of Politics.* New York: Crowell.

Easton, David. 1953. *The Political System.* Chicago and London: The University of Chicago Press.

Eduards, Maud. 1991. "The Swedish Gender Model: Productivity, Pragmatism and Paternalism." *West European Politics* 14.

Edwards, Chris. 1985. *The Fragmented World: Competing Perspectives on Trade, Money and Crisis.* London: Methuen.

Ekholm, Kasja, and Jonathan Friedman. 1982. "'Capital' Imperialism and Exploitation in the Ancient World-Systems." *Review* 6:87–110.

Elder, Neil. 1988. "Corporatism in Sweden." In *The Corporate State: Corporatism and the State Tradition in Western Europe,* eds. A. Cox and N. O'Sullivan. Aldershot: Elgar.

Elias, Norbert. 1939. *State Formation & Civilization.* Vol. 2. Oxford: Basil Blackwell.

Ellman, Michael. 1987. "Eurosclerosis?" In *Unemployment: International Perspectives,* eds. M. Gunderson, N. M. Meltz, and S. Ostrey. Toronto: University of Toronto Press.

El Pais. 1991. *Nostalgia de la tribu. El inquietante retorno de los nacionalismos en Europa.* With contributions by Ralph Dahrendorf, Gabriel Jackson, Regis Debray, Josep Llobera, Ernest Gellner, and Eric Hobsbawn. Temas de Neustra Epocha, Supplement Año 5, no. 203, 10 October.

Emerson, Rupert. 1964. *Malaysia: A Study in Direct and Indirect Rule.* Kuala Lumpur: University of Malaysia Press.

Emmanuel, Arghiri. 1972. *Unequal Exchange.* London: New Left Books.

Engels, Friedrich. 1894. "La futura rivoluzione italiana e il partito socialista." *Critica Sociale* 1 (February).

———. 1895. *Violenza ed economia formazione del nuovo impero tedesco.* Rome.

Engholm, Bjorn. "New Tests—New Opportunities." *Socialist Affairs* 2.

Evans, Peter. 1979. *Dependent Development: The Alliance of Multinational, State, and Local Capital in Brazil.* Princeton, N.J.: Princeton University Press.

———. 1987. "Class, State, and Dependence in East Asia: Lessons for Latin Americanists," in Frederick Deyo, ed., *The Political Economy of the New Asian Industrialism.* Ithaca: Cornell University Press.

Evans, Peter, and John D. Stephens. 1988a. "Development and the World Economy." In *Handbook of Sociology,* ed. Neil J. Smelser. Beverly Hills, Calif.: Sage Publishing.

———. 1988b. "Studying Development Since the Sixties: The Emergence of a New Comparative Political Economy." *Theory and Society* 17:713–745.

———. 1989. "Predatory, Developmental, and Other Apparatuses: A Comparative Political Economy Perspective on the Third World State." *Sociological Forum* 4 (December):561–587.

Evans, Peter, et al. 1985. *Bringing the State Back In.* New York: Cambridge University Press.

Fejtö, François. 1948. "Hungary: The War of Independence." In *The Opening of an Era,* ed. F. Fejtö. New York: Grosset and Dunlap.

Feldman, Robert Alan. 1986. *Japanese Financial Markets: Deficits, Dilemmas, and Deregulation.* Cambridge, Mass.: MIT Press.

Fennema, M. 1982. *International Networks of Banks and Industry.* The Hague: Nijhoff.

Fernández Jilberto, A. E. 1988. "El debate sociologico-politico sobre casi dos siglos de estado nacional en America Latina: un intento de reinterpretacion." *Afers Internacionals* 12/13.

Fine, Ben. 1978. "On the Origins of Capitalist Development." *New Left Review* 109 (May-June):88–95.

Fischer, F. 1984. *Griff nach der Weltmacht. Die Kriegszielpolitik des kaiserlichen Deutschland 1914/18.* Abridged ed., 1961. Düsseldorf: Droste.

Fisher, Herbert. 1989. *The Medieval Empire.* London: Macmillan.

Foerster, Heinz von. 1968. "Cybernetics of Cybernetics." In Foerster, et al., *Purposive Systems: Proceedings of the First Annual Symposium of the American Society for Cybernetics.* New York and Washington, D.C.: Spartan Books.

Foster-Carter, Aidan. 1974. "Neo-Marxist Approaches to Development and Underdevelopment." In *Sociology and Development,* eds. Emanuel de Kadt and Gavin Williams. London: Tavistock.

———. 1978. "The Modes of Production Controversy." *New Left Review* 107:47–77.

Frank, Andre Gunder. 1967. "Sociology of Development and Underdevelopment of Sociology." *Catalyst* (Summer):20–73.

———. 1969. *Capitalism and Underdevelopment in Latin America.* New York: Monthly Review Press.

———. 1977. "Long Live Transideological Enterprise! The Socialist Economies in the Capitalist Division of Labour." *Review* 1:92–140.

———. 1978a. *World Accumulation, 1492–1789.* New York: Monthly Review Press.

———. 1978b. *Dependent Accumulation and Underdevelopment.* New York: Monthly Review Press and London: Macmillan Press.

———. 1980. *Crisis: In the World Economy.* New York: Holmes & Meier and London: Heinemann.

———. 1981. *Reflections on the Economic Crisis.* New York: Monthly Review Press and London: Hutchinson.

———. 1983. *The European Challenge.* Nottingham, England: Spokesman Press.

———. 1984. "Political Ironies in the World Economy." *Studies in Political Economy* 15 (Fall).

———. 1986. "Is the Reagan Recovery Real or the Calm Before the Storm?" *Economic and Political Weekly* (Bombay) 21 (May 24 and 31).

———. 1988. "American Roulette in the Globonomic Casino: Retrospect and Prospect on the World Economic Crisis Today." In *Research in Political Economy,* ed. Paul Zarembka. Greenwich: JAI Press.

———. 1989. "World Debt, The European Challenge and 1992." *ENDpapers* (Nottingham) 19 (Spring):22–29.

———. 1990a. "Revolution in Eastern Europe: Lessons for Democratic Socialist Movements and Socialists." In *The Future of Socialism: Perspectives from the Left,* ed. William K. Tabb. New York: Monthly Review Press.

———. 1990b. "No End to History! History to No End?" *Social Justice* (San Francisco) 17 (December).

———. 1990c. "A Theoretical Introduction to 5,000 Years of World-System History." *Review* (Binghamton) 13 (Spring):155–248.

———. 1991a. "A Plea for World-System History." *Journal of World History* 11 (Spring):1–28.

———. 1991b. "Transitional Ideological Modes: Feudalism, Capitalism, Socialism." *Critique of Anthropology* 11 (Summer):171–188.

———. 1991c. "Third World War in the Gulf: A New World Order Political Economy." *Notebooks for Study and Research* 14 (Amsterdam/Paris) (June 1991):5–34.

———. 1992a. "The Centrality of Central Asia." Center for Asian Studies, Amsterdam, Comparative Asian Studies No. 8 (February 1992). Amsterdam: VU University Press.

———. 1992b. "Fourteen Ninety-Two Once Again." *Political Geography Quarterly* 11 (July).

———. 1992c. "1492 and Latin America at the Margin of World History: East-West Hegemonial Shifts, 1492–1992." Paper presented at International Studies Association Annual Meetings, April 1–5, Atlanta.

Frank, A. G., and M. Fuentes. 1990. "Social Movements in World History." In S. Amin, G. Arrighi, A. G. Frank, and I. Wallerstein, *Transforming the Revolution. Social Movements and the World-System.* New York: Monthly Review Press.

Frank, A. G., and B. K. Gills. 1992. "The Five Thousand Year World System: An Interdisciplinary Introduction." *Humboldt Journal of Social Relations* (Arcata, Calif.) 18 (Spring):1–79.

———., eds. 1993. *The World System: Five Hundred Years or Five Thousand.* London and New York: Routledge.

Franko, Lawrence. 1990. "The Impact of Global Corporate Competition and Multinational Corporate Strategy." In *The Technical Challenges and Opportunities of a United Europe,* ed. Michael S. Steinberg. London: Pinter.

Frieden, Jeffrey A. 1991. "Invested Interests: The Politics of National Economic Policies in a World of Global Finance." *International Organization* 45 (Autumn):425–451.

Friedman, Edward. 1982. "Introduction." In *Ascent and Decline in the World-System,* ed. E. Friedman. Beverly Hills, Calif.: Sage Publications.

Friedman, George, and Meredith Lebard. 1991. *The Coming War with Japan.* New York: St. Martin's Press.

Freidman, Jonathan. 1983. "Civilizational Cycles and the History of Primitivism." *Social Analysis: Journal of Cultural and Social Practice* 14 (December):31–52.

———. 1992. "Narcissism, Roots and Postmodernity: The Constitution of Selfhood in the Global Crisis." In *Modernity and Identity,* eds. S. Lash and J. Friedman. Cambridge, Mass.: Blackwell.

Frobel, Folker, Jurgen Heinrichs, and Otto Kreye. 1980. *The New International Division of Labour.* Cambridge: Cambridge University Press.

Fuentes, M., and A. G. Frank. 1989. "Ten Theses on Social Movements." *World Development* 17 (February).

Fukao, Mitsuhiro, and Masaharu Hanazaki. 1987. "Internationalization of Financial Markets and the Allocation of Capital." *OECD Economic Studies* 8 (Spring): 36–92.

Furet, Françoise. 1978. *Penser la Révolution française.* Paris: Gallimard.

Furtado, Celso. 1964. *Development and Underdevelopment.* Berkeley: University of California Press.

Gallagher, J., and R. Robinson. [1953] 1967. "The Imperialism of Free Trade." In *European Political History 1815–1870. Aspects of Liberalism,* ed. E. C. Black. New York: Harper and Row.

Galtung, Johan. 1967. *Theory and Methods of Social Research.* Oslo: Oslo Universitetsforiaget.

Gardner, Lloyd C. 1971. *Economic Aspects of New Deal Diplomacy.* Boston, Mass.: Beacon Press.

Gardner, Richard N. 1980. *Sterling-Dollar Diplomacy in Current Perspective.* Rev. ed. New York: Columbia University Press.

Garst, Daniel. 1985. "Wallerstein and His Critics." *Theory & Society* 14: 445–468.

Gellner, Ernest. 1983. *Nations and Nationalism.* Ithaca and London: Cornell University Press.

Gereffi, Gary. 1989. "Rethinking Development Theory: Insights from East Asia and Latin America." *Sociological Forum* 4 (December):505–533.

———. 1990. "Paths of Industrialization: An Overview." In *Manufacturing Miracles. Paths of Industrialization in Latin America and East Asia,* eds. G. Gereffi and D. L. Wyman. Princeton, N.J.: Princeton University Press.

Gereffi, Gary, and Donald Wyman. "Determinants of Development Strategies in Latin America and East Asia," in Stephan Haggard and Chung-in Moon, eds., *Pacific Dynamism: The International Politics of Industrial Change.* Boulder, Colo.: Westview Press.

Gernet, Jacques. 1985. *A History of China.* Cambridge, Cambridge University Press.

Giddens, A. 1984. *The Nation State and Violence.* Cambridge, Mass.: Polity.

Gierke, Otto. 1939. *The Development of Political Theory.* Trans. Bernard Freyd. London: George Allen & Unwin.

Gill, Stephen. 1986. "American Hegemony: Its Limits and Prospects in the Reagan Era." *Millennium: Journal of International Studies* 15 (Winter):311–336.

———. 1991. *American Hegemony and the Trilateral Commission.* Cambridge, UK: Cambridge University Press.

———, ed. 1993. *Gramsci, Historical Materialism and International Relations.* Cambridge: Cambridge University Press.

Gill, Stephen, and David Law. 1988. *The Global Political Economy: Perspectives, Problems and Policies.* Hempstead, U.K.: Harvester Wheatsheaf.

Gills, B. K., and A. G. Frank. 1990. "The Cumulation of Accumulation: Theses and Research Agenda for 5000 Years of World System History." *Dialectical Anthropology* (New York/Amsterdam) 15 (July):19–42.

———. 1992. "World System Cycles, Crises, and Hegemonial Shifts 1700 BC to 1700 AD." *Review* 15.

Gilpin, Robert. 1987. *The Political Economy of International Relations.* Princeton, N.J.: Princeton University Press.

Girault, R. [1969] 1975. "Ein neues Bild des französichen Unternehmers um 1914." In *Wirtschaft und Gesellschaft in Frankreich seit 1789,* eds. G. Ziebura with H.-G. Haupt. Cologne: Kiepenheuer and Witsch.

Giroux, Henry A., ed. 1991. *Postmodernism, Feminism, and Cultural Politics: Redrawing Education's Boundaries.* Albany, N.Y.: State University of New York Press.

Giry-Deloison, Philippe, and Philippe Masson. 1988. "Vers un march-financier mondail: les rouages de la globalisation." *Revue Banque* 485 (July/August):725–729.

Goldfrank, Walter L. 1983. "The Limits of an Analogy: Hegemonic Decline in Great Britain and the United States." In *Crises and the World-System,* ed. Albert J. Bergesen. Beverly Hills, Calif.: Sage Publications.

———. 1991. "After the Cold War: The Future of the World-System." Paper presented at the Taft Conference on the Changing World Order, May 3, University of Cincinnati.

Goriely, Benjamin. 1948. "Poland." In *The Opening of an Era,* ed. François Fejtö. New York: Grosset and Dunlap.

Gössner, R. 1989. "Allzweckformel 'Terrorismus.' Zum Prozess gegen Ingrid Stroble." *Blätter für deutsche und internationale Politik* 4.

Gossweiler, K. [1970] 1975. *Grossbanken, industriemonopole, Staat. Ökonomie und Politik des staatsmonopolistischen Kapitalismus in Deutschland 1914–1932.* Berlin: DEB.

Gowland, David H. 1989. "Privatization and Deregulation in Finance." Paper presented to the Interdisciplinary Conference on the Culture of Dependency and the Culture of Enterprise, Institute for Research in the Social Sciences, November, University of New York.

Gramsci, Antonio. 1949. *Il Risorgimento.* Turin: Einaude.

———. 1971. *Selections from the "Prison Notebooks."* Ed. Q. Hoare and G. N. Smith. New York: International Publishers.

Grant, James. 1992. *Money of the Mind: Borrowing and Lending in America from the Civil War to Michael Milken.* New York: Farrar-Straus, Giroux.

Gregg, Susan A. 1988. *Foragers and Farmers: Population Interaction and Agricultural Expansion in Prehistoric Europe.* Chicago: University of Chicago Press.

Gulap, Haldan. 1981. "Frank and Wallerstein Revisited. A Contribution to Brenner's Critique." *Journal of Contemporary Asia* 11:169–188.

Günsche, K.-L., and K. Lantermann. 1977. *Kleine Geschichte der Sozialistischen Internationale.* Bonn: Neue Gesellschaft.

Hagelstange, T. 1988. *Die Entwicklung von Klassenstrukturen in der EG und in Nordamerika.* Frankfurt and New York: Campus.

Haggard, Stephan M. 1986. "The Newly Industrializing Countries in the International System." *World Politics* 38:363–368.

———. 1990. *Pathways from the Periphery: The Politics of Growth in the Newly Industrializing Countries.* Ithaca, N.Y.: Cornell University Press.

Haggard, Stephen, and Tun-jen Cheng. 1987. "State and Foreign Capital in the East Asian NICs." In *The Political Economy of the New Asian Industrialism,* ed. Frederic C. Deyo. Ithaca, N.Y.: Cornell University Press.

Haggard, Stephen, and Chung-in Moon. 1983. "The South Korean State in the International Economy: Economic Dependence and Corporatist Politics." In *The Antinomies of Interdependence,* ed. John G. Ruggie. New York: Columbia University Press.

Hall, H. D. 1971. *Commonwealth. A History of the British Commonwealth of Nations.* London: Van Nostrand Reinhold.

Hall, John A. 1986. *Powers & Liberties: The Causes and Consequences of the Rise of the West.* London: Pelican.

Hall, John A., and G. John Ikenberry. 1989. *The State.* Milton Keynes, U.K.: Open University Press.

Halliday, Fred. 1987. "State and Society in International Relations: A Second Agenda." *Millennium* 16:2.

Halliday, Jon, and Gavan McCormack. 1973. *Japanese Imperialism Today: Co-prosperity in Greater East Asia.* Harmondsworth: Penquin Books.

Hamilton, Adrian. 1986. *The Financial Revolution.* London and New York: Viking Penguin.

Hamilton, Clive. 1984. "Class, State and Industrialization in South Korea." *IDS Bulletin* (April).

———. 1986. *Capitalist Industrialization in Korea.* Boulder, Colo.: Westview Press.

Hamilton, Malcolm. 1989. *Democratic Socialism in Britain and Sweden.* Basingstoke: Macmillan.

Hannson, Par. 1992. "The Discipline of Imports: The Case of Sweden." *The Scandinavian Journal of Economics* 94.

Hardach, Gerd. 1977. *The First World War, 1914–1918.* Berkeley: University of California Press.

Harris, Nigel. 1983. *Of Bread and Guns: The World Economy in Crisis.* Harmondsworth: Penguin Books.

———. 1986. *The End of the Third World: Newly Industrializing Countries and the Decline of an Ideology.* Harmondsworth: Penguin Books.

Harvey, David. 1985. "The Geopolitics of Capitalism." In *Social Relations and Spatial Structures,* eds. Derek Gregory and John Urry. New York: St. Martin's Press.

———. 1989. *The Condition of Postmodernity.* Cambridge, Mass.: Blackwell.

Hart-Landsberg, M. 1987. "South Korea: The Fraudulent Miracle," *Monthly Review* 39.

Heckter, Michael. 1975. *Internal Colonialism: The Celtic Fringe in British National Development, 1536–1966.* Berkeley and Los Angeles: University of California.

Heinrich, A. 1991. "Neue Deutsche Aussenpolitik. Selbstversuche zwischen Zagreb und Brüssel," *Blätter für deutsche und internationale Politik* 12.

Helleiner, Eric N. 1991. "American Hegemony and Global Economic Structure: From Closed to Open Financial Relations in the Postwar World." Ph.D. diss. London School of Economics and Political Science.

———. 1992. "The Waning of American Financial Hegemony." Paper presented to the Annual Meeting of the American Political Science Association, 3–6 September, Chicago.

———. 1993. *When Finance Was the Servant: International Capital Movements in the Bretton Woods Order.* Chap. 2 in *Finance and World Politics: Markets, Regimes and States in the Post-Hegemonic Era,* ed. P. G. Cerny. Cheltenham, Glos., and Brookfield, Vt.: Edward Elgar.

Hellema, D. A. 1984. *Frontlijn van de Koude Oorlog. De Duitse herbewapening en het Atlantisch bondgenootschap.* Amsterdam: Mets.

Hertz, Frederick. 1947. "War and National Character." *Contemporary Review* 171 (May).

Herz, J. H. 1975. *The Nation State and the Crisis of World Politics.* New York: McKay.

Hexter, J. H. 1961. "The Myth of the Middle Class in Tudor England." In *Reappraisals in History.* Reprint. Chicago: University of Chicago Press.

Hilferding, Rudolf. [1909] 1981. *Finance Capital: A Study of the Latest Phase of Capitalist Development.* Ed. Tom Bottomore. Reprint. London: Routledge, and Kegan Paul.

Hill, Christopher. 1981. "A Bourgeois Revolution?" In *Three British Revolutions: 1641, 1688, 1776,* ed. J. G. A. Pocock. Princeton, N.J.: Princeton University Press.

Hilton, R. H. 1976. *The Transition from Feudalism to Capitalism.* London: Verso.

Himmelstrand, U., G. Arhne, L. Lundberg, and L. Lundberg. 1981. *Beyond Welfare Capitalism: Issues, Actors and Forces in Societal Change.* London: Heinemann.

Hintze, Otto. 1975. "Military Organization and the Organization of the State." In *The Historical Essays of Otto Hintze,* ed. Felix Gilbert. New York: Oxford University Press.

Hodgson, Marshall G. S. 1974. *The Venture of Islam.* 3 vols. Chicago: University of Chicago Press.

Hofbauer, Hannes, and Andrea Komlosy. 1991. "Restructuring Eastern Europe. Ms. Illustrierte Zeitung Kulter Sonderausgabe 1944." *Der Europäische Mensch* (Leipzig).

Hoffmann, Stanley. 1963. "Paradoxes of the French Political Community." In Hoffmann, et al., *In Search of France.* Cambridge, Mass.: Harvard University Press.

Holloway, John, and Sol Picciotto, eds. 1978. *State & Capital: A Marxist Debate.* London: Edward Arnold.

Holman, O. 1987. "Semiperipheral Fordism in Southern Europe. The National and International Context of Socialist-led Governments in Spain, Portugal, and Greece in Historical Perspective." *International Journal of Political Economy* 17 (Winter).

———. 1989. "In Search of Hegemony. Socialist Government and the Internationalization of Domestic Politics in Spain." *International Journal of Political Economy* 19 (Fall).

Hood, Neil, and Jan-Erik Vahlne, eds. 1988. *Strategies in Global Competition.* London: Routledge.

Horne, James. 1985. *Japan's Financial Markets: Conflict and Consensus in Policymaking.* Sydney, London, and Boston: Allen & Unwin.

Huffschmid, J. [1969] 1975. *Die Politik des Kapitals. Konzentration und Wirtschaftspolitik in der Bundesrepublik.* Frankfurt: Suhrkamp.

Hughes, John. 1991. *The Social Charter and the Single European Market.* Nottingham: Spokesman.

Huntington, Samuel P. 1968. *Political Order in Changing Societies.* New Haven: Yale University Press.

Husted, Steven, and Michael Melvin. 1990. *International Economics.* New York: Harper Row.

Ikenberry, G. John. 1992. "A World Economy Restored: Expert Consensus and the Anglo-American Postwar Settlement." *International Organization* 46:289–321.

Illustrierte Zeitung Kultur Sonderausgabe 1944. *Der Europaische Mensch.* Leipzig. Reproduced in part with an editorial introduction by Peter Lock in "Rustungswerbung," *Militarpolitik und Dokumentation* Heft 41–42, Frankfurt aM: Haag und Herchen.

Inalcik, H. 1973. "Application of the Tanzimat and Its Social Effects." *Archivum Ottomanicum 5.*

Ingham, Geoffrey. 1985. *Capitalism Divided? The City and Industry in British Social Development.* London: Macmillan.

Jacoby, Neil H. 1966. *U.S. Aid to Taiwan: A Study of Foreign Aid, Self-Help and Development.* New York: Praeger.

Jessop, Robert. 1990. *State Theory: Putting Capitalist States in Their Place.* London: Polity.

Johansson, Gunnar. 1991. Letter to Lawrence Wilde, October 3.

Jones, Leroy, and Il Sakong. 1980. *Government, Business and Entrepreneurship in Economic Development: The Korean Case.* Cambridge, Mass.: Harvard University Press.

Johnson, Chalmers. 1982. *MITI and the Japanese Miracle: The Growth of Industrial Policy, 1925–1975,* Stanford, Calif.: Stanford University Press.

————. 1987. "Political Institutions and Political Performance: The Government-Business Relationship in Japan, South Korea, and Taiwan." In *The Political Economy of the New Asian Industrialism,* ed. Frederic C. Deyo. Ithaca, N.Y.: Cornell University Press.

Kade, G. 1980. *BRD—Modell für Westeuropa?* Berlin: Akademie-Verlag.

Kaiser, David. 1990. *Politics and War: European Conflict from Phillip II to Hitler.* Cambridge, Mass.: Harvard University Press.

Kapstein, Ethan Barnaby. 1992. "Between Power and Purpose: Central Bankers and the Politics of Regulatory Convergence." *International Organization* 46 (Winter): 265–287.

Karpat, Kemal. 1973. *An Inquiry into the Social Foundations of Nationalism in the Ottoman State.* Princeton, N.J.: Woodrow Wilson Center for International Studies.

Kay, William. 1992. "A New Start for Sweden." *The Guardian,* January 3.

Kedourie, Elie. 1960. *Nationalism.* London: Hutchinson.

Kelman, Steven. 1991. "Swedish Model on a Diet." *The Guardian,* 7 August.

Kennedy, J. F. 1957. "A Democratic Looks at Foreign Policy." *Foreign Affairs* 36 (October).

Keohane, R. O., ed. 1986. *Neorealism and Its Critics.* New York: Columbia University Press.

Kiernan, Victor. 1957. "Foreign Mercenaries and Absolute Monarchy." *Past and Present* (April): 66–86.

Kim, Suk-joon. 1989. *The State, Public Policy, and NIC Development.* Seoul: Dae Young Moonwhasa.

Kindelberger, Charles P. 1973. *The World in Depression 1929–1939.* London: Penguin.

Kissinger, Henry. 1957. *A World Restored: Metternich, Castlereagh, and the Problems of Peace 1812–22.* Boston: Houghton Mifflin.

Kleinknecht, Alfred. 1987. *Innovation Patterns in Crisis and Prosperity: Schumpeter's Long Cycle Reconsidered.* New York: St. Martin's Press.

Klerks, P. 1989. *Terreurbestrijding in Nederland 1970–1988.* Amsterdam: Ravign.

Kohl, Phillip. 1987. "The Ancient Economy, Transferable Technologies and the Bronze Age World-System: A View from the Northeastern Frontier of the Ancient Near East." In *Centre and Periphery in the Ancient World,* eds. Michael Rowlands, Mogens Larsen, and Kristian Kristiansen. Cambridge: Cambridge University Press.

Kolko, Joyce, and Gabriel Kolko. 1972. *The Limits of Power: The World and United States Foreign Policy, 1945–1954.* New York: Harper & Row.

Koo, Hagen. 1984. "World System, Class, and State in Third World Development." *Sociological Perspectives* 27 (January):33–52.

————. 1987. "The Interplay of State, Social Class, and World System in East Asian Development: The Case of South Korea and Taiwan," in Frederick Deyo, ed. *The Political Economy of the New Asian Industrialism.* Ithaca: Cornell University Press.

Korpi, Walter. 1978. *The Working Class Under Welfare Capitalism.* London: Routledge and Kegan Paul.

————. 1983. *The Democratic Class Struggle.* London: Routledge and Kegan Paul.

Kowalik, Thadeusz. 1991. "Privatization and Social Participation. The Polish Case." UNRISD/ISS Workshop on Participation and Changes in Property

Relations in East-Central Europe and the Soviet Union, 22–25 May, The Hague.

Krasner, Stephan D., ed. 1978. *Defending the National Interest—Raw Materials Investments and U.S. Foreign Policy.* Princeton, N.J.: Princeton University Press.

———. 1989. "Sovereignty: An Institutional Perspective." In *The Elusive State,* ed. J. A. Caporaso. Beverly Hills, Calif.: Sage Publications.

Kula, Witold, 1976. *An Economic Theory of the Feudal System.* New York: Humanities Press.

Lachman, Richard. 1989. "Origins of Capitalism in Western Europe: Economic and Political Aspects." *Annual Review of Sociology* 15:47–72.

Laclau, Ernesto. 1977. "Feudalism and Capitalism in Latin America." In *Politics and Ideology in Marxist Theory.* London: New Left Books.

Lacost, Yves. 1976. *Géographie du sous-développement.* Paris: Presses Universitaires de France.

Ladeur, K.-H. 1981. "Vom Sinnganzen zum Konsens." In W. Abendroth, et al., *Ordnungsmacht? Über das Verhältnis von Legalität, Konsens und Herrschaft.* Frankfurt: EVA.

Lake, David, and John Graham. 1990. *Global Corporate Financing in the 1990s: How to Succeed in an Era of Relationships and Cautious Credit.* London: The Economist Intelligence Unit.

Lash, Scott. 1985. "The End of Neo-Corporatism? The Breakdown of Centralised Bargaining in Sweden." *British Journal of Industrial Relations* 23.

Lasslet, P. 1965. Editor's Introduction to J. Locke, *Two Treatises on Government [1690].* New York: Mentor.

Lasswell, Harold D. 1977. *On Political Sociology.* Ed. Dwaine Marvick. Chicago and London: Chicago University Press.

Leborgne and Lipietz, 1988. "L'Apres-Fordisme et son espace," *Les Temps Modernes* (April). *Couverture Organge* no. 8807.

Leca, Jean. 1990. "Social Structure and Political Stability: Comparative Evidence from the Algerian, Syrian and Iraqi Cases." In *The Arab States,* ed. Giacomo Luciani. Berkeley and Los Angeles: University of California Press.

Lechner, Norbert. 1983. "Especificando la politica." In Juan Enrique Vega, et al., *Teoria y Politica de America Latina.* Mexico: CIDE.

Lee, Chong-Sik. 1985. *Japan and Korea: The Political Dimension.* Stanford, Calif.: Hoover Institution Press.

LeFebvre, Georges. 1947. *The Coming of the French Revolution.* Princeton, N.J.: Princeton University Press.

Lefebvre, H. 1976. *De l'Etat.* 4 Vol. Paris.

Leggewie, C. 1989. "CDU—Integrationsmodell auf Widerruf? Die Zwei Modernisierungen der deutschen Rechten nach 1945," *Blätter für deutsche und internationale Politik* 3.

Lehmann, David, ed. 1979a. *Development Theory: Four Critical Studies.* London: Cass.

———. 1979b. "Introduction." In Lehmann 1979a.

Lenin, V. I. 1932. *State and Revolution.* New York: International Publishers.

Leroy-Beaulieu, Paul. 1911. *L'état moderne et ses fonctions.* 2d ed. Paris: Guillaumin.

Lewis, Bernard. 1961. *The Emergence of Modern Turkey.* London: Oxford University Press.

Linz, Juan. 1963. "Interests and Politics in Spain." In *Varieties of Corporatism,* ed. Peter J. Williamson. Cambridge: Cambridge University Press.

Lipietz, Alain. 1977. *Le capital et son espace.* Extended ed. 1983. Paris: Maspero.
———. 1979. *Crise et inflation: pourquoi?* Paris: Maspero.
———. 1984a. *L'audace ou l'enlisement.* Paris: La Découverte.
———. 1984b. "La mondialisation de la crise générale du Fordisme: 1967–1984." *Les Temps Modernes,* November.
———. 1987. *Mirages and Miracles: The Crises of Global Fordism.* London: Verso.
———. 1989. *Crisis L'audace.* Paris: La Découverte.
Lipset, S. M. 1983. "Radicalism or Reformism: The Sources of Working-class Politics." *American Political Science Review* 77.
Lombard, Maurice. 1975. *The Golden Age of Islam.* Amsterdam: North Holland.
Loriaux, Michael. 1991. *France After Hegemony: International Change and Financial Reform.* Ithaca, N.Y.: Cornell University Press.
Lowi, Theodore J. 1969. *The End of Liberalism: Ideology, Polity, and the Crisis of Public Authority.* New York: Norton.
Lucas, Colin. 1973. "Nobels, Bourgeois, and the Origins of the French Revolution." *Past and Present* 60 (September):84–126.
Luxemburg, Rosa. 1976. *The National Question. Selected Writings of Rosa Luxemburg.* Ed. Horace B. Davis. New York: Monthly Review Press.
Macartney, C. A. 1934. *National States and National Minorities.* London: Oxford University Press.
MacEwan, Arthur, and William K. Tabb, eds. 1989. *Instability and Change in the World Economy.* New York: Monthly Review Press.
Madison, Angus. 1982. *Phases of Capitalist Development.* Oxford: Oxford University Press.
Mahon, Rianne. 1991. "From Solidaristic Wages to Solidaristic Work: A Post-Fordist Historic Compromise for Sweden." *Economic and Industrial Democracy* 12.
Maier, Charles. 1975. *Recasting Bourgeois Europe. Stabilization in France, Germany, and Italy in the Decade After World War I.* Princeton, N.J.: Princeton University Press.
Mann, Michael. 1984. "The Autonomous Power of the State: Its Origins, Mechanisms and Results." *Archives européenes de sociologie* 25:185–213.
———. 1986. *The Sources of Social Power.* Vol. 1, *A History of Power from the Beginning to A.D. 1760.* Cambridge: Cambridge University Press.
Mann, Michael, and John Hobson, eds. *States, International Markets, and Hegemonic Regimes.* Cheltenham, Glos., and Brookfield, Vt.: Edward Elgar.
Marton, Imre. 1978. *Contribution à une Critique des Interprétationsdes spécificités du Tiers Monde.* Budapest: L'Institut d'économic Mondiale.
Marx, Karl. 1973. *The Revolution of 1848.* Harmondsworth, England: Penguin.
Mason, Edward S., et al. 1980. *The Economic and Social Modernization of the Republic of Korea.* Cambridge, Mass.: Council on East Asian Studies, Harvard University.
Massey, D. 1978. "Regionalism: Some Current Issues." *Capital and Class* 6.
Mayer, Martin. 1988. *Markets: Who Plays . . ., Who Risks . . ., Who Gains . . ., Who Loses . . . .* New York: Simon and Schuster.
Mayer, U. 1979. "Die Verfassungsentwicklunk der Bundesrepublik." In *Beiträge zu einer Geschichte der Bundesrepublik,* eds. U. Albrecht, et al., Cologne: Pahl-Rugenstein.
McIvor, Greg. 1993. "Swedish Welfare State Under Threat." *The Guardian,* January 12.
McKenzie, Richard B., and Dwight R. Lee. 1991. *Quicksilver Capital: How the Rapid Movement of Wealth Has Changed the World.* New York: Free Press.

McLellan, David. 1980. *Marx's Grundrisse*. London and Basingstoke: Macmillan.

McMahon, Hugh. 1991. "1992: A Check List on the Social Dimension." Quoted by Dianne Mahon, "From Solidaristic Wages to Solidaristic Work: A Post-Fordist Historic Compromise for Sweden." *Economic and Industrial Democracy* 12.

McNeill, William. 1964. *The Rise of the West: A History of the Human Community*. Chicago: University of Chicago Press.

———. 1983. *The Pursuit of Power*. Oxford: Basil Blackwell.

Meyer-Fehr, Peter. 1980. "Technologische Kontrolle durch mitinationale Konzerne und Wirtschaftswachtum." In *Multinationale Konzerne, Wirtschaftspolitik und nationale Entwicklung im Weltsvstem*, ed. Volker Bornschier. Frankfurt: Campus Verlag.

Michelet, Jules. 1846. *The People*. Trans. C. Cocks. London: Longman, Brown, Green, Longman.

Micheletti, Michele. 1991. "Swedish Corporatism at a Crossroads: The Impact of New Politics and New Social Movements." *West European Politics* 14.

Migdal, Joel S. 1988. *Strong Societies and Weak States: State-Society Relations and State Capabilities in the Third World*. Princeton, N.J.: Princeton University Press.

Miliband, R. 1969. *The State in Capitalist Society*. London: Quartet.

Milner, Helen. 1991. "The Assumption of Anarchy in International Relations Theory: A Critique." *Review of International Studies* 17 (January):67–85.

Milner, Henry. 1989. *Sweden: Social-Democracy in Practice*. Oxford: Oxford University Press.

Minc, A. 1982. *L'Apres-crise est commence*. Paris: Gallimard.

Moore, Barrington. 1966. *Social Origins of Dictatorship and Democracy: Lord and Peasant in the Making of the Modern World*. Boston: Beacon.

Moran, Michael. 1991. *The Politics of the Financial Services Revolution: The USA, UK and Japan*. London: Macmillan.

Morgenthau, Hans J. 1967. *Politics Among Nations: The Struggle for Power and Peace*. 4th ed. New York: Alfred A. Knopf.

Moseley, K. P. 1983. "East Wind, West Wind." *Theory and Society* 12: 405–411.

———. 1992. "In Defense of the Primitive." In *Rethinking the Third World*, ed. Rosemary Galli. New York: Crane Russak.

Müller, L. 1991. *Gladio—das Erbe des kalten Krieges*. Rhinebeck: Rowohlt.

Müller-Jentsch, W. 1979. "Streiks und Streikbewegungen in der Bundesrepublik 1950–1978." In *Beiträge zur Soziologie der Gewerkschaften*, ed. J. Bermann. Frankfurt: Suhrkamp.

Myrdal, Gunnar. 1969. *Objectivity in Social Research*, London: Duckworth.

Nairn, T. 1978. *The Break-up of Britain*. London: New Left.

Naumann, Friedrich. 1916. *Mitteleuropa*. Berlin: G. Reimer.

Nef, John U. 1967. *Industry and Government in France and England: 1540–1640*. Ithaca, N.Y.: Cornell University Press.

Neff, Stephen C. 1990. *Friends But No Allies: Economic Liberalism and the Law of Nations*. New York: Columbia University Press.

Nelson, Joan M., ed. 1990. *Economic Crisis and Policy Choice: The Politics of Adjustment in the Third World*. Princeton, N.J.: Princeton University Press.

Nester, William R. 1990. *Japan's Growing Power Over East Asia and the World Economy: Ends and Means*. London: Macmillan.

Nisbeth, Robert. 1974. *The Social Philosophers: Community and Conflict in Western Thought*. London: Heinemann.

Ocetto, Achille. 1990. Interview in *The Guardian*, January 25.

O'Connor, James. 1973. *The Fiscal Crisis of the State.* New York: St. Martin's Press.

Offe, Claus. 1984. *Contradictions of the Welfare State.* London: Hutchinson.

Ogle, George. 1990. *South Korea: Dissent Within the Economic Miracle.* London: Zed.

Ohmae, K. 1985. *Macht der Triade. Die neue form weltweiten Wettbewerbs.* Wiesbadan: Gabler.

Oliveira, F. de. 1977. *Elegia para una religiao.* Rio de Janeiro: Paz.

Opitz, R., ed. 1977. *Europastrategien des deutschen Kapitals 1900–1945.* Cologne: Pahl-Rugenstein.

Oriani, Alfredo. 1908. *La rivolta ideale.* Bologna: SEI.

Oudiz, G. 1984. *Strategies economiques europeennes: coordination ou confrontation?* Paris: INSEE. Mimeo 8506.

Palan, R. 1991. "Misguided Nationalism: The Causes and Prospects for Slovenian Independence." *Contemporary Review* (September).

———. 1992a. "The Second Structuralist Theories of International Relations: A Research Note." *International Studies Notes* 17 (Fall).

———. 1992b. "The European Miracle of Capital Accumulation." *Political Geography* 11 (July 1992).

———. 1992c. "The Re-internationalization of Finance Capital: A Sense of Deja Vu?" Paper presented at the Meetings of the International Studies Association, 3 April, Atlanta.

Palan, R. and B. Blair. 1993. "On the Idealist Origins of the Realist Theory of International Relations." *Review of International Studies:* In press.

Palmer, Robert R. 1944. "The National Idea in France Before the Revolution." *Journal of the History of Ideas* 1 (January):95–111.

Parker, Geoffrey. 1988. *The Military Revolution: Military Innovation and the Rise of the West, 1500–1800.* Cambridge: Cambridge University Press.

Pashukanis, Evgent B. 1983. *Law and Marxism.* London: Pluto Press.

Paz, O. 1985. *Une Planete et quatre ou cinq mondes.* Paris: Gillimard.

Peet, Richard. 1991. *Global Capitalism.* London: Routledge.

Penrose, E. F. 1953. *Economic Planning for the Peace.* Princeton, N.J.: Princeton University Press.

Perez, Carlota. 1983. "Structural Change and Assimilation of New Technology in the Economic and Social Systems." *Futures* 15 (October): 357–375.

Pfister, Ulrich, and Christian Suster. 1987. "International Financial Relations as Part of the World System." *International Studies Quarterly* 31:239–272.

Phillips, Anne. 1977. "The Concept of Development." *Review of African Political Economy* 8 (January–April):7–20.

Phillips, Peter D., and Immanuel Wallerstein. 1980. "National and World Identities and the Interstate System." Paper prepared for the United Nations University SCA Project, March.

Pierson, Christopher. 1986. *Marxist Theory and Democratic Politics Polity.* Cambridge: Cambridge University Press.

Piore, M., and C. F. Sabel. 1984. *The Second Industrial Divide.* New York: Basic Books.

Plumb, J. H. 1950. *England in the Eighteenth Century.* Harmondsworth: Penguin.

Poggi, Gianfranco. 1978. *The Development of the Modern State: A Sociological Introduction.* Stanford, Calif.: Stanford University Press.

Polayni, Karl. 1944. *The Great Transformation.* New York: Rinehart.

Pontusson, Jonas. 1984. "Behind and Beyond Social Democracy in Sweden." *New Left Review* 143.

Porter, Michael E., ed. 1986. *Competition in Global Industries.* Cambridge, Mass.: Harvard Business School Press.

Portes, Alejandro, and Douglas Kinkaid. 1989. "Sociology and Development in the 1990s: Critical Challenges and Empirical Trends." *Sociological Forum* 4 (December):479–503.

Poulantzas, Nicos. 1969. "The Problem of the Capitalist State." *New Left Review* 58:119–133.

———. 1973a. *Political Power and Social Classes.* London: Verso.

———. 1973b. "The Problem of the Capitalist State." In *Ideology in Social Science,* ed. Robin Blackburn. New York: Vintage Books.

———. 1975. *Classes in Contemporary Capitalism.* London: New Left Books.

———. 1976. "The Capitalist State: A Reply to Miliband and Laclau." *New Left Review* 95 (January–February):65–83.

Poulantzas, Nicos. 1974. *Fascism and Dictatorship.* London: NLB.

Pounds, N. J. G. 1954. "France and 'les limites naturelles' from the seventeenth to the twentieth centuries." *Annals, Association of American Geographers,* 44, 51–62.

Ragin, Charles. 1987. *The Comparative Method: Moving Beyond Qualitative and Quantitative Strategies.* Berkeley: University of California Press.

Reddaway, William F., ed. 1941. *The Cambridge History of Poland.* Cambridge: Cambridge University Press.

Rehn, Gosta, and Birger Viklund. 1991. "Changes in the Swedish Model." In *European Industrial Relations: The Challenge of Flexibility,* eds. G. Baglioni and C. Crouch. London: Sage.

Reich, Robert B. 1983. *The Next American Frontier.* New York: Times Books.

———. 1991. *The Work of Nations: Preparing Ourselves for 21st-Century Capitalism.* New York: Alfred A. Knopf.

Reuter, J. W. Manoschek, and P. Becker. 1991. "Die jugoslawische Krise," *Blätter für deutsche und internationale Politik* 8.

Rey, Pierre-Philippe. 1971. *Colonialisme, Néo-Colonialisme et transition au capitalisme.* Paris: Maspero.

———. 1973. *Les Alliances de Classes.* Paris: Maspero.

Ricci, David M. 1984. *The Tragedy of Political Science: Politics, Scholarship, and Democracy.* New Haven, Conn.: Yale University Press.

Richelson, J. T., and D. Ball. 1990. *The Ties That Bind: Intelligence Cooperation Between the UKUSA Countries.* 2d ed. Boston: Unwin Hyman.

Robbins, Lionel. 1939. *The Economic Basis of Class Conflict and Other Essays in Political Economy.* London: Macmillan.

Robinson, Cedric J. 1983. *Black Marxism.* London: Zed Press.

Romein, Jan. 1978. *The Watershed of Two Eras: Europe in 1900.* Middletown, Conn.: Wesleyan University Press.

Rosenau, James N. 1989. "The State in an Era of Cascading Politics: Wavering Concept, Widening Competence, Withering Colossus, or Weathering Change?" In *The Elusive State: International and Comparative Perspectives,* ed. James A. Caporaso. Beverly Hills, Calif.: Sage Publications.

Rosenberg, Hans. 1958. *Bureaucracy, Aristocracy, Autocracy. The Prussian Experience: 1660–1815.* Cambridge: Harvard University Press.

Ross, Robert, and Kent Trachte. 1990. *Global Capitalism: The New Leviathan.* Albany: State University of New York Press.

Rothwell, Roy, and Walter Zegveld. 1981. *Industrial Innovation and Public Policy.* London: Pinter Publishers.

Roxborough, Ian. 1979. *Theories of Underdevelopment.* London: MacMillan.

Rubinson, Richard. 1978. "Political Transformations in Germany and the United States." In *Social Change in the Capitalist World Economy,* ed. Barbara Hockey-Kaplan. Beverly Hills/London: Sage Publications.

Rubinson, Richard, ed. 1981. *Dynamics of World Development.* Beverly Hills, Calif.: Sage.

Ruggie, John G. 1982. "International Regimes, Transactions, and Change—Embedded Liberalism in the Post-War Order." *International Organization* 36 (Autumn):379–415.

———. 1992. "Multilateralism: The Anatomy of an Institution." *International Organization* 46 (Summer).

Sainsbury, Diane. 1991. "Swedish Social Democracy in Transition: The Party's Record in the 1980s and the Challenge of the 1990s." *West European Politics* 14.

Sandbrook, Richard. 1985. *The Politics of Africa's Economic Stagnation.* Cambridge: Cambridge University Press.

Sanderson, Stephen K. 1990. *Social Evolutionism.* Cambridge, Mass.: Blackwell.

Santos, M. 1978. *Pro uma Geografia nova.* São Paulo: Hucitec.

Sarkis, J. Khoury. 1990. *The Deregulation of the World Financial Markets: Myths, Realities, and Impact.* London: Pinter.

Sassier, Philippe, and François de Witt. 1985. *Les Française et la corbeille.* Paris: Robert Laffont.

Scase, R. 1980. *The State in Western Europe.* London: Croom Helm.

Schama, Simon. 1989. *Citizens: A Chronicle of the French Revolution.* New York: Alfred A. Knopf.

Schlupp, F. 1979. "Internationalisierung und Krise—das 'Modell Deutschland' im metropolitanen Kapitalismus." *Leviathan* 7.

Schmitt, B. E., and H. C. Vedeler. 1984. *The World in the Crucible 1914–1919.* New York: Harper & Row.

Schneider, Michael. 1990. *Die abgetriebene Revolution. Von der Staatsfirma in die DM-Kolonie.* Berlin: Elefanten Press.

Scott, Allen J., and Michael Storper, eds. 1986. *Production, Work, Territory.* Boston: Allen and Unwin.

Senghaas, Dieter. 1988. "European Development and the Third World: An Assessment." *Review* 11 (Winter):55–66.

Seton-Watson, Hugh. 1977. *Nations and States: An Inquiry into the Origins of Nations and the Politics of Nationalism.* Boulder, Colo.: Westview Press.

Shaw, Stanford. 1977. *History of the Ottoman Empire and Modern Turkey.* Cambridge: Cambridge University Press.

Silverman, Dan P. 1982. *Reconstructing Europe After the Great War.* Cambridge, Mass.: Harvard University Press.

Simon, W. 1976. *Macht und Herrschaft der Unternehmerverbände.* Cologne: Pahl-Rugenstein.

Sklar, H., ed. 1980. *Trilateralism.* Boston: South End Press.

Skoçpol, Theda. 1972. "Wallerstein's World Capitalist System: A Theoretical and Historical Critique." *American Journal of Sociology* 82:1075–1090.

———. 1979. *States and Social Revolutions.* Cambridge: Cambridge University Press.

———. 1985. "Bringing the State Back In: Strategies of Analysis in Current Research." In Peter Evans, et al., *Bringing the State Back In.* New York: Cambridge University Press.

Smith, Anthony. 1976. "The Formation of Nationalist Movements," in *Nationalist Movements,* ed. Anthony D. Smith. London: Macmillan.

Smith, Alan G. R. 1984. *The Emergence of a Nation State: The Commonwealth of England, 1529–1660.* London: Longman.

Smith, Denis Mack. 1971. *Victor Emmanuel, Cavour, and the Risorgimento.* London: Oxford University Press.

Snyder, Louis L. 1964. *The Dynamics of Nationalism*. Princeton, N.J.: D. Van Nostrand Company, Inc.

So, Alvin Y. 1990. *Social Change and Development: Modernization, Dependency, and World-System Theories*. Newbury Park, Calif.: Sage Publications.

Sohn-Rethel, A. 1975. *Grootkapitaal en fascisme: De Duitse industrie achter Hitler*. Amsterdam: Van Gennep.

Sokolovsky, Joan, Jeffrey Kentor, Pamela Walters, Patricia Arregui, and Christopher Chase-Dunn. 1980. "Economic Networks, Political Boundaries and City Systems in the Capitalist World-Economy." Paper presented at the Annual Meetings of the American Political Science Association, 31 August, Washington, D.C.

Sorokin, Pitirim A. 1941. "Social and Cultural Dynamics." In *Fluctuations of Social Relationships, War and Revolution*. Vol. 3. New York: American Book.

Spielmann, Katherine A., ed. 1991. *Farmers, Hunters and Colonists: Interaction Between the Southwest and the Southern Plains*. Tucson: University of Arizona Press.

Spohn, W., and Y. M. Bodemann. 1989. "Federal Republic of Germany." In *The Capitalist Class. An International Study*, eds. T. Bottomore and R. J. Brym. Hemel Hempstead: Harvester.

Stavrianos, L. S. 1958. *The Balkans Since 1453*. New York: Rinehart.

———. 1970. *The World to 1500: A Global History*. Englewood Cliffs, N.J.: Prentice Hall.

———. 1981. *Global Rift: The Third World Comes of Age*. New York: William Morrow & Co.

Stegmann, D. 1976. "Kapitalismus und Faschismus in Deutschland 1929–1934. Thesen und Materialien zur Restituierung des Primats der Grossindustrie zwischen Weltwirtschaftskrise und beginnender Rüstungskonjunktur." *Gesellschaft: Beiträge zur Marxschen Theorie 6*. Frankfurt: Suhrkamp.

Stephens, John. 1979. *The Transition from Capitalism to Socialism*. London: Macmillan.

Stern, Fritz. 1977. "Prussia." In *European Landed Elites in the Nineteenth Century*, ed. David Spring. Baltimore: Johns Hopkins University Press.

Stoinovich, T. 1963. "Social Foundations of Balkan Politics." In *The Balkans in Transition*, eds. Charles Jelavich and Barbara Jelavich. Berkeley and Los Angeles: University of California Press.

Stone, Lawrence. 1981. "The Results of the English Revolutions of the Seventeenth Century." In *Three British Revolutions: 1641, 1688, 1776*, ed. J. G. A. Pocock. Princeton, N.J.: Princeton University Press.

Storper, Michael, and Allen J. Scott, eds. 1986. *Production, Work, Territory: The Geographical Anatomy of Industrial Capitalism*. Boston: Allen & Unwin.

Strange, Susan. 1986. *Casino Capitalism*. Oxford, U.K.: Basil Blackwell.

———. 1988. *States and Markets: An Introduction to International Political Economy*. London: Pinter.

Sunkel, Osvaldo. 1979. "The Development of Development Thinking." In *Transnational Capitalism and National Development*, ed. Jose J. Villamil. Sussex: Harvester Press.

Sunkel, Osvaldo, and Edmundo F. Fuenzalida. 1979. "Transnationalism and Its National Consequences." In *Transnational Capitalism and National Development*, ed. Jose J. Villamil. Sussex: Harvester Press.

Svenson, Peter. 1991. "Labour and the Limits of the Welfare State." *Comparative Politics* 23.

Sylvan, David, and Barry Glassner. 1985. *A Rationalist Methodology for the Social Sciences*. Oxford: Basil Blackwell.

Sylvan, David, Duncan Snidal, Bruce Russett, Steven Jackson, and Raymond Duvall. 1983. "The Peripheral Economies: Penetration and Economic Distortion,
1970–1975." In *Multiple Perspectives on the World System,* ed. William R.
Thompson. Beverly Hills, Calif.: Sage Publications.

Szentes, Thomas. 1976. *The Political Economy of Underdevelopment.* Budapest:
Académiai Kiado.

Szücs, Jenö. 1983. "The Three Historical Regions of Europe." *Acta Historica Aa-
caemiae Scientiarum Hungaricae* 29:131–184.

Tawney, R. H. [1926] 1945. *Religion and the Rise of Capitalism.* New York:
Mentor.

Taylor, John G. 1979. *From Modernization to Modes of Production.* London:
Macmillan.

Taylor, P. J. 1981. "Geographical Scales Within the World Systems Approach."
Review 5. 3–11.

———. 1982. "A Materialist Framework for Political Geography." *Transactions,
Institute of British Geographers,* 7. 15–34.

———. 1987. "The Paradox of Geographical Scale and Marx's Politics." *Antipode*
19: 287–306.

———. 1989. "The Error of Development in Human Geography." In *Horizons in
Human Geography,* eds. Gregory and R. Walford. London: Macmillan.

———. 1991. "The Changing Political Geography," in R. J. Johnston and V. Gar-
diner, eds., *The Changing Geography of the UK.* London: Routledge.

———. 1991. "The Crisis of the Movements: The Enabling State as Quisling." *Antipode* 214–228.

———. 1992. "Political Geography Within World-Systems Analysis." *Review*
14:387–402.

———. 1993. "Contra Political Geography." *Tijdschrift voor Economische en Sociale Geografie* 84.

Teichova, Alice. 1974. *An Economic Background to Munich: International Business and Czechoslovakia 1918–1938.* London: Cambridge University Press.

Terray, E. 1973. "L'idee de nation et les transformations du capitalisme." *Les
Temps Modernes* 324 (August).

Therborn, Göran. 1978. *What Does the Ruling Class Do When It Rules?* London:
New Left Books.

———. 1991. "Swedish Social-Democracy and the Transition from Industrial to
Post-Industrial Politics." In *Labor Parties in Post-Industrial Societies,* ed.
Frances Fox-Piven. Cambridge, Mass.: Polity.

Thomas, W. A. 1989. *The Securities Market.* London: Philip Allan.

Thompson, E. P. [1963] 1968. *The Making of the English Working Class.* Harmondsworth: Pelican.

Thompson, Janice E. 1990. "State Practice, International Norms, and the Decline
of Mercenarism. *International Studies Quarterly* 34:23–47.

Thompson, William R. 1990. "Long Waves, Technological Innovation and Relative Decline." *International Organization* 44:201–233.

Tihany, Leslie C. 1976. *A History of Middle Europe.* New Brunswick, N.J.: Rutgers University Press.

Tilly, Charles. 1975. "Reflections on the History of European State-Making." In
The Formation of National States in Western Europe, ed. C. Tilly. Princeton,
N.J.: Princeton University Press.

———. 1985. "Warmaking and State Making as Organized Crime." In Peter
Evans, et al., *Bringing the State Back In.* New York: Cambridge University
Press.

————. 1990. *Coercion, Capital, and European States.* Oxford: Basil Blackwell.
Tolchin, M., and S. Tolchin. 1989. *Buying into America.* New York: Berkley.
Trimberger, Ellen Kay. 1978. *Revolution from Above: Military Bureaucrats and Development in Japan, Turkey, Egypt, and Peru.* New Brunswick, N.J.: Transaction Books.
Underhill, Geoffrey R. 1991. "Markets Beyond Politics? The State and the Internationalization of Financial Markets." In *The Politics of Transnational Regulation: Deregulation or Reregulation?* ed. P. G. Cerny. Special issue of the *European Journal of Political Research* 19 (March/April):197–226.
Van der Pijl, K. 1984. *The Making of an Atlantic Ruling Class.* London: Verso.
————., ed. 1989. "Transnational Relations and Class Strategy." *International Journal of Political Economy* 19: (Fall).
Van der Wurff, R. 1992. "Neo-Liberalism in West-Germany: The *Wende* in Perspective." In *Restructuring Hegemony: Neoliberalism in the Global Political Economy,* ed. H. Overbeek. London: Routledge.
Veblen, Thorstein. 1942. *Imperial Germany and the Industrial Revolution.* New York: Harper & Row.
von Braunmühl, C. 1973. *Kalter Krieg und friedliche Koexistenz: Die Aussenpolitik der SPD in der grossen Koalition.* Frankfurt: Suhrkamp.
Vulliamy, Ed. 1990. "Sad Death of a Swedish Model." *The Guardian,* February 16.
Wade, Robert. 1988. "The Role of Government in Overcoming Market Failure: Taiwan, Republic of Korea and Japan," in Helen Hughes, ed., *Achieving Industrialisation in East Asia.* Cambridge: Cambridge University Press.
————. 1990. *Governing the Market: The Economic Theory and the Role of the Government in East Asian Industrialization.* Princeton, N.J.: Princeton University Press.
Wade, Robert, and Bong Sik Kim. 1977. *The Political Economy of Success: Public Policy and Economic Development in the Republic of Korea.* Seoul: Kyung Hee University Press.
Waldheim, Kurt. 1944. *Kie Reichsidee bei Konstation Frantz.* Inaugural—Dissertation zur Erlangung des Doktorgrades der Rechts—und Staatswissenschaftlichen Fakultät der Universität Wien.
Walker, R. B. J. 1988. *One World, Many Worlds: Struggles for a Just World Peace.* Boulder, Colo.: Lynne Rienner Publishers.
Wallerstein, Immanuel. 1974. *The Modern World-System.* Vol. 1, *Capitalist Agriculture and the Origins of the European World-Economy in the Sixteenth Century.* New York: Academic Press.
————. 1979. *The Capitalist World Economy.* Cambridge: Cambridge University Press.
————. 1980. *The Modern World-System.* Vol. 2, *Mercantilism and the Consolidation of the European World Economy, 1600–1750.* New York: Academic Press.
————. 1982. "Crisis as Transition." In Amin Samir, Giovanni Arrighi, Andre Gunder Frank, and Immanuel Wallerstein, *Dynamics of Global Crisis.* London: Macmillan.
————. 1983. *Historical Capitalism.* London: Verso.
————. 1984. *The Politics of the World-Economy: The States, the Movements and the Civilizations.* Cambridge: Cambridge University Press.
————. 1985. "The Relevance of the Concept of Semiperiphery to Southern Europe." In *Semiperipheral Development: The Politics of Southern Europe in the Twentieth Century,* ed. Giovanni Arrighi. Beverly Hills, Calif.: Sage.

————. 1988. "Development: Lodestar or Illusion." *Economic and Social Weekly* 23 (September):2017–2023.

————. 1989. *The Modern World-System.* Vol. 3. San Diego: Academic Press.

————. 1990. "The West, Capitalism, and the Modern World-System." In J. Needham, *Science and Civilization in China,* Vol. 7. In press.

————. 1991. *Geopolitics and Geoculture. Essays on the Changing World-System.* Cambridge: Cambridge University Press.

Walters, Peter. 1987. "The Legacy of Olof Palme: The Condition of the Swedish Model." *Government and Opposition* 22:70.

Warren, Bill. 1973. "Imperialism and Capitalist Industrialization." *New Left Review* 81 (September-October):3–44.

————. 1980. *Imperialism, Pioneer of Capitalism.* London: Verso.

Waters, Richard. 1992. "Preliminary Agreement on Capital Adequacy for Securities Markets." *Financial Times—Financial Regulation Report,* February:8–10.

Weber, Max. 1946. *From Max Weber: Essays in Sociology.* Eds. H. H. Gerth and C. Wright Mills. New York: Oxford University Press.

————. [1904–1905] 1958. *The Protestant Ethic and the Spirit of Capitalism.* New York: Scribners.

————. 1978. *Economy and Society.* Vol. 2. Eds. Guenther Roth and Claus Wittich. Berkeley: University of California Press.

Weiss, John. 1977. *Conservatism in Europe, 1770–1945.* New York: Harcourt Brace Jovanovich.

White, Gordon. 1984. "Developmental States and Socialist Industrialization in the Third World." In *Third World Industrialisation in the 1980s,* ed. Raphael Kaplinsky. London: Cass.

————. 1988. *Developmental States in East Asia.* London: Macmillan.

Wiener, Norbert. 1948. *Cybernetics: Or Control and Communication in the Animal and the Machine.* New York: Technology Press, John Wiley & Sons.

Wight, Martin. 1977. *Systems of States.* Leicester: Leicester University Press.

Wilkinson, David. 1987. "Central Civilization." *Comparative Civilizations Review* 17 (Fall):31–59.

————. 1988. "Universal Empires: Pathos and Engineering." *Comparative Civilizations Review* (Spring):22–44.

Willoughby, John. 1986. *Capitalist Imperialism, Crisis and the State.* Chur, Switzerland: Harwood Academic Publishers.

Wolf, Erick. 1982. *Europe and the People Without History.* Berkeley: University of California Press.

Woo, June-en. 1991. *Race to the Swift: State and Finance in Korean Industrialization.* New York: Columbia University Press.

Worseley, Peter. 1980. "One World or Three? A Critique of the World-System Theory of Immanuel Wallerstein." In *The Socialist Register 1980,* eds. Ralph Milibard and John Seville. London: Merlin Books.

Wright, Erik Olin. 1976. "Modes of Class Struggle and the Capitalist State." *Kapitalistate* (Summer).

Zernatto, Guido. 1944. "Nation: The History of a Word." *Review of Politics* 6.

Ziegler, R., D. Bender, and H. Biehler. 1985. "Industry and Banking in the German Corporate Network," in F. N. Stokman, R. Ziegler, and J. Scott, *Networks of Corporate Power.* Cambridge, Mass.: Polity.

Ziemann, W., and M. Lanzendorfer. 1977. "The State in Peripheral Societies." In *The Socialist Register 1977,* eds. Ralph Miliband and John Saville. London: Merlin Books.

Zolberg, Aristide R. 1981. "Origins of the Modern World System: A Missing Link." *World Politics* 33:253–281.

Zysman, John. 1983. *Governments, Markets, and Growth: Financial Systems and the Politics of Industrial Change.* Ithaca, N.Y.: Cornell University Press.

Zysman, John, and Laura Tyson, eds. 1983. *American Industry in International Competition: Government Policies and Corporate Strategies.* Ithaca, N.Y.: Cornell University Press.

Contributors

PHILIP G. CERNY is senior lecturer in politics at the University of York. He is the author of *The Politics of Grandeur: Ideological Aspects of De Gaulle's Foreign Policy* (1980) and *The Changing Architecture of Politics: Structure, Agency and the Future of the State* (1990), and the editor of *Finance and World Politics: Markets, Regimes and States in the Post-Hegemonic Era* (1993).

CHRISTOPHER CHASE-DUNN is professor of sociology at Johns Hopkins University. He is author of *Global Formation* (1989) and editor, with Tom Hall, of *Core/Periphery Relations in Precapitalist Worlds* (1991). His current research is on comparing world-systems and the role of upwardly mobile semiperipheries in the transformation of systems logic.

ANDRE GUNDER FRANK is professor of development economics and social science at the University of Amsterdam. His publications, in twenty-five languages, include *World Accumulation 1492–1789* (1978), *Crisis in the World Economy* (1980), *Underdevelopment of Development: An Autobiographical Essay* (1991), and *The World System: 500 Years or 5000?*, with Barry Gills (1993).

BARRY GILLS is lecturer in international politics at the University of Newcastle upon Tyne and a fellow of the Transnational Institute, Amsterdam. He is a joint editor of *Review of International Political Economy*. His recent publications include *Low Intensity Democracy: Political Power in the New World Order*, with Joel Rocamora and Richard Wilson (1993), *The World System: 500 Years or 5000?*, with Andre Gunder Frank (1993), and *The Crisis of Socialism in the Third World*, with Shahid Qadir (1994).

SANDRA HALPERIN is assistant professor of political science at the University of Pittsburgh, specializing in international relations theory and Middle East politics. She is currently at work on a study that compares conflict and social change in nineteenth-century Europe and in the contemporary Middle East.

ALAIN LIPIETZ is a researcher at CEPREMAP, Paris. He is a leading exponent of the French school of regulation and has been the representative of the Green Party in the Paris Council., His publications in English include *The Enchanted World* (1983), *Mirages and Miracles* (1987), and *Towards a New Economic Order: Post-Fordism, Ecology and Democracy* (1993).

WARREN MASON is professor of political science at Miami University, Ohio. He is a former director of the Dolibois European Centre in Luxembourg and is the current director of Miami University's Transatlantic Seminar. His writings in comparative politics include *Demythologizing an Elite: American Presidents in Empirical, Comparative and Historical Perspective*, with Mostafa Rejia and Kay Phillips (1993).

K. P. MOSELEY is a development sociologist based in Washington, D.C. and a specialist on North Africa. She is currently conducting research at the Institut des Etudes Africaines in Rabat, Morocco, on trans-Saharan trade networks and the Mediterranean from 1500 to 1900.

RONEN P. PALAN is lecturer in international politics at the University of Newcastle upon Tyne. His current research and publications are in the area of state theory and international political economy. He is a joint editor of *Review of International Political Economy*.

SUSAN STRANGE is professor of political science at the European University Institute in Florence. As professor of international relations at the London School of Economics, a cofounder of the British International Studies Associations, and past vice-president of the International Studies Association, she pioneered the study of IPE in Britain. She has written widely on the international economy and international finance and is author of the popular textbook *States and Markets: An Introduction to International Political Economy*.

PETER J. TAYLOR is professor of political geography at the University of Newcastle upon Tyne and has published widely in world-systems analysis and political geography. His books include *Political Geography: World-Economy, Nation-State and Locality* (third edition, 1993), *Britain and the Cold War: 1945 as Geopolitical Transition* (1990), and *Political Geography in the Twentieth Century* (1993). He is editor of the journal *Political Geography* and a coeditor of *Review of International Political Economy*.

KEES VAN DER PIJL is reader in international relations at the University of Amsterdam. He has published widely on issues of transnational class formations, including *The Making of an Atlantic Ruling Class* (1984) and *Transnational Relations and Class Strategies* (editor, 1989). He is currently preparing an English edition of a history of International Relations theory previously published in Dutch and German in 1992. Other projects included a study of the rise and demise of the movement for a New International Economic Order.

LAWRENCE WILDE is reader in politics at Nottingham Trent University. He is the author of *Marx and Contradictions* (1989) and *Modern European Socialism* (1994).

Index

Accumulation: logic of, 87; modes of, 10, 85–86, 89; regime of, 29, 32, 34

Almond, Gabriel, 19

Apter, David, 19, 21

Asiatic mode of production, 88

BAIRs (bureaucratic authoritarian industrializing regimes), 138

"Billiard ball" model, 1

Brandt, Willy, 176–177, 179, 182, 186

Bretton Woods, 225, 234–235, 239–240, 243, 245

Bureaucracy, 74–76

Capital: accumulation, 11, 107, 223; internationalization of, 95–96; materialization of, 9

Capitalism, 8–9, 11–12, 16, 25, 48, 68, 80, 85–86, 88, 90–93, 97, 131, 140, 149; class, 17, 68, 76, 111, 192; contradiction, 13; industrialization, 92; state, 118; system, 9, 89; world-economy, 95

Cartelization, 79–80

CDU (German Christian Democratic Union), 174–177, 179, 186

Cerny, Philip, 13

Chase-Dunn, Christopher, 10

Cold War, 7, 8, 15, 19, 21, 96

Colonization, 29, 65

COMECON, 156, 160

Command economies, 88

Commercial competition, 57

Competition state, 223

Core-periphery relations, 87, 93, 102

Credit crunch, 243

Culturalist perspective, 21

Debt crisis, 37

Debt service, 147

Democracy, 66–68

Dependency, 17, 55; analysis, 135; development, 136; industrialization, 139; theory, 2, 54; underdevelopment school, 135; underdevelopment theory, 140; unequal exchange, 135

Deregulation, 236–245

Development, 3, 133

Dialectical historicism, 15, 19

Distribution of income, 18

Duvall, Raymond, 21

East Asian model, 13

Eastern Europe, 145–168

EC (European Community), 39, 162

Economic determinism, 23

Economic nationalism, 99

Economic regions, 26

Economy, the, 77–80

Education, 80

"Embedded financial orthodoxy," 226–227

EOI (export-oriented industrialization), 203–222

EPZs (export priority zones), 211

ERM (exchange rate mechanism), 227, 233

European unification, 39

Exchange-rate stabilization, 229

Expansion, (Kondratieff B-phase), 96

Fascism, 12, 79, 165

279

About the Book

Advancing a new and distinct conception of IR, the authors of this collection aim to supplement the purely globalist framework of the world-system with a comprehensive theory of politics and the state. Each contributor seeks to establish a framework for the study of domestic and global processes as interactive structures that affect one another continuously. Their systematic attention to domestic-global interrelationships, both political and socioeconomic, sets in place a new agenda for IR research.

Other Books in the Series

Politics Without Principle: Sovereignty, Ethics, and the Narratives of the Gulf War
David Campbell

Discourses of Global Politics: A Critical (Re)Introduction to International Relations
Jim George

The Global Economy as Political Space
Stephen J. Rosow, Naeem Inayatullah, and Mark Rupert, editors